M.J. Hummel®

Dido Nitz

M.J. Hummel®
Ich will Freude machen!
Eine schicksalhafte Frauenkarriere
Eine Biografie

I Want to Give Joy! A Fateful Woman's Career
A Biography

English Translation: Ernest Bernhardt

Einleitung / Introduction	6
Hummel Bertl – zeichne mich! Eine Kindheit in Niederbayern Hummel Bertl – will you draw me? – A Childhood in Lower Bavaria	8
Centa Hummel – Erinnerungen an eine Jugend Centa Hummel – Childhood Reminiscences	32
Ein außergewöhnliches Talent An der Staatsschule für angewandte Kunst in München An Exceptional Talent – At the State School of Arts and Crafts in Munich	34
Chronik einer glücklosen Zeit Chronicle of a Luckless Time	64
Der andere Weg Entscheidung für ein Klosterleben The Other Way – Decision for a Convent Life	66
Tagesordnung im Kloster Sießen Daily Schedule at Convent Siessen	84
Klosterkind und Künstlerin Anfänge einer Weltkarriere Convent Child and Craftswoman – The Beginnings of a World Career	86
70 Jahre Handarbeit – Die berühmten Hummel-Figuren 70 Years of Handcraft – The Famous Hummel Figurines	120

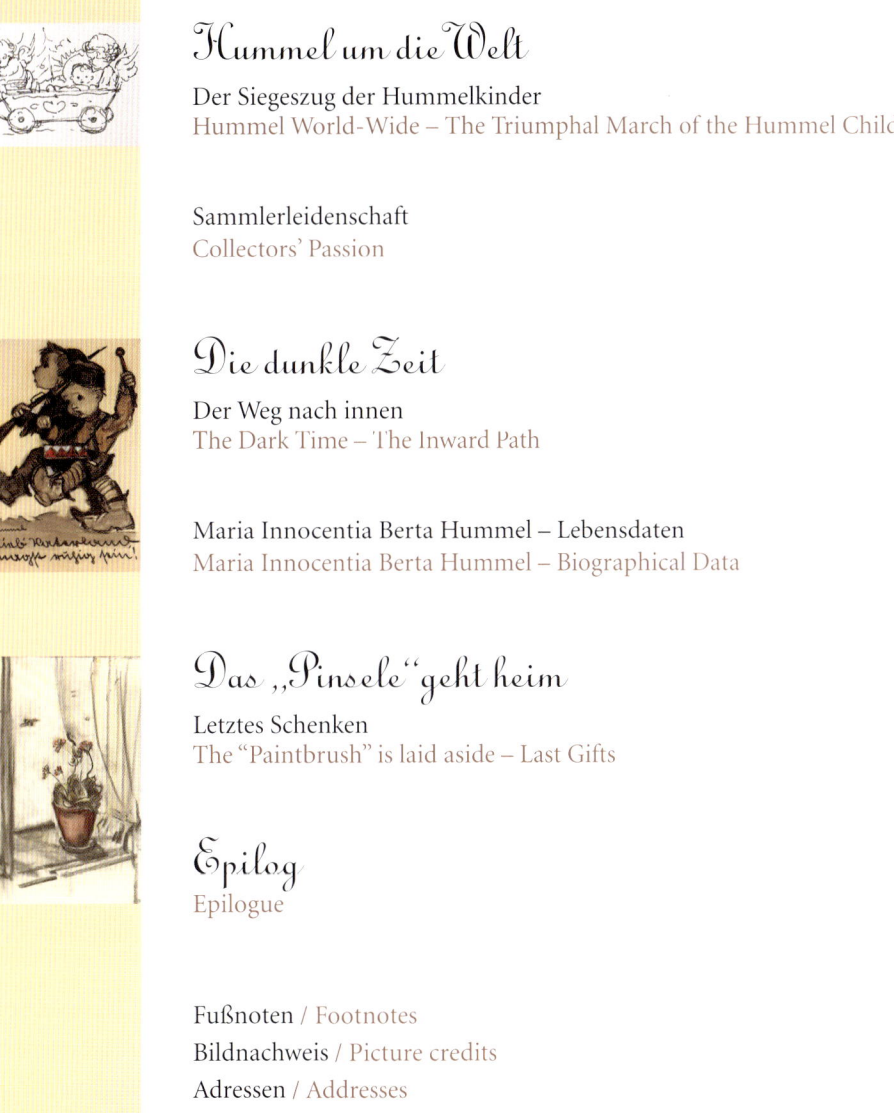

Hummel um die Welt — 122
Der Siegeszug der Hummelkinder
Hummel World-Wide – The Triumphal March of the Hummel Children

Sammlerleidenschaft — 144
Collectors' Passion

Die dunkle Zeit — 146
Der Weg nach innen
The Dark Time – The Inward Path

Maria Innocentia Berta Hummel – Lebensdaten — 174
Maria Innocentia Berta Hummel – Biographical Data

Das „Pinsele" geht heim — 176
Letztes Schenken
The "Paintbrush" is laid aside – Last Gifts

Epilog — 208
Epilogue

Fußnoten / Footnotes — 210
Bildnachweis / Picture credits — 218
Adressen / Addresses — 221
Impressum / Imprint — 224

Einleitung

M.I. Hummel – ein Name, der durch Porzellankinder zur weltweit bekannten Marke avancierte. Jeder kennt die Hummel-Figuren mit ihren verstrubbelten Haaren und den voll naiver Unschuld vorgereckten Bäuchen. Die stämmigen Beine in heruntergerutschten Strümpfen fest auf ihrem nostalgischen grünen Fleckchen heile Welt. Liebreiz für die einen, Kitsch as Kitsch can für die anderen, seit 70 Jahren.

Berta Maria Innocentia Hummel – eine Frau Anfang des 20. Jahrhunderts. Eine frohsinnige, leidenschaftliche studierte Künstlerin, die Gesehenes blitzschnell umsetzen konnte. Porträts, Landschaftsbilder, Karikaturen. Eine bis ins Innerste bewegte und gehorsame Klosterfrau. „Wenn wir nur ganz das sind, was wir sein sollen", schrieb sie und wählte – wenn sie denn die Wahl hatte – keinen leichten Weg für ihr kurzes Leben.

Auf einmal war sie dann berühmt durch ihre Kinderpastelle. Die Menschen in jenen harten 30er-Jahren liebten daran die Lebendigkeit des Augenblicks, ein Fensterchen in eine scheinbar sorglose kleine Vergangenheit. Die Zeichnungen wurden in die Dreidimensionalität übertragen.

Damit begann noch zu Lebzeiten der Künstlerin der unaufhaltsame Siegeszug der „Hummelkinder", optisches Gemeingut, mit dem Generationen aufwuchsen. Die Biografie hinter dieser Popularität ist faszinierend. Sie ist hier zum ersten Mal umfangreich und mit viel noch unbekanntem Bildmaterial aus den Archiven ausgearbeitet. Sie ist Erfolgsstory, Zeitzeugnis und Tragödie zugleich. Sie zeigt ein Leben zwischen Glauben und Kunst und Kunst und Kommerz, in einer Zeit, die das dunkelste Kapitel der deutschen Geschichte darstellt.

Kurz vor Drucklegung dieses Buches ging die Nachricht durch die Presse, dass die Porzellanmanufaktur Goebel im oberfränkischen Rödental ihre Hummel-Produktion einstellt. Stille in den weitläufigen Fertigungshallen, in denen in guten Zeiten bis zu 2000 Mitarbeiter von Hand modelliert, gegossen und kirschrote Kindermünder gemalt haben? Für die Firma waren beinahe 70 Jahre gut verlaufen. Eine Ära des Erfolgs eines der beliebtesten und bekanntesten volkskundlichen Phänomene unserer Zeit.

Introduction

M.I. Hummel: a name that a host of porcelain children elevated into a trademark known the world over. Every one knows the Hummel figures with their tousled hair and their tummies protruding in naive innocence, their sturdy legs in sagging stockings firmly placed on a nostalgically green spot of unspoilt world. Sheer winsomeness for some, kitsch as kitsch can for others, for 70 whole years.

Berta Maria Innocentia Hummel: a woman of the first half of the 20th century. A cheerful, passionate trained artist, able to transmute what she saw with lightning speed into portraits, landscape paintings, caricatures. A deeply stirred and dutiful nun. "If only we are completely what we are meant to be," she wrote and chose – to the extent that she had a choice – no easy way for her brief life.

Then suddenly she was famous for her pastel drawings of children. People of those hard years of the thirties loved the liveliness of the moment in these drawings, their being like little windows into a seemingly untroubled diminutive past. And then the drawings were transformed into three-dimensionality.

Therewith began – while the artist was still alive – the unstoppable triumphal march of the "Hummel Children," a common visual property, with which generations grew up. The biography behind the popular figure is fascinating. It is presented here for the first time in comprehensive form, enriched with a great many hitherto unknown pictorial materials from the archives. It is at once success story, historical testimony, and tragedy. It paints a life between religion and art and between art and commercialism, lived during a time that represents the darkest chapter in German history.

Shortly before the book went to press, news came through the media that the porcelain manufacturing firm Goebel of Rödental in Upper Franconia is discontinuing its Hummel production. Quietness in those spacious production halls, in which during good times up to 2000 employees hand-modeled and cast the figurines and painted cherry-red children's mouths? The firm flourished for a period of nearly 70 years – an era of success, and of one of the most beloved and best-known folkloristic phenomena of our time.

Hummel Bertl – zeichne mich!

Eine Kindheit in Niederbayern

Hummel Bertl – will you draw me? – A Childhood in Lower Bavaria

Wappen der Familie Hummel, 1942
Das Hummel-Haus, 1913
The Hummel family coat of arms, 1942
The Hummel House, 1913

Ein Haus voller Hummeln. Sechs Kinder sind es: Kätl, Viki, Bertl, Ady, Cenerl und Franzl. Eine Rasselbande, mittendrin die Wildeste, ja, die kann springen! „Das Hummele" Bertl, lautes Kinderlachen, kaum zu bändigen, den hübschen Kopf voller Lausmädelideen. Manchmal aber schaut sie ganz ernst, zum Beispiel wenn sie fotografiert wird, dann guckt sie schräg von unten her, die Augen fast ein wenig misstrauisch auf die Linse gerichtet. Sie hat das typische Gesicht ihrer Familie, mit den hohen Wangenknochen, die ihren klaren Gesichtszügen später als Erwachsene einen kräftigen Ausdruck verleihen werden.

Massing an der Rott war während Bertls Kindheit ein winziger Marktflecken in Niederbayern mit rund 700 Seelen. Schaut man heute die großzügig breite Hauptstraße hinunter, bekommt man einen Eindruck von behaglicher Bürgerlichkeit. Das war am 21. Mai 1909 kaum anders, als Berta hier geboren wurde, im großen Hummel-Haus am Ende des Platzes. Während nur 100 Kilometer entfernt in München eine blühende Kulturepoche unweigerlich ihrem Finale durch den Ersten Weltkrieg entgegensteuerte, verharrte der bäuerliche Marktflecken im malerischen Rottal noch ein paar unbehelligte Jahre in seiner abgeschirmten Idylle.

Berta mit Matrosenkragen, 1919
Berta with a sailor collar, 1919

Bertas Eltern waren Kaufleute. Der Vater, Adolf Hummel, hatte als einziger Sohn das Geschäft von seinem Vater übernommen, wie das damals üblich war.

*Fotografie: Massing,
Marktplatz, 1928/1929
Zeichnung: Massing, Marktplatz
im Winter, Dezember 1928*

*Photograph: Massing, market square
Drawing: Massing, market square
in winter, December 1928*

Großvater Jakob Hummel, ein fahrender Händler, war 1875 über die hügeligen Felder und Wiesen nach Massing gekommen. Von Geschäft zu Geschäft bot er, wie schon sein Vater und sein Großvater, seine Waren feil. Seit über 400 Jahren waren seine Vorfahren im Nachbarkönigreich Württemberg angestammt und hatten von dort aus den süddeutschen Raum bereist.[1] Doch ab und an gab auch einmal einer dieser Händler sein unabhängiges Leben auf und wurde an geeignetem Ort sesshaft.

A house humming with Hummels! There are six children: Kätl, Viki, Bertl, Ady, Cenerl, and Franzl. A mischievous lot! The wildest one among them, who can really run, is "Hummele" Bertl, full of childish laughter, all but untamable, her pretty head chock-full of pranks. Sometimes, though, she will look quite earnestly, for example, when she is being photographed. Then she will glance askance from below, her eyes a bit suspicious of the camera lens. She has the typical face of the family, with the high cheekbones that in her adulthood will make for strong features.

Massing on the Rott River was then a tiny market town in Lower Bavaria, with a population of about 700. Today a look down the generously wide Market Street gives the impression of comfortable civic life. It was pretty much the same on May 21, 1909, when Berta was born here, in the big Hummel house at the end of the square. While in Munich, some sixty miles away, a flourishing cultural epoch was already approaching its grim finale brought on by World War I, the rural market town in the picturesque Rott Valley remained a sheltered idyll for a few more years.

Berta's parents were merchants. Her father, Adolf Hummel, being an only son, had inherited the business from his father, as was customary. The grandfather, Jakob Hummel, had been a peddler, who, in 1875, had come to Massing across the surrounding hilly fields and meadows, hawking his wares from store to store like his father and grandfather before him. For more than 400 years his forebears had resided in the neighboring kingdom of Württemberg, from which they had traveled throughout the area of Southern Germany.[1] Now and then, however, one or the other of these traders was happy to abandon the footloose life and settle down at a suitable location.

Das Talent liegt in der Familie: Zeichnung des Vaters Adolf Hummel
The talent runs in the family: drawing by the father, Adolf Hummel

Großeltern Anglsperger, lesend, 1928, mit fotografischer Vorlage
Grandparents Anglsperger, reading, 1928, and photographic model

Mit seiner jungen Frau Katharina, die aus Haag in Oberbayern kam, hatte nun Jakob Hummel das Haus am Ende des dörflichen Marktplatzes bezogen und bei der lokalen Behörde die „halbe Krämergerechtigkeit"² erworben. Das heruntergewirtschaftete Ladenlokal im Erdgeschoss baute er zu einem „gemischten Warengeschäft" aus, sehr zur Freude der Massinger, die jetzt ihren Bedarf an verschiedensten Alltäglichkeiten bei ihm abdecken konnten. 1904 starb Jakob Hummel als geachteter Bürger seiner Wahlheimat und hinterließ ein gut etabliertes Geschäft.

Sein Sohn Adolf wäre lieber Holzschnitzer oder Bildhauer geworden. Das Talent lag in der Familie, auch Jakob hatte man beachtliche künstlerische Fähigkeiten nachgesagt. Adolf heiratete die Bäckertochter Viktoria Anglsperger. Während seine Familie sich – durch den Händlerberuf seit jeher kontaktfreudig – durch eine gewisse Weltoffenheit auszeichnete, entstammte Viktoria einem alteingesessenen, sehr traditionell und zutiefst religiös geprägten Umfeld. 1906 übernahm Adolf das von seiner Mutter weitergeführte Geschäft. Das junge Ehepaar steckte nun jede Minute in den kleinen Laden, um ihn zu modernisieren und auszubauen. Die Mühe lohnte sich und versetzte Adolf und Viktoria in die angenehme Lage, ein mittelständisches Leben führen zu können. In dieses Umfeld, geprägt von zäher Arbeit auf der einen Seite und gut situierter Bürgerlichkeit auf der anderen, wurden die sechs Kinder hineingeboren. Katharina (Kätl, Kathi) 1907, Viktoria (Viki, Vicki) 1908, Berta (Bertl) 1909, Adolf (Ady) 1910, Crescentia (Centa, Cenerl, Zennerl) 1911 und Franz (Franzl) 1912. Berta ist also die Drittälteste.³

With his young wife Katharina, who was from Haag in Upper Bavaria, Jakob Hummel had moved into the house at the end of the village market square and had acquired a "limited merchant's right"² from the local authorities. He expanded the run-down shop area on the ground floor into a "general merchandise store," much to the satisfaction of the Massingers, who now were able to obtain their everyday needs from him. Jakob Hummel died in 1904 as a respected citizen of his elective hometown, leaving behind a well-established business.

His son Adolf would rather have become a woodcarver or sculptor. There was talent in the family; Jakob, too, had been said to have artistic potential. Adolf

Bertas Taufschleife vom 23. Mai 1909, zwei Tage nach ihrer Geburt
Berta's christening bow of May 23, 1909, two days after her birth

Abschrift (1940) der Eheurkunde von Adolf und Viktoria Hummel
Die kleine Berta, 1910/1911
Copy (1940) of the marriage license of Adolf and Viktoria Hummel
Little Berta, 1910/11

married the baker's daughter Viktoria Anglsperger. While his family – outgoing by virtue of their trading profession – were quite cosmopolitan in outlook, Viktoria sprang from a rooted, tradition-bound, and deeply religious environment. In 1906 Adolf took over the business from his mother, who had been carrying it on in the meantime. The young couple used every free minute to modernize and enlarge the store. The effort paid off: Adolf and Viktoria were able to lead a comfortable, well-to-do life. Into this environment of both hard work and solid middle-class affluence their six children were born: Katharina (Kätl, Kathi) 1907, Viktoria (Viki, Vicki) 1908, Berta (Bertl) 1909, Adolf (Ady) 1910, Crescentia (Centa, Cenerl, Zennerl) 1911, and Franz (Franzl) 1912. Berta was thus the third-eldest.³

Stammbaum „zum 40-jährigen Hochzeitsjubiläum" der Großeltern Anglsperger
Family tree "for the fortieth wedding anniversary" of the grandparents Anglsperger

Adolf Hummel in seiner Uniform des Ersten Weltkriegs
Adolf Hummel in his World War I uniform

Viktoria Hummel mit ihren ältesten Töchtern Kätl und Viki vor dem Hummel-Haus, 1913
Hummel House, Viktoria Hummel with her eldest daughters Kätl and Viki, 1913

Doch das friedliche Leben währte nicht lange. Im Schicksalsjahr 1914 hatte das politische Geschehen nun auch Massing eingeholt. Am 28. Juni erreichte den Wittelsbacher Ludwig III. in München die Nachricht des tödlichen Attentats auf seinen Verwandten Erzherzog Franz Ferdinand, den österreichisch-ungarischen Thronfolger, womit der Erste Weltkrieg eingeläutet wurde. Die Ereignisse in Berlin und München überstürzten sich. Am 31. Juli verkündete König Ludwig vom Balkon der Residenz seinem bayerischen Volk die drohende Kriegsgefahr. Am nächsten Abend folgte der Befehl, die Truppen mobilzumachen. Offiziere durchkämmten trommelwirbelnd Münchens Straßen, um die Wehrpflichtigen zu den Waffen zu rufen. Vom 2. bis 5. August rückten mit wehenden Fahnen, blumenbekränzt und von munterer Marschmusik begleitet, die bayerischen Feldregimenter in Richtung des neu erklärten Gegners Frankreich aus. Unter ihnen war auch Adolf Hummel, Geschäft und Haus musste er für die nächsten fünf Jahre seiner Frau überlassen.

Und die führte das Haus mit großem Geschick und unerschütterlicher Frömmigkeit. Bertas jüngere Schwester Centa erinnert sich: „Sie war eine enorm tüchtige Geschäftsfrau." Jeden Tag im Laden, von morgens bis spät am Abend, verkaufen, bestellen, Buchführung, dazu der Haushalt, das Personal. Das war nicht leicht und setzte eine straffe Führung voraus. Die Kinder sah die junge Mutter im turbulenten Tagesgeschehen selten. „Aber dass die Mutter einen Kinderwagen schiebt – undenkbar!" Viel später musste Viktoria Hummel selbst das Resümee ziehen: „Ich bin nie geliebt worden, immer nur gefürchtet." Inwiefern die Geschwister unter der kühlen Strenge gelitten haben, lässt sich kaum sagen. Offensichtlich jedoch waren die Schrecken und Mangelerscheinungen des Krieges im Hause Hummel kaum präsent, und das, obwohl der Vater an der Front kämpfte. Viktoria schaffte es, für alle den bisherigen Lebensstandard weitgehend aufrechtzuerhalten.[4]

But this peaceful existence was not to last. By 1914, political developments at last also caught up with Massing. On June 28, the Wittelsbach king Ludwig III of Bavaria received the news, in Munich, of the assassination of his relative, Archduke Franz Ferdinand, the heir to the throne of the Austro-Hungarian Empire – the tragic incident that would ring in World War One. Events in Berlin and Munich followed in rapid succession. On July 31, Ludwig proclaimed the imminence of war to his Bavarians from the balcony of his Munich residence. An order to mobilize was issued the following evening. Officers combed the streets of Munich to the roll of drums to call all conscripts to arms. Between August 2 and August 5, the Bavarian regiments, wreathed with flowers and accompanied by waving flags and snappy marching bands, set out to meet the newly declared enemy France. Adolf Hummel was among them. For the next five years, home and business would be left to the care of his wife.

Viktoria managed both with great skill and unshakable religious faith. Berta's younger sister Centa remembered her as an "enormously capable business-woman." She was in the store every day from morning until night, selling, ordering, book-keeping, while also running the household and supervising the servants. It was not easy and required a firm hand. Caught up in the turbulence of her daily chores, the young mother saw little of her children. "That mother should ever have pushed a baby carriage – unthinkable." Years later, Viktoria Hummel herself had to conclude: "I was never loved, always only feared." It is hard to say how much the children may have suffered under the mother's cool sternness. Evidently however, though the father was at the front, the horrors and hardships of the war were hardly present in the Hummel household. Viktoria managed to keep the accustomed standard of living nearly undiminished.[4]

Großmutter Katharina Hummel mit ihren vier Enkelkindern, 1910
Grandmother Katharina Hummel with her four grandchildren, 1910

Viktoria Hummel mit ihren sechs Kindern auf der Schaukel, 1916/1917 (von links oben nach rechts unten: Kätl, Viki, Berta, Ady, Centa, Franzl)
Viktoria Hummel with her six children on a swing, 1916/1917 (from upper left to lower right corner: Kätl, Viki, Berta, Ady, Centa, Franzl)

Porträt Großmutter Kreszentia Anglsperger, 1927
Portrait of Grandmother Kreszentia Anglsperger, 1927

Porträt Viktoria Hummel, April 1927
Portrait of Viktoria Hummel, April 1927

Kätl, Viki und Berta im Winterdirndl vor dem Schaufenster des Hummel-Hauses, 1915
Kätl, Viki and Berta in winter dirndls in front of the Hummel store window, 1915

Essecke der Familie Hummel
The Hummel dining area

Berta entwickelt sich zu einem lebhaften Kind, Stillsitzen ist ihre Sache nicht. Nur manchmal, wenn sie etwas sieht, was sie in seinen Bann zieht, dann vergisst sie alles um sich herum und schaut. Schaut und starrt mit aller Konzentration auf das Objekt, das ihr ins Visier gekommen ist, merkt nicht das Lachen der Geschwister, weil sie mal wieder den Anschluss an die Realität verloren hat. „Geh weiter, du Schauerfreitag"[5], necken sie dann die anderen, bis sie wieder bei ihnen ist und eine ihrer schlagfertigen Antworten gibt. Schon früh zeichnet sie auf jeden Fetzen Papier, dessen sie habhaft werden kann.

Um die freundliche Lisi, die Köchin, scharten sich die kleinen Hummeln gern, sie konnte hervorragendes Zuckerwerk backen. Und selbstverständlich gab es für die sechs Geschwister auch Kindermädchen. Keine leichte Aufgabe, die aufgeweckten Bengel im Zaum zu halten. Eine der Kinderfrauen konnte Berta nicht leiden und trat mit den Füßen nach dem Mädchen. Bertas Schwester Centa erinnert sich, dass die Mutter, wenn die Geschäfte es erlaubten, immer wieder einen Blick ins Spielzimmer warf, um sich zu vergewissern, dass alles in üblicher Ordnung war. Als sie einmal das zornige Kindermädchen dabei erwischte, wie es sich an der kleinen Berta ausließ, folgte auf der Stelle die Kündigung und eine andere Betreuerin wurde eingestellt.

Ein großes Spielzimmer stand allen Kindern zur Verfügung und Schlafräume, in denen sie jeweils zu zweit untergebracht waren. Berta teilte ihr Zimmer mit der jüngeren Centa, die bis an ihr Lebensende die engste Vertraute unter den Geschwistern bleiben sollte. Der Zusammenhalt unter den Kindern war groß. Die Älteste, Katharina, stand damals ein wenig außen vor, weil sie gelegentlich ihre Position mithilfe saftiger Maulschellen verteidigte. Noch in der Pubertät und seiner Schwester längst körperlich gewachsen, würde der Bruder Adolf die „Kätl" feixend herausfordern: „Sag einmal, wann habe ich denn eigentlich die letzte Watsch'n von dir bekommen?"

Berta was becoming a very lively child. Sitting still was not to her taste. Only sometimes, when she would see something that fascinated her, she would forget everything around her and just look. She would stare in complete concentration at the object that had captured her attention, never noticing her siblings' laughing because she had once again lost touch with reality. "Get a move on, Schauerfreitag,"[5] they would tease her, until she would come back to them with one of her quick-witted replies. Early on she began to draw on any scrap of paper she could get hold of.

The little Hummels loved to crowd around Lisi, the good-natured cook, who was an outstanding confectioner. And of course, there were nursemaids for the children. Not an easy task, to keep those bright rascals under control. One of the nannies couldn't stand Berta and would kick at her with her feet. Berta's sister Centa recalled how their mother would regularly look in at the nursery, whenever business allowed, to make sure that everything was in order. At one of these times she caught the ill-tempered nursemaid letting out her anger on little Berta. The woman was fired on the spot and another caretaker hired.

There was a large nursery for all the children, as well as bedrooms for two each to share. Berta roomed with little Centa, who to the end of her life remained her closest confidante among all her siblings. The bond between the children was strong. Only the oldest, Katharina, was somewhat of an outsider, because she was apt to assert her position of preeminence by now and then boxing her siblings' ears. When her brother Adolf was already in puberty and long since his sister's equal in height, he would still challenge her with a grin: "Hey, Kathi, when was the last time I got smacked by you?"

Im Hummel-Haus ging es lebhaft zu. Berta karikierte ein paar Jahre später sich selbst und ihre Geschwister, jede mit unverwechselbarem Attribut, als emsige kleine Hummeln, 1923/1925.
Humming Hummel home: Berta's caricatures of herself and her siblings as busy little Hummeln (bumblebees), each with its own unique attribute, 1923/1925.

Hummelkinder (v. l. n. r.): Berta, Viki, Franzl, Kätl
Hummel children (from the left): Berta, Viki, Franzl, Kätl

Zwei streitende Buben, 1929/1930
Two boys quarreling, 1929/1930

Die schlimmste Demütigung, die von den Erwachsenen zu befürchten war, waren nicht die Ohrfeigen, sondern das „Eckerlsitzen". Angewandt in der höchsten Not, wenn die gestresste Gouvernante der sechs Rabauken einmal wieder nicht Herr werden konnte! Die Kinder sollten nicht alleine auf die Straße laufen, aber es war ihnen erlaubt, ihre Freunde mit nach Hause zu bringen. Wenn die nun alle im Haus herumtobten und der Lärmpegel einmal wieder jedes erträgliche Maß überschritt, dann griff das Kindermädchen zur bewährten Züchtigung. Die Unruhestifter samt aller auswärtigen Kinder mussten sich mit dem Gesicht zur Wand in die Ecken des Zimmers verteilen, und da es nun einmal nicht genug Ecken waren, möglichst weit voneinander entfernt an der Wand entlang. Dort hatten sie so lange schweigend auszuharren, bis die Kinderfrau endlich Milde walten ließ. Kaum hatte die jedoch einmal den Raum verlassen, rutschten alle blitzartig auf dem Hosenboden in die Mitte, um sich tuschelnd zu verständigen. Waren Schritte vor der Tür zu hören, ging es auf die gleiche Weise schnellstens wieder in die geforderte Stellung, und man tat mit heiliger Unschuldsmiene, als hätte sich nichts ereignet.

Der Krieg tobte nun schon bald ein Dreivierteljahr. Im Februar und März 1915 hatten die Franzosen während der Winterschlacht in der Champagne ein massives Trommelfeuer eröffnet. Die deutsche Antwort war schrecklich gewesen, eine der furchtbarsten Waffen des Ersten Weltkriegs – Chlorgas – hatte sich erstmals in die Gräben vor dem flandrischen Städtchen Ypern gesenkt und 15.000 französische Soldaten das Leben gekostet.

Hummelkind Ady, 1923/1925
Hummel child Ady, 1923/1925

The worst humiliations the children had to fear from the grownups were not any slaps but "corner-sitting," meted out at moments of crisis, when the stressed-out governess could think of no other way to get the six rascals under control. Though forbidden to run in the streets by themselves, the children were allowed to bring their friends into the house. If, as they romped about the place, the decibels rose above all tolerance levels, the nanny would resort to the tried method of chastisement. The noisemakers, along with their visitors, were ordered to sit on the floor in the corners of the room with their faces to the wall and, since there were never enough corners to go around, at maximal distances along the walls themselves. There they would have to endure in silence until the nursemaid at last took pity on them. If, in the meantime, she left the room, however, they would instantly scurry to the center of the room on their seats to confer in whispers. As soon as steps became audible outside the door, they speedily returned in the same fashion to their required posts, all looking as innocent as if nothing untoward had occurred.

Meanwhile the war had already been raging for the better part of a year. In the winter battle in the Champagne of February/March, 1815, the French had launched a heavy drumfire assault. The German response was terrible: chlorine gas, one of the most lethal weapons of World War I, had for the first time descended into the trenches near the Flemish town of Ypres and had taken the lives of 15,000 French soldiers.

Liebe Grüße von daheim: „Feldpost"
mit Bertas Kinderzeichnungen
With love from home: "field-post" letter
with youthful drawings by Berta

Am 1. Mai 1915 wurde Berta in die ortseigene Volksschule der Armen Schulschwestern[6] eingeschult. Sie ging mit ihren beiden älteren Schwestern in die Klasse, denn wie damals auf niederen Schulen üblich, wurde in Altersgruppen in zwei großen Räumen unterrichtet. Selbstredend erwies sich eine adäquate Beurteilung oder gar Förderung der Schützlinge als schwierig. Als Berta beinahe zwanzig Jahre später berühmt wurde, verfasste die Schulleiterin im Nachhinein einen „Bericht über Berta Hummel", in dem es heißt: „Unsere Handarbeitslehrerin (…) rühmt sie als ein gut begabtes, sehr fleißiges, lebhaftes, heiteres, fein, ja sehr zart fühlendes Kind, das eine sehr geschickte Hand zur Handarbeit hatte, doch viel Abwechslung liebte. Der Zensurbogen zeugt von dem hervorragenden Zeichentalent. Schon in der Unterklasse benotete die Lehrerin die kleine Schülerin im Zeichnen mit Note 1 ½; die Lehrerin der Oberklasse, Schwester Maria Theresilla Höhenleitner, zensiert sie im Zeichnen ‚mit Note 1', d.i. hervorragend."[7]

„Bericht über Frl. Berta Hummel". Im Nachhinein, als die Öffentlichkeit sich für das Leben der Künstlerin zu interessieren begann, verfasste Bertas Handarbeitslehrerin 1934 diese kurze Charakterbeschreibung. Klassenfoto 1919 (Berta steht in der hintersten Reihe, Dritte von links)
"Report on Miss Berta Hummel." Ex post facto character sketch composed by Berta's needlework teacher in 1934, after Berta had begun to be an object of public interest. Class photo, 1919 (Berta in the back row, third from left)

Die kleine Berta steht vorne an der Tafel, um sie herum ein johlender Haufen Schulkameraden. „Hummel Bertl, zeichne mich", rufen sie und quietschen vor Vergnügen, wenn mal wieder eins von ihnen in charakteristischen Umrissen an der Tafel zu sehen ist.

Die Klassenleitung durch jene Schwester Theresilla in den letzten drei Volksschuljahren muss für Berta eine ungeheure Erleichterung gewesen sein, denn eigentlich spielte ein Kunsttalent damals überhaupt keine Rolle. Und in den ersten Jahren war Berta noch dazu mit einer Lehrerin konfrontiert, die mit dem Temperament der Schülerin nicht zurechtkam und sie bei jeder Gelegenheit kleinhielt. Berta sei in dieser Zeit „immer stiller geworden und leiser und vollkommen verschreckt", erinnert sich Centa Hummel, „aber Schwester Theresilla hat sie verstanden. Und das Mädchen ist aufgeblüht." Noch viel später schrieb sie der alten Lehrerin oder ließ ihr in Briefen an die Familie Grüße ausrichten. Sechs Jahre blieb Berta insgesamt an der Massinger Volksschule.

Bertas Klosterschule in Massing, Aufnahme von 1928/1929
Berta's convent school, Massing, photograph of 1928/1929

Die Schwestern Kätl und Viki am Klavier, 1920. Berta übte fleißig die Geige.
Berta's sisters Kätl and Viki at the piano, 1920. Berta played the violin.

On May 1 of 1915, Berta entered the local elementary school of the School Sisters of Notre Dame.[6] She was in the same class with her two older siblings, it then being customary in the lower schools to instruct pupils in two age groups in two large rooms. It goes without saying that an adequate evaluation, let alone support, of the individual child was all but impossible. Twenty years later, after Berta had become famous, the school principal composed an ex-post-facto "Report on Berta Hummel," which reads in part: "Our needlework teacher (…) lauds her as a talented, vivacious, cheerful, sensitive, even delicate child, who had a skillful hand with needlework but liked to have lots of variety. Her report card indicates an outstanding talent for drawing. Even in the lower class the teacher gave her little pupil a mark of 1 ½ [A/B]; the upper-class teacher, Sister Maria Theresilla Höhenleitner, marked her 'with a grade of 1 [A]', i.e. outstanding."[7]

Little Berta would be standing in front of the blackboard, surrounded by a group of hooting schoolmates. "Hummel Bertl, draw me," they would cry and squeal with delight every time the telling outlines of one of them materialized on the board.

The last three years of elementary school under Sister Theresilla must have been a great relief for Berta, since artistic talent was generally ignored there in those years. Moreover, during the early years Berta had been confronted with a teacher who had no idea how to deal with the temperament of her pupil and put her down at every opportunity. Centa recalled that Berta had grown progressively quiet and subdued and totally cowed during that time, "but Sister Theresilla showed understanding for her, and the girl blossomed." Years later Berta would still write to her old teacher or send her regards in letters to her family. She remained at the Massing Elementary School for a total of six years.

Berta am Tag ihrer Erstkommunion, 1918
Berta at her first communion, 1918

Strafarbeit der lebhaften Schülerin Berta, 1921
Penalty assignment for an overly vivacious Berta, 1921

Urkunde des bayerischen Königs an Adolf Hummel. Bereits 1916 erhielt er das Militär-Verdienstkreuz 2. Klasse für seine Verdienste als Geschützführer und Schirrmeister im Ersten Weltkrieg.
Certificate from the king of Bavaria, awarding Adolf Hummel the Distinguished Service Cross, second class, as early as 1916 for meritorious service as No. 1 gunner and motor sergeant in WWI.

Familie Hummel vor dem Sommerhaus (v. l. n. r.: Centa, Kätl, Ady, Viki, Berta, Viktoria und Adolf Hummel, Franzl), Pfingsten 1922
The Hummel family in front of their summer house (from the left: Centa, Kätl, Ady, Viki, Berta, Viktoria and Adolf Hummel, Franzl), Pentecost, 1922

In den Kriegsjahren hatte sich die Welt verändert. Am 11. November 1918 war endlich ein Waffenstillstandsvertrag unterzeichnet worden. Der Krieg hatte weltweit fast 10 Millionen Todesopfer und 20 Millionen Verwundete gefordert. Die deutsche Delegation fügte sich im Januar 1919 in Versailles bedingungslos in ihre Kapitulation. Adolf Hummel war am Ende des Krieges heimgekommen, unversehrt zur großen Erleichterung der Familie. Und das Leben war weitergegangen, man hatte in die Hände gespuckt und sich unermüdlich wieder den geschäftlichen Dingen zugewandt.

An der Höheren Mädchenschule in Simbach am Inn begann für Berta ab dem 2. Mai 1921 ein neues Leben. Die „Marienhöhe" war ein traditionelles Internat, das vom Institut der Englischen Fräulein[8] geleitet wurde. Die Schülerinnen waren nun in Klassen eingeteilt und Bertas Talent wurde von Anfang an erkannt und gefördert. Seltsamerweise schickten die Eltern die Töchter – vor Berta waren es Katharina und Viktoria – erst nach dem sechsten Jahr Volksschule in die weiterführende Ausbildung, dafür aber sollten sie eine Klasse in der neuen Schule überspringen. Dieses Vorgehen brachte Schwierigkeiten mit sich, denn es galt einiges an Lernstoff nachzuholen. Berta jedoch war eine gute und aufmerksame Schülerin. Immer wieder, auch in späteren Zeugnissen an der Hochschule, wurde ihr eine ganz eigene Kombination aus großem Fleiß, äußerst lebhaftem Gemüt und höchster Sensibilität bescheinigt. Gerade der stets so betonte Hinweis auf ihr feinfühliges Wesen lässt aufhorchen, ist er doch ein erster Anhaltspunkt auf die andere, die ernste und nach innen gekehrte Seite des lustigen, schlagfertigen Lausmädels.

Aufgang zur Volksschule Massing, August 1928
Elementary school, Massing, August 1928

Für die Heimfahrt in den Ferien: Antrag auf Fahrpreisermäßigung auf der Strecke Simbach-Massing
Going home for summer vacation: application for reduced train fare, Simbach-Massing

Das Institut „Marienhöhe" in Simbach, Ansichtskarte
The Institute "Marienhöhe" ("St. Mary's Heights"), picture postcard

Meanwhile the war had transformed the world. On November 11, 1918, an armistice had been signed at last. The war had cost ten million dead and 20 million invalids worldwide. In January of 1919, at Versailles, the German delegation had surrendered unconditionally. Adolf Hummel had returned unharmed at the end of the war, much to the relief of the family. Life resumed; one rolled up one's sleeves and, with renewed energy, turned to business again.

For Berta a new phase commenced on May 2, 1921, at the High School for Girls in Simbach on the Inn. "Marienhöhe" (St. Mary's Heights) was a traditional boarding school, run by the Institute of the English Conventuals.[8] Students were now divided into regular classes, and Berta's talent was recognized and furthered from the start. Oddly enough the parents sent all of their daughters to elementary school for six years – Katharina and Viktoria as well as Berta – before letting them proceed to secondary education, but then wanted them to skip a grade in the new school. This procedure was not without difficulties, as the girls would have to catch up on quite a bit of subject matter. But Berta was a good and attentive student. Time and again, both here and later at the university, she was credited with a unique combination of unflagging industry, liveliness of disposition and extreme sensibility. The repeated reference, from earliest times on, to her delicacy of mind is noteworthy as a first hint of the merry, quick-witted tomboy's other side of earnestness and inwardness.

Schülerarbeiten im Zeichenunterricht, 1921 und 1923
Drawing class works, 1921 and 1923

„Marienhöhe", Simbach, 1927/1928
"St. Mary's Heights," Simbach, 1927/1928

Eine lebenslang enge Verbindung:
die Schwestern Berta und Centa
Lifelong intimates:
the sisters Berta and Centa

Zwergerl auf dem Reck, 1934
Little gnome on the horizontal bar, 1934

Ehrenurkunde nach einem Sportfest, 1923
Certificate of outstanding performance
in a sports meeting, 1923

Trotz der liebevollen Zuwendung von Schwester Theresilla war Berta heilfroh gewesen, zu „den Großen" auf die neue Schule zu kommen. Heimweh kannte sie nicht. Schon drei Tage nach ihrer Ankunft schrieb sie restlos begeistert nach Hause: „Liebe Eltern! Nun bin ich in Simbach gut angekommen und es gefällt mir sehr gut. An das Zeitlang[9] denke ich gar nicht daran. Auch bin ich schon ganz eingewöhnt." Bertas Klassenkameradinnen wussten ihren quirligen Einfallsreichtum sehr zu schätzen, und ihre Mutter berichtete später, sie sei niemals fern gewesen, wenn es darum ging, etwas auszuhecken. Immer wieder muss sie zur Ordnung gerufen werden und „das langsame gesittete Gehen auf den Gängen fiel ihr besonders schwer"[10].

Sportlehrerin will Berta werden. Turnen ist ihr liebstes Fach. Die Stunde beginnt mit Gymnastik. Vorbeugen! Seitbeugen!, ruft die Lehrerin, dann geht es vielleicht ein wenig an die Ringe oder den Barren und zum Schluss ist Ballspielen angesagt. Die Schuluniform zwickt, man trägt die gleiche Bluse wie in der übrigen Schulzeit auch. Aber es ist herrlich, endlich nicht mehr stillsitzen zu müssen!

Erstaunlicherweise hegte die kleine Schwester Centa zu dieser Zeit den Wunsch, Zeichenlehrerin zu werden. Deshalb war auch das „Cenerl" die possierliche Hummel mit Pinseln und Palette, als Berta jedes ihrer Geschwister auf Papier bannte, jedes mit seinen typischen Accessoires dem Familiennamen Ehre machend. Doch Centa traute sich mit der Zeit und in wachsender Konkurrenz zur Begabung der großen Schwester nicht mehr so recht an Farben und Bleistift heran. Berta ihrerseits wurde von Centa im Turntalent bald überflügelt, sodass ihr nun doch die Aussicht, Zeichenlehrerin zu werden, verlockender erschien. Eine Wahl, die auch der kunstliebende Vater guthieß und ermutigte. Ein paar Jahre später übrigens, als Centa nach der Schule fest zur Ausbildung als Turnlehrerin entschlossen war, riet Berta ihr dringend dazu, doch auch lieber ein Kunststudium zu machen. Ihre Begründung: Turnlehrerin sei nicht gut, weil schnell vorbei, wenn man älter würde, Zeichenlehrerin dagegen ganz einfach und dauerhaft möglich.

Briefe an die Eltern in Massing. Oft schmückt sie den Briefbogen mit einer kleinen Zeichnung im oberen linken Eck, eine liebevolle Geste, die Berta ihr Leben lang beibehalten wird.
Letters to the parents in Massing. Berta often decorated the page with a little drawing in the upper left corner, a loving gesture she continued all her life.

Despite Sister Theresilla's loving attention, Berta was really glad to join the "big kids" in the new school. Pining for home was not her style. A mere three days after her arrival, she wrote full of enthusiasm to her family: "Dear parents! I am safely arrived in Simbach, and I like it very much. I have no thought of homesickness. And I am already completely settled in." Her classmates appreciated her exuberant inventiveness, and her mother later told how Berta had never been far off when there was a prank to be hatched. Time and again she had to be called to order. "Walking slowly and demurely in the hallways was particularly difficult for her."[9]

She wanted to become a sports teacher, gym being her favorite subject. The lesson always began with gymnastics. Bend forward! Bend sideways! the teacher would call out. Then perhaps there would be some work on the rings or on the parallel bars, and at the end there was always a ballgame. The school uniform pinched – one wore the same blouse as during the rest of the school day. But what a treat not to have to sit still for a change!

Ironically enough, it was the younger sister Centa who at this time had the desire to become an art teacher. When Berta portrayed each of her siblings with a characteristic attribute to honor the family name, it was "Cenerl" who appeared attractively armed with brush and palette. But with the increasing competition from the talent of her older sister, Centa gradually grew less and less eager to venture near paint and pencil. Conversely Centa soon outstripped her sister in gymnastic ability, so that the prospect of a career as an art teacher became more attractive to Berta – a choice that her art-loving father also approved and encouraged. Several years later, incidentally, when Centa left the school firmly resolved to embark on a training in physical education, Berta urged her to study art instead. The job of a gym teacher, she thought, had the drawback of being over too soon once one got older, whereas one could easily remain an art instructor.

Bewertungsblatt der schulischen Leistungen, das den Eltern zur Unterschrift vorgelegt werden musste
School report card, which had to be presented to the parents for their signature

Hummelkind Centa, 1923/1925
Hummel child Centa, 1923/1925

Personalausweis der 16-jährigen Berta
Berta mit Kätzchen in der Schuluniform des Instituts „Marienhöhe", 1925
Berta's identity card at age 16
Berta, with kitten, in the school uniform of "St. Mary's Heights," 1925

Nach Friedrich Wilhelm Webers „Dreizehnlinden", einer beliebten Schullektüre Anfang des 20. Jahrhunderts: Elmar, Kopfstudie, 1925/26
After Friedrich Wilhelm Weber's Dreizehnlinden ("Thirteen-Lindens"), a popular work of juvenile fiction much used in schools in the early 20th century: Elmar, head sketch, 1925/26

Als Centa zwei Jahre nach Berta auf die „Marienhöhe" kam, waren alle vier Hummel-Mädchen auf dem Internat. Ganz anders als die ältere Schwester war das arme Mädchen furchtbar von Heimweh geplagt. Die Kleinen waren im Erdgeschoss untergebracht, während Berta schon zu den „Oberen" im ersten Stock gehörte. Wenn Centa einmal wieder gar so viel „Zeitlang" nach Hause hatte, fragten sie ihre Klassenkameradinnen: „Du hast doch eine Schwester hier. Warum gehst du nicht hinauf zu ihr?" Aber jedes Mal, wenn Centa dann in der Hoffnung, ihr Heimweh lindern zu können, kleinlaut bei Berta ankam, wies diese sie mit den Worten ab: „Geh wieder hinunter, du musst dich an deine Klasse gewöhnen!" Sie wollte ihrer kleinen Schwester sicherlich das Beste und konnte sich einfach nicht vorstellen, dass man im Internat mit so vielen anderen Mädchen zusammen nicht zufrieden sein könnte.

Ihr Wohlbefinden auf der „Marienhöhe" gab Berta gern in ihren Briefen nach Hause wieder. Oft fand sich eine Zeichnung auf dem Briefbogen, mal ein paar Schafhirten, mal ein Haus mit Birke, mal eine Rose. Daneben erzählte sie dann in plaudernder Spontaneität von Schulausflügen in die Berge und nach Salzburg, vom feierlichen Geburtstag der Mater Oberin, einem Aufsatz mit dem Titel „Des Weibes Welt ist das Haus", von den Fingerübungen, die ihr die Violinlehrerin aufgab, und ob es regnete oder nicht.

Beinahe nie vergaß sie, in den Mitteilungen an die Eltern mit „Euer dankbares Kind Berta" zu unterschreiben, eine Grußformel, die damals durchaus gängig war und die auch ihre Schwester benutzte. Dennoch verstärkt sich beim Lesen ihrer Briefe der Eindruck, dass sie ihre Dankbarkeit schon als Heranwachsende außergewöhnlich ernst nahm und dass sie im Gegenzug zu den „Opfern" ihrer Eltern unbedingt etwas zurückgeben wollte, sei es Fleiß und gute Noten, seien es Gebete für ihre Angehörigen zu Hause.

With Centa's arrival, two years after Berta, at "St. Mary's Heights," all four of the Hummel girls were enrolled in the boarding school. Quite unlike her older sister, the poor youngster was plagued by homesickness. The little ones were quartered on the ground floor, while Berta already ranked among the "upper classes" on the first floor. Whenever Centa grew particularly sick for home, her classmates would tell her: "You have a sister here with you. Why don't you go up to her?" But every time the downcast Centa would appear before Berta in hopes of soothing her loneliness, she was turned away with the words: "Go back down, you have to make friends with the girls in your class!" Berta surely meant well by her little sister; she simply could not imagine how with so many other girls around one should not be happy at the boarding school.

How comfortable she herself was at "St. Mary's Heights" Berta frequently conveyed in her reports back home. Often a drawing was added to the letter, whether a group of shepherds, or a house with a birch tree, or a rose. Alongside these, she would write down spontaneous accounts of school excursions into the mountains or to Salzburg, of the birthday celebration for the Mother Superior, or she might attach an essay entitled "A Woman's World is the Home," or tell about the finger exercises her violin teacher made her do, rain or shine.

She rarely forgot to sign her communications to her parents with "your grateful child, Berta." It was a formula common at the time, which her sister also used. Nevertheless Berta from early on in her adolescence conveyed the impression that she took her gratitude more seriously than most and that she wished to give something in return for her parents' "sacrifices," whether in the form of her industry and good marks or in that of prayers for those at home.

Eine gute Schülerin: Jahreszeugnis 1925
An excellent student:
year-end report card, 1925

Schulausflug nach
Braunau, 1925 (Berta ganz links)
Class excursion to
Braunau, 1925 (Berta on far left)

Hausordnung mit detailliertem
Tagesablauf im Institut „Marienhöhe"
House rules and daily schedule at
"St. Mary's Heights"

Immer mitten im Geschehen: Berta im Harlekinkostüm, 1925
Always in the midst of things: Berta in a harlequin costume, 1925

Berta sprach von „malerisch", wenn ihr eine Landschaftsszenerie besonders gut gefiel. Am 11. Dezember 1924 schrieb sie an die Eltern ihren größten Weihnachtswunsch: „Ich weiß daß die Zeit schwer ist u. Ihr liebe Eltern Euch so große Opfer für mich auferlegt, so will ich Euch liebe Eltern meine Wünsche fast nicht vorbringen; denn so gerne hätte ich einen Ölfarbenkasten mit Palette. Liebste Eltern, ich aber will mich doppelt bemühen Euch eine große Freude durch mein Zeugnis [zu] bereiten." Und ein Jahr später: „Ich bin Euch, liebste Eltern so viel Dank schuldig u. darum finde ich es fast nicht recht, dass ich Euch meinen leisesten Wunsch schreibe; nämlich das Buch ‚Der Kunstschatz' zu haben; in diesem sind die bedeutendsten Künstler bezw. Maler u. ihre berühmtesten Werke enthalten."[11]

Weihnachten! Zu Weihnachten ging es für alle Kinder nach Hause. Was war das für ein Fest voller Zauber! An diesem Feiertag waren alle beisammen, die Eltern ließen das Geschäft sein und widmeten sich nur der Familie. Alles war liebevollst arrangiert und üppig geschmückt. Geschenke „vom Christkind" für die sechs Geschwister gab es reichlich. Als sie klein waren, bekamen alle vier Mädchen Puppen mit echten Haaren, damals eine teure Besonderheit.

Ersehntes Weihnachtsgeschenk: Bertas erster Ölmalkasten
Longed-for Christmas present: Berta's first oil paint box

Vorfreude auf das Weihnachtsfest, 1925
Looking forward to Christmas, 1925

Maria im Walde, 1926/1927
The Virgin in the Woods, 1926/1927

Ein paar Jahre später hatte der Vater mit großem handwerklichem Geschick eine prächtige Kasperlebühne für alle gebaut, einen großen Guckkasten mit zweigeteiltem Vorhang, Kulissen und Figuren. Voller Hingabe wurden nun fieberhaft Stücke ausgedacht und vorgeführt, jeder, der nur irgendwie den Weg kreuzte, wurde sofort auf einen Zuschauerplatz genötigt. Einmal, ein Onkel war diesmal chancenloses Opfer gewesen, kamen Berta und Centa nach Beendigung der Vorstellung hinter ihrem Vorhang hervor, um sich den wohlverdienten Applaus abzuholen. Wie waren sie enttäuscht, als sie feststellen mussten, dass sich ihr Publikum die Dunkelheit des Zuschauerraums zunutze gemacht und sich heimlich davongemacht hatte!

Berta vor ihrem ersten
großen Ölbild, Segelschiff, 1926/1927
Berta working on her first large-format
oil painting, Sailingship, 1926/1927

Landscapes that she liked particularly well Berta called "picturesque." On December 11, 1924, she wrote her parents her biggest Christmas wish. "I know that the times are hard and that you, dear parents, take such great sacrifices upon yourselves for me, and so I hardly dare, dear parents, to tell you my wishes. But I would so love to have a set of oil paints and a palette. Dearest parents I will redouble my efforts in return so I can make you very happy with my report card." And a year later: "I owe you such gratitude, dear parents, and therefore almost think it wrong to write you my least wish, to have the book *Der Kunstschatz* ("A Treasury of Art"), which contains the most important artists and painters and their most famous works."[10]

Christmas! All the children went home for Christmas. What a magic-filled holiday, when they would all be together, and the parents forgot about business and devoted themselves wholly to the family. Everything was arranged lovingly and richly decorated. There were plenty of presents "from the Christ Child" for all six siblings. When they were little, the four girls got dolls with real hair, a costly rarity at the time. A few years later, the father had built a magnificently crafted Punch and Judy theater for all the children – a large proscenium stage with a split curtain, backdrops and figures. With feverish dedication the children now concocted and performed plays, and whoever was somehow within reach was promptly pressed into a spectator's seat. Once, when an uncle had been the hapless victim, Berta and Centa came out from behind the curtain at the end of the performance to garner their well-earned applause, only to discover to their utter disappointment that their audience had secretly made off under cover of the darkness in the auditorium!

Einladung zur musikalischen Schlussfeier der stolzen Absolventinnen, Absolvia 1926
Invitation of the proud graduates to the musical graduation ceremony, Graduation 1926

Eine selbstbewusste junge Frau: Berta (links) 1926/1927
A self-assured young woman: Berta (left) 1926/1927

Familie Hummel, 1926 (v. l. n. r.: Viktoria und Adolf Hummel, Franzl, Viki, Ady, Centa, Kätl, Berta)
The Hummel family, 1926 (from the left: Viktoria and Adolf Hummel, Franzl, Viki, Ady, Centa, Kätl, Berta)

Bertas so schüchtern geäußertem Wunsch nach dem Ölmalkasten hatte der Vater nur allzu gerne stattgegeben. Voller Stolz auf das Talent seiner Tochter war er fest entschlossen, ihr den Weg in eine künstlerische Zukunft zu ebnen und ihr nach der Schule eine Ausbildung zur Zeichenlehrerin zu ermöglichen.

Berta ist die einzige Schülerin, die den Zeichensaal auch außerhalb der Schulstunden benutzen darf. Oft sitzt sie hoch konzentriert da in ihrer Freizeit und zeichnet und malt. Wenn etwas gar nicht gelingen will, hilft ihr Schwester Stefania, die Kunstlehrerin.

Auf der „Marienhöhe" war man von Bertas Begabung überzeugt. Die Lehrerinnen förderten sie, wo sie nur konnten. Am 25. März 1925 erhielt Berta ihr Abschlusszeugnis. Darin heißt es: „Das Gemüt dieses Mädchens ist äußerst empfindsam, ihre einmal gefassten guten Willensentschlüsse setzt sie mit großer Energie in die Tat um. (...) Sie besitzt ein angeborenes Talent für Formenschönheit."[12] Berta konnte nun zum ersten Mal die Weichen ihres Lebenswegs stellen. Sie würde nach München gehen, auf die renommierte Staatliche Kunstgewerbeschule. Die Aufnahmeprüfung galt als hart. Zwischen dem Schulabschluss und dieser Prüfung blieb sie noch ein weiteres Jahr in Simbach, um sich mithilfe ihrer Kunstlehrerin auf die kommende Aufgabe vorzubereiten.

Berta mit dem Familienhund „Lord", am Fenster ihr jüngster Bruder Franzl, 1926/1927
Berta with the family dog "Lord," at the window her youngest brother Franzl, 1926/1927

erta's father had been only too glad to fulfill her shyly uttered request for a paint box. Full of pride about his daughter's talent, he was resolved to ease her way toward a future as an artist and to facilitate an art teacher training after high school for her.

The only student allowed to use the art room after school hours, Berta would often spend her free time there, drawing and painting in utter concentration. If something did not want to go right at all, Sister Stefania, her art teacher, would offer some tips.

The teachers at "St. Mary's Heights" were convinced of Berta's talent and would help and encourage her wherever they could. In 1925, Berta graduated. Her certificate read in part: "The girl is of an exceptionally sensitive disposition. Sound decisions, once made, she implements with great energy. She has an innate aptitude for beauty of form."[11] Berta was now able for the first time to set her own course. She would attend the renowned Academy of Arts and Crafts in Munich. The admission test was said to be hard. During the year between her graduation and this admission exam, she appears to have stayed in Simbach at least part of the time to prepare for the impending task with the aid of her art teacher.

Vorbereitungen auf die Aufnahmeprüfung an der Kunstgewerbeschule: Bertas Schwestern Kätl und Viki am Klavier, 1926
Preparations for the admission test at the School of Arts and Crafts Berta's sisters Kätl and Viki at the piano, 1926

Dirigent im Frack, Juli 1926
Conductor, July 1926

Centa Hummel

Erinnerungen an eine Jugend

Sie sind diejenige aus der Familie, die Berta ihr Leben lang am nächsten stand … Wir hatten unsere ganze Jugend zusammen. In der Volksschule, auf der höheren Mädchenschule, da waren wir einige Jahre beieinander. Dann bin ich nach München gegangen, dort waren wir auch gleichzeitig. Sie hat die Kunstschule gemacht und ich war beim Turnen. Und dann war ich oft und lang in Sießen. Das weiß ja keiner.

Wie haben Sie Ihre Eltern und das Zuhause Ihrer Kindheit in Erinnerung? Wissen Sie, das war ein Geschäftshaus daheim. Mein Vater war Geschäftsmann, meine Mutter eine enorm tüchtige Geschäftsfrau. Wir hatten ein Kindermädel, das wurde auch gebraucht, weil wir ja gleich zu sechst waren. Ich kann nicht sagen, dass wir keine schöne Jugend gehabt haben. Da gibt es viel zu erzählen über das Zusammenhalten der Kinder untereinander. Die zwei Buben, die haben wir Mädchen schon in Schach gehalten! Ich kann mich erinnern, dass wir sehr viel gespielt haben, und ganz selten einmal hat meine Mutter mitgemacht. Theater haben wir gespielt. Mein Vater war ja so künstlerisch veranlagt, der hat uns an Weihnachten ein Kasperltheater gebaut. Die Stücke haben wir uns selber ausgedacht.
Und Ihre Schwester Berta? Sie war lustig und lebhaft. Und sehr beliebt.

Die Zeiten Ihrer Kindheit waren schwierig. Haben Sie den Ersten Weltkrieg bewusst miterlebt? Eigentlich weniger. Nur mit ein paar lächerlichen Sachen. Da haben wir mal zur Nacht einen Kakao gekriegt, den mochten wir einfach nicht. Komisch, das hat sich so eingeprägt. Da hieß es dann: „Andere Kinder wären froh, wenn sie einen Kakao bekommen würden." Das ist das Ganze vom Krieg. Von Hamburg sind Kinder zu uns verschickt worden. Aber die Sprache haben wir nicht verstanden (lacht). Einer kam Jahre später wieder nach Massing zu uns und hat gesagt: „Ich bin bei euch gewesen als ‚Landverschickter'."

Als für die Hummelkinder der Ernst des Lebens begann – was haben Ihre Eltern zu Ihrer Berufswahl gesagt? Vor allem für Mädchen waren derart eigene Pläne doch keine Selbstverständlichkeit. Da kann ich mich an keinen Widerstand erinnern. Der eine Bruder, der jüngere, ist Arzt geworden und der andere hat das Geschäft gekriegt. Studiert hat ein jedes von uns. Mein Vater war der einzige Bub in der Familie gewesen, der musste das Geschäft übernehmen. Er wäre so gern Bildhauer geworden. Oder Steinmetz. Er hat sich sehr eingesetzt, dass Bertl nach München gekommen ist und ist sogar mit ihr hinge-

Berta und Centa: ein lebenslang enges Schwesternverhältnis

fahren. Es wird immer so betont, dass ein Mädchen vom Land so selten nach München in die Großstadt kommt – aber sie hat das Talent einfach in sich gehabt.

Childhood Reminiscences

Of the family, you were the one that was closest to Berta throughout her life … We had all of our childhood and adolescence together. For a number of years we were together in elementary school and again in boarding-school. When I went to Munich, we again were there at the same time. She attended art school, I was in gymnastics. And then I was often in Siessen, and for long periods of time. Nobody knows about that.

What do you remember about your parents and your childhood? You know, our home was really a place of business. My father was a businessman, my mother an enormously capable businesswoman. We had a nursemaid, which was really needed, because there were six of us. I can't say that we did not have a happy childhood. There is much to tell about us kids sticking together. And as to the two boys, we four girls certainly managed to keep them in check! We played a lot, and once in a great while my mother joined in. We did a lot of theater. My father had such artistic talent, he built us a Punch and Judy theater for Christmas. We made up the plays ourselves.

And your sister Berta? She was so jolly and vivacious. And very popular.

Your childhood years were difficult ones. Were you very conscious of World War One? Actually not much. Just a few ridiculous things. Once we got some cocoa before bedtime that we just didn't like. Funny how that sticks in your mind. So then we were told: "Other children would be happy to get any cocoa." That's all there was about the war. Kids were evacuated to us from Hamburg. But we didn't understand their language (laughs). Years later, one of them came back to us to Massing and said: "I was here with you as an 'evacuee.'"

When the real world caught up with the Hummel children – what did your parents say to your vocational choices? Especially for girls, after all, it was by no means a matter of course to have plans of one's own. I don't recall there being any objections. One of my brothers, the younger one, became a physician, and the other got the business. All of us went to college. My father had been the only boy in the family, so he had to take over the store. He had wanted so much to be a sculptor or a stone mason. He did all he could to enable Bertl to go to Munich, he even accompanied her on her journey there. It is always said that girls from the country seldom get to a big city like Munich – but she simply had the talent it takes.

Berta and Centa: sisters and lifelong friends

Ein außergewöhnliches Talent

An der Staatsschule für angewandte Kunst in München

An Exceptional Talent – At the State School of Arts and Crafts in Munich

Selbstporträt, 1928
Self-portrait, 1928

Ein Selbstporträt 1928: ein ernstes Gesicht, zurückhaltend, beinahe verschlossen, den eigenen Blick jedoch genau beobachtend. Berta wirkt ruhig, aber hoch konzentriert, forschend, fast ein wenig trotzig schaut sie dem Betrachter entgegen. Auffällig die kräftige Schraffur, mit der sie ihr Gesicht umgibt, ihre klaren Gesichtszüge treten aus einer dunklen Wirrnis heraus. Haare und Halspartie dagegen lassen sich nur erahnen. Was mag in der 19-Jährigen vorgegangen sein? Was erwartet sie sich von ihrem Leben?

Die Zeiten waren hart. Manch einer ahnte schon lange, welche dunklen Wolken sich über München am Ende der 20er-Jahre zusammengezogen hatten. München, das einst so sorglose „Isar-Athen", war nach dem Ersten Weltkrieg verändert, traumatisiert und materiell schwer angeschlagen über das Fiasko der Räterepublik in die Weimarer Republik hineingeschlittert. Dabei war die weiß-blaue Stadt so vielgerühmt gewesen für ihr freisinniges Laisser-faire, die sprichwörtliche „Liberalitas Bavariae". In der Tat, „München leuchtete"[1] im 19. Jahrhundert, als die Wittelsbacherkönige die schönen Künste zur Staatsräson erklärt hatten. Eine Stadt der Musen und Mäzene, wo die reich entlohnten Maler und Bildhauer sich hochherrschaftliche Villen vor die Tore der Metropole stellen lassen konnten[2]. Eine Stadt, die den Ruf genoss, dass man nirgendwo auf der Welt besser die akademische Kunst studieren könne. Diesem Ruf waren neben vielen anderen Wilhelm Busch und Lovis Corinth gefolgt. 1898 schrieb sogar der junge Picasso von der Iberischen Halbinsel: „Wenn ich einen Sohn hätte, der Maler werden möchte, würde ich ihn nicht einen Augenblick lang in Spanien festhalten, und glauben Sie nicht, dass ich ihn nach Paris schicken würde (wo ich selber gerne wäre), sondern nach München."[3]

Um die Jahrhundertwende und kurz danach waren Alfred Kubin und Giorgio de Chirico an der Königlichen Akademie gewesen, ein paar Jahre später Wassily Kandinsky und Paul Klee, beide in der Klasse des letzten Münchner „Malerfürsten" Franz von Stuck. Kandinskys wegweisend abstrakte Improvisation Nr. 5 und die avantgardistische Künstlervereinigung „Der Blaue Reiter" waren an der

Isar entstanden und heiß erörtert worden. Das kulturelle Geschehen gehörte zum Alltag der gebildeten Münchner und Wahlmünchner.

Münchner Dächer, 1928/1930
Munich, bird's-eye view, 1928/1930

München, im Stadtteil Au, 1929
Munich, city district Au, 1929

In a self-portrait from the year 1928, we see a serious face, aloof, reserved, but closely observant of her own gaze. Berta appears calm, but highly concentrated, scrutinizing, almost a little defiant, as she looks at the viewer. The bold cross-hatching surrounding her face, making her clear features emerge from a dark tangle, is striking; hair and neck are only hinted at. What might have been going on in the mind of the 19-year-old? What does she expect her life to be like?

These were hard times. Many could already foresee the dark clouds that were gathering over the Munich of the late 1920s. Munich, once the carefree "Athens on the Isar," but now changed, traumatized, and shattered in the aftermath of the World War, had slithered via the fiasco of the Bavarian Räterepublik ("Republic governed by commissars") into the Weimar Republic. The white-blue city had been famed for its liberal laisser-faire, the proverbial "Liberalitas Bavariae." "Munich was radiant"[1] indeed during the 19th century, when the Wittelsbach kings had made the fine arts a state matter. It was a city of painters and patrons, where richly paid artists and sculptors were able to build noble mansions for themselves outside the gates of the metropolis.[2] A city with the reputation that there was no better place in the world for the study of academic art. Wilhelm Busch and Lovis Corinth, among many others, had followed that call. Even the young Picasso wrote in 1898 from the Iberian Peninsula: "If I had a son who wanted to become a painter, I would not keep him in Spain for a moment, and don't you think I would send him to Paris, either (where I would love to be myself), but to Munich."[3]

Around the turn of the century and sometime thereafter, Alfred Kubin and Giorgio de Chirico had been at the Bavarian Royal Academy, Vassily Kandinsky and Paul Klee a few years later, both of them in the class of the last of the Munich's "princes of painting," Franz von Stuck. Both Kandinsky's path-breaking abstract Improvisation No. 5 and the avant-garde artists' association "Der Blaue Reiter" ("The Blue Rider") had originated and been hotly debated at the Isar. Cultural events were part of the everyday life of educated Munich residents.

München, Viktualienmarkt, 1929/1930
Market in Munich, 1929/1930

Man diskutierte, theoretisierte, polemisierte. Ästhetische Erwägungen waren nachzulesen in den Magazinen „Jugend"[4] und „Die Insel"[5]. Der beißende antiwilhelminische Spott der Zeitschrift „Simplicissimus", gegründet 1896, die die Crème de la Crème begnadeter Schreiber und Zeichner in ihrem Mitarbeiterstab[6] versammelte, fand mit der Zeit auch über die bayerischen Landesgrenzen hinaus begeisterten Absatz. Albert Langen, einer der Gründer des berühmten Satireblatts[7], hatte Heinrich Manns heiklen Roman „Professor Unrat oder das Ende eines Tyrannen" verlegt und damit im ganzen Deutschen Reich einen Skandal provoziert. Es war die Zeit der berüchtigten Schwabinger Boheme. Man lebte, konferierte, feierte in Extremen. Entrückte Poesie und wilder Weltverbesserungswahn. Der kapriziöse Stefan George versammelte jährlich einen erlauchten Kreis ergebener Jünger bei seinem ebenso exzentrischen Münchner Mäzen Karl Wolfskehl. Derweil der Seemannsdichter Ringelnatz jeden Abend im „Simpl" vortrug, jener legendären rauch- und inspirationsgeschwängerten Kneipe, die Namen und Logo von der oben genannten Satirezeitschrift entlehnt hatte. Ein paar Straßen weiter, vielleicht auf einem der beliebten Kostümfeste, warfen sich der freigeistigen Gräfin Franziska zu Reventlow die Schriftsteller, Dichter und Denker zu Füßen. Ein Rausch der Sinne im Namen der Kunst!
Und dann 1914 das jähe Ende, als auch ein großer Teil der Künstler in verhängnisvoller Begeisterung dem Aufruf zum Krieg folgte.

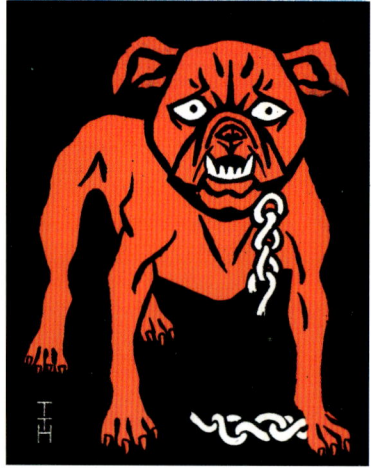

Die berühmte Bulldogge auf dem Cover des „Simplicissimus"
The famous bulldog cover, Simplicissimus

Ab diesem Zeitpunkt veränderte sich die Lage grundlegend. Die künstlerische Aufbruchstimmung war dahin, man begnügte sich in der Regel mit dem Ruhm vergangener Tage. Die Avantgarde der „Goldenen Zwanziger" tobte jetzt in Berlin. Auf einmal waren in bürgerlichen Salons reaktionäre und antidemokratische Meinungen en vogue. Radikale Ansichten bekamen fruchtbaren Nährboden. Der „letzte Hautausschlag Münchens – nach den eisernen die Hakenkreuze"[8] war nicht mehr auszurotten. Die Nationalsozialisten setzten mithilfe ihrer expandierenden Presseorgane alles unter Druck, was nicht ihrer eigenen Ästhetik entsprach. Zielscheibe war jegliche abstrahierende Kunstrichtung. Und man hatte eine genaue Vorstellung, wie dem Unerwünschten beizukommen sei. So tönte der „Völkische Beobachter": „Seit 10 Jahren wütet eine eigenartige Geistesseuche in unserer Stadt, neue Kunst, Expressionismus, von uns Kunstpest genannt. (…) Dabei ist erfreulich, dass diese Pest nicht zu einer allgemeinen septischen Verseuchung führte, sondern sich in Abszessen sammelte, die man nur aufzuschneiden braucht."[9]

Bekanntgabe der Mobilmachung vor der Feldherrnhalle in München, 1914
Proclamation of the mobilization in Munich, 1914

Debate, theory, polemic flourished. Speculations in aesthetics could be read about in the periodicals *Jugend* ("Youth")[4] and *Die Insel* ("The Island")[5]. The caustic anti-Wilhelminian satire of the *Simplicissimus*, founded in 1896, which attracted the crème de la crème of talented writers and caricaturists to its staff,[6] in time gained an enthusiastic readership far beyond the Bavarian borders. Albert Langen, one of the founders of the famed satirical magazine,[7] had published Heinrich Mann's risqué novel *Professor Unrat oder das Ende eines Tyrannen* (*The Blue Angel*), which had provoked a scandal throughout the German Reich. It was the period of the notorious Schwabing Bohème, a time of extreme living, debating, partying, of enraptured poesy and wild, starry-eyed idealism. The capricious poet Stefan George annually gathered a select circle of devoted disciples at the home of his equally eccentric Munich patron Karl Wolfskehl. Meanwhile the sailor poet Joachim Ringelnatz held forth nightly in the "Simpl," the legendary smoke- and inspiration-filled dive that derived its name and logo from the *Simplicissimus*. A few blocks away, perhaps at one of the popular costume parties, writers, poets and thinkers sat at the feet of the free-thinking Countess Franziska zu Reventlow. A never-ending orgy of sensuality in the name of art!

Then, in 1914, came the sudden end, when even a large majority of the artists followed the call to arms with fatal enthusiasm.

Gautag München-Oberbayern der NSDAP am 3. Juli 1932, Vorbeimarsch SA und SS an Adolf Hitler in der Münchner Widenmayerstraße, hinter Hitler im Auto Ernst Röhm und Rudolf Heß
NSDAP gau celebration Munich-Upper Bavaria in July 3, 1932. Defile of the SA and SS past Adolf Hitler, in the car behind Hitler Ernst Röhm and Rudolf Hess

Everything changed thereafter. The spirit of a new beginning in art was gone, people were for the most part content to rest on their past laurels. The avant-garde of the "Golden Twenties" was now the rage in Berlin. In Munich's bourgeois salons, reactionary and anti-democratic sentiments were suddenly fashionable, so that radical views found a fertile soil. "Munich's final skin eruption – after the Iron Crosses the Crooked ones [swastikas]"[8] became incurable. The National Socialists used their expanding press to exert pressure on anything that did not match their own aesthetics. Their target was any tendency toward abstraction in art. And they knew exactly how to get at this undesirable development. Thus the *Völkische Beobachter* orated: "For ten years now a peculiar intellectual disease has been raging in our city, a new art form called Expressionism – we call it art plague. (…) Fortunately, this scourge has not yet led to a pandemic sepsis but has remained localized in certain abscesses that only need to be lanced."[9]

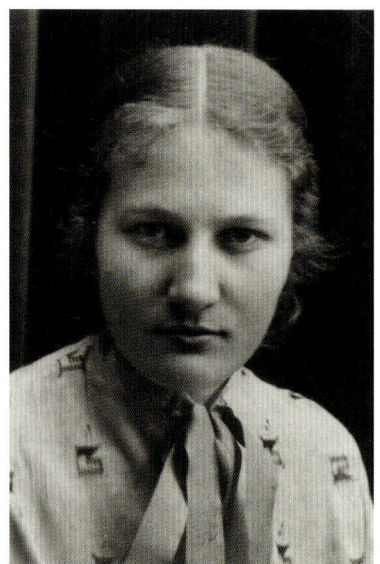

Bertas Passbild, 1928
Berta's passport picture, 1928

Aus den Bestimmungen der Staatlichen Kunstgewerbeschule München
From the Rules of the State School of Arts and Crafts, Munich

Auch der fehlgeschlagene Hitler-Putsch von 1923 konnte das kommende Terrorregime nicht aufhalten. Den Münchner Publizisten Wilhelm Hausenstein[10] beunruhigte der Stimmungsumschwung zutiefst: „Die Wandlung ist ungeheuerlich, diese Wandlung, die einer Zerstörung gleichkommt."[11] Die Weichen waren gestellt. Adolf Hitler hatte „sein" München längst zur „Hauptstadt der Bewegung"[12] auserkoren.

In diese Situation stolperte das Mädchen Berta nun Ende der 20er-Jahre hinein. Anfangs wird sie sich kaum über Münchens Probleme jener Tage den Kopf zerbrochen haben. Sie hatte sich zu der Aufnahmeprüfung an der Staatlichen Kunstgewerbeschule[13] angemeldet, um ihre Ausbildung zur Zeichenlehrerin zu beginnen. Zur Einschreibung war eine Mappe vorzulegen, „künstlerische Begabung muß durch Vorlage von Zeichnungen, Entwürfen, Skizzen und sonstigen früher oder später entstandenen Versuchen nachgewiesen werden", hieß es in den Bestimmungen des Instituts. „An Arbeitsmaterial ist zur Prüfung mitzubringen: Gerät zum Zeichnen und Malen (Bleistift, Kohle oder Kreide, Gummi, Aquarell- oder Temperafarben), acht bis zehn Bogen Zeichenpapier auf Block oder Reißbrett." Ferner: zwei Passbilder, 10 Mark Prüfungsgebühr („dieser Betrag verfällt bei nichtbestandener Prüfung"), 10 Mark Einschreibegebühr und bei bestandener Prüfung 30 Mark Schulgeld für das laufende Semester. Derartig ausgerüstet kam nun Berta also im April 1927 im unbekannten München an.

Ihr Vater hat sich ausnahmsweise von den geschäftlichen Verpflichtungen daheim freimachen können und begleitet sie. Nun soll ein ganz neues Leben beginnen. Voller Hoffnung, aus der Begabung das Beste herauszuholen. Voller Bangen vor der unbekannten Fremde, zum ersten Mal fern von häuslicher und schulischer Obhut.

Am Abend des 27. April, allein in der fremden Stadt, schrieb sie erschöpft nach Hause: „Meine liebsten Eltern! Nun, Gott sei Dank ist der 3. Tag vorbei. Mir gefällt es bis jetzt gar nicht in München, fühle mich furchtbar einsam." Am ersten Tag der Prüfungen sei innerhalb von drei Stunden ein alter Lehnstuhl mit darübergeworfener Decke zu zeichnen gewesen, am nächsten Tag habe man sich thematisch mit dem Motto „Geburtstag" beschäftigen sollen und dann mit einem Ornamentikentwurf für einen Spiegelrahmen. Die letzte Zeichenprüfung, eine Bewegungsstudie, stünde noch aus.

Zur Ausbildung gehörten auch Entwürfe in Ornamentik: Kindertapete, 1927

The training program included ornamental design: Wallpaper for children, 1927

Even the failed Hitler putsch of 1923 could not arrest the coming terror regime. The Munich journalist Wilhelm Hausenstein[10] was deeply disturbed by the reversal in outlook: "The change is horrendous, a change that is tantamount to wholesale destruction."[11] The new course was set: Hitler had long since chosen "his" Munich to be the "capital of the movement."[12]

Into this situation young Berta stumbled at the end of the twenties. At first she probably did not trouble her head much about Munich's problems of the day. She had registered for the admission exam at the State School of Arts and Crafts[13] in order to embark upon her training as an art teacher. Along with her registration she had to turn in a portfolio. "Artistic talent must be documented by submitting drawings, outlines, sketches, and other earlier or later attempts," the School's instructions read. "The following art supplies are to be brought to the exam: utensils for drawing and painting (pencil, charcoal or chalk, eraser, water colors and tempera), eight or ten sheets of drawing paper on a pad or drawing-board." Also required were two passport pictures, an examination fee of 10 marks ("non-refundable if the exam is failed"), a 10 marks registration fee, and, upon passing the test, 30 marks for tuition for the first semester. Thus equipped, Berta arrived in April of 1927 in the strange city of Munich.

Her father had for once been able to free himself of his business obligations in order to accompany her. An entirely new life was about to begin, one full of hope to make the most of her talent, full of apprehension about the unknown environment, far from all protection of home and boarding-school.

On the evening of April 27, now alone in the alien city, Berta wrote wearily: "My dearest parents! A third day is done, thank God. So far I do not like Munich at all; I feel terribly bereft." On the first day of the examination, they had to draw an old armchair with a blanket thrown over it. On the next day they had to work on the theme of "birthday" and then design ornaments for a mirror frame. The final drawing test, a motion study, was still to come.

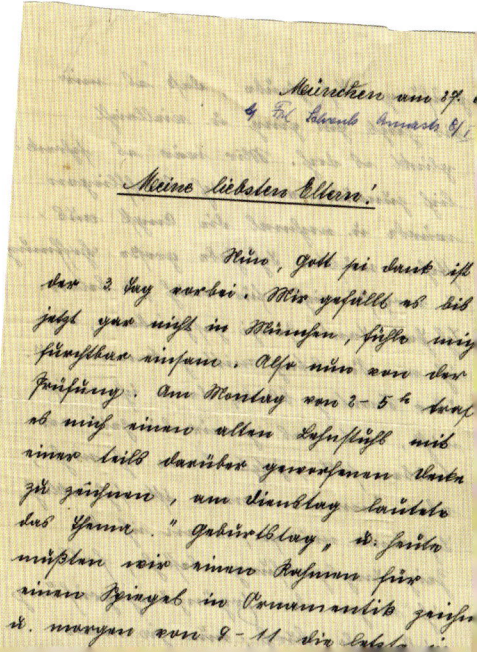

Heimweh: der erste Brief aus München an die Eltern

Homesickness: the first letter to the parents from Munich

*Die Kunstgewerbe-
schule in der Luisenstraße*
The State School on Luisenstrasse

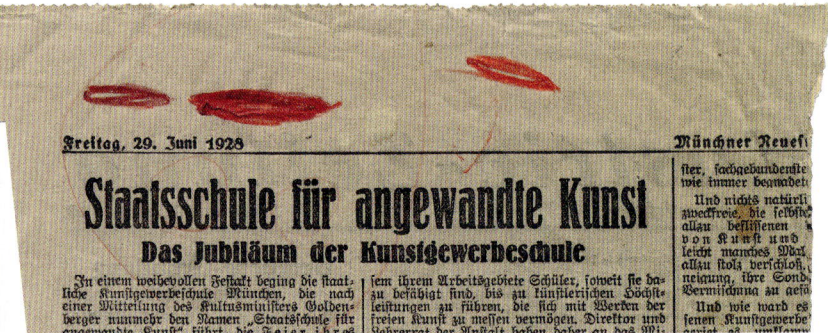

*Zeitungsartikel anlässlich der Umbenennung der Staatlichen
Kunstgewerbeschule in „Staatsschule für angewandte Kunst", 1928*
*Newspaper article about the renaming of the State School of Arts
and Crafts to "State School of Applied Art," 1928*

*Antrag auf Fahrpreisermäßigung
für die Strecke München – Massing*
*Application for reduced train
fare Munich – Massing*

Porträt eines alten Mannes, 1930
Portrait of an old man, 1930

Über diese Prüfung äußerte sie sich einige Zeit später in einem Brief an eine Schulfreundin beinahe ein wenig schockiert. Es ging um einen Anblick, der zwar für die Großstadt der 20er zum Alltag gehörte und auch in der Kunst von Egon Schiele bis Käthe Kollwitz als gängiges Sujet diente, ihr in der behüteten Kleinstadtidylle jedoch sicherlich noch nie begegnet war: „Dann mussten wir einen ganz ausgehungerten Mann zeichnen." Der Anblick von schlecht ernährten Menschen, die sich ihren kärglichen Lebensunterhalt als Modell verdienen, sollte die junge Künstlerin allerdings für die nächsten Jahre begleiten.

Doch auch wenn Berta das fremde München gewöhnungsbedürftig erschien, erwartete sie voller Ungeduld die Prüfungsergebnisse. Sie wollte ihr Ziel um jeden Preis erreichen. „Mir wäre es schrecklich zumute, wenn ich durchfliegen würde u. noch mal die Angst ausstehen müßte. Ich habe große Hoffnung u. vergeßt nicht für mich zu beten." Sie bestand die Prüfung mit Bravour, als Zweitbeste ihres Jahrgangs!

„Die Staatliche Kunstgewerbeschule in München bietet Unterricht in allen Zweigen der bildenden Kunst, die sich in den Dienst der Architektur, des Handwerks und der Industrie stellen, und vermittelt die künstlerische und handwerkliche Ausbildung, besonders in der Richtung gründlicher geschmacklicher Schulung, selbständigen künstlerischen Entwerfens, Erfindens und Gestaltens,

„Die hässliche Margret" war in der Staatsschule wegen ihrer eigenwilligen Physiognomie ein geschätztes Modell, 1930
"Ugly Margret" was a model at the State School prized for her unusual physiognomy, 1930

Porträt Margret, 1930
Portrait Margret, 1930

Margret, sitzend, 1930
Margret, seated, 1930

der Einführung in besondere, seltenere und verfeinerte Techniken und der Erhaltung und der Wiederbelebung guter, alter Techniken." So lautete ein mit „Zweck" überschriebener Teil aus der Schulsatzung. In München war das Studium für das Lehramt strikt getrennt von der „freien", zweckungebundenen Kunst, die an der Akademie unterrichtet wurde.[14] 1868 hatte König Ludwig II. das Institut für die „angewandte" Kunst als staatliche Einrichtung gegründet, und vier Jahre später wurde eigens eine weibliche Abteilung eingerichtet, um die „Heranbildung von Zeichnen-Lehrerinnen"[15] zu fördern. An der Kunstakademie dagegen waren Frauen erst seit 1919 zum Studium zugelassen.

Some time later she wrote about this part in a letter to a school friend, sounding almost a little shocked. The subject was one common enough in any large city in the twenties as well as in the art of an Egon Schiele or Käthe Kollwitz, but one she had undoubtedly not encountered in the sheltered small-town idyll of Massing. "Then we had to draw a completely emaciated man." The sight of malnourished individuals who eked out a living by modeling would accompany the young artist for the next several years.

But although the alien city took getting used to for Berta, she also impatiently awaited the test results. She wanted to reach her goal at any price. "It would be terrible if I flunked and had to go through all that anxiety again. But I am full of hope, and please do not forget to pray for me." She passed the examination with flying colors as second-best in her age group!

"The State School of Arts and Crafts in Munich offers instruction in all those branches of the pictorial arts that serve architecture, handicrafts, and industry. It provides training for artists and craftsmen, especially in terms of a thorough education in taste, independent artistic design, invention, and execution, and introduces the student to special, uncommon, and refined techniques, as well as preserving and revitalizing proven older ones." Thus reads the portion of the school's articles entitled "Mission." Teacher training in Munich was strictly separate from the "liberal" or "pure" art taught at the Academy.[14] King Ludwig II had founded the institute for "applied" art as a state institution in 1868, to which four years later a separate section for women was added to promote the "training of women art teachers."[15] Women were not admitted to the Art Academy, on the other hand, until 1919.

Betrunkenen-Perspektive, 1929
Neujahrsmusikanten, 1929
Topsy-turvy, 1929
New Year's music, 1929

*J*mmerhin hätte Berta, wäre ihre Entscheidung für ein „freies" Studium gefallen, womöglich noch bei Franz von Stuck Malerei[16] oder bei Olaf Gulbransson[17] Zeichnen studieren können; gerade Letzterer wäre von ihrem Talent zur Karikatur sicherlich begeistert gewesen. Doch scheint für sie die sogenannte „hohe" Kunstlaufbahn mit Akademiestudium nie infrage gekommen zu sein. Sie liebte Kinder und freute sich auf die Aussicht, sie unterrichten zu dürfen. Sie selbst hatte wohl – trotz des Aufsehens, das sie mit ihrer Zeichenbegabung im Internat erregt hatte – ihre Bilder bis dato ungern als „Kunst" gesehen. Ihre Schwester Centa berichtet von einer Klassenkollegin, die recht gewandt im Scherenschnitt war und sich stolz als „Künstlerin" feiern ließ. Berta dagegen habe derartige Stilisierungen stets von sich gewiesen.

Dennoch war sie seit jeher – und blieb es auch in den Jahren ihres Erfolgs – extrem kritisch in der Beurteilung ihrer eigenen Arbeiten gewesen. Oft ging sie hart mit sich ins Gericht. Die fachgemäße Ausübung der verschiedenen Arbeitstechniken war ihr ein großes Anliegen. Sie arbeitete meist nach einer konkreten Themenstellung, auch wenn sie in der Umsetzung gerne mit ihren Materialien experimentierte. Weniger scheint sie ein ideeller Überbau inspiriert zu haben, wie er die Avantgarde-Bewegungen ausmacht. Insofern kam ihr der streng traditionelle Lehrplan ihrer neuen Schule bestens entgegen. Seit der Anfangszeit des Instituts waren die Schülerinnen in „Linearzeichnen mit den nöthigsten Erläuterungen aus der Geometrie, Ornamentenzeichnen, Figurenzeichnen, Blumenzeichnen, Holzschneidekunst, Kunstgeschichte, Perspective und Schattenlehre"[18] unterrichtet worden, und in all diesen Fächern wurde auch Berta über 50 Jahre später immer noch unterwiesen.

*H*ad Berta decided upon a "liberal" art study, she might have been able to study painting with Franz von Stuck[16] or drawing with Olaf Gulbransson.[17] The latter, in particular, would have been greatly taken by her talent for caricature. But she seems never to have entertained a thought of a career in "high" art and a study at the Academy. She loved children and looked forward to being able to teach them. Despite the attention her talent for drawing had received at the boarding-school, she herself had been reluctant until now to regard her own pictures as "art." Her sister Centa reported how a classmate skilled in making silhouettes had herself proudly extolled as an "artist," while Berta always rejected such a title.

Yet she had always been extremely critical of her own work – and always remained so, even during the years of achieved success. She often took herself severely to task. She was anxious for a workmanlike execution of the various techniques. She generally commenced with a concrete subject, though she liked to experiment with her materials in the execution. Abstract ideas, like those that characterized the avant-garde movement, seem to have touched her very little. The strongly traditional curriculum of her new school thus suited her perfectly. From the founding years of the institute, the students had been instructed in "line drawing with the necessary principles of geometry, ornament drawing, figure drawing, flower drawing, wood-carving, art history, perspective and silhouette."[18] Fifty years later, Berta was being trained in the self-same subjects.

Skizzenblatt mit Karikaturen, Viehmarkt und Fronleichnamsprozession in Massing, 1931
Caricature sketches, Massing, cattle market and Corpus Christi Procession, 1931

Schon sehr bald konnte sie von ersten Erfolgen berichten. Bereits drei Monate nach ihrer Aufnahmeprüfung schrieb sie eifrig an ihren Vater: „Habe jetzt immer viel zu tun in der Schule, da unsere Klasse eine Zeitschrift herausgibt ‚Winkel', in welche die besten Zeichnungen, Holzschnitte und Lithographien kommen. Herr Professor versprach mir schon, daß meine erste Lithographie hineinkommt. Das würde mich schon freuen."[19] Ihrer Freundin gegenüber gestand sie allerdings gleichzeitig ein wenig gedämpfter, dass ihre Errungenschaften nicht von selbst dahergeflogen kämen: „Ja, ja, durch Kampf zum Sieg. Nun bin ich schon ganz gut eingearbeitet u. bekam schon oft Lob u. sogar eine Auszeichnung für meine Zeichnungen." Stolz erzählte sie von ihren neu erlernten Techniken, mit denen sich die Arbeiten sogar mehrfach reproduzieren lassen: „Zeichnungen kannst von mir genug haben; denn ich lernte schon verschiedene [Techniken] (…) wie Holzschneiden, Lithographieren u.s.w. nach welchen man dann druckt u. seine Zeichnungen vervielfältigen kann."[20] Oft machte sie nun den Lieben daheim mit ihren selbst entworfenen Postkarten eine Freude.

Chinoiserie, 1927
Brandgasse Massing, 1928
Pfau, 1927
Chinoiserie, 1927
Massing, Brandgasse, 1928
Peacock, 1927

Verschiedene Kopfskizzen, 1928
Head Studies, 1928

Very quickly she was able to report her first successes. Only three months after her admission, she eagerly wrote to her father: "I have always much to do at school now, as our class edits a newsletter called 'Angle,' in which the best drawings, woodcuts and lithographs are published. My professor promised me that my very first lithograph would be included. I would really like that."[19] At the same time she confessed to a girlfriend in a more muted manner that her achievements did not come to her without an effort: "Through struggle to victory, yes, yes. I am pretty well broken in now and have received frequent praise and even an award for my drawings."[20] Full of pride she told about her newly learned techniques enabling her to reproduce pieces in multiple copies: "You can have any number of drawings from me, for I have learned several [techniques], such as wood-cutting, lithographing, etc., which one can then use to print and duplicate one's drawings." Often now she would delight her family at home with originally designed postcards.

Bertas Visitenkarte
Berta's calling card

*Malausflug mit Professor Dasio,
1927/1928 (Berta rechts)*
*Painting excursion with Professor Dasio,
1927/1928 (Berta on the right)*

*Professor Friedrich Wirnhier
(1868 – 1952) lehrte an der Staatsschule
„einführende Arbeiten und Naturzeichnen, Graphik, Flächendekorierung für
Stoffe, Glas usw." (Aus dem Lehrplan)*
*Professor Friedrich Wirnhier
(1868 – 1952) taught "Introductory
exercises and Drawing from Nature,
Graphics, Plane Decoration for Fabrics,
Glass, etc." (from the Curriculum)*

Nach einem guten Jahr rühmte ihr Klassenlehrer Professor Friedrich Wirnhier sie im Semesterzeugnis: „Eine Musterschülerin! Mit malerischer Begabung, sehr eifrig, verlässlich, ist sehr gut vorwärtsgekommen." Bald darauf, nach drei Semestern, nahm sie all ihren Mut zusammen und bat um Aufnahme in die Zeichenklasse des berühmten und von ihr sehr bewunderten Geheimrats Professor Maximilian Dasio. Der nun schneller als erwartet „verlassene" Professor Wirnhier ließ seinen Schützling freilich nur ungern ziehen. „Wirnhier war natürlich sehr unangenehm überrascht, er konnte es gar nicht glauben, er meinte, ich könnte bei Dasio auch nicht mehr sehen, da ich auch dort zu den Allerbesten gehöre. (…) Mir tut es natürlich auch fürchterlich leid, aber ich kann es nicht ändern, ich muss auf meinen Vorteil bedacht sein. Die Aquarelle soll ich aber Wirnhier noch immer zur Korrektur bringen, das würde ihn noch freuen, sagte er, das tu ich auch natürlich."[21] Nach bereits vier Semestern konnte Berta stolz ihren Eltern berichten: „Möchte Euch nur rasch die Mitteilung machen, daß ich durch meine Prüfung in die Oberstufe aufgenommen wurde, was mich natürlich schon sehr freut, da ich es mir eigentlich nicht erwartete u. zu alledem die einzige von meinem Kurs bin."[22]

Mit Professor Dasio und der Oberstufe begann ein neuer Abschnitt in Bertas künstlerischem Leben. Schon Gabriele Münter hatte einst bei Dasio Kopf- und Aktzeichnen studiert und sich von dem engagierten Lehrer zum ersten Mal in ihrem Leben in ihrem Talent bestätigt gefühlt.[23] Er selbst pflegte einen renaissanceorientierten linearen Stil, ließ aber gute Entwürfe seiner Schülerinnen gelten, auch wenn sie sich von seiner bevorzugten Arbeitsweise unterschieden.

At the end of a year, her class teacher, Professor Friedrich Wirnhier, praised her in her semester report card: "A model student! With talent in painting, very industrious, dependable, and has made excellent progress." Soon thereafter, after her third semester, she mustered the courage to ask for admission to the drawing class of the famous Privy Councilor Professor Maximilian Dasio, whom she greatly admired. Wirnhier, of course, finding himself thus unexpectedly "forsaken," was reluctant to let go of his protégée. "Wirnhier was unpleasantly surprised, of course, he could hardly believe it, he thought I would not be able to see more at Dasio's, since I ranked among the very best there as well. (…) Naturally I am very sorry, but I can't help it, I have to look out for my own advantage. I should continue to take my water colors to Wirnhier for cor-

Professor Maximilian Dasio (1865 – 1954) unterrichtete die fortgeschrittene Zeichenklasse, außerdem Medaillen und Steinschneiden

Professor Maximilian Dasio (1865 – 1954) taught Advanced Drawing, Medal and Stone Cutting

rection, however; he said that would make him happy. I'll do that, of course."[21] After only four semesters, Berta proudly reported to her parents: "Just wanted to let you know quickly that through my exam I have been admitted to the upper division. I am naturally very happy, as I had not expected it and because I am the only one from my course."[22]

Berta's advancement to Professor Dasio and the upper division signaled a new phase in her artistic life. Already Gabriele Münter had once upon a time studied drawing of heads and nudes with this dedicated teacher and for the first time in her life had felt that her talent was being recognized.[23] He himself cultivated a Renaissance-oriented linear style, but he was capable of acknowledging the merit of good design by his pupils, even if they differed from his own preferred way of working.

Bauer mit Hut, 1930
Peasant with hat, 1930

Porträt Maria Graser, Massing, 1928
Portrait of Maria Graser, Massing, 1928

𝔇ie Münter konnte zu ihrem Leidwesen diese neue positive Erfahrung nur ein paar Monate lang genießen, denn 1901 wechselte der Professor von der von ihr besuchten privaten Studienanstalt an die Staatliche Kunst- und Gewerbeschule. Dort blieb er tätig, bis er 1931 endgültig in den Ruhestand gehen musste.[24] Als Berta anfing zu studieren, war der Geheimrat als hoch geachtetes Urgestein nicht mehr aus der Kunstschulszene wegzudenken.

Berta war selig, als sie in seine Klasse aufgenommen wurde. Sie arbeitete viel: Akte, Bewegungsstudien, Ornamente, Drucke, Stoffmuster. Wenn sie in den Ferien nach Massing heimkehrte, hatte der stolze Vater schon neue Aufgaben für sie gesammelt. Er suchte mit den Künstleraugen seiner Tochter und hielt bei den Bauern in der Umgebung Ausschau: „Ich hab wieder ein paar Charakterköpfe für dich, da fahr ich dich hin", freute er sich, wenn sie kam.

Zeichnen, immer zeichnen! Landschaften, Stillleben, Kopfstudien. Porträts, fein gearbeitet, doch mit entschiedener Verve die kantigen Gesichter auf Papier gebannt. Mit einem Blick den ungeschönten Augenblick erfassen, in Kohle, Rötel, Aquarell. Techniken, die einen raschen Strich ermöglichen. Der Dorfschuster bei der Arbeit, eine Bäuerin bei der Wäsche, eine alte Frau beim Stricken, ein Nachtwächter bei seiner Runde, Kinder – Kinder über Kinder – schlafend oder spielend, die Schwestern, die Großeltern, die Verwandten, der geliebte Hund „Lord". Und immer wieder Massing, Häuser, die Straße zum Haus, den Marktplatz, das Marterl am Feldweg, die Hügel der Heimat.

𝔐ünter sadly had been able to enjoy her positive experience with Dasio only for a few months, for in 1901, the professor had moved from her private study institute to the State School of Arts and Crafts. There he remained until 1931, when he was forced to go into retirement.[24] Thus when Berta started her studies, the art school scene had long since become unthinkable without the highly respected figure of the Privy Councilor.

Berta was in seventh heaven about being admitted to his class. She did a great deal of work: nudes, motion studies, ornaments, prints, textile patterns. Whenever she went home to Massing for vacation, her proud father had new tasks lined up for her. Looking with the artist's eyes of his daughter, he searched for models among the neighboring peasants. "I have a few characteristic heads for you again," he would announce gleefully upon her arrival; "I'll take you there."

Drawing, always drawing! Landscapes, still lifes, head studies, portraits, finely worked, but the angular faces conjured onto the paper with great verve. Capturing at one glance the unvarnished moment, in charcoal, red chalk, or water color – techniques that allow quick strokes. A village cobbler at work, a peasant woman doing laundry, an old woman knitting, a night watchman making his rounds, children, lots of children, sleeping or playing, the sisters, the grandparents, the relatives, the pet dog "Lord." And time and again Massing, its houses, the street leading to the Hummel house, the market square, a shrine along a country lane, the native hills.

Massinger Charaktere:
Bäuerinnen, 1927/1928
Massing Characters:
Peasant women, 1927/1928

Johann Huber, der Nachtwächter von Massing, 1928
Johann Huber, night watchman, 1928

Kleinkinderstudien, 1928
Infants, 1928

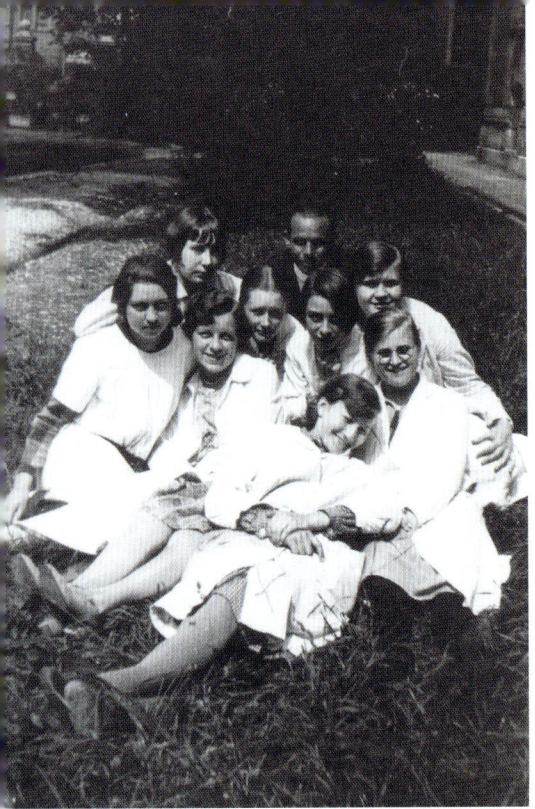

Berta (vorne) mit ihrer Malklasse, 1927
Berta (front) with her painting class, 1927

Die lebhafte Berta war in ihrer Klasse äußerst beliebt. Schon nach einem Jahr wurde sie zur ersten Klassensprecherin gewählt, vergnügt schrieb sie nach Hause: „Habe es sehr wichtig." Wie schon im Internat kam ihr Talent zur Karikatur ihrer ganzen Umgebung zugute. Ihre Mitstudentin M. Laura Brugger erzählte folgende Anekdote, die ihre übermütige Freundin Berta, den brummigen Geheimrat und die Atmosphäre an der Schule wunderbar abbildet: „Als sie in ihrer Studienzeit die sogenannte ‚Dasio'-Klasse besuchte (…), pflegte sie die charakteristische Erscheinung des Professors in verschiedenen Karikaturen festzuhalten. Professor Dasio war von seiner Klasse geliebt ob seiner Tüchtigkeit und gleichzeitig gefürchtet ob seiner unerbittlichen Kritik. Einmal wöchentlich pflegte er die Arbeiten seiner Schüler ohne Namensangabe einzusammeln. Dann setzte er sich gemütlich in die Mitte des Hörsaals, versammelte seine Schüler möglichst nahe um sich und kritisierte Blatt um Blatt. Er merkte aber nicht, dass sein Hummele den Tisch hinter ihn gerückt hatte und hoch oben thronte, den Professor scharf beobachtend, ihre beiden Getreuen zur Seite. Diese hielten ihr Pinsel, Wasser und Farbe und sie zeichnete mit Inbrunst den verehrten Lehrer. Aus dieser Karikatur machte sie anschließend einen Holzschnitt, auf welchem sie die Originalität und Eigenart des großen Lehrers meisterhaft und treffsicher festhielt. Den Probeabzug warf sie in den Papierkorb. Der Hausmeister (…) entdeckte beim Leeren desselben den Versuch, erkannte darauf sofort den Dasio, glättete und bügelte das zerknitterte Papierstückchen und zeigte es triumphierend Frau Professor Else Brauneis. Diese erkannte den genialen Wurf (…) und sagte lächelnd: ‚Das kann nur eine sein: das Lausmädel in der Dasio-Klasse.' Dasio selbst erhielt auch Kenntnis davon und sagte ohne jegliche Spur von Empfindlichkeit: ‚Sagen Sie dem Lausmädel, sie hätte ruhig die Schublade noch weiter herausziehen dürfen.' (Mit Schublade meinte er seine gewohnheitsmäßig vorgeschobene Unterlippe)."[25]

Porträts Maximilian Dasio, 1930
Portraits of Maximilian Dasio, 1930

Professor Dasio schätzte die Fertigkeit seiner Lieblingsschülerin sehr. „I bin allweil do!", lud er sie in breitestem Münchner Dialekt ein, ihn jederzeit in seinem Atelier zu porträtieren.
Professor Dasio thought highly of his favorite pupil's skills and invited her, in his broadest Munich dialect, to portray him anytime in his studio: "A'm always theah!"

Porträt Maximilian Dasio mit Zeitung, 1930
Portrait of Maximilian Dasio reading his newspaper, 1930

Der Massinger Schuster Johann Huber bei der Arbeit, März 1929
The cobbler Johann Huber at his work, March 1929

Being as lively as she was, Berta was very popular in her class. After only one year she was elected class representative. "Am Very Important," she informed her family merrily. As before at boarding-school, her talent for caricature was an unfailing source of entertainment for all around her. Her fellow student M. Laura Brugger told the following anecdote, which perfectly captures the sportive Berta, the grumpy Privy Councilor, and the overall atmosphere at the school. "While attending the so-called Dasio class during her study years, she would arrest the characteristic appearance of the professor in various caricatures. Professor Dasio was loved by his class for his competence but also feared for his pitiless criticism. Once a week he would collect the works of his students, unmarked. Then he would settle in the center of the lecture room, gather his students closely around him, and pass judgement on one leaf after another. What he failed to notice was that his 'Hummele' had set up the table behind him and was perched on high, sharply observing the professor, her two cohorts by her side. They were holding brush, water and paint for her while, with great ardor, she sketched the beloved teacher. Afterwards she made a woodcut from this caricature, in which she exactly and masterfully caught the originality and peculiarity of the revered teacher. A test copy she tossed into the wastebasket. While emptying the basket, the janitor (...) discovered the test print, recognized Dasio, smoothed and ironed out the crumpled paper and triumphantly showed it to Professor Else Brauneis. The latter instantly recognized the genius of the design, and said smilingly: 'That can only be by that rascally girl in the Dasio class.' When Dasio himself learned of it, he said without a trace of pique: 'Tell the rascal, she could easily have pulled the drawer out even more.' (By drawer he meant his habitually protruding lower lip.)"[25]

Porträt Mann mit Hut, 1929/1930
Potrait of a man with hat, 1929/1930

Eine andere Professorin, die Berta entscheidend beeinflussen sollte, war Else Brauneis. Sie lehrte perspektivisches Zeichnen und Aquarell und hatte eine besonders enge Beziehung zu Berta aufgebaut. Oft organisierte sie Exkursionen, alle Studentinnen packten dann Blöcke und Pinsel ein und ließen sich einen Tag lachend und schwatzend – und vor allem natürlich eifrig aquarellierend – im malerischen Münchner Umland, in dramatischer Bergkulisse oder im hübschen Salzburg inspirieren. Einmal schrieb Berta nach Hause, sie hätte gepfefferte Ohrfeigen an ein paar aufdringliche Buben verteilt, die nicht ablassen konnten, die jungen Künstlerinnen durch freche Zurufe bei ihrer Arbeit zu stören.[26] Die Empörung war ihr auch Tage danach noch deutlich anzumerken.

Schnell den flüchtigen Eindruck aufs Papier bannen. Ein paar Bleistiftstriche umreißen die Gestalt, dann kommen die Farben. Weiß lassen, wo das Licht ist. Eine junge Frau im roten Kleid. Mit erotischer Lässigkeit steht sie da, dem Betrachter den schlanken Rücken zugewandt. Durch das Standbein die Hüfte betont, den einen Arm leger gegen die Wand gelehnt. Langer Hals, schwarze Haare, Bubikopf. Sie ist sehr hübsch, das kann man sehen, auch wenn ihr Gesicht nicht zu erkennen ist.

Dame in Rot, 1930
Lady in red, 1930

A second major influence on Berta was Professor Else Brauneis. She taught perspective drawing and water colors and had established an especially close relationship with Berta. Often she would organize excursions. All of the students would then pack their brushes and drawing blocks and, laughing, chattering, and, above all, sketching, let themselves be inspired by the picturesque surroundings of Munich, a dramatic mountain scenery, or pretty Salzburg. After one of these occasions, Berta wrote home that she had dealt out resounding boxes on the ears of some impudent boys who would not stop disrupting the work of the young artists with saucy catcalls.[26] Her anger was still noticeable several days later.

Quickly getting the fleeting moment onto paper: a few pencil strokes outline the figure, then the colors. White space where the light is. A young woman in a red dress, standing in erotic nonchalance with her slim back to the viewer. The standing leg emphasizes the hip, one arm is propped casually against the wall. Elongated neck, black, bobbed hair. One can see that she is very pretty, though her face cannot be made out.

Salzburg, Blick auf den Dom, 1929/1930
Salzburg, view of the cathedral, 1929/1930

Studienausflug, 1927/1928
Study excursion, 1927/1928

Porträt einer jungen Frau mit Kopftuch, 1929/1930
Portrait of a young woman with head-scarf, 1929/1930

Biedermeier-Zimmer, 1929/1930
Biedermeier interior, 1929/1930

Berta freundete sich allmählich mit der Großstadt an. Ein Wertmutstropfen, der ihr zu schaffen machte, war ihre Unterkunft. Sie wohnte zur Untermiete in der Annastraße im Stadtteil Lehel, wo ihr das „Fräulein Schenk", die Vermieterin, das Leben oft schwer machte. Einige Male wohl kam es vor, dass Berta nach ihrem langen Tag in der Hochschule nach Hause kam und die ältere Dame in ihrem Zimmer sitzend vorfand, uneinsichtig, dass in einem teuer bezahlten Raum eine gewisse Privatsphäre gewahrt bleiben sollte. Berta fühlte sich beobachtet und eingeengt. Dennoch berichtet ihre Schwester Centa, dass sie die Vorzüge der Großstadt mit der Zeit in vollen Zügen genossen habe. Sie sei mit ihren Kommilitoninnen gerne ins Kino und ins Theater gegangen. Bereits in einem der ersten Briefe berichtete Berta ihrem Vater begeistert von einer Freikarte zu Wagners „Walküre". Dann gab es natürlich noch die zahlreichen Museen und Ausstellungen.

Und da war einiges zu sehen: nicht wie früher und nicht wie in Berlin. Aber in bayerischer Gemütlichkeit ließ sich doch so manch neue Tendenz mit bodenständiger Tradition friedvoll vereinen. In der Zeitschrift „Jugend", die in einem neuen Konzept erschien, gab es ein schönes Miteinander von Otto Dix und George Grosz Seite an Seite mit idyllischen Salonkünstlern oder von Oskar Maria Graf und Kurt Tucholsky neben harmlosen Unterhaltungsliteraten.[27] Man konnte, nicht weit von der Kunstgewerbeschule entfernt, die alten Meister in der Alten Pinakothek und die Impressionisten in der Neuen Staatsgalerie am Königsplatz studieren. Und sich dann, zu Fuß in zehn Minuten zu erreichen, die neue Kandinsky-Ausstellung in der Galerie Goltz an der Brienner Straße ansehen. Daneben gab es die verschiedenen örtlichen Kunstverbände. So etwa die traditionelle Münchner Künstlergenossenschaft, der auch Bertas Professoren Brauneis, Dasio und Wirnhier angehörten, und andererseits die „Secession", die sich der gemäßigten Moderne verpflichtet fühlte, und die „Juryfreien", um die sich die Progressiven versammelten. Alljährlich war deren unterschiedliches Programm in der „Münchner Kunstausstellung" zu bewundern. Diese Sammelausstellung der Künstlervereine fand damals noch im berühmten Glaspalast am Alten Botanischen Garten statt, bevor das fragile Gebäude in der Nacht vom 6. auf den 7. Juni 1931 völlig niederbrannte, „eine nationale Katastrophe"[28], die Berta nach Ende ihres Studiums gerade nicht mehr miterleben musste.

Signaturen
Signatures

Berta was beginning to like the city, though one fly in the ointment was her accommodation. She had a room in the apartment of a Miss Schenk on Annastrasse, in the Lehel district, who often made her life miserable. It could happen that when she returned home after a long day at the school, she would find the old lady sitting in her room with no consideration that so expensive a room should guarantee a measure of privacy. She felt hemmed in and spied upon. Her sister Centa nevertheless reports that Berta gradually came to enjoy the advantages of a large city to the full. She liked going to the movies and the theater with her fellow students. Already in her first letter to her father she told of being thrilled about a free ticket she had received to Wagner's *Valkyrie*. And, of course, there were the numerous museums and exhibitions to visit.

There was still a lot to see. Not as in earlier years and not like Berlin. Nevertheless, Bavarian geniality allowed the juxtaposition of many a new tendency along with old, rooted traditions. In the journal *Jugend* ("Youth"), appearing in a new concept, one could find Otto Dix and George Grosz peacefully side by side with idyllic salon artists, or Oskar Maria Graf and Kurt Tucholsky next to purveyors of innocuous entertainment writing.[27] Not far from the School of Arts and Crafts, one could study the old masters in the Old Pinakothek and the Impressionists in the New State Gallery on Königsplatz. A ten-minute walk would then bring one to the new Kandinsky Exhibition at Gallery Goltz on Brienner Strasse. There were also the various local art associations. Among them was the traditional Munich Artists Guild, to which Berta's professors Brauneis, Dasio, and Wirnhier belonged. On the other hand, there was the "Secession," committed to a moderate modernity, and the "Jury-Free" group representing the Progressives. Their diverse programs could be admired annually at the "Munich Art Exhibition." This collective exhibition of all the artist associations was still taking place in the famed Glass Palace in the Old Botanical Garden, until a fire destroyed the fragile building in the night from the 6th to the 7th of June, 1931 – a "national catastrophe,"[28] which Berta, her studies completed, just missed having to witness.

Bertas Studienausweis für das Sommersemester 1927
Berta's student ID for the summer semester of 1927

Aktzeichnungen, 1927/1930
Nudes, 1927/1930

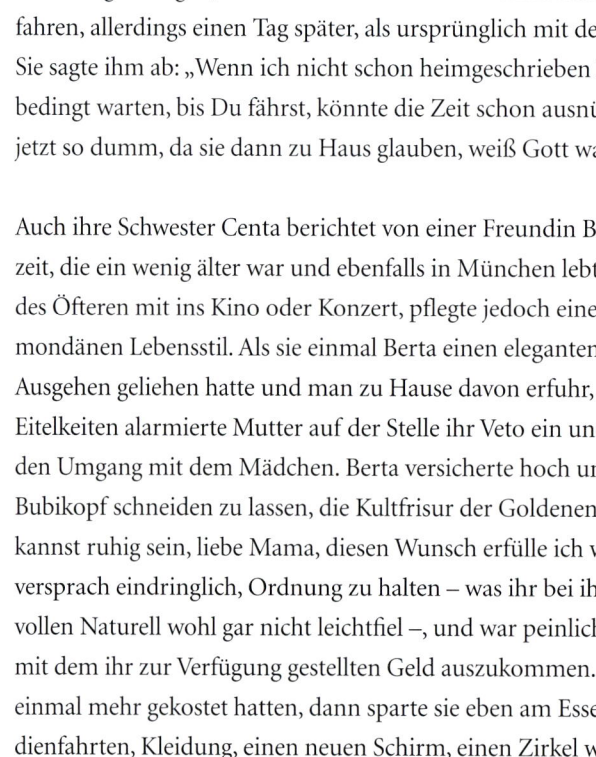

Doch so interessant und aufwühlend das alles gewesen sein mag, Berta blieb konsequent zurückhaltend, wenn sie ihrer Familie in Massing über ihr Münchner Leben Bericht erstattete. Vielleicht aus Furcht, den Lieben daheim Sorge zu bereiten. Vielleicht, weil ihr das, was sich in München bewegte, doch recht fern von dem Tagesgeschehen in Massing erschien. Oder vielleicht auch ein wenig, weil sie fühlte, dass nicht alles, was die Großstadt zu bieten hatte, bei der strengen und stets besorgten Mutter Anklang finden würde. Einmal gestand sie ihrem Bruder Ady ihre Angst vor Missverständnissen daheim. Er hatte vorgeschlagen, mit ihr zusammen in die Weihnachtsferien nach Hause zu fahren, allerdings einen Tag später, als ursprünglich mit den Eltern verabredet. Sie sagte ihm ab: „Wenn ich nicht schon heimgeschrieben hätte, würde ich unbedingt warten, bis Du fährst, könnte die Zeit schon ausnützen. Aber es ist halt jetzt so dumm, da sie dann zu Haus glauben, weiß Gott was ich mache."[29]

Auch ihre Schwester Centa berichtet von einer Freundin Bertas aus der Schulzeit, die ein wenig älter war und ebenfalls in München lebte. Diese nahm Berta des Öfteren mit ins Kino oder Konzert, pflegte jedoch einen verhältnismäßig mondänen Lebensstil. Als sie einmal Berta einen eleganten Pelzkragen zum Ausgehen geliehen hatte und man zu Hause davon erfuhr, legte die von diesen Eitelkeiten alarmierte Mutter auf der Stelle ihr Veto ein und verbot ihrer Tochter den Umgang mit dem Mädchen. Berta versicherte hoch und heilig, sich keinen Bubikopf schneiden zu lassen, die Kultfrisur der Goldenen Zwanziger: „Da kannst ruhig sein, liebe Mama, diesen Wunsch erfülle ich wohl bestimmt."[30] Sie versprach eindringlich, Ordnung zu halten – was ihr bei ihrem temperamentvollen Naturell wohl gar nicht leichtfiel –, und war peinlichst darauf bedacht, mit dem ihr zur Verfügung gestellten Geld auszukommen. Wenn die Farben einmal mehr gekostet hatten, dann sparte sie eben am Essen. Jede Bitte um Studienfahrten, Kleidung, einen neuen Schirm, einen Zirkel war äußerst vorsichtig und bescheiden vorgetragen, immer beinahe von Entschuldigung begleitet.

*B*ut regardless of how interesting and stirring all this may have been, Berta remained reticent about it in the reports about her life in Munich she sent to her family in Massing, whether out of fear her loved ones back home might worry, or because everything that went on in Munich appeared too remote from the daily life of those in Massing. Perhaps also she felt that not everything the city had to offer would meet with the approval of her stern and ever concerned mother. Once she confided to her brother Ady her fear of being misunderstood at home. He had suggested they travel home together for the Christmas vacation, a day later than originally arranged with the parents. She said no. "If I had not already written home about it, I would certainly wait to travel with you: I could well use the extra day here. But it's awkward now, because at home they will think I am doing God knows what."[29]

Her sister Centa tells about a slightly older friend of Berta's at school who also lived in Munich but kept a more worldly lifestyle, and who occasionally would take Berta to the movies or a concert. Once, when she had loaned Berta an elegant fur collar for going out and the family found out about it, her mother, much alarmed about such vanities, instantly forbade her daughter all contact with the girl. Berta swore a solemn oath she would never wear her hair close-cropped, the cult hairstyle of the 'twenties. "You can rest assured, dear Mama, I'll definitely follow your wishes in this."[30] She promised faithfully to keep order – probably not an easy task for a girl of her temperament – and was meticulously concerned to make ends meet with the money put at her disposal. If her paints came to more than anticipated, she spent less on food. Every financial request for study excursions, clothing, a new umbrella, or a pair of compasses was submitted warily and modestly, almost always accompanied by apologies.

Engel mit Blumen, 1931
Angel with flowers, 1931

Schaufensterdekoration für das elterliche Geschäft in Massing, Weihnachten, 1928
Window decoration for the parents' store in Massing, Christmas, 1928

Berta, 1930/1931
Berta, 1930/1931

Ob Berta wohl einmal auf einer Lesung des berühmten Thomas Mann gewesen ist oder auf einer der „Brettlbühnen" den anarchischen Witz des wundervollen Tragikomikers Karl Valentin erlebt hat? Ob sie vielleicht einmal im „Hofbräuhaus" eine Maß Bier getrunken hat oder auf dem Oktoberfest Karussell gefahren ist? Ob sie sich an Diskussionen über Kunst oder Politik beteiligt hat? Ob sie Zeitung gelesen hat, einmal Schnaps und Zigarren probiert hat? Einmal einen Liebesbrief bekommen hat?

Und die andere, die dunkle Seite im München dieser Tage. Ob sie Frank Wedekinds „Lulu" in Otto Falckenbergs „Kammerspielen" gesehen hat? Diese Aufführungen waren ein Skandal, ein Angriff auf die bürgerliche Scheinmoral, von gewaltbereiten Nazis lautstark niedergebrüllt. Ob Berta manchmal Angst hatte nach dem Kino oder Theater auf den nächtlichen Straßen, zu einer Zeit, wo überall SA-Schlägertrupps patrouillierten und vom Zaun gebrochene Schlägereien an der Tagesordnung waren? Wir wissen es nicht. Nichts von alledem schreibt sie in ihren Briefen nach Hause. Dennoch – Berta war eine lebhafte Persönlichkeit und mittendrin dabei. Sie wird die Stimmungen und Strömungen aufgesogen haben, wach beobachtend, wie es ihre Art war.

Porträt einer Frau, 1929/1930
Portrait of a woman, 1929/1930

Porträt einer jungen Frau, 1929/1930
Portrait of a young woman, 1929/1930

Dame in Blau, 1929/1930
Lady in blue, 1929/1930

Schlägerei zwischen Nationalsozialisten und Passanten in der Sendlingerstr. am 5. März 1923

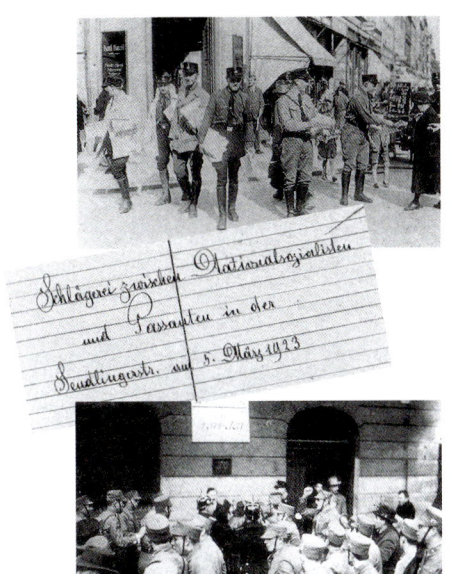

SS-Angehörige beim Verteilen von Flugblättern in München, Aktennotiz, Auseinandersetzung zwischen SA-Männern und Polizisten, um 1930
SS members distributing pamphlets in Munich, official notice, confrontation between SA-men and the police, about 1930

Did Berta ever attend a reading by the famous Thomas Mann? Or experience the anarchical wit of the wonderful tragicomedian Karl Valentin at one of the cabaret stages? Did she ever have a mug of beer at the Hofbräuhaus? Or ride a merry-go-round at the Octoberfest? Did she take part in debates about art and politics? Did she read the newspapers, try schnapps and cigars once? Did she ever receive a love letter?

And did she witness the other, darker side of the Munich of the day? Did she see Frank Wedekind's Lulu at Otto Falckenberg's Kammerspiele (Studio Theater)? The production was a scandal, an attack on phony bourgeois morality that was shouted down by Nazi rowdies. Did Berta ever have reasons to be afraid in the streets at night after a movie or the theater, at a time when everywhere gangs of SA roamed the city, and willfully provoked fights were daily happenings in the streets of Munich? We do not know. Her letters home say nothing about any of this. Yet Berta was an alert young woman and in the midst of it all. Watchful as was her habit, she will no doubt have absorbed and observed the moods and currents of the day.

Die Münchner Ludwigstraße zum Siegestor, 1929
Munich, Ludwigstrasse, view towards the Siegestor, 1929

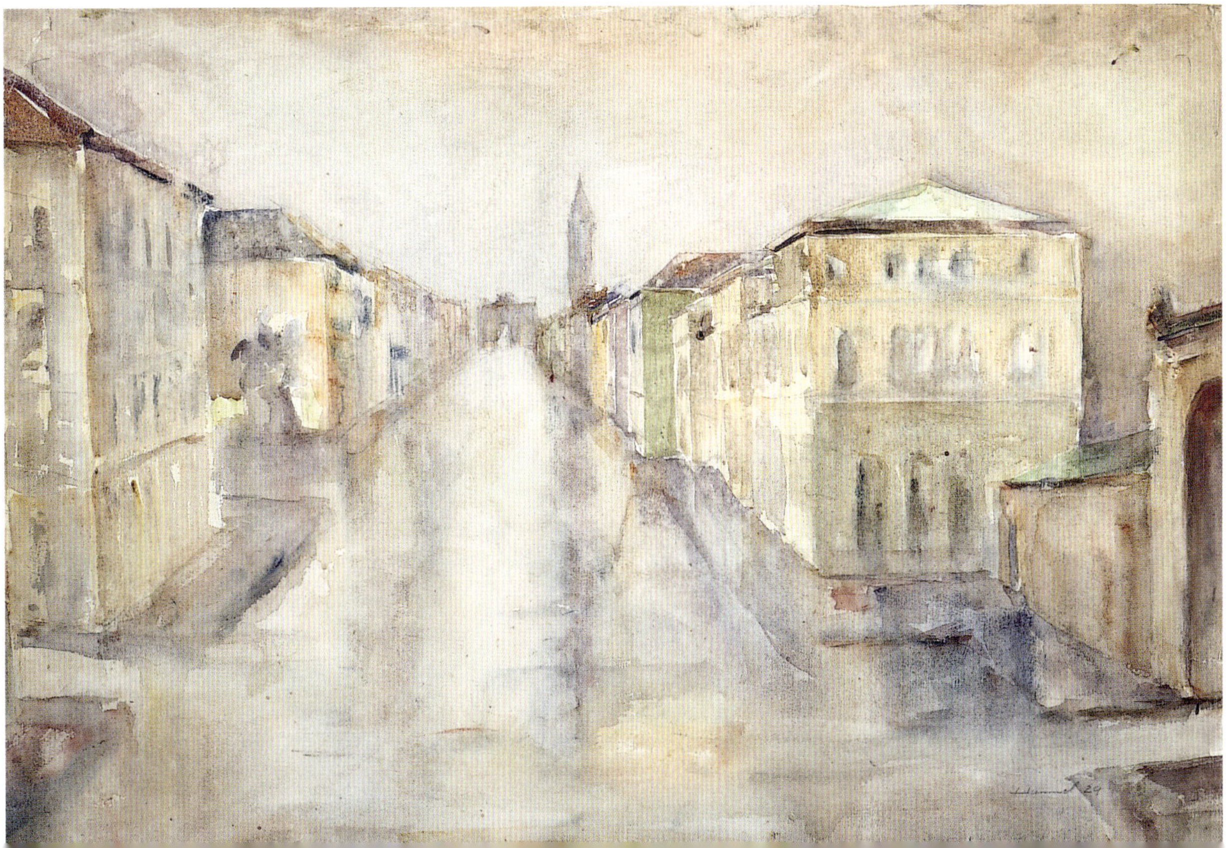

Berta beendete ihr Studium mit dem besten Zeugnis ihrer Klasse. In allen Fächern erzielte sie exzellente Bewertungen. Die Welt stand ihr offen und die Möglichkeiten waren zahlreich. Sie hatte durch ihren Abschluss „die Befähigung zur Verwendung als Zeichenlehrerin an Volksschulen, Mädchenmittelschulen, höheren Mädchenschulen, Mädchenlyzeen und den 9klassigen höheren Lehranstalten für Mädchen (Mädchengymnasien, -Realgymnasien, -Oberrealschulen), ferner an Lehrerinnen Bildungsanstalten, Handarbeitslehrerinnen-Seminaren und Frauenarbeitsschulen nachgewiesen"[31]. Noch dazu hatten ihr die Professoren Klein, Dasio, Jaskolla und Brauneis eine Assistententätigkeit angeboten. Eine Chance also, die ihr den Weg zur Hochschullehrerin ebnen würde.

Ein Selbstporträt 1929: Sie schaut den Betrachter an, auffällig die Augen bei aller Bescheidenheit, man kann sich dem Blick nicht entziehen. Ein wenig melancholisch. In zartem Rötelstrich gezeichnet die gescheitelte Ponyfrisur, die hohen Wangenknochen, kräftige Nase, kräftiges Kinn. Ein schönes, klares Gesicht. Eine junge Frau an der Schwelle ihrer größten Entscheidung.

„Sehr gut befähigt": Abschlusszeugnis der Staatsschule für angewandte Kunst „Examen mit Note 1 bestanden" Telegramm an die Eltern, 15. März 1931

"Very highly qualified": final report from the State School of Applied Art "Exam passed with the grade of 1 [A]" Telegram to the parents, March 15, 1931

Berta graduated with the highest average in her class, with grades of Outstanding in all her subjects. The world was now open to her, and her options were legion. By completing her studies, she had "demonstrated her employability as art teacher in elementary schools, girls' middle schools, girls' high schools, lycées, and the nine-grade secondary schools for girls, whether classical or science-oriented (*Mädchengymnasien, Realgymnasien, Oberrealschulen*), as well as teacher-training schools, needlecraft teachers' seminars, and women's vocational schools"[31]. On top of that, her professors Klein, Dasio, Jaskolla, and Brauneis had offered her an assistant's position – a first step toward an academic teaching career.

In a self-portrait of 1929 she looks straight at the viewer, her eyes conspicuous, compelling with all due modesty, not to be avoided. She looks a little melancholic, bangs and parted hair evoked by soft strokes of red chalk, high cheekbones, prominent nose, a strong chin – a beautiful, clear face, a young woman at the threshold of her greatest decision.

Silberhochzeit der Eltern, 1931
Gabentisch, im Hintergrund
ein großer Textilbehang mit der
dörflichen Szenerie Massing
Silver wedding of the parents, 1931
Table for presents; in the background
a large wall hanging by Berta
showing the village scenery of Massing

Selbstporträt, 1929
Self-portrait, 1929

Chronik einer glücklosen Zeit
München und die Republik zwischen den Weltkriegen

7. November 1918 In der bayerischen Landeshauptstadt formiert sich ein Aufstand der Arbeiter und kriegsmüden Soldaten unter Kurt Eisner. Ein Arbeiter- und Soldatenrat wird konstituiert, König Ludwig III. für abgesetzt erklärt und die Bayerische Republik ausgerufen.

9. November 1918 Ende der Monarchie auch in Berlin. Kaiser Wilhelm II. von Preußen dankt ab.

12. Januar 1919 Bayerische Landtagswahlen ergeben eine Mehrheit der bürgerlichen Parteien und erteilen der Linken unter Eisner eine radikale Abfuhr.

6. Februar 1919 In Weimar kommt erstmals die neu gewählte Nationalversammlung zusammen. Einen Monat später wird der Sozialdemokrat Friedrich Ebert zum deutschen Reichskanzler gewählt.

21. Februar 1919 Eisner wird auf dem Weg zum bayerischen Landtag ermordet, die Situation eskaliert erneut. In München herrscht gewalttätiges Chaos, als links stehende Sozialisten, Kommunisten und Spartakisten versuchen, eine Räterepublik nach russischem Vorbild zu installieren.

Anfang Mai 1919 wird die Münchner Räterepublik mithilfe preußischer Truppen niedergeschlagen, auf beiden Seiten sind etliche Todesopfer zu beklagen.

28. Juni 1919 Deutschland und die Alliierten unterzeichnen den Versailler Friedensvertrag. Das Deutsche Reich verliert dabei ein Siebtel seines Gebiets.

12. August 1919 Die „Weimarer Verfassung" unter Preußens Führung gab den einzelnen deutschen Ländern eine zentralisierte Staatsform vor und enthob sie damit weitgehend ihrer eigenstaatlichen Gesetzgebungskompetenz. Bayern behält eine Eigenstaatlichkeit im Rahmen des Deutschen Reiches.

27. April 1921 Die Alliierten fordern 132 Milliarden Goldmark Reparationszahlung für die von Deutschland verursachten Kriegsschäden, Nährboden für die Parolen der sich formierenden rechtsradikalen NS-Partei unter Adolf Hitler, den „Schandvertrag" von Versailles und die „Zinsknechtschaft" zu beseitigen.

8./9. November 1923 Die rechtsradikalen Kräfte haben in den Turbulenzen der letzten Jahre in ganz Deutschland regen Zulauf erfahren. Im Münchner „Bürgerbräukeller" ruft Hitler die „nationale Revolution" aus. Mit seinen NSDAP-Anhängern marschiert er zur Feldherrnhalle, wo der Staatsstreich von der bayerischen Landespolizei niedergeschlagen wird.

1. April 1924 Hitler wird wegen seines Putschversuchs zu fünf Jahren Festungshaft verurteilt, wird jedoch am 20. Dezember vorzeitig entlassen. In der Zeit seiner Haftstrafe schreibt er an seinem Grundlagenwerk „Mein Kampf".

26. April 1925 Paul von Hindenburg wird nach Eberts Tod neuer Reichspräsident.

Ende Oktober 1929 Nach dem Kurssturz an der New Yorker Börse beginnt die Weltwirtschaftskrise.

29. März 1930 Heinrich Brüning wird deutscher Reichskanzler und verfolgt eine rigorose Sparpolitik zur Bekämpfung der immensen Staatsverschuldung.

14. September 1930 Bei der Wahl des Reichstags kann die rechtsradikale NSDAP deutschlandweit ihr Ergebnis von 2,6 auf 18,3 Prozent steigern.

Februar 1932 Die Arbeitslosenzahl im Deutschen Reich erreicht ihren Höchststand.

31. Juli 1932 Bei der Reichstagswahl wird die NSDAP deutschlandweit stärkste Partei.

6. November 1932 Die NSDAP verliert erheblich an Stimmen, bleibt aber dennoch stärkste Partei.

30. Januar 1933 Hindenburg ernennt Hitler zum Reichskanzler.

Chronicle of a Luckless Time
Munich and the Republic between the World Wars

November 7, 1918 An uprising of workers and soldiers tired of war forms in the Bavarian capital under Kurt Eisner. A council of workers and soldiers is constituted, Ludwig III is declared deposed and the Bavarian Republic is proclaimed.

November 9, 1918 Fall of the Monarchy in Berlin: Emperor Wilhelm II abdicates.

January 12, 1919 Bavarian parliamentary elections result in a majority of bourgeois parties radically rebuffing the Left under Eisner. The election had been preceded by violent demonstrations of jobless people and street battles.

February 6, 1919 The newly elected National Congress assembles in Weimar. One month later the Social Democrat Friedrich Ebert is elected Reich Chancellor.

February 21, 1919 Eisner is assassinated on his way to the parliament; the situation escalates again. Chaotic violence reigns in Munich, as Leftist Socialists, Communists and Spartakists attempt to install a soviet-type Council of Commissars on the Russian model.

Early May, 1919 With the aid of Prussian troops, Munich's *Räterepublik* is forcibly put down, with casualties on both sides.

June 28, 1919 Germany and the Allies sign the Treaty of Versailles. Germany loses one seventh of its territory.

August 12, 1919 Under Prussian auspices, the "Weimar Constitution" imposed a centralized form of government upon the individual German states, thereby largely depriving them of an autonomous legislative competency. Only Bavaria retains its status as a Free State within the framework of the German Reich.

April 27, 1921 The Allies demand 132 billion gold marks in reparations for the war damages caused by Germany – a fertile ground for the slogans of the radical rightist National Socialist German Workers' Party (NSDAP) under Adolf Hitler calling for the eradication of the "infamous treaty" of Versailles and Germany's "tax bondage."

November 8/9, 1923 During the turbulences of the last several years, the forces of the radical right have been increasingly sought after throughout Germany. In Munich's "Bürgerbräukeller" Hitler proclaims a "national revolution." With his NSDAP followers he marches to the "Feldherrnhalle" (Hall of Commanders), where his putsch is put down by the Bavarian state police.

April 1, 1924 Hitler is sentenced to five years of prison for his putsch attempt, but is given an early release on December 20. During the period of his incarceration he writes his foundational work *Mein Kampf*.

April 26, 1925 Upon Ebert's death, Paul von Hindenburg becomes Reich President.

Late October, 1929 The crash of the New York Stock Exchange sets off the world-wide Depression.

March 29, 1930 Heinrich Brüning becomes Reich Chancellor and pursues a policy of rigorous economizing to combat the immense national debt.

September 14, 1930 In the Reichstag (Parliamentary) election, the percentage of the right-wing NSDAP increases from 2.6 to 18.3 percent.

February, 1932 Unemployment in the German Reich reaches its peak.

July 31, 1932 In the Reichstag election, the NSDAP becomes the strongest party nationwide.

November 6, 1932 The NSDAP loses a good many votes, but still remains the strongest party.

January 30, 1933 Hindenburg appoints Hitler as Reich Chancellor.

Der andere Weg

Entscheidung für ein Klosterleben

The Other Way – Decision for a Convent Life

Vogelpredigt des hl. Franziskus, 1935
St. Francis preaching to the birds, 1935

„Die tiefsinnige und hochherzige Armutsauffassung des hl. Franziskus begnügte sich nicht mit dem Verzicht auf alle materiellen Güter. Um wahrhaft arm zu sein nach dem Vorbilde des Heilandes, wollte der Poverello auch die Demut als Gefährtin erküren, die Armut im Geiste, die Liebe zum Kleinsein. Es ist ohne weiteres klar, daß dieses selbstgewollte Kleinsein zur echten und wahren Armut gehört. Es ist wie die Seele und Grundlage, so auch die notwendige Folge der echten Armut. Armsein und Kleinsein sind fast dasselbe. Mit Recht ist gesagt worden: Demut – das ist die vollkommene Armut."[1]

Die Kunst in den Dienst Gottes stellen. Damit hat in Bertas Umfeld keiner gerechnet. Bei dieser Begabung! Diesen Möglichkeiten, sich künstlerisch weiter entfalten zu können – in guter Aussicht auf materielle Sicherheit! Doch Berta hat sich längst entschieden. Sie will alles eintauschen für ein Leben in Armut, Keuschheit und Gehorsam gegenüber Gott.

Bereits am 14. August 1930, also beinahe ein Jahr vor ihrem Abschlussexamen, hatte Berta ein Aufnahmegesuch an das Franziskanerinnenkloster im württembergischen Sießen gestellt. Nur die Allernächsten, natürlich vor allem die Eltern, wussten Bescheid und hatten ihre Einwilligung gegeben. Berta erklärte schriftlich, dass ihre Familie keine „Unterstützung" benötigte und dass niemand in Notlage hilfsbedürftig zurückgelassen würde. Denn das Ordensleben forderte „die selbstlose Hingabe aller Kräfte und Fähigkeiten" an die klostereigenen Aufgaben: „a) Erziehung und Unterricht in Kindergärten, Schulen, Pensionaten und Mädchenheimen, b) Herstellung von Paramenten[2], c) Pflege der Kranken (…), d) Uebung der ewigen Anbetung in der Klosterkapelle des Mutterhauses, e) Missionstätigkeit in Südafrika und Brasilien."[3] In den Aufnahmebedingungen hieß es weiter: „Die Bestimmung über die Verwendung der einzelnen Kandidatinnen steht den Vorgesetzten zu, die sich dabei nur von der Rücksicht auf die Bedürfnisse der Kongregation und auf die Anlagen und Fähigkeiten der Kandidatinnen und deren etwaige Vorkenntnisse leiten lassen." Berta hatte also eine genaue Vorstellung davon, was sie erwartete. Ihr war bewusst, dass die Möglichkeit bestand, nicht ihrer kreativen Leidenschaft entsprechend eingesetzt zu werden.

Auf dem Weg zur Innerlichkeit:
„Bertls Lieblings Büchlein",
Eintrag von der Mutter (links zu sehen)
„Das kleine Geheimnis" von Cassian Carg
The path toward inwardness:
"Bertl's favorite little book,"
Mother's entry (left side)
"The Little Secret" by Cassian Carg

"Saint Francis' profound and high-minded conception of poverty was not limited to the renunciation of worldly goods. In order to be truly poor after the model of the Savior, the poverello also wanted to choose humility as his companion, poverty in the spirit, the love of being small. This voluntary smallness is quite clearly part of a true and genuine poverty. It is as it were the soul and basis as well as the necessary consequence of true poverty. Being poor and being small are nearly identical. Rightly it has been said: humilitas – that is perfect poverty."[1]

To put art in the service of God: no one in Berta's circle had reckoned with that. With such a talent! Such possibilities for further development as an artist – with excellent prospects of material security! But Berta had long since decided. She would exchange everything for a life in poverty, chastity, and obedience to God.

Already on August 14, 1930, almost a year prior to her graduating examination, Berta had submitted an application for admission to the convent of Franciscan nuns in Siessen in Württemberg. Only those nearest to her, especially, of course, her parents, had knowledge and had given their consent. Berta declared in writing that her family needed no "support," and that no one would be left behind in dire straits and need of help. For the life of a nun demanded "the selfless dedication of all one's resources and abilities" to the mission of the convent: "a) education and instruction in kindergartens, schools, boarding-schools, and girls' homes, b) the making of paraments[2], c) nursing the sick (...), d) practice of perpetual adoration in the convent chapel of the motherhouse, e) missionary activity in South Africa and Brazil."[3] The conditions of acceptance specified further: "The determination how to employ the individual candidate is reserved to the superiors who are to be guided wholly by concern for the needs of the congregation and the talents, aptitudes, and previous experiences of the candidates." Thus Berta had a precise idea of what awaited her. She was aware of the possibility that she might not be deployed in accordance with her creative passion.

Kruzifix mit Kerze und Büchern, 1929/1930
Crucifix with candle and books, 1929/1930

Gebirgslandschaft mit Wald, 1929/1930
Wooded mountain landscape, 1929/1930

Porträt Jakob Huber mit Herrgottswinkel, 1929
Portrait of Jakob Huber with "Lord's corner," 1929

$\mathcal{B}$erta hatte sich zwar gerade deshalb für das Kloster Sießen entschieden, weil sie hoffen konnte, dort in ihrem Beruf als Zeichenlehrerin zu arbeiten. Und hatte sich im letzten Jahr an der Hochschule mit dem Hintergedanken an die klösterliche Paramentenabteilung mit Textilkunst auseinandergesetzt. Hatte immer schon Kruzifixe, Madonnen, Engel und Kirchenarchitektur gezeichnet und gemalt. Aber niemals, bis zum Studienende, wäre man aufgrund ihrer Bildauswahl darauf gekommen, dass sie einen ausgesprochenen Hang zu religiösen Motiven gehabt hätte. All die Landschaften, Porträts, Karikaturen! Nie wieder würde sie so frei arbeiten können, ihre Staffelei mitten ins Feld stellen und einfach in ihrem unbefangenen Pinselstrich erfassen, was ihr in den Sinn und vor den Aquarellblock kam. Sie würde sich und ihr Talent vollkommen unterordnen. Künstlerisch gesehen bedeutete ihr Entschluss also in jedem Fall eine enorme Einschränkung.

Warum also? Man unterschätzt wohl leicht die starke Prägung, die Berta durch das bayerisch-katholische Brauchtum in ihrem Umfeld mitbekommen hatte. Sie stammte aus einem frommen Elternhaus. Dort gab es einen „Herrgottswinkel"[4], man betete vor den Mahlzeiten, ging regelmäßig in die Kirche und gedachte am Namenstag des Heiligen, nach dem man benannt war. Berta war mit dem Klosterleben von klein auf vertraut, denn sie hatte in der Obhut von Klosterfrauen ihre ganze Schulzeit verbracht. Auch in der Familie gab es aufseiten beider Elternteile Ordensschwestern, und besonders zu ihrer Tante Maria Ludgera, Lehrerin in Kaiserslautern, pflegte Berta engen Kontakt. Diese Tante nämlich hatte sie in Kindertagen an das Pastellzeichnen herangeführt. Schon in Bertas frühesten Briefen aus dem Internat war eine unbefangene, tiefe kindliche Gläubigkeit zu spüren, immer wieder sprach sie davon, für ihre Lieben beten zu wollen, oder bat um Unterstützung durch Gebet für Prüfungen oder Ähnliches.

$\mathcal{S}$he had nevertheless chosen the convent at Siessen for the very reason that she could hope to be able to work there in her profession as an art teacher. During her last year at the college she had also preoccupied herself with textile art with an eye to the convent's paraments department. And she had always been fond of drawing crucifixes, figures of the Madonna, angels, and church architecture. But to the very end of her studies, no one would on the basis of her choices of pictorial themes have thought that she might have any pronounced penchant for religious motifs. All those landscapes, portraits, caricatures! Never

Roter Fäustling, 1927
Red mitten, 1927

again would she be able to work so freely, set up her easel in the middle of a field and simply capture with uninhibited brushstrokes whatever popped into her mind or appeared in front of her watercolor pad. She would have utterly to subordinate herself and her talent. In artistic terms, her decision would entail enormous restrictions in every respect.

Why therefore? Perhaps one underestimates too easily the enormous impact that the customs and habits of her Bavarian-Catholic background would have had on her. She came from a pious home. It had a *Herrgottswinkel*[4] ("Lord's Corner"), prayers were said before meals, one regularly attended church, and observed the day of the saint after whom one was named. Berta had been familiar with convent life from childhood on, having spent all of her school years under the tutelage of convent women. There were nuns also on both sides of the family, and Berta had an especially close connection to her aunt Maria Ludgera, a teacher in Kaiserslautern, as it was this aunt who had introduced her to pastel drawing in early childhood. Already her earliest letters intimated a deep, childlike devoutness. Time and again she spoke about wanting to pray for her loved ones or asked for support through prayer before examinations or the like.

Fotografie: Der Herrgottswinkel im Hummel-Haus, und Bild: Stube mit Herrgottswinkel, 1929/1930
Photograph: "Lord's corner" at the Hummel home, and painting: Living room with crucifix, 1929/1930

Kniende Madonna mit Kind, wahrscheinlich ein Entwurf für eine Textilarbeit, 1931
Kneeling Virgin with Child, probably a draft for a textile design, 1931

*Einsiedler vor der Klause
(Schülerarbeit), 1927
Hermitage with hermit
(student work), 1927*

ls Berta elf Jahre alt war, nahm sie das erste Mal an Exerzitien teil. Im klösterlichen Internat war es üblich, dass die Schülerinnen sich ein paar Tage allein der Besinnung auf Gott widmeten. „Schweigen ging schwer. Am 1. Tag habe ich geschwiegen, am 2. Tag geschrieben, am 3. Tag geschwätzt", schrieb das Mädchen noch ein wenig hilflos nach Hause. Jahre später, während ihrer Studienzeit, verabredete sie sich immer noch mit Freundinnen von daheim, um an den geistlichen Übungen teilzunehmen. Wiederholt betonte sie, wie sehr sie sich darauf freute. Ihr unverbrüchlicher Glaube war für Berta ein beständiges Stück Heimat in der Fremde.

So ist es nicht verwunderlich, dass die Begegnung mit zwei besonderen Studienkolleginnen ihre Aufmerksamkeit fesselte. Im September 1928 bat Professor Dasio Berta in ihrer Eigenschaft als Obmännin der Klasse, sich dieses Semester zweier neuer Studentinnen anzunehmen. Die beiden seien Franziskanerinnen aus Sießen im Württembergischen. Sie würden von der Klosterleitung zur Weiterbildung ihrer künstlerischen Ausbildung nach München gesandt. Als dann anderntags Schwester M. Kostka Hartmann allein am Schwarzen Brett stand und sich mit dem Veranstaltungsplan nicht recht auskannte, wurde sie von Berta angesprochen: „Sie sind ja ganz neu, gehen Sie auch mit?"[5] Die beiden verabredeten sich am Münchner Ostbahnhof, um gemeinsam zu einer Exkursion ins Münchner Umland zu fahren. Im November kam dann Schwester M. Laura Brugger aus Sießen in München an. Die Ordensfrauen wohnten im Maria-Theresien-Wohnheim der Schwestern der Heiligen Familie in der Blumenstraße. Berta besuchte die beiden dort, und schnell entstand eine enge Freundschaft. Und da sie sich in ihrem recht teuren Studentenzimmer unwohl und einsam fühlte, beschloss sie, auch in dasselbe Heim zu wechseln. Endlich wieder zu Hause in einer richtigen Gemeinschaft, wie daheim mit den Geschwistern und in der Schule mit den Klassenkameradinnen!

t the age of eleven, she first participated in spiritual exercises. At the convent-like boarding-school it was customary for the pupils to devote a few days to reflections about God. "Silence was hard. On the 1st day I kept silent, on the 2nd day I wrote, on the 3rd day I talked," the girl reported, still a little helplessly, to those at home. Years later, during her studies, she would still

Romanischer Kreuzgang, 1929/1930
Romanesque cloister, 1929/1930

arrange to take part in the spiritual exercises together with childhood girlfriends and repeatedly emphasized how much she looked forward to these. A firm faith was a steady home away from home for Berta.

It is thus not altogether strange that the encounter with two special fellow students arrested her lasting attention. In September of 1928, Professor Dasio asked Berta in her role as class leader to take two new students under her wing for the semester, both of them Franciscan nuns from Siessen in Württemberg, who were being sent to Munich for postgraduate art training. When on the following day Sister M. Kostka Hartmann was standing alone at the bulletin board, not quite able to find her way through the schedule of classes and events, she was addressed by Berta: "You are brand-new here, would you like to come along?"[5] The two arranged to meet at Munich's East Station for a joint excursion into the surrounding countryside. Then, in November, Sister M. Laura Brugger arrived from Siessen. The two nuns lodged at the Maria Theresia boardinghouse of the Sisters of the Holy Family on Blumenstrasse. Berta visited them there, and a close friendship quickly developed between them. And since she felt uncomfortable and lonely in her rather expensive rented room, she decided to move to the same living-quarters. There she could at last feel at home again in a real community, as she had with her siblings and at the boarding school with her classmates.

Malausflug an den Chiemsee
Painting excursion to the Chiemsee

Dampfer auf dem Chiemsee, 1929/1930
Chiemsee steamer, 1929/1930

St. Anna im Münchner Stadtteil Lehel, in der Nähe befand sich Bertas erstes Zimmer
St. Anna in the Munich district of Lehel, not far from Berta's first rooming house

Maria-Theresien-Wohnheim in der Blumenstraße
Passbild Berta Hummel
Boarding house Maria Theresia on Blumenstrasse
Passport photograph of Berta Hummel

Berta musste zwar eine Weile warten, bis ein Zimmer frei wurde, aber im Juni 1929 konnte sie nach Hause berichten: „War eben in der Pension u. besichtigte das Zimmer. Es ist klein aber hell u. nett." Des Weiteren erwähnte sie, dass die Bewohnerinnen das Zimmer „selbst machen u. auch Schuhe putzen" mussten, und bat ihre Mutter um Schuhputzzeug.[6]

Die Franziskanerinnen waren beide älter als Berta, Schwester Kostka nur drei Jahre, Schwester Laura immerhin um 16. Wer ahnte schon damals, dass M. Laura Brugger in nicht allzu langer Zeit die wichtigste Assistentin für ihre weltberühmte Kommilitonin werden würde? Die drei verstanden sich jedenfalls prächtig. Berta fühlte sich in ihrem neuen Zuhause rundum wohl. Zu Fasching erlaubte sie sich sogar einen Scherz mit der Heimleitung und meldete der Schwester Oberin, im Sprechzimmer sei „hoher Besuch" angekommen. Als diese ganz konsterniert hineinging, um die Gäste zu begrüßen, lachten sie auf den Besucherstühlen platzierte lebensechte Pappmachéfiguren von den Professoren der Kunstschule an. Es muss für Berta eine schöne Zeit gewesen sein! Sie war äußerst erfolgreich und beliebt in ihrer Ausbildungsstätte. Sie war umgeben von einem breiten kulturellen Angebot. Und sie fühlte sich verstanden in ihrem Bedürfnis nach den traditionellen spirituellen Werten ihrer Herkunft.

Oft gehen Berta und ihre neuen Gefährtinnen gemeinsam zur Staatsschule in die Luisenstraße. Wenn Zeit ist, bummeln sie dabei durch die Innenstadt, anstatt die Trambahn zu nehmen. Ganz besonders interessant ist die elegante Brienner Straße mit ihren mondänen Boutiquen, Cafés und Galerien. Ein kurzes Gebet in der üppig-barocken Asamkirche in der Sendlinger Straße gehört zum Spazierprogramm, ebenso wie ein Besuch in der Herzog-Spital-Kirche, wo ganztags Anbetung gehalten wird.

M. Kostka Hartmann OSF (1906 – 1997)
M. Kostka Hartmann OSF (1906 – 1997)

Though she had to wait for a while for a room to become vacant, she was able to report home in June of 1929: "Was at the boarding-house just now to look at the room. It is small but light and pleasant." She also mentioned that the residents had to "make up" their rooms "themselves and polish their own shoes" and asked her mother for shoeshine utensils.[6]

Both of the Franciscans were older than Berta, Sister Kostka a mere three years, Sister Laura all of 16. Who could have guessed then that in the not too distant future M. Laura Brugger would become her by then world-famous fellow student's principal assistant? In any event, the three of them got along famously, and Berta felt comfortable all the way round at her new home. For Mardi Gras, she even permitted herself a practical joke on the house authorities, announcing to the Sister Superior that "high visitors" had arrived in the parlor. When the latter showed up there quite flustered to greet the guests, she found life-size papier-mâché effigies of the professors at the art school grinning at her from the visitors' chairs. It must have been a good time for Berta. She was exceptionally successful and popular at her place of training. She was surrounded by a broad cultural offering. And she felt understood in her needs for the traditional spiritual values of her background.

Often Berta and her new companions went together to the State School on Luisenstrasse. If there was enough time, they would stroll though the city center rather than taking the streetcar. Of special interest was the elegant Brienner Strasse with its fashionable boutiques, cafés, and galleries. A brief prayer in the sumptuous baroque Asam church on Sendlingerstrasse was a regular part of the walk, as was a stop at the Herzog-Spital church, where worship went on all day.

Schmerzensmutter nach dem berühmten Gnadenbild in der Münchner Herzog-Spital-Kirche, 1935
Mater dolorosa after the famous miracle-working image at Munich's Herzog-Spital church, 1935

𝔄m Sonntag besuchten die drei Freundinnen gemeinsam das Hochamt in St. Michael, dort wurde Berta zum ersten Mal mit den unkonventionellen Predigten des Jesuitenpaters Rupert Mayer konfrontiert.[7] Er war ein Mann des Volkes, äußerst beliebt bei den Münchnern, denn er brachte frischen Wind in die Kirche. Er setzte sich kompromisslos für die Armen ein und konnte seine Zuhörerschaft durch mitreißende Predigten begeistern. Bereits 1929 hatte er die Zeichen seines Umfelds erkannt und rief zum Engagement gegen die Nationalsozialisten auf. So bekam Berta in jener Zeit vielleicht Folgendes zu hören: „Jeder trägt die Heiligkeit im Tornister. Niemand kann sagen: Heiligkeit ist zu hoch für mich. Es gehören dazu keine auffallenden Heldentaten, kein besonderes Lebensalter, keine bestimmten Verhältnisse, kein todernstes Gesicht. (...) Heiligsprechungsprozesse können wir uns nicht leisten (...), dazu fehlt uns das Geld. Aber heilig werden müssen wir alle."[8]

Berta beobachtet die Franziskanerinnen. Was sie tun, was sie reden und wie sie sich verhalten. Sie stellt Fragen. Sie ist fasziniert, hingezogen, etwas scheint in ihrem eigenen Dasein zu fehlen, sie hat noch viel Sehnsucht. Das ganze Leben geben an eine Sache! Die Kunst um der Kunst willen kann es nicht sein, nicht für sie, so sehr sie die Ausübung liebt, die Aktion an sich, das Lernen und Tun dank ihres außergewöhnlichen Talents – doch es fehlt eben das Gerüst, die höhere Aufgabe, in deren Dienst es zu stellen ist.

Rosen, 1927/1928
Roses, 1927/1928

Eines Tages teilte sie ihren beiden Freundinnen mit, dass sie sich mit dem Gedanken trage, auch Ordensfrau zu werden. Von da an bemühten sich die Schwestern, ihr einen Einblick zu geben. Wollten ihr nicht eine schwärmerische Idealvorstellung, sondern das tägliche Klosterleben näherbringen. „Den Sinn und das Wesen der Ordensgelübde und der restlosen Bindung an Gott und den Dienst an den Mitmenschen", erinnert sich Schwester Kostka. „Wir sagten ihr auch ganz klar, dass sie zu jeder Arbeit bereit sein müsse, dass es ungewiss sei, ob sie einen künstlerischen Beruf ausüben dürfe. Auf jeden Fall: wir waren sehr darauf bedacht, keinerlei direkten Einfluss auf ihre Entscheidung auszuüben, im Bewusstsein der großen Verantwortung, die wir trugen, sowohl für die Persönlichkeit der Berta Hummel, wie auch für unsere eigene Kongregation."[9]

Der Jesuit Pater Rupert Mayer (1876 – 1945) beim Spendensammeln
The Jesuit priest Rupert Mayer (1876 – 1945) collecting funds

Stillleben mit Obst und Blumenstock, 1928/1930
Still life with fruit and potted plant, 1928/1930

On Sundays, the trio would jointly attend High Mass at St. Michael's, where Berta first encountered the unconventional sermons of the Jesuit priest Father Rupert Mayer.[7] He was a man of the people, much beloved in Munich for bringing a fresh current into the church. He was an uncompromising champion of the poor and was able to inspire his listeners by his stirring sermons. Already in 1929 he could read the signs of the times and called upon people to oppose the National Socialists. Thus Berta may have heard words like these: "Everyone carries holiness in his knapsack. No one can say: holiness is too high for me. No conspicuous deeds of heroism are required, no particular age in life, no specific conditions, no holier-than-thou face. (...) We cannot afford canonizations (...), we lack the money for that. But saints we must all become."[8]

Berta closely observed the Franciscans. What they did, what they said, how they comported themselves. She asked questions. She felt fascinated, drawn, something was missing in her own existence, she still had such longings. To give one's whole life for a cause! It could not be art for art's sake, not for her, as much as she loved its execution, the action itself, the learning and doing, driven by her exceptional talent. But as yet there was lacking a framework, a higher mission that her art could subserve.

One day she told her two friends that she was entertaining the thought of becoming a nun as well. From then on the sisters endeavored to provide her with a realistic insight, not a starry-eyed ideal but a picture of the actual daily life at a convent – "the meaning and nature of a nun's vow," as Sr. Kostka recalled, "and the unreserved commitment to God and to the service of one's fellow human beings". "We also told her quite clearly that she must be prepared for any work, that it was by no means certain that she would be able to pursue her artistic calling. At all events we were conscientious about exerting no direct influence on her decision, aware, as we were, of the great responsibility we had, both for the person of Berta Hummel and for our own congregation."[9]

Ostern 1928:
Familienausflug: die Geschwister Hummel
vor der Befreiungshalle in Kehlheim
(Berta zweite von links und links)
Easter 1928:
Family excursion: the Hummel children in
front of the Liberation Hall in Kehlheim
(Berta second from the left and left)

Die vier Hummel-Schwestern (Berta links)
The four Hummel sisters (Berta on the left)

Jede Franziskanerin besitzt ein Büchlein, in dem Anordnungen, Gedanken und Regeln für das Ordensleben enthalten sind. Dieses Buch ist zur ganz persönlichen Auseinandersetzung bestimmt. Eines Tages ist das Regelbuch einer der Schwestern verschwunden, und kurz darauf kommt Berta triumphierend damit ins Zimmer und verkündet ihren verblüfften Freundinnen: „So, jetzt weiß ich alles, jetzt ist mir alles klar und – mein Entschluss steht fest!"[10]

Im Frühling 1930 stellte sich Berta in Sießen vor. Die Kandidatinnenmeisterin war sehr überrascht, dass die junge Frau kaum Fragen stellte. Berta schaute sich nur um, schaute und schaute, wie es seit jeher ihre Art gewesen war. Die erfahrene Schwester konnte ja nicht wissen, dass die Bewerberin das Regelbüchlein entwendet hatte und sich deshalb so gut im klösterlichen Leben auskannte. Berta war jedenfalls begeistert von ihrem Besuch. „In Sießen war es wunderschön", schwärmte sie ihren Eltern vor, „das Ganze machte auf mich einen sehr guten Eindruck. War zweimal bei Mutter Oberin, die eine Heilige sein soll." Ein kleiner Fauxpas machte ihr allerdings schwer zu schaffen. Sie war ohne Hut im Kloster angekommen, der war ihr nämlich im Zug aus dem Fenster geflogen. Was die wohlerzogene junge Frau in allerhöchst „peinliche Verlegenheit" stürzte, gerade nachdem sie sich in aller Korrektheit präsentieren wollte! [11]

Bertas Entschluss löste an der Kunstschule zunächst Bestürzung aus. Vor allem Professor Dasio zeigte sich entsetzt, dass seine Lieblingsschülerin der Welt entsagen wollte, so sehr, dass er es sich nicht verkneifen konnte, ihr sein Missfallen deutlich zu zeigen: Er kommunizierte schlichtweg nicht mehr mit ihr. Nun hieß es Lebewohl sagen. Vor allem bei ihrer Mentorin Professor Brauneis fiel Berta das ausgesprochen schwer: „Ich war bei ihr, um mich zu verabschieden; dabei gab sie mir die Versicherung eines großen künstlerischen Könnens mit. Sie weinte und bat mich, zeitlebens mit ihr in Verbindung zu bleiben. (…) Sie weiß, daß ich in das Kloster gehe, es kam ihr schwer an; weil ich nach Sießen gehe, freute sie sich, dort muß ein guter Geist sein, meinte sie. (…) aber künstlerisch dürfen Sie niemals einbüßen, ich will Ihnen immer helfen, sagte sie. (…) Eine Lehrerin wie die Brauneis hatte ich noch nie; und da wurde es mir schon schwer, auch Abschied nehmen zu müssen, um ganz von München zu gehen."[12]

Chrysantheme, 1929/1930
Chrysanthemum, 1929/1930

Rote Primeln, 1929/1930
Red primula, 1929/1930

Every Franciscan nun is given a booklet containing instructions, reflections, and rules governing life in the order. It is a manual for individual self-examination. One day one of the sisters' rulebooks had disappeared. But soon afterwards Berta entered the room triumphantly and announced to the friends' astonishment: "All right, now I know everything, everything is clear to me, and – my decision is made!"[10]

In the spring of 1930, Berta presented herself at Siessen. The mistress of candidates was puzzled that the young woman hardly asked any questions. Berta merely looked around, looked and looked, as had ever been her habit. The knowledgeable sister could not know that the applicant had purloined the rule manual and therefore already knew all about monastic life. In any case, Berta was ecstatic about her visit. "Siessen was wonderful," she told her parents enthusiastically, "the entire place made an excellent impression on me. Twice spoke with the Mother Superior, who is said to be a saint." A small faux pas had troubled her deeply, though. She had arrived at the convent without her hat, which had been blown out of the window on the train. It caused the very proper young woman, who had been so intent on presenting herself absolutely correctly,[11] a most "painful embarrassment."

Berta's decision caused great consternation at the art school. Especially Professor Dasio was appalled that his favorite pupil wanted to renounce the world, and he made no secret of his extreme displeasure: he simply stopped talking to her. Now the time for parting had come. That was very hard for Berta, especially with regard to her mentoress, Professor Brauneis. "I went to see her to say good-bye, and she assured me of my great artistic ability. She cried and begged me always to remain in contact with her. (...) She knows I am going into a convent, and it was hard for her; but she was glad that I am going to Siessen, the spirit of the place must be good, she thought. (...) 'But you must never let go of your artistic ability: I will always help you,' she said. (...) I never had a teacher like Brauneis before, and so it was hard for me to say good-bye and to leave Munich forever."[12]

Porträt Professor Else Brauneis, 1930
Portrait of Professor Else Brauneis, 1930

Porträt Professor Maximilian Dasio, 1930
Portrait of Professor Maximilian Dasio, 1930

Die Abreise vom Wohnheim in der Blumenstraße dagegen fiel zum Glück weniger schwermütig aus. Die bestandene Abschlussprüfung wurde gebührend gefeiert: „Torte extra angefertigt und Wein und Kaffee wird aufgetragen, man kann es sich nicht besser denken."[13] Viel Organisatorisches war noch zu erledigen. In der ganzen Münchner Zeit hatte sich in Bertas Zimmerchen einiges angesammelt, es „hätte sich beinahe rentiert mich mit dem Auto zu holen, so viel Gepäck habe ich, weiß gar nicht wohin damit"[14]. Die Mappen mit ihren Bildern aus der Studienzeit allerdings durfte sie nur zum Teil mitnehmen, denn laut Vertrag konnte die Schule die Bilder für ein Jahr zurückbehalten und ausstellen. So sehr sich Berta darüber ärgerte, dass sie nicht alles beisammenhatte, so stolz war sie doch auch, dass von ihren Sachen das meiste öffentlich gezeigt werden sollte. Und das trotz der ewigen Debatte, dass die angewandte nicht den gleichen Status genoss wie die freie Kunst. Man kann Berta beinahe herzhaft seufzen hören, wenn sie schrieb: „Durch die Ausstellung soll eben gezeigt werden, daß auch Zeichenlehrerinnen Künstlerisches leisten können."[15]

Es war eines der letzten Male für Berta, die Ferien bei der Familie in Massing zu verbringen. Vier Wochen, dann würde es in eine herbeigesehnte und doch mit Bangen erwartete Zukunft gehen.

In diesem Sommer besuchte Berta zusammen mit Schwester Kostka und Schwester Laura noch einen einwöchigen Kurs in Starnberg, den sie als gute Vorbereitung auf ihre Schultätigkeit sah. Bereits vor einem Jahr hatte sie ihren Eltern gegenüber ihr Interesse an der neuartigen pädagogischen Methodik bekundet, die dort gelehrt würde[16]: „In Starnberg ist eine neue Schule d.h. schon alt, aber die Auffassung ist neu v. Kor[n]mann, dieser weiht einen sehr gerne unverbindlich in seine Theorie ein, die ganz hervorragend sein soll u. mich auch wahnsinnig interessiert. Diese Lernmethode, die im Kind schon das Künstlerische wecken will, geht im Lauf der Jahre ganz durch, in Württemberg ist es bereits schon so."[17] Wohlgemerkt hatte sie damals schon an den Lehrplan ihres zukünftigen Heimatlandes gedacht.

The departure from the boarding-house on Blumenstrasse was fortunately less melancholy. The passing of the final examination was duly celebrated: "A special fancy cake was served, with wine and coffee: nothing finer can be imagined."[13] A great many details still needed to be seen to. A lot had accumulated in Berta's room during her stay in Munich. "It might almost have been worthwhile to be picked up by car, I have so much baggage, I don't know where to put it all."[14] Actually she was able to take only some of the portfolios containing her work as a student, as the school was entitled by contract to retain and exhibit her pictures for one year. Although Berta was annoyed that she could not have all her things together, she was also very proud that more of her works would be shown than of any one else's. And this despite the everlasting debate about applied art not having the same status as "liberal" art! One can almost hear Berta heaving a deep sigh when she writes: "The exhibition should finally demonstrate that women art teachers, too, are capable of achieving genuine art."[15]

It was one of the last few chances for Berta to spend a vacation with her family in Massing. Within four weeks she would step into a future at once longed for and yet also dreaded.

During this summer, Berta, together with Sister Kostka and Sister Laura, attended a one-week course in Starnberg, which she thought would be a good preparation for her teaching career. Already a year earlier she had mentioned to her parents her interest in the innovative pedagogical method that was taught there:[16] "There is a new school in Starnberg, that is to say, the school is old, but its concept is new, developed by Kor[n]mann, who readily and without obligation initiates you into his theories, which are supposed to be outstanding and which hugely interest me. This teaching method, designed to develop an artistic vein already in childhood, has been spreading for some years and is already established in Württemberg."[17] One notices that even then she was thinking about the curriculum in her future homeland.

Der Münchner Hauptbahnhof
Munich central station

Klassenfoto (Berta Vierte von links) mit ihren Lieblingslehrern Professor Brauneis (in der Mitte sitzend) und Professor Dasio (stehend dahinter). Links neben der Professorin M. Laura Brugger in Ordenstracht.
Class picture (Berta fourth from the left) with the favorite teachers Professors Brauneis (center, seated) and Dasio (behind her, standing). To the left of Professor Brauneis, M. Laura Brugger in nun's habit.

Alte Massinger Häuser, 1929/1930
Massing, old houses, 1929/1930

Ansonsten ist über diese vier Wochen in Massing so gut wie nichts bekannt. Wie Berta sie wohl verbrachte, so kurz, bevor sie den Eintritt in ihr neues Leben wagen wollte? Sie war auf ihre Kandidatur gut vorbereitet und hatte den Sießener Bewerberinnenprospekt gründlich gelesen: „Wenn dir nun, liebe Jungfrau, die Aufnahme bewilligt werden konnte, so danke dem lieben Gott von ganzem Herzen dafür; denn der Ordensberuf ist nach dem wahren Glauben die größte Gnade. Verbringe die Zeit bis zu deinem Eintritt in stiller Zurückgezogenheit und treuer Pflichterfüllung und flehe zu Gott um den rechten Ordensgeist." Ob sie wohl in jenen Wochen auch zweifelte an ihrem Entschluss? Man weiß es nicht. Einmal, einige Zeit später, kann man aus einem Brief herauslesen, wie spannungsreich diese Ferien für sie gewesen sein müssen. Sie schrieb entschuldigend an ihre Mutter, dass sie vor dem Klostereintritt keine Möglichkeit gehabt hätte, sich bei allen Verwandten zu verabschieden. Und sie wirkt ein wenig müde, immer wieder ihre Entscheidung begründen zu müssen: „Du weißt doch selbst, wie zu Hause alles drunter u. drüber ging u. ich nicht gerade Lust hatte in den letzten Tagen, meine gemischten Gefühle aufs Papier zu bringen."[18] Wie dem auch gewesen sein mag, ihre Schwester Centa jedenfalls bescheinigt ihr, sie hätte niemals etwas aufgegeben, was sie sich einmal in den Kopf gesetzt hatte. „Sie hat immer alles durchgezogen, von Anfang bis Ende."

Am Schluss des Kandidatinnenprospekts heißt es: „Wenn aber der ersehnte Tag kommt, an dem die Klosterpforte sich öffnet für dich, dann komm mit der Gesinnung des Psalmisten: ‚Wie hab' ich mich gefreut, als man mir sagte: Zum Hause Gottes wallen[19] wir'."[20]

Virtually nothing is known otherwise about those four weeks in Massing. How might Berta have spent them, so shortly before taking her daring step into a new life? She was well prepared for her candidacy and had thoroughly studied the Siessen application brochure: "If, dear virgin, acceptance has been accorded to you, thank the good Lord with all your heart; for the calling to a religious order is, according to our true faith, the greatest of mercies. Spend the time until your arrival in quiet retreat and faithful discharge of your duties, and pray to God for the true spirit of the order." Might she have had any doubts about her decision during those weeks? We do not know. In a letter written some time later one can sense how tense a time this vacation must have been. She wrote to her mother to apologize that she had not had a chance prior to entering the convent to say good-bye to all her relatives. And she seems a little tired of constantly having to defend her decision: "You yourself know how everything at home was so topsy-turvy and I had no desire, during those last days, to put down my mixed feelings on paper."[18] However that may have been, her sister Centa attested that Berta never abandoned anything she had once put her mind to. "She always saw everything through from beginning to end."

The candidates' prospectus concludes with the words: "When the longed-for day arrives on which the convent gates open for you, then come in the frame of mind of the psalmist: 'I was glad when they said unto me, Let us go into the house of the Lord.'"[19]

Berta mit ihrem geliebten Boxer „Lord" und Porträt „Lord", 1929/1930
Berta with her beloved boxer "Lord" and Portrait "Lord," 1929/1930

Tagesordnung im Kloster Sießen

aus der Zeit von Maria Innocentia Hummel bis nach 1960

5.00 Uhr	Aufstehen, die Novizinnen gehen mit der Glocke durch das Haus
5.30 Uhr	Laudes, Morgenlob in der Kapelle
6.00 Uhr	Eucharistiefeier
	Prim und Terz
	Die klassischen sieben Tagzeiten:
	Matutin – nachts (wurde antizipiert),
	Laudes – in der Früh,
	Prim – die erste Stunde um sechs,
	Terz – die dritte um neun,
	Sext – die sechste um zwölf,
	Non – die neunte um drei,
	Vesper – die zwölfte – Abendlob,
	Komplet – Nachtgebet
6.55 Uhr	Betrachtung
7.30 Uhr	Frühstück
8.00 Uhr	Arbeitszeit
9.30 Uhr	Zehn-Uhr-Pause
12.00 Uhr	Sext im Chor und Partikularexamen (kurze innere Einkehr)
12.15 Uhr	Mittagessen
13.00 Uhr	Freizeit oder allgemeine Dienste
14.00 Uhr	Arbeitszeit
16.00 Uhr	Non und Vesper im Chor
16.30 Uhr	Abendbrot
17.00 Uhr	Kurze Arbeitszeit und persönliches Gebet (z. B. Kreuzweg, Rosenkranz)
18.00 Uhr	Geistliche Lesung und Matutin in der Kapelle
18.45 Uhr	Eucharistischer Segen
19.00 Uhr	Abendessen
19.30 Uhr	Freizeit oder allgemeine Dienste
20.30 Uhr	Komplet im Chor
21.00 Uhr	Nachtruhe Stillschweigen bis nach dem Frühstück

Anbetung halten die Schwestern, je zwei in Vertretung aller, im stündlichen Wechsel von 7 Uhr bis 19 Uhr, zu bestimmten Zeiten, etwa jeden ersten Freitag des Monats, auch nachts.

Zwölf Kalenderblätter, 1935

Daily Schedule at Convent Siessen
at the time of Maria Innocentia Hummel until after 1960

5:00 a.m.	Rise. the novices go through the house ringing a bell	2:00 p.m.	Work
5:30 a.m.	Lauds, morning service of praise in the chapel	4:00 p.m.	Nones and vespers in choir
6:00 a.m.	Holy Mass Prime and Tierce	4:30 p.m.	Dinner
		5:00 p.m.	Short work period and private prayer (e.g., Way of the Cross, Rosary)
	The seven classic canonical hours: Matins – at night (was moved up), Lauds – early mornings, Prime – the first hour at 6 a.m., Tierce – the third hour at nine. Sext – the sixth hour at noon, Nones – the ninth hour at 3 p.m., Vespers – the twelfth hour at 6 p.m., Compline – evening prayer.	6:00 p.m.	Spiritual reading and matins in the chapel
		6:45 p.m.	Eucharistic benediction
		7:00 p.m.	Supper
		7:30 p.m.	Recreation or general chores
		8:30 p.m.	Compline in choir
6:55 a.m.	Contemplation	9:00 p.m.	Bedtime
7:30 a.m.	Breakfast		Silence until after breakfast
8:00 a.m.	Work		
9:30 a.m.	Ten o'clock break		
12 noon	Sext in the choir and particular examination (brief self-communion)		
12:15 p.m.	Midday meal		
1:00 p.m.	Recreation or general chores		

At certain times, for example, every first Friday of the month, including at night, two sisters each, representing all and changing hourly, offer worship every hour from 7 a.m. to 7 p.m.

Twelve calendar sheets, 1935

Klosterkind und Künstlerin

Anfänge einer Weltkarriere

Convent Child and Craftswoman – The Beginnings of a World Career

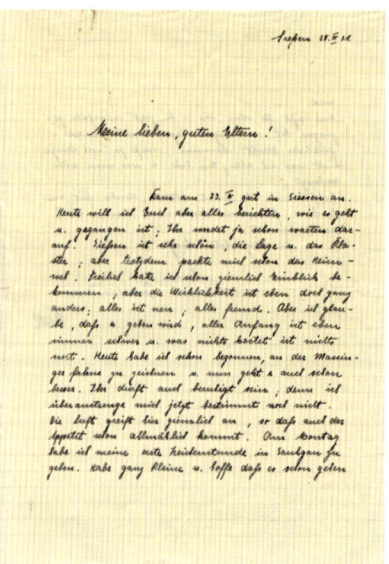

Bertas erster Brief aus Sießen
Berta's first letter from Siessen

„Meine lieben, guten Eltern! Kam am 23.IV. gut in Siessen an. Heute will ich Euch aber alles berichten, wie es geht und gegangen ist; Ihr werdet ja schon warten darauf. Sießen ist sehr schön, die Lage und das Kloster; aber trotzdem packte mich schon das Heimweh. Freilich hatte ich schon ziemlich Einblick bekommen; aber die Wirklichkeit ist eben doch ganz anders; alles ist neu; alles fremd. Aber ich glaube, dass es gehen wird; aller Anfang ist eben immer schwer u. was nichts kostet ist nichts wert."[1]

Um nach Sießen zu gelangen, musste Berta mit dem Zug nach Saulgau fahren, ein romantisches Fachwerkstädtchen in der oberschwäbischen Hügellandschaft. Von dort aus sind es noch 40 Minuten zu Fuß, und wenn sie den sanften Biegungen des schmalen Birkenwegs folgte und nach oben blickte, konnte sie die imposante Anlage sehen. An dieser Stelle hatte schon seit dem hohen Mittelalter ein Kloster gestanden. 1260 hatten Dominikanerinnen sich hier niedergelassen. Über die Jahrhunderte hatten sie ihren Orden immer wieder mit äußerster Anstrengung durch harte Kriegszeiten gebracht. Die Anlage war im Laufe der Jahre vergrößert und die Gebäude ausgebaut worden, was in der Errichtung der prächtigen Kirche durch den Meister des bayerischen Rokoko, Dominikus Zimmermann, gipfelte. Er entwarf unter anderem später die weltberühmte Wieskirche. Durch die Säkularisation war das Kloster Anfang des 19. Jahrhunderts enteignet worden. 1860 schließlich waren die verwaisten Gebäude von Franziskanerinnen aus Oggelsbeuren gekauft worden, man war auf der Suche nach geeigneten Räumlichkeiten gewesen. Diese Schwestern hatten sich die schulische und religiöse Erziehung von Mädchen zur Aufgabe gemacht. Nun stand Berta also an jenem Apriltag vor den Toren ihrer neuen Heimat.

Fußweg durch die Birkenallee nach Sießen, 1949
The birch-lined footpath to Siessen, 1949

"My dear kind parents! Arrived safely in Siessen on April 23. Today I will tell you everything that is happening and has happened, as you will be anxious to hear. Siessen is beautiful, both the location and the convent itself; even so I am already homesick. Though I had already gained a lot of insight, the reality is inevitably quite different, everything is new and strange. But I think I will be all right. All beginnings are hard, and where there is no price there is no value."[1]

To get to Siessen, Berta had to go by train to Saulgau, a romantic village of half-timbered houses in the hilly landscape of Upper Swabia. From there it is another 40 minutes on foot to the convent, and when Berta followed the gently curving, birch-lined footpath she could see the imposing complex whenever she glanced up. There has been a monastery at this location ever since the high Middle Ages. Around 1260, Dominican nuns settled here. Through the centuries they had to struggle time and again to preserve the order in times of war. Over the years, the complex was enlarged and the buildings expanded, culminating in the erection of the gorgeous church by the master of Bavarian Rococo, Dominikus Zimmermann, who later designed the world-famous Wies church. As a result of the secularization, the convent was expropriated at the beginning of the 19th century. Then, in 1860, the deserted buildings were purchased by Franciscan nuns who had been searching for a suitable facility. These sisters had chosen the schooling and religious education of girls as their mission. And now, on this day in April, Berta was standing at the gates of her new home.

*Das Franziskanerinnenkloster
Sießen, Luftbild von Südosten, 1962*
The Franciscan convent of Siessen, aerial photograph from the southeast, 1962

89

*Die erste Arbeit in Sießen:
Bruder-Konrad-Fahne der
Jungmänner von Massing, 1931*
First work in Siessen:
Brother Konrad Banner of the men's
congregation in Massing, 1931

Kaselentwurf, Kreuz und IHS, 1931/1933
Design for a chasuble, cross
and IHS, 1931/1933

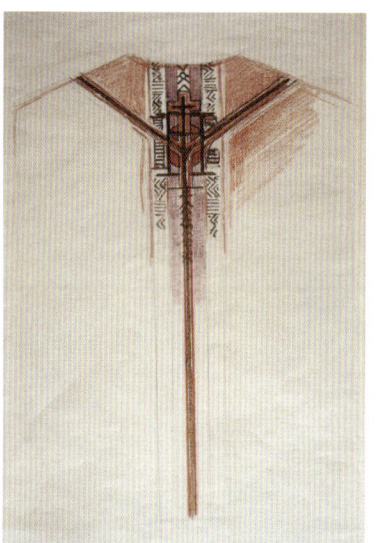

Das Klosterleben begann für jede Aufnahmesuchende als Kandidatin. Berta nahm am ganz normalen Klosteralltag teil. Sie hatte zwar von Anfang an ihre Aufgaben und Pflichten, dennoch war sie während der zweijährigen Probezeit an keine Versprechen gebunden. Vom ersten Tag an arbeitete Berta in der Paramentenwerkstatt, sie durfte eigene Vorlagen entwerfen, nach denen dann im Sticksaal gearbeitet wurde. Ein Tag im Kloster folgte strengen Regeln, um fünf wurden alle Schwestern geweckt und zum Morgenlob um halb sechs in die Kapelle gerufen. Der Tag war gegliedert durch feste Gebets- und Schweigezeiten, drei Mahlzeiten und zwei Zwischenmahlzeiten, die alle Schwestern zusammen im Speisesaal einnahmen. Was für eine Veränderung muss das für Berta gewesen sein! Sie war es ja gewohnt, völlig eigenmächtig zu arbeiten und erst dann damit aufzuhören, wenn sie das Gefühl hatte, eine Aufgabe erledigt zu haben. So seufzte sie auch ein wenig ungeduldig nach Hause: „Nur das eine kostet schon so kleine Öpferle, daß man oft und oft am Tag aufhören muß und oft gerade dann, wenn man im besten Schaffen ist."²

Doch es gab nicht nur die künstlerische Arbeit, denn natürlich schützte auch ein Klosterleben nicht vor hausfraulichen Pflichten. Tischdienst, Spüldienst und Hausdienst wurden von allen Schwestern erledigt, unabhängig von der beruflichen Tätigkeit. An bestimmten Tagen wurde die Wäsche gemacht, die schließlich aufgehängt und gelegt werden musste. Die Tracht der Ordensfrauen war nicht unkompliziert zu handhaben. So bestand etwa der Weil, der ausladende Schleier der Franziskanerinnen, aus mehreren Stofflagen, die sorgfältig geplättet und zusammengefaltet werden mussten. Oder das weiße Hülltuch, welches das Gesicht umrahmte, musste im noch nassen Zustand fein plissiert werden. Berta beschrieb ihren anfänglichen Werktag in komischer Verzweiflung: dass sie sich in die Hausarbeiten einarbeiten müsse, wo sie noch „tüchtig lernen" müsse und sie bei sich „gar keine praktische Veranlagung" sehe. „Habe wohl den Willen auch zu arbeiten u. auch mitzutun; aber in dem Fall geht der Wille nicht fürs Werk; das muß bei mir erst gelernt sein. Bis jetzt habe ich fast überhaupt noch nichts Derartiges getan; so gern ich es täte; aber ich geniere mich fürchterlich. Ehrw. Schw. Laura sitzt nebenan u. lacht über diese meine große Sorge, so ernst sie mir auch erscheint. Aber auch das wird im Laufe der Zeit besser werden."³ Ein anderer anpassungsbedürftiger Punkt war das Dasein in der Gemeinschaft. „Das Zusammenleben u. Zusammensein lerne ich; muß mich auch daran wieder erst gewöhnen; war ich doch nur zu sehr gewöhnt, frei und selbständig zu handeln."

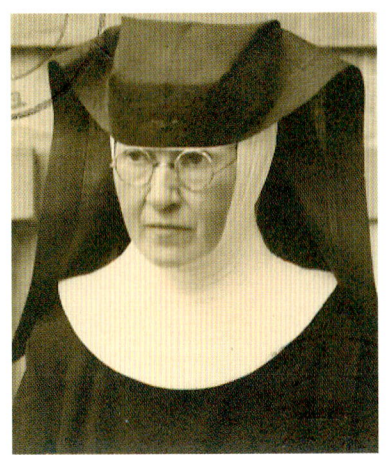

M. Laura Brugger OSF (1893 – 1960)
M. Laura Brugger OSF (1893 – 1960)

Every applicant began her life at the convent as a candidate. Berta fully participated in the daily convent routine. Though she had specific tasks and duties from the start, her two-year trial period did not entail any binding promises. From the first day, she worked in the paraments workshop and was allowed to design her own patterns, which were then executed in the embroidery room. The day at the convent proceeded according to strict rules. The sisters were awakened at five o'clock and were called to the chapel for Lauds at five-thirty. The day was articulated by fixed periods of prayer and silence, three main meals, and two snacks, which the sisters took jointly in the refectory. What a change that must have been for Berta, who was used to work completely independently and to stop only when she felt that a task was complete. Thus she sighed a little impatiently in a letter to her parents: "Just that one thing is a bit of a sacrifice, that one is interrupted so often during the day, frequently when one is at one's most productive."[2]

There was not just art work, however: convent life did not mean freedom from domestic chores. Service at table, in the scullery, and around the house was shared by all the sisters, irrespective of their vocational work. Certain days were laundry days, and the laundry had to be hung and finally folded. Nuns' habits were not easy to handle. The widely flaring veil of the Franciscans consisted of several layers of cloth, which had to be carefully ironed and folded. The white wimple, which framed the face, had to be meticulously pleated while still wet. In comical despair, Berta wrote of her new workday that she had to train herself for the domestic chores and had to "learn a lot," since she could not detect "any practical talent" in herself. "I certainly have the will to work and cooperate, but the will is no substitute for the work, I still have to learn that. As much as I would like to, I have hardly ever done anything like it before – I am terribly embarrassed. The Hon. Sr. Laura is sitting next to me and is laughing about my great concern, as serious as that appears to me. But things will improve in time."[3] Another area where Berta needed to adapt was the community. "I am learning to live together and be together; I have to get used to that again, having been all-too accustomed to act freely and independently."

Entwurf für ein Messgewand: Pelikan, Kelch und Brot, 1930/1931
Design for a vestment: Pelican, chalice and bread, 1930/1931

Kloster Sießen, Ansicht von Osten, 1954
Convent Siessen from the east, 1954

*Erinnerung an die Klassen-
kameradinnen: Postkarte mit Unterschriften aus der „Marienhöhe"*
Souvenir of the classmates: postcard with
signatures from "St. Mary's Heights"

Postkarte Alleinsein war nie ihre Sache gewesen. Die Geschwister, die Klassenkameradinnen, die fidelen Kunstmädel an der Hochschule. Aber
dies ist etwas anderes – allzeit Rücksicht nehmen, immer die gemeinsamen
Regeln akzeptieren! Jede noch so winzige Entscheidung abfragen! Die Gemeinschaft zu begreifen als ständigen Teil des Lebens, sei es beim Beten, beim
Schweigen, beim Essen, bei der Arbeit und in den freien Minuten. Und sich
umgekehrt nicht mehr nur als Individuum, sondern als Teil des Ganzen zu
betrachten. Freundschaften sind nicht gern gesehen. Es gilt keinen Unterschied
zu machen, ob man jemandem eine Neigung entgegenbringt oder nicht! Alle
sind gleich.

Berta biss die Zähne zusammen. Sie fing an, in ihren neuen Aufgaben aufzu-
gehen. Stolz berichtete sie im Juni nach Hause, dass sie jetzt das „Krägelchen"
tragen dürfe, das sie offiziell als Klosteranwärterin auswies. „Damit bin ich einen
Schritt oder eine Stufe näher meinem großen Ziel und nun muss ich nur trach-
ten, dass es auch wächst."[4]

Für die Sommerferien ersuchte Berta ihre Eltern, wieder nach Starnberg zu
einem Kornmann-Kurs fahren zu dürfen. Die Auslagen dafür wurden, solange

sie noch Kandidatin war, von zu Hause getragen: 20 Mark für die Tagung, Pensionspreis drei Mark für etwa zehn Tage und 5 Mark Fahrtkosten. Noch konnte Berta Alltagskleidung tragen, sie bat die Mutter, ihr den „blauen plissierten Rock" mitzuschicken, „vielleicht auch mein blaues Mouslinkleid". Dezente Kleidung also, aber im Klostergewand mochte sie für diesmal noch nicht anreisen: „In meiner ‚Uniform' kann ich dort nicht gut auftreten, der Kontrast von vorigem Jahr wäre wohl zu groß."⁵ In diesem Jahr durfte Berta in den Sommerferien noch nach Hause fahren. Sie wusste, dass die Zeit kommen würde, in der Besuche nicht mehr möglich sein würden, da das Ordensleben sie ganz in Anspruch nehmen würde.

Berta und ihre Schwester Centa, 1931
Berta and her sister Centa, 1931

Solitude had never been her lot, what with the siblings, the classmates, the merry art girls at the college. But this was something else: always having to be considerate, always to accept the common rules! Having to ask about the least little decision! To accept the community as a constant part of life, whether for prayer, during periods of silence, at meals, at work, and even during one's free minutes. And conversely to see oneself no longer as an individual, but as part of a whole. Friendships are frowned upon. The idea was not to distinguish between liking and disliking a person: all were to be equal.

Berta gritted her teeth. She began to be absorbed by her new tasks. In June, she proudly reported home that she was now allowed to wear the "little collar" that formally identified her as a convent applicant. "With that I am one step closer to my great goal, and must now only see to it that it keeps growing."⁴

For the summer vacation, Berta asked her parents to be able to go back to Starnberg for another Kornmann seminar. While she was still a candidate, the expenses had to be paid by the family: 20 marks for the congress, three marks for room and board for ten days, and 5 marks for travel. As yet Berta was able to wear regular clothing: she asked her mother to send her "the pleated skirt and maybe my blue muslin dress." Modest garb, that is, but as yet she did not want to arrive in convent dress. "I cannot very well appear in my 'uniform,' the contrast to last year would be too drastic."⁵ This year Berta was still able to go home for the summer vacation. She knew the time would come when such visits would no longer be possible, as life in the order would command all of her time.

J. Hummel Firmenzeichen, 1929
J. Hummel trademark, 1929

*Porträt Adolf Hummel
mit Zigarre, März 1931*
Portrait of Adolf Hummel, March 1931

Adolf Hummel unterstützte nach wie vor das Schaffen seiner Tochter mit allen Kräften. Dank seiner guten Kontakte war er in der Lage, ihr – und damit dem Kloster – etliche Aufträge zu verschaffen. Im September nach den Ferien war von einer zweiten Prozessionsfahne die Rede. Zu der ersten Bruder-Konrad-Fahne[6] sollte ein Gegenstück mit der Muttergottes gefertigt werden. Berta ging mit Feuereifer ans Werk. Ein reger Briefwechsel über Skizzen entwickelte sich, Fragen nach Motivwünschen, Vorlagen und Stoffmustern, nach Preisen und Qualitätsansprüchen. Die Schreiben an den Vater waren nun geprägt von künstlerischen Themen, der einerseits noch kindlichen Zuwendung gesellte sich ein ernst-fachlicher Austausch zu. Dem unermüdlichen Interesse von Bertas Vater und in Nachfolge ihres Bruders Adolf verdanken wir heute eine umfangreiche Sammlung ihrer Arbeit. Zweimal wurde in der Kunstabteilung des Klosters alles mit der großen Plattenkamera fotografiert, bevor das fertige Werk an die Auftraggeber ging. Eine Platte blieb dann in Sießen und eine wurde nach Massing geschickt und dort von Vater und Bruder noch einmal vergrößert und archiviert.[7]

Bertas Briefe nach Hause zeigten sich mit der Zeit immer stärker beseelt von einer glühenden Innigkeit. Die wachsende Gewissheit, das Richtige getan zu haben! Die anfängliche Unsicherheit schien völlig verschwunden. In ihren Briefen sprach sie jetzt davon, „glücklich" zu sein. Beinahe atemlos versuchte sie, ihren Gefühlen Ausdruck zu verleihen: „Lieber Papa, ich bin so glücklich und freue mich jeden Tag mehr, hier sein zu dürfen, wenn auch die Opfer groß sind, die Freude und das Glück wird um so größer."[8] Im Oktober durfte Berta zum ersten Mal dabei sein, als andere Schwestern feierlich ihre Gelübde ablegten: „In dieser Woche war hier Einkleidung u. Profeß. Hatte zum ersten Mal diese heiligen Handlungen gesehen; war tief ergriffen davon u. wurde noch mehr erfüllt von dem Sehnen auch zu diesem großen, hohen Ziele zu gelangen u. von Neuem wieder anzufangen zu arbeiten an mir. Was waren doch die jungen Novizen so glücklich u. mit ihnen die Eltern. Freuet Euch mit mir, ich danke jeden Tag, daß ich mich darauf vorbereiten darf, es ist bestimmt die größte Gnade, die der liebe Gott geben kann. Sehe es jeden Tag mehr ein u. gerade deshalb um so mehr, weil ich doch gesehen, wie es auch in der Welt ist u. was sie Glück heißt."[9]

Entwurf für die Fahne der Anzenberg-Kongregation: Maria mit Kind, Engel und Anzenbergkirche, 1931
Design for Banner of the Congregation Anzenberg: Madonna and child, angel and the Anzenberg Church, 1931

Adolf Hummel continued to support his daughter's creative work with all his might. Thanks to his contacts, he was able furnish her – and thus the convent – with a number of commissions. In September, after the vacation, there was talk of a second procession banner. The first, a Brother Konrad banner,[6] was to have a pendant depicting the Mother of God. Berta went to work with great ardor. A lively correspondence ensued about sketches, motifs desired, patterns, and textile samples, prices and quality expectations. The letters to the father were thus dominated by artistic concerns, so that a sober professional exchange supervened upon continued filial affection. It is to the tireless interest of Berta's father and, subsequently, her brother Adolf that we owe today's voluminous collection of her work. Before a finished work went to the client, it was photographed twice with a large plate camera by the convent's art department. One plate remained in Siessen, the other was sent to Massing, where it was once again enlarged and then archived by the father and the brother.[7]

Berta's letters to her family were increasingly filled with a fervent inwardness and a growing assurance to have done the right thing. The initial uncertainty seemed to have vanished. In her letters she now spoke of being "happy." Almost breathlessly, she tried to express her feelings. "Dear Papa, I am so happy, and happier from day to day to be able to be here; though the sacrifices are great, the joy and happiness are that much greater."[8] In October Berta was allowed for the first time to be present as other sisters made their final vows. "This week we had Assumption of the Habit and Profession ceremonies. It's the first time I have witnessed these sacred rites, and was deeply moved by them and filled even more by a longing to attain to this great, high goal and to begin anew to work on myself. How happy the young novices were and their parents with them. Rejoice with me, I am thankful every day that I am allowed to prepare for this, it is assuredly the greatest mercy that God can bestow upon me. I realize that more clearly every day and all the more because I have seen how it is in the world and what the world calls happiness."[9]

Die Bruder-Konrad-Fahne für die Pfarrkirche Massing, ausgestellt im Schaufenster des Hummel-Hauses, 1931
The Brother Konrad banner for the Church in Massing, exhibited in the Hummel House, 1931

Skizze: Madonna im Rundbogen, 1931/1933
Sketch: Madonna under a round arch, 1931/1933

Im November fand in der prächtig im oberen Donautal gelegenen Benediktinerabtei Beuron eine große Künstlertagung statt. Drei Mitarbeiterinnen des klösterlichen Zeichensaals durften hinfahren, und auch auf Berta war die Wahl gefallen. Die Einladung zur „Religiösen Einkehr für Bildende Künstler" stellte den anspruchsvollen Leitgedanken vor: „Symbol und Wirklichkeit in Kunst und Religion". Dazu hörte man von Freitagabend bis Montag zum Mittagstisch Vorträge. Es war ein durchgehendes und anstrengendes Programm, das nur von gemeinsamem Gebet und Gottesdienst unterbrochen war. Diese Veranstaltung des Kunstvereins der Diözese Rottenburg hatte sich bereits in Künstlerkreisen einen Namen gemacht, denn das Kloster Beuron war bekannt für sein Engagement für zeitgenössische sakrale Kunst. Alle Plätze waren ausgebucht. Eine Unterschriftenliste weist die Teilnehmer – mehr Männer als Frauen – als Maler, Bildhauer oder Grafiker aus dem württembergischen Raum aus. Der Beuroner Abt wies bei der Eröffnungsrede ausdrücklich auf den apostolischen Stellenwert hin, den die Kunst in diesen Tagen zu erfüllen hätte. Also auch hier keine l'art pour l'art, sondern die Kunst ganz Gott geweiht.

Interessant, dass sich Berta nicht wie ihre beiden Kolleginnen mit „Kloster Sießen" in die Teilnehmerliste eintrug, sondern noch unter der einfachen Bezeichnung „Kunstgewerblerin". Am zweiten Tag hatten die Künstler Gelegenheit, ihre Arbeiten zur allgemeinen Beurteilung vorzulegen. Zunächst fiel es Berta schwer, ihre Schüchternheit zu überwinden. Zu viel Respekt hatten ihr, vielleicht der jüngsten Teilnehmerin, die hochgebildeten Vorträge eingeflößt. Die Referenten waren weltgewandt und prominent aufgetreten, so etwa der „Malermönch" Pater Willibrord Verkade, der vor seiner Benediktinerzeit mit Gauguin befreundet gewesen war. Doch dann wurde die Tagung für Berta zu einer weiteren bemerkenswerten Bestätigung ihrer Begabung. Ganz erfüllt von den Ereignissen konnte sie nach Hause berichten: „Und denkt Euch, liebste Eltern hatte so Segen und Erfolg, man gratulierte mir auf das Wärmste u. bestätigte ich hätte die besten Arbeiten von allen, worauf sich mehrere Architekten eingehend erkundigten, sich meine Adresse geben ließen u. aber noch bemerkten, ich soll nur noch gründlich überlegen ob ich ins Kloster gehe, das wollte ihnen gar nicht eingehen."[10]

In November, a large artists' congress took place at the Benedictine abbey of Beuron, splendidly situated in the upper Danube valley. Three of the workers in the convent's art room were allowed to attend, and Berta was one of the choices. The invitation to "religious contemplation for pictorial artists" had cited "Symbol and Reality in Art and Religion" as its lofty central theme. Lectures on this theme succeeded each other from Friday evening until midday on Monday. It was a strenuous ongoing program, interrupted only by communal prayer and divine service. This annual event of the Art Association of the Diocese of Rottenburg had gained a reputation in artistic circles: the Beuron monastery was known for its engagement on behalf of contemporary sacred art. The conference was fully booked. A subscription list identifies the participants – more men than women – as painters, sculptors, and graphic artists from around Württemberg. In his keynote address, the abbot of Beuron stressed the apostolic function art had to fulfill in these times. Thus no art for art's sake here either, but art wholly consecrated to God.

Interestingly enough, Berta, unlike her colleagues, inscribed herself on the list of participants, not as from "Convent Siessen," but still with the simple title "artisan." On the second day, the artists were able to submit their work to the conference's judgment. At first, Berta, possibly the youngest participant there, had trouble overcoming her shyness, overawed as she may have been by the erudite lectures she had heard. The speakers had been impressively knowledgeable and prominent – for instance the "painting monk" Father Willibrord Verkade, who prior to becoming a Benedictine had been a friend of Gauguin's. But then the congress turned into yet another remarkable confirmation of Berta's talent. Quite overwhelmed she wrote home: "And just think, dearest parents, I had such blessing and success, I was congratulated most warmly and reassured that mine were the best works of all, whereupon several architects made close inquiries, asked for my address, but also remarked I should really think twice about going into a convent, they couldn't see it at all."[10]

*Muttergottesfahne,
genaues Datum unbekannt*
Mother of God banner,
date unknown

Sogar die rezensierende Zeitung erwähnte das Kloster Sießen im Zusammenhang mit der talentierten Kandidatin. Und eine Begegnung sollte Berta in der Folge besonders wichtig werden, denn einer der Vortragenden, Pfarrer Albert Pfeffer, Mitbegründer des Rottenburger Kunstvereins und Vorstand des Verlags Ver Sacrum, hatte sich ausgesprochen interessiert an den Arbeiten der jungen Zeichnerin gezeigt.

Auch aus München kam Erfolgsmeldung. Die treue Professorin Brauneis hatte einen langen Brief geschickt, hocherfreut über den Erfolg einer Ausstellung, in der auch Arbeiten ihrer Lieblingsstudentin zu sehen gewesen waren. 80 Mark legte sie für den Verkauf zweier Bilder bei, in fünf verschiedenen Tageszeitungen seien „vorzügliche Kritiken" erschienen, und auch viele Künstlerkollegen hätten sich positiv geäußert – außer denen von der Hochschule selbst. Dort habe sich der Umgangston gewandelt: „Nur nicht ein Wort von meinem Direktor (…) – aber wir leben ja alle nur nebeneinander hier und nie miteinander. Manchmal friert man hier bei uns."[11] Professor Dasio hatte die Institution verlassen. Der Einfluss des ehrgeizigen Nationalsozialisten Richard Klein hatte die Atmosphäre an der Staatsschule sehr verändert.

„Und die Bertel?", schreibt die Professorin, drängend nach Bertas persönlicher Stellungnahme, „Was tun Sie? Sind Sie befriedigt von Ihrer Arbeit und arbeiten Sie manchmal frei künstlerisch?" „Nicht liegen lassen Bertl bitte", fleht sie ihre Schülerin geradezu an. „Einmal im vorigen Jahr sagten Sie von sich – ich stecke ja noch halb in den Kinderschuhen und das stimmt – bleiben Sie noch etwas drin." Doch Berta ist sich ihrer Sache sicher, so sehr wie nie zuvor in ihrem Leben.

Fliegeraufnahme Kloster Sießen, 1931
Eine schwungvolle Künstlerschrift: Brief von Else Brauneis
Convent Siessen from the air, 1931
The vigorous handwriting of an artist: letter from Else Brauneis

Even the newspaper reviews mentioned the Siessen convent in connection with its talented candidate. One encounter at the congress was to become particularly important later on: one of the lecturers, Father Albert Pfeffer, co-founder of the Rottenburg Art Association and head of the Ver Sacrum press, had shown particular interest in the works of the young artist.

From Munich, too, came news of success. The faithful Professor Brauneis sent a long letter, delighted about the exhibition that had included works by her favorite student. She included 80 marks from the sale of two of Berta's pictures. Five different dailies had published "excellent critiques," and many fellow artists had expressed themselves very positively – except those at the college itself. There the tone had changed radically: "Not one word from my director (...) – all of us just live alongside, but not with, each other now. One could freeze here at times."[11] Professor Dasio had left the institution. The impact of the ambitious Nazi Richard Klein poisoned the atmosphere at the state school.

"And my Bertel?" the professor writes, pressing for personal news from Berta, "what are you doing? Are you satisfied with your work, and do you sometimes work creatively?" "Don't put it aside, Bertl, please," she downright implores her pupil. "Last year you once said about yourself 'I am still half a child,' and that is true – stay one a little while longer." But Berta was sure of her decision – surer than she had ever been in her life.

Berta, 1932
Berta, 1932

Porträt Professor Else Brauneis, 1930
Portrait of Professor Else Brauneis, 1930

Zu Weihnachten durften die Kandidatinnen nicht nach Hause fahren. Berta verbrachte die Feiertage weitgehend im Krankenzimmer, eine schwere Grippe machte ihr zu schaffen. Als sie versuchte, an den Gottesdiensten teilzunehmen, fiel sie zweimal in Ohnmacht und musste von da an das Bett hüten. Weihnachten im Kloster wurde zu jener Zeit äußerst karg begangen, Geschenke etwa gab es kaum. Was für ein Unterschied zu all den Jahren, die sie in der Familie gefeiert hatte! Gerade dieses Fest, da alle einmal im Jahr zusammenkamen, eine Zeit, um zu reden und zu lachen. Jenes erste Weihnachten in Sießen muss einsam für Berta gewesen sein. Doch sie riss sich zusammen: „Wenn der Fisch ins Wasser geworfen wird muß er eben schwimmen u. so ging es mir auch."[12] Das neue Jahr begann schweigend, für den 1. Januar waren Exerzitien angesetzt. Niemand konnte ahnen, dass dieses Jahr 1932 den Beginn einer beispiellosen Erfolgsgeschichte bringen sollte.

Christkind mit Hirt, 1931
Christ Child with shepherd, 1931

Einmal in der Woche lief Berta den Birkenweg nach Saulgau hinunter, um in der Mädchenschule St. Anna Zeichenunterricht zu geben. Sie wurde von einer Schwester begleitet, die ebenfalls an der Schule unterrichtete. Offensichtlich war es den Lehrerinnen überlassen, wie sie die Klassen untereinander aufteilten. Denn die Kollegin hatte Berta angeboten, wegen ihrer anspruchsvolleren Qualifikation doch die älteren Schülerinnen zu übernehmen. Aber Berta hatte bescheiden abgelehnt, da die andere, obwohl etwa gleich alt, innerhalb des Konvents den höheren Rang innehatte – also schon eine „richtige" Schwester war. So blieb Berta fürs Erste für die Schulanfänger zuständig.

Christkind mit König, 1931
Christ Child with king, 1931

Christkind, Engel mit Kerze, 1931
Christ Child, angel with candle, 1931

Lesendes Kind, 1928
Child reading, 1928

For Christmas the candidates were not allowed to go home. Berta spent the holidays mostly in sickbay with a severe case of influenza. Twice, while trying to attend service, she fainted and from then on had to keep to her bed. Christmas was observed very meagerly in the convent at the time. There were no presents to speak of, and everything turned around the birth of Christ. What a difference from all the years of celebrating in the family – this one holiday in particular, when everyone assembled once a year to talk and to laugh together. That first Christmas in Siessen must have been very lonely for Berta. But she pulled herself together: "If a fish gets thrown into the water, it will just have to swim, and so it was with me as well."[12] The New Year began in silence, as spiritual exercises had been scheduled for the first of January. No one could know that this year of 1932 would bring the beginning of an unparalleled success story.

Once a week Berta walked down the birch tree path to Saulgau to teach drawing at the girls' school of St. Anne. She was accompanied by a sister who also taught at the school. Evidently it was left to the teachers how to divide the classes between them. For in view of Berta's superior qualifications, her colleague had offered to let her teach the older pupils. But Berta had declined modestly, as the other, although about her age, was already a "real" sister and therefore ranked higher within the convent hierarchy. Thus for the moment Berta remained in charge of the beginners.

*Umringt von „ihren Kleinen":
Maria Innocentia in Ordenstracht im
klösterlichen Kreuzgarten, 1934
In ihrem Atelier musste niemand stillsitzen.
Sie ließ die Kinder auch beim Porträtieren schwatzen und herumtollen.
Surrounded by her "little ones":
Maria Innocentia in her
habit in the cloister garden, 1934
No one had to sit still in her studio.
She let the children chatter and romp about
even while they were being portrayed.*

Eine Momentaufnahme, einige Zeit später entstanden: Hier bereits in Ordenstracht, sitzt Berta inmitten einer Schar Kinder auf einer Bank. Mit ehrlicher Ernsthaftigkeit wendet sie sich dem Jungen auf seinem Dreirad zu, der seinerseits die ganze Aufmerksamkeit auf sie gerichtet hat. Die kräftigen Beinchen in kurzen Trachtenhosen fest auf dem Boden, mit heruntergerutschten Kniestrümpfen in den festen schwarzen Schuhen schaut er erwartungsvoll zur Schwester hoch. Die Übrigen in ganz enger Runde drum herum, mit Zöpfen und Schleifen, Schürzenkleidchen und dicken Wolljankern.

Berta liebte ihre „Kleinen", wie sie sie nannte. Wer sich besonders gut betragen hatte, konnte damals üblicherweise Fleißkärtchen sammeln, auf denen ein hübsches Bild zu sehen war, manchmal mit einem kleinen Vers dazu. Was lag für Berta näher, als ihre eigenen Fleißbildchen zu entwerfen? Motiv waren ihr die Kinder selbst, keine perfekt geschniegelt lächelnden Gestalten, sondern Kinder, wie sie eben waren, mit verstrubbelten Haaren und vorgereckten Bäuchen, die kleinen Münder ein wenig geöffnet und völlig konzentriert auf das, was sie gerade sahen oder taten.

Die niedlichen Motive erregten rasch Aufmerksamkeit. „Jetzt darf ich nebenbei entwerfen für kleine Kompositionen, das macht mir immer Spaß. Ein Pater riet uns kürzlich sehr an, solche in den Verlag Ars sacra zu geben daß welche in Bildchen herauskommen."¹³ Ars sacra war einer der führenden katholischen Verlage mit Sitz in München. Doch noch war es nicht so weit.

Kinderstudien, Schreibendes Mädchen und Lesendes Mädchen, 1932/1933
Sketches of children, Girl writing and Girl reading, 1932/1933

A snapshot taken somewhat later shows Berta, already in full habit, sitting on a bench, surrounded by a group of children. In genuine earnestness she is looking at a boy on a tricycle, who in turn is the center of everyone's attention. The sturdy little legs in short lederhosen firmly on the ground, with sagging knee-socks and solid black shoes, he looks expectantly up at the sister. The others surround the two in a close circle, with braids and bows, apron dresses and thick woolen cardigans.

Berta loved her "little ones," as she called them. Children who had behaved especially well, were usually able to collect little "diligence cards" at the time, with pretty pictures and sometimes a short verse. What more natural for Berta than to design her own diligence cards? Her motifs were the children themselves, no perfectly starched and ironed smiling figures, but children as they really are, with tousled hair and protruding bellies, their little mouths a little open and utterly absorbed in what they were seeing or doing at the moment.

These sweet, charming motifs soon attracted attention. "I am allowed now to design small compositions, that is always great fun. A monk recently urged me to send some of these to the publishing house Ars Sacra, to get them turned into little printed pictures."¹³ Ars sacra, seated in Munich, was one of the leading Catholic publishers. But things had not yet reached that point.

Hochzeit der Schwester Kätl im Kreise der Familie (Berta schräg links hinter der Braut), 6. August 1932
Wedding of Berta's sister Kätl, with family (Berta to the left behind the bride), August 6, 1932

```
Grüss Gott zum Hochzeitsfeste
Wir sind koa gelad'ne Gäste
doch ich denk es freut Euch sehr
wenn wir kommen auch daher.

Doch wozu wir alle kommen
habt,s ja alle schon vernommen
es feiert man hier Hochzeitsfest
dazu wünschen wir das Best

Noch unzählige lange Jahre
dazu viel Glück und Segen alle Jahre
soll man Euch nur Freude machen
nich Verdruss und andre Sachen.

Will die Ehe glücklich sein
muss das Weibchen kochen fein
alles was dem Manne schmeckt
da die Lieb im Magen steckt.

Doch schwer ist das zu machen
wenn liebt der Mo ganz andre Sachen
als das Kätchen gerne hat
wie Wurst Sardellen und Salat.

Spinat und Wirsching ist sei Spezialität
das liebt er sehr
ach,des grad kann sie net riecha
dafür viel Schinken u. andre Viecher

Ach was soll man jetzt da machen
wenn stehn so schlimm die Sachen
ich rat Euch lasst das Essen sein
sonst passt alles z'amm so fein

Doch skäterl kann kocha famos
Kochkunst die hat's los
Käse Wurt und Delekatess
kann's richten mit feinser Finess

Auch eine Platte wunderbar
einladend ist's fürwahr
doch was ist denn nur das
Wurst Fleisch oder Kas

Doch nichts von alledem
die Gabel bleibt fest drinn stehn
in den Semmeln fein
die unten schön im Teller sein
```

Das Duo Berta (links) und Centa verfasste ein Hochzeitsgedicht über die Kochkünste der Braut.
The duo Berta (left) and Centa composed a wedding poem about the bride's culinary skills.

Das Jahr verging wie im Flug. Wieder standen die Sommerferien ins Haus und Berta durfte nach Hause fahren. Diesmal stand ein besonderes Ereignis im Mittelpunkt: die Hochzeit ihrer Schwester Katharina. Die hatte sie gebeten, ob sie nicht ihre Brautjungfer sein würde, noch einmal in hellem Kleid. Doch dies wurde Berta von der Mutter Oberin als unpassend abgeschlagen: „Sie meinte, wenn mir die Eltern die Erlaubnis gaben, in das Kloster zu gehen, so werdet Ihr auch jetzt nichts dagegen haben, wenn ich nur als Kandidatin teilnehmen darf, d.h. in ‚schwarz'."[14]

Bei der diesjährigen Professfeier in Sießen fanden Bertas ausgestellte Kinderzeichnungen enormen Anklang. Die Festgäste „äußerten sich ganz begeistert (...) und freuten sich ganz besonders, mit der Künstlerin selbst sprechen zu dürfen".[15] Alle Bilder wurden verkauft.

Und dann die Fleißbildchen. Maria mit dem Jesuskind. Die ersten Seriendrucke wurden im Verlag der Gesellschaft für christliche Kunst gefertigt und vom Kloster selbst vertrieben. Das Paket à 100 Stück kostete zwei Mark fünfzig. In kürzester Zeit erfreuten sich Bertas „kleine Kompositionen" allergrößter Beliebtheit. Es sollte nachgedruckt werden und die Kunden baten dringlich um Nachschub an Motiven. Was für ein Erfolg! Man muss sich einmal die Verbreitung dieser Fleißbildchen vor Augen halten: Zu Hunderten wurden diese in Pfarreien und Schulen verteilt – eine größere Streuung in so kurzer Zeit ist wohl kaum möglich.

Ausgestellt bei der Professfeier, 1932:
Tierliebe
Exhibited at Profession ceremony, 1932:
Pet Loving

The year went by in no time. Summer vacation was imminent again, and Berta was allowed to go home. The central event this time was the wedding of her sister Katharina. The latter had asked her to be her bridesmaid, once more in a bright dress. But that was ruled out by the Mother Superior as inappropriate: "She said since our parents gave their consent for me to enter the convent, you will surely have no objection to my taking part as a candidate, i.e. in 'black.'"[14]

An exhibition, on the occasion of the year's Profession ceremony, of Berta's drawings of children met with a lively response. The guests at the ceremony "commented enthusiastically (...) and were particularly delighted to be able to speak with the artist herself."[15] Every picture was sold.

And then the diligence cards: the Virgin with the infant Jesus. The first series was printed by the press of the Society for Christian Art and distributed by the convent itself. A packet of 100 sold for two marks and fifty pfennig. In a short time, Berta's "little compositions" became hugely popular. They were presently to be reprinted, and the customers urgently requested additional motifs. What a success! One has to try to imagine the extent of the distribution of the pictures: by the hundreds they were sent to parishes and schools – a larger spread in such a short time span seems hardly possible.

Eines der ersten Andachts-
bildchen, gedruckt im Verlag der
Gesellschaft für christliche Kunst:
Missionsmadonna, 1932/33
One of the earliest devotional
pictures, printed by the Society
for Christian Art Press
Madonna of the Missions, 1932/33

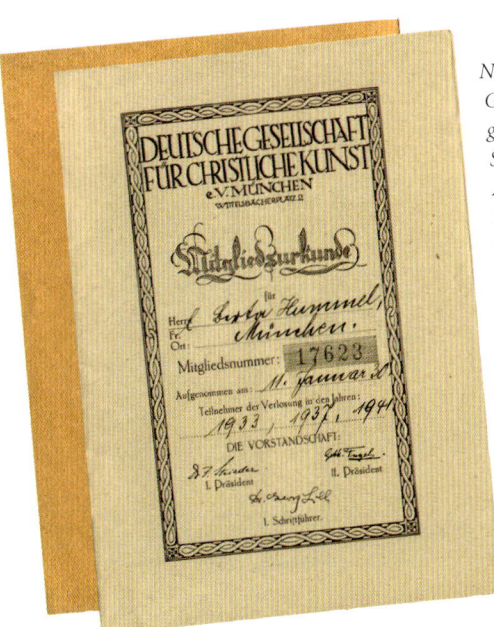

Nicht zu verwechseln mit der Deutschen
Gesellschaft für Christliche Kunst (Mit-
gliedsurkunde), in der Berta seit ihrer
Studienzeit Mitglied war und an deren
Ausstellungen sie damals teilnahm
Not to be confused with the German
Society for Christian Art (membership certificate), of which Berta had
been a member ever since her student
years and in whose exhibitions she
participated during those years

Im November 1932 fand abermals das alljährliche Treffen in Beuron statt, ein weiterer künstlerischer Schritt für Berta. Der Tagungsleiter Albert Pfeffer hatte die junge Zeichnerin nicht vergessen und reservierte sich nun endgültig Bilder für seinen Verlag Ver Sacrum in Rottenburg. Zwölf verschiedene Kindermotive sollten es sein mit Erscheinungstermin vom 16. Januar 1933.[16]

An daheim denkt Berta viel. Die lieben guten Eltern! Die Geschäfte laufen gut in Massing. Oftmals, wenn man etwas braucht im Kloster, einen bestimmten Stoff vielleicht, einige Wechselrähmchen oder ein Klebeband, schreibt sie heim und lässt es vom Vater schicken. Wie die Zeit verfliegt! Wieder ein Jahr zu Ende. „Auf Weihnachten dürfen wir Kandidatinnen nicht heim; so sehr ich das bedaure. Du schreibst, ich solle meine Wünsche schreiben. So will ich es tun, aber nur dann, wenn es Euch leicht möglich ist bitte ich um ein Photoalbum ganz einfacher Ausführung (da meine zwei schon bereits voll sind) u. um ein Paar Strümpfe, wenn wir [im Geschäft] Söckchen in schwarz hätten wäre ich sehr dankbar dafür. Das sind meine Wünsche liebste Eltern u. hoffe daß sie Euch keine zu großen Auslagen sind."[17]

Fotografie: Der Marktplatz in Massing, um 1930
Bild: Massinger Straße, heute „Berta-Hummel-Straße" genannt, April 1929
Photograph: Massing, Market square, ca. 1930
Painting: Street in Massing, now Berta-Hummel-Street, April 1929

Beuron und die religiöse Kunst der Gegenwart

Einkehr für bildende Künstler

ap. Beuron, 23. November.

Vom 13.—22. November wurde in Beuron die fünfte religiöse Einkehr für bildende Künstler durchgeführt. Das Interesse an dieser Tagung in Oberschwaben zeigt schon ein Blick in die Anwesenheitsliste. Da finden wir, um mit Ulm zu beginnen, W. Geyer und A. Vollmar, A. Dursch aus Laupheim; aus der Ravensburger Gegend Franz Bayer=Klötern; aus dem Allgäu August und Joseph Braun aus Wangen, H. Tiebert=Isny, H. Vogel=Waltershofen, M. Ullrich=Schomburg-Wangen, aus dem Donaubereiche E. Kneer=Munderkingen; endlich sind auf dem Gebiet kirchlicher Paramentik zu nennen die Schwestern M. Laura Brugger und M. Theodata Barreiter mit Kandidatin Berta Hummel aus Sießen; Maria Ehrhart=Munderfingen, Frau Maria Strobel=Waldsee, endlich Bildhauer Strobel=Waldsee. Dazu kommen aus Sigmaringen Franz Marmon, Restaurator Steidle und Luise Hoff.

Die meisten der genannten Künstler hatten auch ausgestellt, wobei die ausgestellten Arbeiten auf dem Gebiete der Paramentik besonders ins Auge fielen. Daß Frau Maria Strobel den handgewebten Stoff in Kirchenteppichen, Altar=Ueberbehängen, Bodenteppichen und Läufern und Paramentenstoffen neu zu Ehren bringt, ist als besonderes Verdienst zu buchen. Ueberhaupt zeigt sich auf dem Gebiet der kirchlichen Gewandstils in Oberschwaben ein entschiedenes Bekenntnis zur neuen Formgestaltung, so maßvoll und wohlabgewogen das Neue auch in Erscheinung tritt. Waren die Geschwister Burger auf dem Gebiet kirchlicher Stoffe nach Farbe und ornamentaler Ausstattung hervorragend vertreten, so Kloster Sießen auf dem Gebiet der Altarspitzen, der Ausstattung eines Pluviale mit dem Motiv des thronenden Christus (Wolle mit Seide auf Altgold); endlich die zahlreichen Meßgewänder, Fahnenentwürfe, Engels= und Kindermotive mit köstlicher Erfassung des Stimmungs= und Gedankengehalts von B. Hummel zu nennen. — Auf die weiter ausgestellten Arbeiten auf dem Gebiet der Malerei und Plastik wird in anderem Zusammenhang zurückzukommen sein.

Zeitungsrezension der Beuroner Tagung, 1932
Newspaper reviews of the congress in Beuron, 1932

In November of 1932, the annual meeting at Beuron took place again and signaled another step forward in Berta's artistic career. The director of the congress, Albert Pfeffer, had not forgotten the young draftswoman and now definitively reserved the pictures for his press Ver Sacrum in Rottenburg. Twelve different child motifs were to be included, publication date to be January 16, 1933.[16]

Berta often thinks about home. Her dear, kind parents! Business is going well in Massing. Whenever something is needed at the convent, a certain textile, a picture frame or an adhesive strip, she writes home and has her father send it. How time flies! Another year has run its course. "We candidates are not allowed to go home for Christmas, much to my regret. You said in your letter I should write you my wishes. I will do so, but only if it is no trouble for you: could I please have a photo album of the simplest kind (as my two albums are already full), and a pair of stockings? If we have any black socklets [i.e., at the family store], I would be very grateful for some. Those are my wishes, dearest parents, and I hope they are not too much of an expense for you."[17]

Die ersten Fleißbildchen, Kinder und Schutzengel, 1932: Auf dem Schulweg
The earliest "diligence cards," Children and guardian angels, 1932: On the Way to School

Beim Beten
Child's Prayer

Beim Spielen
Making Repairs

Meine lieben, guten Eltern!

Anfang des Jahres 1933 schrieb Berta glückselig nach Hause: „Und so darf ich Euch heute liebste Eltern mitteilen, daß ich auch zu den 35 Auserwählten zähle, die am 19. Februar in das Postulat aufgenommen werden u. so Gott will im August das hl. Ordenskleid erhalten sollen. So freut Euch liebste Eltern mit mir u. mein Glück; daß es nun wahr werden sollte, was ich ersehnte."[18] Die Entscheidung, wer wann für die Aufnahme in die Klostergemeinschaft geeignet war, fiel der Klosterleitung zu. Nun würde sie also im August ihre Einkleidung feiern dürfen. Dann würde sie endlich Novizin sein, in Vorbereitung auf die Profess im darauffolgenden Jahr, wenn sie die zeitlichen Gelübde für die Dauer von drei Jahren abzulegen hatte[19]. Vom Tag der Einkleidung an würde sie die Ordenstracht der Franziskanerinnen tragen. Vor dem Beginn des Postulats, der intensiven Vorbereitung auf die Einkleidung, wurde den Kandidatinnen Ende Januar noch einmal gestattet – „es ist diesesmal noch nicht das letztemal"[20] –, in die Heimat zu reisen, „wo wir uns gut erholen sollten"[21].

Jenes Jahr 1933, das für Berta so wunderbar hoffnungsfroh begann, sollte zu einem der verhängnisvollsten der Weltgeschichte werden. Berta war also zu Hause bei ihrer Familie, als am 30. Januar 1933 Adolf Hitler in Berlin die Macht ergriff. So sehr klarsichtige Beobachter diesen Tag vorhergesehen und gefürchtet hatten, so überraschend war er für andere gekommen. Bei Wahlen im November 1932 waren die Stimmen für die NSDAP immerhin so stark zurückgegangen, dass dies in weiten Teilen der Bevölkerung als ein Anfang vom Ende der Partei gedeutet wurde. Mit Karikaturen und Spottversen gegen die vermeintlichen Möchtegern-Machthaber wurde nicht gespart. Noch am 8. Januar 1933 war im Münchner „Simplicissimus" ein entsprechender „Neujahrsgruß" erschienen:

Hitlerkritische „Simplicissimus"-Blätter
Anti-Hitler-Pages from the Simplicissimus

„Geht mit euren Horoskopen,
denn ihr prophezeiet schlecht,
Pessimisten, Misanthropen
haben meistens leider recht.
Eins nur lässt sich sicher sagen,
und das freut uns ringsherum:
Hitlern geht es an den Kragen,
dieses Führers Zeit ist um!"[22]

Reichskanzler Adolf Hitler und Reichspräsident Paul von Hindenburg beim Staatsakt zur Eröffnung des Reichstages am 21. März 1933. Grafische Umsetzung von Karl Langhorst
Reich Chancellor Adolf Hitler and Reich President Paul von Hindenburg at the state ceremony opening the Reichstag on March 21, 1933. Graphic realization by Karl Langhorst

At the beginning of the year 1933, Berta wrote ecstatically: "Today I can report to you, dearest parents, that I am one of the 35 elect who on February 19 are to be taken into the postulancy and, God willing, will receive the habit of the order in August. So rejoice with me and my happiness, dearest parents, that what I have longed for is now to become reality."[18] The decision, who would be ready for acceptance into the cloistral community, and when, was made by the convent authorities. In August, Berta would be able to celebrate the Assumption of the Habit. Then she would be a novice at last and prepare for the Simple Profession a year later when she would have to make temporal vows for a period of three years.[19] From the day of her investment, she would be wearing the habit of the Franciscans. Prior to the postulancy, the period of intensive preparation for the Assumption of the Habit, the candidates were permitted, at the end of January, to go home once more – "though it is not yet the last time"[20] – "to get a good rest and recovery."[21]

The year 1933, which began so full of glad hope for Berta, was to be one of the most ill-fated in world history. Berta was at home with her family when, on January 30, 1933, Adolf Hitler seized power in Berlin. Though perceptive observers had foreseen and feared this day, others were taken wholly by surprise. In the election of November 1932, the votes for the NSDAP had shrunk enough so that large segments of the population thought it would be the beginning of the end for the party. There was no dearth of caricatures and satiric verses against the would-be potentates. As late as January 8 of 1933, Munich's *Simplicissimus* had published a lampoon entitled "New Year's Greeting":

"Take away your horoscopes,
for your prophecies are trite,
pessimists and misanthropes
are sadly mostly in the right.
One thing, though, is all but certain,
and this gladdens everyone,
on Hitler soon descends the curtain,
for this Führer's show is done!"[22]

Drei Wochen nach dieser Zeitschriftenausgabe war die Weimarer Republik am Ende. Am 28. Januar 1933 trat die Reichsregierung unter Kurt von Schleicher zurück. Am Abend desselben Tages verbreitete sich die Nachricht, dass der greise Reichspräsident Hindenburg den Chef der NSDAP zum Reichskanzler ernennen würde. „Hitler ist fabelhaft sicher", frohlockte dessen Berliner Gauleiter Joseph Goebbels am 29. Januar in seinem Tagebuch. Am nächsten Morgen gegen zehn Uhr brach Hitler von seinem Berliner Quartier, dem Hotel „Kaiserhof", auf. Eine Stunde später war seine Vereidigung zum Kanzler angesetzt. An diesem frostigen Montag – trotz Sonne hatte der Wetterdienst als höchste Temperatur im Reich minus 3,4 Grad gemessen – nahmen die schreckensreichen zwölf Jahre des Dritten Reichs ihren Anfang.

Berta besaß, abgeschottet im Kloster, wenig Zugang zu politischen Informationen, eine Tatsache, die sie am Anfang auch einmal offen bedauert: „Fern von allem Getriebe geht man Tag für Tag der Arbeit nach, ganz ungeachtet was draußen außerhalb der Mauern vor sich geht, mit Ausnahme ganz weniger Stichproben, die man manchmal vorgelesen bekommt. Aber dann macht sich mein politisches Fühlen und Denken wieder stark bemerkbar u. mir kommt es dann ganz leidlich zu Bewusstsein, wie wenig ich am Laufenden bin; so sehr ich daran nichts ändern könnte."[23] Der letzte Satz klingt resigniert, denn wohl scheint Berta die Zeichen ihrer Zeit mit Besorgnis gesehen zu haben. Sie wird sich erinnert haben an das von den Nationalsozialisten geprägte München vor drei Jahren, an den antisemitischen Ton, an einige Mitstudenten, die für die NSDAP auf Stimmenfang waren.

Three weeks after the appearance of this issue, the Weimar Republic was at an end. On January 28, 1933, the administration, under Kurt von Schleicher, resigned. On the same day news came that the aged Reich president Hindenburg would appoint the head of the NSDAP, the National Socialist German Workers Party, as Reich Chancellor. "Hitler is fabulously certain," the *gauleiter* of Berlin, Joseph Goebbels, wrote in his diary on January 29. At about ten o'clock of the following morning, Hitler left his Berlin quarters in the hotel "Kaiserhof." The swearing in for the chancellorship was set for an hour later. On this frosty morning– the weather service had measured a high of only some 38 degrees F – the twelve terror years of the Third Reich had their beginning.

In her isolated convent existence, Berta had little access to political information, a fact she once openly regretted early on. "Far from all commotion, we ply our work day by day, altogether oblivious of what is happening outside our walls, except for very occasional snippets that might get read to us. But then my political feelings and thoughts come strongly to the fore again, and I become quite conscious how little au courant I am, though there is nothing I can do about it."[23] The last sentence sounds resigned, for Berta is bound to have read the signs of the time with apprehension. She will have remembered the brown-shirted Munich of three years ago, the anti-Semitic tone, the several fellow students who had been out to drum up votes for the NSDAP.

Aus einem Skizzenblock: Stempelentwürfe für das Kloster Sießen, 1931/1933
From a sketchpad: rubber stamp designs for the Siessen convent, 1931/1933

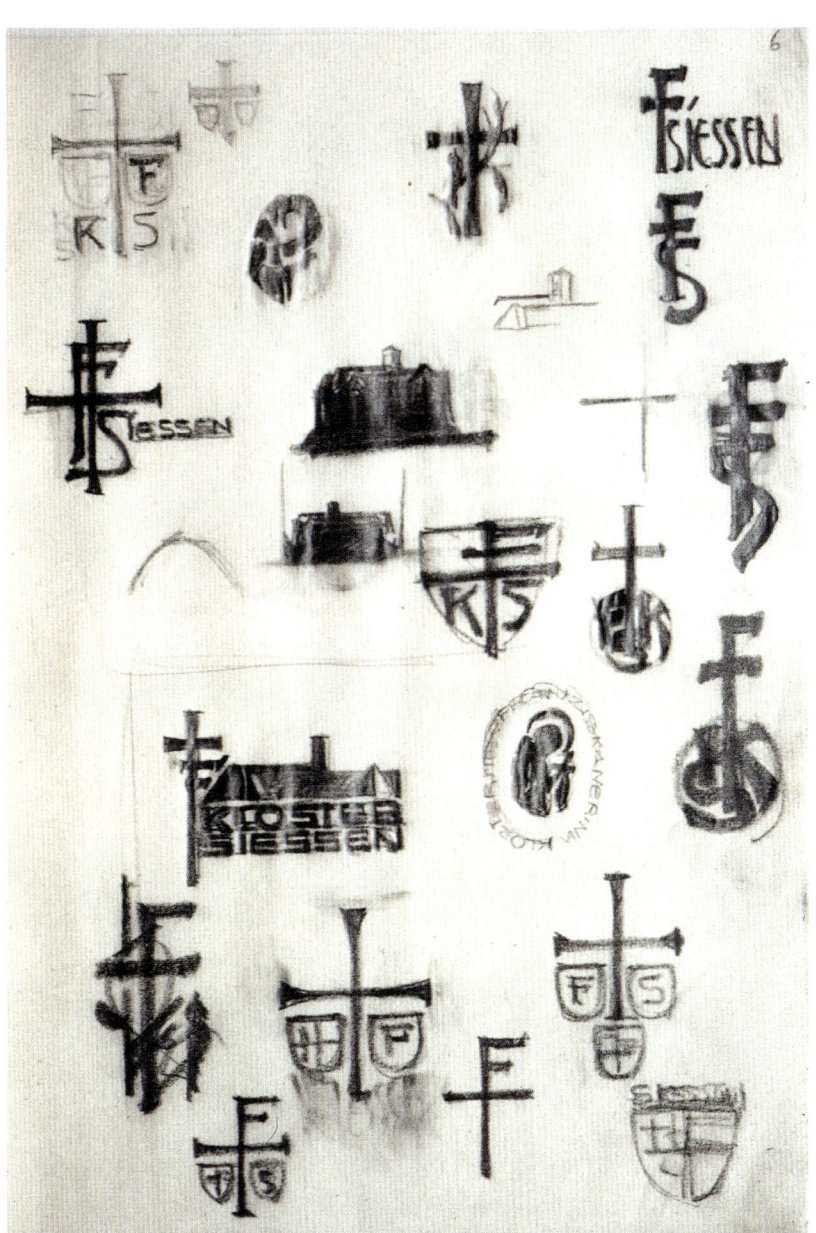

Marktszene am Hummel-Haus in Massing mit Druckstock, Juni 1928
Massing, Hummel house with market scene and printing block, June 1928

„Meine lieben, guten Eltern! Heute darf ich Euch liebste Eltern mitteilen, daß wir Postulantinnen am Dienstag den 30. Mai zum letzten Ferienbesuch nach Hause fahren dürfen u. ich freue mich, Pfingsten noch mit Euch feiern zu können als ein frohes Familienfest, zu dem doch sicher alles nach Hause kommt. Hoffe, daß ich Euch alle gesund u. wohl zu Hause antreffe."[24] Nicht viel hatte Berta in der Zeit nach ihrem letzten Besuch in Massing schreiben können; den Postulantinnen war es in Erwartung der vollkommenen klösterlichen Abgeschiedenheit nicht mehr gestattet, allzu intensiven Kontakt nach außen zu pflegen. Bald würde Berta, „Bertl", nicht mehr das Massinger Mädel sein, sondern ein „Klosterkind" in Armut und Demut, „das nicht mehr tun und geben kann, was es gerne wollte".[25] Sie war sich der Veränderung, die dieser nächste Schritt mit sich bringen würde, voll und ganz bewusst. „Denken wir jetzt nicht mehr an das, was vorüber ist, sondern freuet Euch bitte jetzt mit mir auf das was kommt und dann gibt es so Gott will auch ein frohes herzliches Wiedersehen."[26] Man kann sich vorstellen, dass diese endgültige Trennung von ihrem Kind die Eltern schwer angekommen sein mag, vor allem der Vater hatte wiederholt Bedenken geäußert. Und auch Berta wird der Abschied nicht leichtgefallen sein. Umso mehr waren ihre Briefe nach Massing von jetzt an geprägt von vielen und langen Dankesbezeugungen, weit mehr als je zuvor, als wollte sie den Verlust dadurch ein wenig ausgleichen. Und das „Opfer", ab jetzt immer wieder: „Ich darf Euch versichern, dass alles was ihr an diesem Tag mit mir dem lieben Gott opfern werdet, Euch zum größten Glück und Segen sein wird."[27]

"My dear, kind parents! Today I can report to you, dearest parents, that on Tuesday, May 30, we postulants may go home for our last vacation visit, and I am glad to be able to celebrate Pentecost one more time with you as a merry family holiday, for which surely everyone will return home. Hope that I will find all of you happy and healthy at home."[24]

Berta had been able to write little since her last visit to Massing: in anticipation of their coming complete monastic seclusion, postulants were no longer permitted to maintain extensive contacts with the outside. Soon Berta, "Bertl," would no longer be the Massing lass, but a "convent child" in poverty and humility, "who no longer may do and give as she would like to."[25] She was fully conscious of the change this next step would bring with it. "Let us not think any more of what is past, but be glad with me of that which is to be, and then, God willing, the day will also come when we meet again in joy and cordiality."²⁶ One can imagine that this final separation from their child must have been hard for the parents; especially the father had repeatedly expressed reservations. For Berta, too, the parting will not have been easy. All the more, her letters to Massing were now filled with long professions of thanks, far more than ever before, as though she could thereby compensate a little for the imminent loss. And time and again now we hear about "sacrifice." "I can reassure you that everything you will be sacrificing to God on that day will redound to the greatest possible happiness and blessing."²⁷

Die Postulantin Berta, Juni 1933
Postulant Berta, June 1933

Die Familie vor dem Sommerhaus, Juni 1933
The family at the summer house, June 1933

Berta mit Postulantinnenkragen, Centa, Viktoria Hummel, Franz, Kätl Edenhofer (geb. Hummel), Adolf Hummel, Georg Edenhofer, Ady, 1933
Berta with the postulant´s collar, Centa, Viktoria Hummel, Franz, Kätl Edenhofer (née Hummel), Adolf Hummel, Georg Edenhofer, Ady, 1933

*Mit dem Auto nach Sießen:
Straßenkarte: „Die wichtigsten Autostrecken mit Kilometerangabe"
Mittagessen für eine Reichsmark:
Speisekarte des Hotels Kleber Post*

*To Siessen by car:
Road map: "The principal automobile routes with distances in kilometers"
Lunch for one mark: menu of the Hotel Kleber Post*

Am 21. August 1933. Es regnet. 710 Kilometer sind es mit dem Auto von Massing nach Sießen und zurück. Zu fünft sind sie: die Eltern, Centa, Ady und Franzl. Um fünf Uhr morgens ist Abfahrt, um Viertel vor sieben ist man in München, um neun in Landsberg, um zwanzig vor zehn in Memmingen. Mittag im Gasthaus zur Post in Saulgau. Gegen zwei Uhr Ankunft im Kloster Sießen. In Anwesenheit ihrer Familie wird Bertl am nächsten Tag das Ordenskleid erhalten. Am heutigen Tag jedoch darf sie niemanden sehen.

Die Eltern Hummel besichtigten an diesem Nachmittag die alljährliche Werkschau in den klösterlichen Präsentationsräumen. Bertas Vater brachte stolz seine Eindrücke zu Papier, er war eine Sammlernatur, der auch Erinnerungen in allen Details für die Zukunft bewahrt wissen wollte. „Die wunderschöne Ausstellung fand allgemeine Bewunderung und war auch in den Ausstellungstagen überaus gut besucht. Uns wurden als Eltern der Künstlerin alle Ehrungen zuteil."[28] Die Bildauswahl war von den Arbeiten der Tochter bestimmt: „1. Saal: Bilder von Berta. 2. Saal: Paramente Entwürfe von Berta. 3. Saal: Schülerarbeiten." Der Tag verging rasch, später kamen noch einige entferntere Verwandte. Die Familie Hummel fühlte sich bestens bewirtet und wie Ehrengäste behandelt, es war sogar eigens das schönste Zimmer für ihre Mahlzeiten reserviert worden. Logiert wurde im Gasthaus des Klosters. Was dem Vater wohl in jener Nacht durch den Kopf gegangen sein mag, wissend, was für ein Einschnitt seinem Künstlerkind am nächsten Morgen bevorstand?

On August 21, 1933, it rained. It is 450 miles by automobile from Massing to Siessen and back. There were five of them in the car: the parents, Centa, Ady and Franzl. They started at five in the morning, were in Munich at a quarter to seven, in Landsberg at 9, in Memmingen at twenty to ten. Lunch at the hotel "Zur Post" in Saulgau. Shortly before two, they arrived at the convent. Berta would receive her habit on the following day in the presence of her family. Today, however, she could not see anyone.

In the afternoon the Hummels visited the annual work show in the convent's presentation rooms. Berta's father proudly recorded his impressions. He was a collector by nature, who also wished to have memories preserved for the future in every detail. "The wonderful exhibition was greatly admired by all and very well attended throughout the length of the show. As the parents of the artist, we were being greatly honored."[28] The selection of material was dominated by the work of their daughter: "1st room: pictures by Berta. 2nd room: parament designs by Berta. 3rd room: student work." The day passed quickly. Some more distant relatives joined later. The Hummel family felt entertained to perfection and treated like guests of honor; the best room had even been reserved for them to take their meals in. They lodged in the convent's guest house. What may have gone through the mind of the father, knowing the rupture the next day would bring for his artist child?

Bericht des berührten Vaters: Adolf Hummel zur Einkleidung seiner Tochter, 22. August 1933
A father's emotional account: Adolf Hummel on his daughter's Assumption of the Habit, August 22, 1933

Prozession der eingekleideten Novizinnen (Fotografien der unveränderten Zeremonie aus den 50er-Jahren)
Procession to the Assumption of the Habit ceremony (photographs from the 1950's of the unchanged ceremony)

„Liebe Ordensschwestern alle! Diese 32 Postulantinnen nehmt ihr heute auf in eure Reihen und ihr wollt mit ihnen sein – Beterinnen, so wie jene starke Frau im alten Bunde, die Judith, von der es heißt: Sie ging in ihr Betgemach, zog Bußkleider an, bestreute ihr Haupt mit Asche, unaufhörlich flehte sie für ihr Volk. Ihr sollt mit diesen Postulantinnen sein wie eine Anna des alten und neuen Bundes, von der es heißt: Sie kam nimmer heraus aus dem Tempel, sie betete und diente Gott unaufhörlich. Draußen wartet die Welt auf euch, Tausende und Tausende in ihren schweren Sorgen und Anliegen, Ihr sollt sie kreuzesstark beten. Tausende liegen in den Ketten der Sünden, Ihr sollt sie frei beten. Hunderte liegen im Todeskampf, Ihr sollt sie in den Himmel hineinbeten."[29]

Um halb neun am 22. August hielten 32 Postulantinnen feierlichen Einzug in die prächtig geschmückte Pfarrkirche des Klosters. Weiß wie weltliche Bräute gekleidet, sogar die feinen Handschuhe fehlten nicht, die jungen Häupter geschmückt mit Myrtenkranz und Schleier. Ihnen voraus liefen die kleinen „Bräutchen"[30], ein Kind für jede Postulantin. Die Kirche war voll, viele Angehörige waren gekommen, die nun erwartungsvoll auf den reservierten Plätzen saßen. Nachdem die Postulantinnen den Mittelgang durchschritten und sich um den Hochaltar versammelt hatten, begann die Predigt. Dann das Hochamt und das Evangelium. Danach nahmen die Einkleidungszeremonien ihren Anfang. „Ich bitte um der Liebe Gottes willen, mich zum Kleide des dritten Ordens des heiligen Franziskus in der Kongregation der Franziskanerinnen von Sießen zuzulassen." Jede Postulantin kniete mit gefalteten Händen an den Stufen des Altars. Verzicht auf die Welt. Schleier, Myrtenkranz und Handschuhe wurden nun der assistierenden Schwester übergeben. Zwei Haarlocken wurden abgeschnitten, Symbol für Entsagung. Eintritt in ein neues Leben. Die Postulantin empfing ihr Gewand, den Habit. „Der Herr bekleide dich mit dem neuen Menschen, der nach Gott geschaffen ist in Gerechtigkeit und wahrer Heiligkeit." Den Gürtel für die Reinheit, den Mantel für die Demut. Den weißen Schleier zum Zeichen für die Treue gegen Christus.

Dear sisters of the order! You are receiving these 32 postulants into your group, and with them you want to be – champions of prayer, like that strong woman of the Old Covenant, Judith, of whom it is written: 'She went into her praying closet, put on penitential clothes, strewed her head with ashes and prayed to God continually for her people.' You shall be, with these postu-

Der Festprediger:
Porträt Pater Adalbero Hugo, 1930
Preacher at the ceremony:
Portrait of Father Adalbero Hugo, 1930

lants, like an Anna of the Old and New Covenant, of whom it is written: 'She never left the temple but prayed and served God unceasingly'. Without, the world is waiting for you, thousands upon thousands with their heavy burdens and wants. You are to make them strong to bear their cross by your prayers. Hundreds are lying in the agony of death: you are to pray them into Heaven."[29]

At half past eight on August 22, the 32 postulants made their solemn entrance into the richly decorated parish church of the convent. Dressed in white like secular brides – even to the fine white gloves – their young heads wreathed with myrtle and a veil. Ahead of them tripped the little "bridelets,"[30] one child for each postulant. The church was full: a great many relatives had come, who were now sitting expectantly on the seats reserved for them. When the postulants had passed down the center aisle and assembled around the high altar, the sermon commenced, followed by the high mass and the reading of the gospel. Then the ceremony of the Assumption of the Habit began. "I ask for the love of God to be admitted to the habit of the third order of St. Francis in the congregation of the Franciscan sisters of Siessen." All the postulants knelt with folded hands at the steps to the altar. Renunciation of the world. Veil, myrtle wreath, and gloves were now handed to the assisting sister. Two locks of hair were cut to symbolize renunciation of the world. Entrance into a new life. The postulant received her dress, the habit. "The Lord clothe you with the New Man, who is created in the image of God in righteousness and true holiness." The cincture for purity, the cloak for humility. The white veil in token of fidelity to Christ.

Feierlicher Einzug in die Klosterkapelle
Festive entrance into the church

Um halb elf war die Zeremonie zu Ende. Die Familie Hummel zog sich in das reservierte Zimmer zurück und bald kam auch die „neugebackene Klosterfrau"[31] dazu, bis zum Abend durfte sie bei ihren Eltern bleiben. Der Vater nahm großen Anteil, als er seine Tochter in ihrer selbst gewählten Umgebung beobachtete. „Allzuschnell vergingen die feierlichen Stunden im schönen Kloster Sießen u. die Abschiedsstunde kam. Wenn auch schwer, so war die Trennungsstunde auch wieder leicht, denn ein schöneres Plätzchen in eigener Berufswahl kann man einem Kinde auf dieser Welt nicht wünschen. Ihr selbstgestecktes Ziel ist nun erreicht."[32] Am nächsten Morgen besuchten Adolf und Viktoria Hummel die Frühmesse in der Klosterkapelle. „Glaubten nocheinmal Bertl gesehen zu haben", notierte der Vater später in seinen Aufzeichnungen.

Novizin. Nun ist ihr Leben ganz in Gottes Hand, der sie leiten wird, sie gebrauchen wird als sein Werkzeug: im Leben bis zum Tod. Die Festpredigt hatte mit den Worten geschlossen: „Liebe Postulantinnen! Der Meister ist da und ruft euch! So wird der Priester (...) wieder einmal zu euch sagen: Schwester, der Meister ist jetzt da und ruft dich! Und da sollen deine Augen strahlen wie heute am Einkleidungstag und dann wird der Meister sprechen: O du meine Braut komme jetzt und empfange den Lohn, den zwanzig-, vierzig-, sechzig-, hundertfältigen, für dein Beten, für dein frohes Dienen und für dein freiwilliges Opfern. Amen."

Mit dem Ablegen der weltlichen Kleider legte die Postulantin auch ihren alten Namen ab. Berta hieß von nun an „Innocentia", die „Unschuldige". Unschuldig wie die vielen gezeichneten Kinder, die sie unvergessen machen würden.

Bertas „Bräutchen":
Gruß der kleinen Maria Hugo an
die neugebackene Novizin
und Porträt Maria Hugo, 1928
Berta's "bridelet":
Greeting of little Maria Hugo
to the new novice
and Portrait of Maria Hugo, 1928

The ceremony ended at half past ten. The Hummel family retreated into the room reserved for it and was soon joined by the "brand-new conventual"[31] who was allowed to stay with her parents until the evening. The father was deeply moved as he watched his daughter in her chosen setting. "The festive hours at the beautiful convent of Siessen passed all-too quickly, and the hour of

Zur Erinnerung an einen feierlichen Tag
Memento of a solemn day

parting arrived. Though hard, the parting was yet also easy, for a more beautiful place for her chosen profession one cannot wish for one's child in this world. Her longed-for goal is now attained."[32] On the following morning, Adolf and Viktoria Hummel attended early mass in the convent chapel. "Thought we glimpsed Bertl once more," the father later wrote in his notebook.

Novice: her life is now altogether in God's hands, who will guide her and employ her as his tool throughout her life until death. The ceremonial sermon had concluded with the words: "Dear postulants! The Master is come and is calling you! Thus the priest will (…) someday say to you again: Sister, the Master is come and is calling you! And then your eyes will shine, as now on the day of your assumption of the habit, and then the Master will say: O you my bride, come now and receive your reward twenty-, forty-, sixty-, a hundredfold, for your prayers, for your glad service, for your voluntary sacrifices. Amen."

Along with her worldly clothes, the postulant also put off her old name. Berta was now called Innocentia, the "innocent." Innocent like the many children in her drawings that would make her unforgotten.

Abschied von der Mutter;
mit „Bräutchen" Maria Hugo und Familienauto
Farewell to the mother;
with "bridelet" Maria Hugo and family car

70 Jahre Handarbeit

Die berühmten Hummel-Figuren

Die Porzellankinder der Firma Goebel aus Rödental haben den Namen „M.I. Hummel" zur Marke gemacht. Über 70 Jahre lang gleichbedeutend mit aufwendigster Handarbeit, die unverändert in der typischen Farbgebung wie zu Maria Innocentias Lebzeiten praktiziert wurde. Die Herstellungsprozedur erfordert von 75 Einzelschritten bei der einfachsten Figur bis zu fast 500 bei der komplexesten.

Der Modelleur formt den ersten Entwurf nach einer Originalzeichnung von Maria Innocentia Hummel aus dem schwarzen, besonders fein formbaren Ton aus der Gegend von Rödental. Danach wird eine Negativform erstellt, in die flüssige Keramikmasse gegossen wird. Dafür muss das Modell zuvor in mehrere Teile zerlegt werden, damit man später die fest gewordene Keramikmasse wieder aus der Negativform entnehmen kann, ohne dass sie an einem Überhang festsitzt. Komplizierte Figuren mit vielen Überschneidungen – z. B. bei einem Wanderstab oder einer Laterne – können bis zu 40 Einzelteile nötig machen. Die gewonnenen Keramikstücke werden wieder zusammengesetzt – zu exakt der gleichen Figur, die der Modelleur eingangs als Entwurf gefertigt hat, nur eben jetzt in brennbarem Keramikton. Die durch das Zusammenfügen entstandenen Nähte werden nach sorgfältiger Austrocknung geglättet, bevor die Figuren in den Ofen wandern dürfen und bei 1140 Grad Celsius gehärtet werden. Anschließend wird eine transparente Glasur aufgetragen und bei 1080 Grad eingebrannt. Nun kommt die Figur aus dem sogenannten „Weißbetrieb" zum Mustermaler, um einen Prototypen zu erstellen. Er dekoriert in „Aufglasurmalerei" aus einer Palette von 130 Farbtönen, die seit den 30er-Jahren den Originalzeichnungen entsprechen. Diese altbewährte Technik wurde von den kunstfertigen chinesischen Porzellanmalern bereits im 15. Jahrhundert angewandt. Nach der Vorlage des Mustermalers werden die Figuren in der Manufaktur mit Farbe versehen, teils aufgespritzt, teils mit feinstem Pinsel von Hand gemalt. Der Maler, der Augen und Form des Mundes – die ausdrucksstärksten Details also – aufträgt, darf die Figur auf dem Boden mit seinem Zeichen signieren.

Abschließend geht es noch einmal in den Brennofen, wo die Farben bei 700 Grad ihre dauerhafte Härte erhalten.

70 Years of Handcraft

The Famous Hummel Figurines

The porcelain children of the Goebel Company of Rödental transformed the name "M.I. Hummel" into a trademark – one synonymous, for 70 years, with the most elaborate handcraftsmanship, carried on unchanged in its characteristic coloration since the days of Maria Innocentia. The manufacturing process requires from 75 individual steps for the simplest figures to nearly 500 for the most complex. The following simplified description of the major steps may serve to illustrate the process.

The modeler creates the first rough copy of an original drawing by Maria Innocentia Hummel, using the black, especially malleable clay found in the area around Rödental. From that a mold is formed, into which liquid ceramic mass is poured. The model must first be divided into seperate pieces so that the hardened ceramic mass can be removed from the mold without being held in by any projections. Complicated figures with overlapping parts – for example, a walking staff or a lantern – may require dissection into as many as 40 components. The finished pieces are reassembled into the exact same figure the modeler had initially designed, but now in ceramic clay that can be fired. After a careful drying process, the seams formed where the pieces are joined together are smoothed away, and then the figures are placed into a kiln, where they are hardened at a temperature of some 2100 degrees Fahrenheit. Afterwards a transparent glaze is applied and burnt on at 1975 degrees.

Now the figure moves from the so-called "white production unit" to the shop of the model painter, who creates a prototype. He decorates the figures with "on-glaze painting," using a palette of 130 different shades of color corresponding exactly to the hues of the original drawings. This tried technique was used by highly skilled Chinese porcelain painters as early as the 15th century. Following the pattern furnished by the model painter, the figures are then colored in the factory, partly sprayed, partly painted by hand with a very fine brush. The artist who paints the eyes and the form of the mouth – the figure's most expressive details – has the privilege of signing the underside of the figure with his mark.

Thereupon the figure is sent back once more to a 1300 degree kiln to give the color its durable hardness.

Hummel um die Welt

Der Siegeszug der Hummelkinder

Hummel World-Wide – The Triumphal March of the Hummel Children

Die Hummel-Motive wurden als Fotokarten im Handabzug vertrieben: Resele mit Ball
The Hummel motifs were sold as hand-produced photo cards: Resele with ball

Schwester Maria Innocentia, spielst du mit mir? Die kleine Resele reckt ihr eifrig einen bunten Ball entgegen. Offensichtlich des Kindes ganzer Stolz. Maria Innocentia muss laut lachen. Nahe den Klostergrundstücken gibt es ein paar Bauernfamilien. Man kennt sich gut, hält oft ein Schwätzchen, begegnet sich sonntags in der Pfarrkirche. Von der allgemeinen Aufregung, die durch die Kinderbilder losgetreten wurde, ist hier zum Glück nichts zu spüren. Wie gerne würde sie den süßen Lockenkopf jetzt auf den Arm nehmen, so wie früher ihre kleinen Nichten und Neffen. Aber das ist ihr als Ordensfrau verwehrt. Körperlicher Kontakt zu den Kindern könnte Muttergefühle wecken. Maria Innocentia wirft dem Resele den Ball wieder zu. Sie wird sie nachher zeichnen, im Gras sitzend, den bunten Ball auf dem Schoß.

Ein paar Monate zuvor war auf einmal alles sehr schnell gegangen. Am 9. März 1933 ging ein kurzes Schreiben nach München, adressiert an Herrn Josef Müller, Inhaber des renommierten katholischen Verlags Ars sacra: „In der Anlage finden Sie 3 Abzüge der neuesten Entwürfe unserer jungen Künstlerin B. Hummel. Wir fragen höflichst an, ob und unter welchen Bedingungen eine Herausgabe von Andachtsbildchen in schwarz und dann auch in farbig geschehen könnte? Einer baldmöglichen Antwort unter gleichzeitiger Bemusterung von Papier u. Format, zeichnet inzwischen hochachtend Sr. Eligia Stadler."[1] Ein knapper Text – ein großer Schritt. Die „Graphischen Kunstwerkstätten des Verlages Ars sacra" boten Fachkenntnisse in „Buchdruck, Offsetdruck, Tiefdruck, Buchbinderei, Clicheherstellung, Specialität: Farben, Druck in allen modernen Reproduktionsarten" an. In den letzten Jahren, als durch die Weltwirtschaftskrise etliche andere Betriebe ihre Pforten hatten schließen müssen, war die Firma außerordentlich erfolgreich gewesen und beschäftigte Anfang der 30er-Jahre über 100 Mitarbeiter.

Selbst schüchterne Kinder verloren ihre Scheu vor Maria Innocentia. So berichtete ein Vater, wie sich sein ansonsten sehr zurückhaltendes Söhnchen einmal von der Hand seiner Mutter losriss, um der Schwester einen langen Gang entgegenzulaufen.
Even timid children quickly lost their shyness with Maria Innocentia. Thus a father reports how his usually very reserved little boy tore himself from his mother's hand and ran down the long corridor toward the approaching sister.

Sister Maria Innocentia, will you play with me? Little Resele eagerly holds a colored ball toward her, evidently the child's pride and joy. Maria Innocentia has to laugh out loud. Near the convent property live several farm families, who are well acquainted with the sisters, have little chats with them, see them at the parish church on Sundays. Of the wide-spread excitement caused by the children's pictures, luckily little is felt here. How Berta would love to take the sweet curly-head on her arm, as she used to do with her little cousins. But as a conventual she is debarred from that. Bodily contact with the children might awaken maternal feelings. Maria Innocentia throws the ball back to the little girl. Later she will draw her as she sits in the grass, holding the colorful toy in her lap.

A few months ago, things had suddenly begun to happen very fast. On March 9, 1933, a letter had been sent to Munich, addressed to Josef Müller, the owner of the renowned Catholic press Ars Sacra. "Attached please find 3 copies of the latest designs by our young artist B. Hummel. We would like to inquire whether and under what conditions it might be possible to publish a series of devotional pictures in black and white and then also in color. In hopes of receiving a favorable response, along with samples of paper and format, I am respectfully yours, Sr. Eligia Stadler."[1] A terse text – a tremendous step. The "Graphic Arts Workshop of the Ars Sacra Press" offered professional expertise in "letter press, offset print, gravure, book-binding, and stereotype production. Our specialty: color printing in all modern forms of reproduction." Though the world-wide economic depression of the last several years had forced a number of other presses into bankruptcy, Ars Sacra had been exceptionally successful, with a staff, in the early 30's, of more than a hundred employees.

Schmuckstück des Jugendstils: das Verlagshaus der Ars sacra in der Münchner Friedrichstraße
Die „Kinderbildchen (...) sind wirklich allerliebst": Antwortschreiben Ars sacra auf neuerlich eingesandte Motive
A jewel of Art Noveau architecture: the building housing the Ars Sacra Press on Munich's Friedrichstrasse
The "little children's pictures (...) are really just lovely": response of Ars Sacra to motifs newly sent in

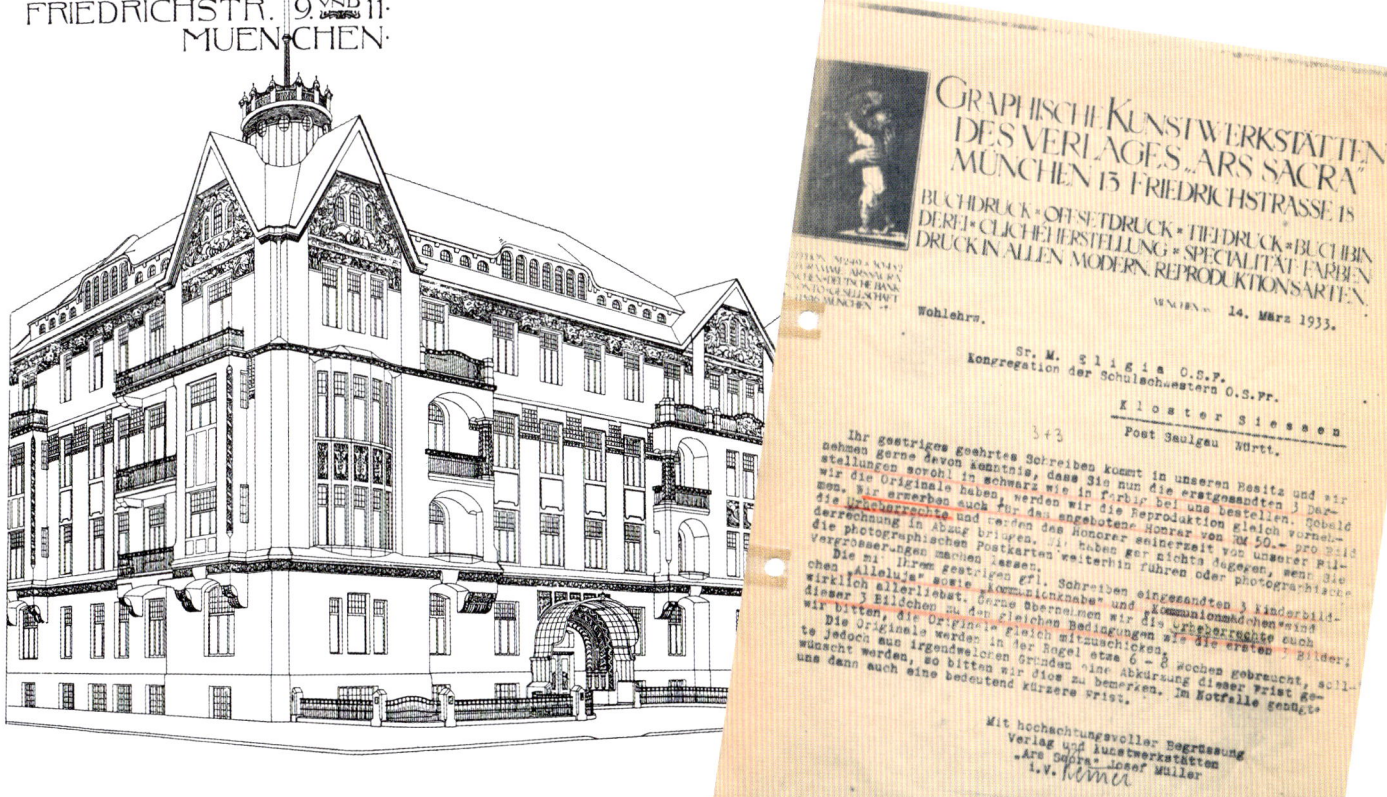

Liebreich Holdseligste, 1933
Virgin Mother, 1933

St. Franziskus, 1933
St. Francis, 1933

𝔐an hatte sich auf ein weit gestreutes, religiös-populäres Programm für Erwachsene und Kinder ausgerichtet, nach dem Motto: „Vermittlung christlicher Werte in Bild und Text"[2]. Kein Buch erschien ohne Illustration, und die Inhaber scheuten weder Kosten noch Mühen, Erfolg versprechende Künstler aufzuspüren und an den Verlag zu binden.

Jetzt waren also drei Andachtsmotive der jungen Kandidatin „B. Hummel" auf einem der Verlagsschreibtische gelandet. Der zuständige Lektor biss an. Postwendend erfolgte die Antwort auf die Sießener Anfrage: „Können Sie uns das Recht erteilen, die Bilder auch in unserem eigenen Verlag zu vertreiben, so würden wir für die Überlassung der Urheberrechte[3] RM 50.- für jedes Bild vergüten. (...) Die eingeschickten Bilder zeigen nach verschiedener Richtung sehr schätzenswerte Qualitäten, die Bilder werden heute schon sicherlich großen Anklang finden und bei dem sicher noch zu gewärtigenden Fortschritt hinsichtlich korrekter figuraler Zeichnung werden sich die Bilder bald beliebt machen."[4] Jene aussichtsreiche Antwort war der Auftakt zu einem regen Schriftverkehr zwischen Sießen und München. Das Kloster schickte drei weitere Fotos von Zeichnungen, Eingang in München 14. März. Auch diesmal ging sogleich ein Brief zurück, die „Kinderbildchen" seien „wirklich allerliebst" und man möchte hiervon die Urheberrechte[5] ebenfalls gerne erwerben. Abermals ermutigt, sandten die Schwestern am 15. März drei weitere Abzüge an den Verlag, sodass sich in München innerhalb dieser ersten Woche peu à peu 10 Hummel-Motive, darunter 6 Originalzeichnungen[6] ansammelten. Der Lektor bedankte sich herzlich mit der Bitte, weitere „neue Entwürfe jeweils gleich zur Ansicht [zu] überschicken"[7].

Nun schalteten sich auch der Verlagsleiter und seine Frau ein. Was hatte es mit diesen Hummel-Bildern auf sich? Darstellungen von Kindern waren an sich nichts Neues. In der eigenen Edition feierte man große Erfolge mit den populären Illustrationen von Else Wenz-Vietor und Ida Bohatta[8]. Von Gemälden Philipp Otto Runges und Hans Thomas über Illustrationen von Wilhelm Busch[9], Ludwig Richter und Wilhelm Kaulbach bis hin zur Werbegrafik eines Ludwig Hohlwein waren Maßstäbe in der Kinderdarstellung gesetzt worden.[10]

Alleluja-Engel, 1932/1933
Alleluja Angel, 1932/1933

Under the motto: "Dissemination of Christian Values in Text and Image,"[2] the press specialized in a broad religious-popular program for both adults and children. All of their books were illustrated, and the owners spared no expense or effort in ferreting out promising artists and engaging them for their publishing enterprise.

Now three devotional motifs of the young convent candidate "B. Hummel" had landed on a desk at the press. The lector in charge took the bait. By return mail, Siessen received the following response: "If you authorize us to publish the pictures through our own house, we will pay you 50 reichsmark per picture for the copyright.[3] (…) The pictures submitted exhibit promising qualities in several respects. They will certainly evoke a lively response even now, and with further progress in correct figure draftsmanship are bound to become very popular."[4] This promising letter was the beginning of a lively correspondence between Siessen and Munich. The convent sent three additional photographs of drawings, which arrived in Munich on March 14. Again an answer came promptly, saying these "children's pictures" were "really just lovely" and the press would like to have the copyright[5] of them as well. Thus encouraged, the sisters, on May 15, sent the press copies of yet another three designs, so that within one week ten Hummel motifs, including six original drawings,[6] had collected in Munich. The lector conveyed his thanks together with a request "to send all new designs immediately for our consideration."[7]

At this point Ars Sacra's director and his wife became involved in the proceedings. What was it about these Hummel pictures? Representations of children as such were nothing new. The press had had great successes with their editions of popular illustrations by Else Wenz-Vietor and Ida Bohatta[8]. From the paintings of a Philipp Otto Runge or Hans Thoma, through illustrations by Wilhelm Busch[9], Ludwig Richter and Wilhelm Kaulbach, to the commercial graphic art of a Ludwig Hohlwein, the pictorial representation of children had already attained to a considerable level.[10]

Frohe Ostern, 1932/1933
Happy Easter, 1932/1933

Das Ehepaar Müller mit Tochter Lilly und dem Familienpapagei, um 1921 in Lugano
Josef and Maximiliane Müller with their daughter Lilly and the family parrot, ca. 1921 in Lugano

𝒟ennoch: Gerade diese Hummel'schen Schelme mit ihren stämmigen Beinchen und dem verschmitzten Blick hatten einen ganz besonderen Charme. Und sie waren exzellent gezeichnet. In wenigen kräftigen Strichen offenbarte sich ihre kleine heile Welt, jene pausbäckige Unschuld, an die man sich selbst aus eigenen Tagen gerne erinnerte.

Trotz seines übervollen Terminkalenders nahm das Ehepaar Josef und Maximiliane Müller Ende März die gut 350 Kilometer Hin- und Rückfahrt in Kauf, um ein paar Stunden im klösterlichen Atelier zu verbringen und um zu sichten, zu beurteilen, zu sondieren, was für den Verlag geeignet sein könnte. Mit der Künstlerin persönlich sprachen sie über Fleißbildchen, Postkarten, Kommunionandenken und über die langjährige Erfahrung von Ars sacra in der Reproduktion einer differenzierten Farbgebung. Mit ihren Vorgesetzten wurde das Geschäftliche erörtert: die ungeheure Verbreitungsmöglichkeit, die ein derart großer Verlag wie Ars sacra den Bildern im In- und Ausland verschaffen könne. Über Startauflagen von bis zu 12.000 Bildchen wurde gesprochen, über Pressearbeit und Werbeaufwand und über die Überlassung des alleinigen Reproduktionsrechts an den zukünftigen Werken.

Man wurde sich schnell einig. „So hoffen wir ganz zuversichtlich auf eine segensreiche und recht ersprießliche Zusammenarbeit und wir begrüßen Sie, Fräulein Hummel, sowie die Schwester der Kunstabteilung, Ehrw. Frau Oberin und Hochw. Herrn Pater Superior aufs Herzlichste. Mit vorzüglicher Hochachtung Verlag und Kunstwerkstätten ‚Ars sacra' gez. Josef Müller."[11] „Jetzt gilt es dann für ‚Ars sacra'"[12], versprach hierauf M. Eligia Stadler, die Leiterin der künstlerischen Werkstatt.

Englein mit Christkind im Wägelchen, 1929/1932
Christ Child with angels in toy cart, 1929/1932

But these Hummel poppets with their sturdy legs and mischievous looks in their eyes had a unique charm. Moreover, they were exquisitely drawn. A few bold strokes evoked a small, intact world, a chubby-faced innocence such as one might want to remember from one's own past.

Despite their very busy schedule, Josef and Maximiliane Müller braved the 220 miles to Siessen and back at the end of March in order to spend a few hours at the convent studio, inspecting, evaluating, and selecting whatever appeared suitable for the press. They talked at length with the artist about diligence pictures, postcards, and communion souvenirs, and about Ars Sacra's many years of expertise in the reproduction of nuanced color. The business aspect was taken up with Berta's superiors, specifically the enormous distribution, inland and abroad, that a large publishing house like Ars Sacra would make possible. The discussion envisioned initial editions of up to 12,000 prints and covered such issues as press work, advertising, and the granting of exclusive reproduction rights for all future creations.

Alleluja-Engel, 1932/1933
Alleluja Angel, 1932/1933

A consensus was quickly reached. "We confidently look forward to a mutually beneficial and fruitful collaboration, and we cordially salute you, Miss Hummel, as well as the sisters of the art department, the Reverend Mother Superior and the Reverend Father Superior. Respectfully, 'Ars Sacra,' Publishing and Arts Workshops, signed Josef Müller."[11] "We are on for 'Ars sacra,'"[12] M. Eligia Stadler, the director of the convent's arts workshop, vowed.

International: Briefkopf der New Yorker Filiale des Verlags Ars sacra, seit ca. 1907
International: letterhead of the press's New York branch, est. ca. 1907

In den nächsten Monaten wurde alles, was geeignet erschien, an den Verlag gegeben. „Überhaupt sind wir dankbar, wenn bald wieder etwas zurückkommt, da unser Atelier ganz ausgeraubt ist"¹³, klagte Schwester Eligia angesichts der leeren Wände. Josef Müller hatte den Vorschlag gemacht, die meisten Originale nicht mehr hin- und herzuschicken, sondern neben dem jeweiligen Reproduktionsrecht auch das Bild selbst zu erwerben. Dann könne es dem Verlag für verschiedene Formate und eine eventuelle spätere Monografie zur Verfügung stehen. 50 Reichsmark schlage man vor, das hieße 100 Reichsmark für Reproduktionsrecht und Original zusammen. Im Kloster zeigte man sich einverstanden. Man würde sich nur gerne vorbehalten, die Bilder vom 22. bis zum 31. August zur Ausstellung anlässlich der Einkleidungsfeier der Postulantin B. Hummel zeigen zu dürfen.

Verlegerporträt Josef Müllers
(1872 – 1930) aus den 20er-Jahren
Portrait of Josef Müller (1872 – 1930)
dating from the twenties

Vom Tag der Einkleidung an änderte sich mit dem Namen der Künstlerin auch ihre Unterschrift. Die Bilder trugen nun die Signatur „Hummel" oder „M.I.Hummel".¹⁴

In der folgenden Zeit gab es viel zu tun. Neben der Produktion für Ars sacra ging das ganz normale Tagesgeschäft seinen Gang: Aufträge für Altargemälde in Öl und neue Entwürfe für Paramente ließen nicht auf sich warten. Seit Maria Innocentia in Sießen war, wurde in der Werkstatt „mit neuen Besen gekehrt", die frühere Gestaltung der Messgewänder hatte die studierte Künstlerin als „kitschig" verworfen, und nun bemühte man sich um neue, modernere Formen.

Aus München kamen neue Anregungen. Maximiliane Müller verstand es, ihre Künstler immer wieder zu motivieren, es schien kaum möglich, sich ihrer herzlich vorgetragenen Wünsche zu widersetzen. Nun bat sie um weitere Motive zum Jahreswechsel: „Die Neujahrskarte ‚Nachtwächter' könnte zu einer Serie ergänzt werden mit folgenden Darstellungen: Kaminfegerlein, Neujahrsgratulanten, Bub und Mädchen oder nur Mädchen allein; das neue Jahr ‚Anschiessen'¹⁵ oder – wenn das Fräulein Hummel lieber ist – zwei Buben blasen als Musikanten das neue Jahr ein. (...) Wenn Fräulein Hummel, die ich bestens zu grüssen bitte, etwas Gescheiteres weiss als meine Vorschläge, desto besser!"¹⁶ Die Antwort kam prompt: „Für die neue Bestellung dankt Frl. Hummel und ein Kaminfegerlein steht schon in Kohle auf der Staffelei!"¹⁷

„Unsere ‚Hummel'-Bilder": ganzseitige Rezension der
katholisch-vaterländischen Zeitschrift „Weiße Rose", Advent 1933
"Our 'Hummel'-Pictures": fullpage commentary of the
Catholic-national newspaper Weiße Rose, *Advent 1933*

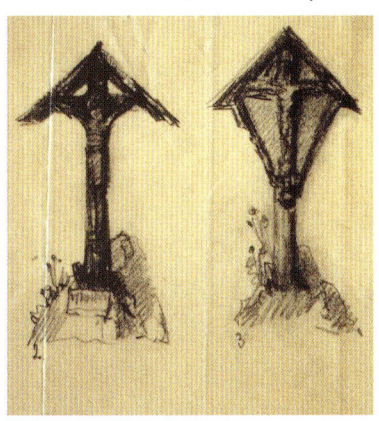

Grabkreuz-Entwürfe für die 1933 verstorbene ältere Schwester Viki. Am 3. Januar 1934 schrieb Maria Innocentia ihren Eltern, sie wäre für eine "stilechte u. einfache" Lösung, "damit sie immer standhält".
Sketches for a cross for the grave of Berta's elder sister Viki, who died 1933. On January 3, 1934, Maria Innocentia wrote to her parents she favored a "simple, traditional" solution that "will stand the test of time."

During the next several months, everything that appeared suitable was transmitted to the press. "We'll be only too happy if something is returned to us soon, as our studio is altogether depleted,"[13] Sister Eligia lamented about the emptied walls. Josef Müller had proposed not to send the originals back and forth any longer but for him to acquire the pictures themselves along with the copyright. The press would then have them available for diverse formats and perhaps for a monograph later on. He offered 50 reichsmark per picture, which meant 100 reichsmark for reproduction rights and original combined. The convent consented, with the request to be able to keep the pictures until the end of the month for an exhibition to be held from August 22 to 31 on the occasion of the postulant B. Hummel's receiving the habit.

From the day of her becoming a novice, the artist's signature changed along with her name. The pictures were henceforth signed either simply "Hummel" or else "M.I.Hummel."[14]

The months following brought a great deal of work. Besides the production for Ars Sacra, the normal daily output had to continue: orders for church paintings in oil and new designs for paraments. Ever since Maria Innocentia's arrival in Siessen, the workshop was being "swept with a new broom." The academically trained artist had rejected previous chasuble styles as "kitschy," and a great effort was underway to come up with new, more modern forms.

Additional impulses came from Munich. Maximiliane Müller had a knack for motivating her artists time and again – it was virtually impossible to resist her cordially expressed wishes. Now she was asking for fresh motifs for the New Year. "The New Year's card 'Night Watchman' could be expanded to an entire series with the following images: little chimney sweeps, a boy and girl – or just a girl – offering New Year's wishes; New Year's 'Anschiessen' (shooting in)[15] or – if Miss Hummel prefers – two boy musicians blowing a salute to the New Year. (...) If Miss Hummel, to whom I send my best regards, can think of something smarter than my suggestions, so much the better!"[16] An answer came back promptly: "Miss Hummel thanks you for the new order: a little charcoal chimney sweep is already on the easel!"[17]

Im Kreuzgarten:
Maria Innocentia mit Kind, 1934
In the cloister garden:
Maria Innocentia with a child, 1934

Anneliese, 1933/1934
Anneliese (Heidi), 1933/1934

Schwester Maria Innocentia, zeichnest du mich? Das kleine Resele kam mit ihrer Freundin aufgeregt den Weg heruntergelaufen. Aber mich musst du mit meinen neuen Sonntagsschuhen malen, ja? Lächelnd stimmt die Schwester zu. Ja freilich, zieh sie nur an, deine schönen Schuhe! Als das Kind nachher sein Bild anschaut, ist in schwungvollen Kohlestrichen nur das hübsche Köpfchen abgebildet.[18]

Ars sacra legte Ende des Jahres 1933 Rechenschaft ab: 37 Original-Pastellbilder seien in Druck gegangen. Werbemittel mit Hummelmotiven seien zu Hunderttausenden an die Händler im ganzen Land geschickt worden. Hunderte von Zeitungen und Zeitschriften haben Musterbilder zur Rezension erhalten. Einige haben sie unerfreulicherweise auch ohne Genehmigung abgedruckt. Es seien jedoch „schon sehr viele günstige Besprechungen eingegangen"[19]. Dieses erfolgreiche Jahr konnte also zufrieden abgeschlossen werden. Maximiliane Müller schickte dankbar ein reichlich gepacktes Weihnachtspaket an das Kloster.

Doch bald stellten sich Schwierigkeiten ein. „Es wäre (…) sehr erwünscht, wenn die letztgesandten 8 Nummern ja nicht farbiger herauskämen als die Originale. (…) Mit deutschem Gruß Sr. M. Eligia Stadler."[20] Im klösterlichen Atelier regte sich Unmut über die Druckausführung. Es sei „nicht die Art der Reproduktion, sondern die zu ‚brillante' Farbwirkung, die der Künstlerin nicht sympathisch ist."[21] Man hatte bei Ars sacra begonnen, im teureren Offsetverfahren zu arbeiten, um eine möglichst große Brillanz der Pastellkreide zu erzielen.[22] „Sie macht jetzt ihre Bilder immer gedämpfter in der Farbe"[23], hieß es aus Sießen.

Sister Maria Innocentia, will you draw me? All excited, little Resele comes running down the path, together with her friend. But you must paint me in my new Sunday shoes, yes? Smilingly, the sister agrees. By all means, put on your pretty shoes! When the child later looked at the finished picture, she found only her pretty little head limned in vigorous charcoal strokes.[18]

At the end of the year 1933, Ars Sacra reported that 37 pastel pictures had gone into print. Advertising copy with Hummel motifs had been sent to dealers throughout the country by the hundreds of thousands. Hundreds of newspapers and journals had received sample pictures for review; annoyingly, some had printed them off without permission. But "already a large number of favorable critiques have come in."[19] The year could thus be judged to have been very successful. As a token of her gratitude, Maximiliane Müller sent a generous Christmas package to the convent.

Before long, however, problems began to emerge. "It would be (...) greatly desirable for the 8 numbers sent you most recently not to come out in louder colors than the originals. (...) With German salute, Sr. M. Eligia Stadler."[20] The convent studio was displeased with the printer's execution. What the artist found disagreeable was "not the type of reproduction, but the too 'brilliant' color effect."[21] Aiming at a maximum brilliance for the pastel chalks,[22] Ars Sacra had begun to apply the more expensive offset process. "She now does her pictures in increasingly subdued colors,"[23] Siessen informed the press.

Glück auf zum Neuen Jahr!, 1932/1933
Gebet vor der Schlacht, 1933
Ich bring dir Glück, 1933
Town Crier, 1931/1933
Prayer before Battle, 1933
Good Luck Chimney Sweep, 1933

Schwester Maria Innocentia, 1934
Sister Maria Innocentia, 1934

Auch andere Verlage hatten begonnen, sich für die Hummel-Bilder zu interessieren. So sprach eines Tages „ein Herr Fink aus Stuttgart"²⁴ in Sießen vor und regte den Gedanken an, in seinem Verlag ein „Hummel-Buch" mit 40 bis 50 Bildtafeln herauszugeben, eine Monografie also, der Künstlerin allein gewidmet. Die Schwestern sagten zu.

Im Münchner Verlag Ars sacra zeigte man sich entsetzt. War man doch als „Hummel'scher Hofverleger"²⁵ stets von einem Exklusivrecht ausgegangen! Man habe schließlich Vorleistungen gehabt, habe den ganzen Vertrieb und die Pressemaschinerie angekurbelt. Ob die Schwestern es sich nicht noch einmal überlegen wollten! Es sei besser, noch ein wenig zu warten, bis Material für „ein feines großes Hummelbuch"²⁶ zusammengekommen sei. Dies herauszubringen habe man sich in München auch schon überlegt.

Doch die Zusage an den Fink Verlag war gegeben. Die klösterliche Werkstattleitung argumentierte mit der feineren künstlerischen Umsetzung des Stuttgarter Verlags, und ohnehin ginge es lediglich um „wenige andere" Bilder und ansonsten um solche, die für Ars sacra „aus irgend einem Grunde nicht in Frage kommen"²⁷. Nach einigem Hin und Her reiste das Ehepaar Müller erneut nach Sießen, um zumindest das Verfahren mit den zukünftigen Werken zu klären: „Wie weiterhin besprochen, werden wir für die Zukunft die ganze Neuproduktion in Hummel-Originalen zur Reproduktion übernehmen."²⁸ Eindringlich warb der Verlag dafür, die künstlerische Produktion in einer Hand zu lassen: „Ein so bedeutendes und dazu noch sehr entwicklungsfähiges künstlerisches Können wie das der Schwester Innocentia (…) gehört vielmehr in die Gesellschaft erster Autoren und Künstler und in den angesehensten führenden religiösen Kunstverlag, der in Deutschland doch zweifellos der ‚Ars sacra' Verlag ist."²⁹

Moreover, other publishers had begun to take an interest in the Hummel pictures. One day "a Mr. Fink from Stuttgart"²⁴ called at the convent and proposed to publish a "Hummel book" at his press, with 40 to 50 color plates – in other words a monograph solely dedicated to this artist. The sisters agreed.

In Munich, Ars Sacra was aghast. As the "Hummel court publisher,"²⁵ the press had always presumed to have exclusive rights! After all, there had been consider-

able outlay in increased sales activity and printing machinery. Would the sisters please think the matter over once more? It would be better to wait a little longer, until enough material had accumulated for "a really nice big Hummel book."²⁶ They had already considered putting out such a book in Munich.

But the consent to the Fink press had been given. In their defense, the convent authorities argued that the work of the Stuttgart press was artistically subtler. Besides, only "a few new" pictures were involved, the rest were such as "for one reason or another are not suitable for Ars Sacra."²⁷ After some back and forth, the Müllers again traveled to Siessen in order at least to clarify procedures about future works. "As further discussed, we will in future take over the reproduction of all new Hummel originals."²⁸ The press urgently requested to leave the artistic production in the hands of a single publisher: "An artistic ability as important and still capable of further growth as that of Sister Innocentia belongs into the company of leading authors and artists and thus into the foremost, most respected publishing house for religious art, which in Germany is surely the 'Ars Sacra' Press."²⁹

Im Kreuzgarten: Maria Innocentia mit Kindern, 1934
In the cloister garden: Maria Innocentia with children, 1934

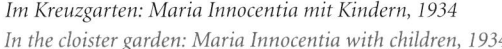

Manchmal scheint die Welt ganz fern. Maria Innocentia hört, wie das Kinderlachen leiser wird, als Reseles Lockenköpfchen hinter einem Meer von gelbem Weizen verschwindet. Es ist der 23. August 1934. In einer Woche wird sie die Erstprofess ablegen. Die Eltern werden kommen, Cenerl, Kätl, Ady und Franzl. Ein Jahr hat sie sie nicht gesehen. Sie wird den schwarzen Schleier nehmen, um die Augen vor den Eitelkeiten der Welt zu verschließen. Den Ring als Zeichen der Treue. Die brennende Kerze als Zeichen der Unsterblichkeit. Sie wird vor dem Altar ausgestreckt am Boden liegen als Zeichen ihrer vollkommenen Hingabe an Gott: „Ich, Schwester Maria Innocentia, gelobe und verspreche Gott, dem Allmächtigen, in freiwilliger Armut, jungfräulicher Keuschheit und klösterlichem Gehorsam zu leben, gemäß der Regel des Dritten Ordens des heiligen Franziskus und den Konstitutionen unserer Gemeinschaft."[30]

Maximiliane Müller schickte zur Professfeier zwei Bände über Fra Angelico nach Sießen, da sie wusste, wie sehr Maria Innocentia diesen italienischen Künstler liebte. In München war Ars sacra währenddessen vor ganz andere Probleme gestellt. Mit der Machtergreifung Hitlers gestaltete sich die Situation für den populär-katholischen Verlag zunehmend schwierig. Als sich das Ehepaar Müller an einem nationalsozialistischen Feiertag geweigert hatte, Hakenkreuzfahnen aus dem Fenster zu hängen, flatterte eine Androhung des zuständigen Blockwarts ins Haus. Eine linientreue Nachbarfirma ließ wissen, dass „es uns doch in der heutigen Zeit nicht angenehm sein konnte, mit einem ultramontanen, antinationalsozialistisch eingestellten Verlag unter einem Dache zu hausen".[31]

Bericht von Adolf Hummel zur Profess am 30. August 1934
Die Klosterkapelle, 1954
Über den Seitenaltären sind zwei Pastellbilder von Maria Innocentia aus dem Jahr 1940 zu sehen.
Adolf Hummel's account of the Profession ceremony of August 30, 1934
The convent chapel, 1954
Above the side altars, two crayon pictures by Maria Innocentia from 1940

Sometimes the world seems far away. Maria Innocentia hears Resele's laughter fading as the child's curly-head disappears in a sea of yellow wheat. It is the 23rd of August, 1934. A week from now she will have taken the next official step in her convent life, the Simple Profession. Her parents will come, Cenerl, Kätl, Ady, and Franzl. She has not seen them for a whole year. She will

*Erinnerungen für das Familienalbum;
Maria Innocentia mit M. Laura
Brugger, ihrer engsten Mitarbeiterin*
*Mementos for the family album;
Maria Innocentia with her closest
work associate M. Laura Brugger*

take the black veil, so as to shield her eyes from the vanities of the world, the ring as token of fidelity, the burning candle as symbol of immortality. She will lie prone on the floor in front of the altar, as a gesture of her complete submission to God. "I, Sister Maria Innocentia, swear and promise to God the Almighty, to live in voluntary poverty, virginal chastity, and monastic obedience, according to the rule of the Third Order of St. Francis and the constitution of our community."[30]

Maximiliane Müller sent two volumes about Fra Angelico to Siessen for the profession ceremony, knowing how much Maria Innocentia loved the Italian painter. In Munich, meanwhile, Ars Sacra was confronted with very different problems. Ever since Hitler's coming to power, the situation of the popular Catholic press had become increasingly precarious. When the Müllers refused, during a National Socialist holiday, to hang swastika flags out the windows, they promptly received a warning from the block warden. At the same time, a neighboring firm loyal to the party let them know that "in these times it could not but be awkward for them to have to share the same roof with an ultramontanist, anti-National-Socialist publishing house."[31]

*Maria Innocentia im Kreis ihrer Lieben; hinter ihr Maria Ludgera Anglsperger,
die Schwester der Mutter und Maria Possidia Hummel, die Schwester des Vaters*
*Maria Innocentia surrounded by her loved ones; behind her, Maria Ludgera
Anglsperger, sister of the mother and Maria Possidia, sister of the father*

Titelblatt (Entwurf) des „Hummel-Buchs", erschienen am 4. November 1934 im Stuttgarter Fink Verlag
Title page (sketch) of the Hummel-Buch, *published on November 4, 1934 by the Fink Press in Stuttgart*

Zum 50. Geburtstag des Vaters, 1934
For the father's fiftieth birthday, 1934

Das angekündigte Stuttgarter „Hummel-Buch" blieb Stein des Anstoßes. Abermals hatte das Kloster dem Fink Verlag weitere Bildrechte zugesagt. Die Abmachungen waren von Sießener Seite bisher nur mündlich erfolgt und man berief sich auf Unabhängigkeit in der Rechtevergabe. In München war man tief enttäuscht und zählte noch einmal die nötigen Aufwendungen auf, von denen nun andere profitieren würden: „Vorige Woche versandten wir z.B. 60'000 Hummelpostkarten als Gratismuster an Handlungen, augenblicklich versenden wir 70'000 Karten von beiliegendem Nachtwächterlein an Privatkunden, ebenso 70'000 farbige Bildchen, nächste Woche verschicken wir wiederum 60'000 Karten an Handlungen, das sind also von voriger Woche bis einschliesslich nächster Woche 190'000 Hummelpostkarten gratis und 70'000 farbige Bildchen ebenfalls gratis."[32] Das Schreiben schließt mit der dringlichen Bitte, „Stellung zu nehmen und uns zu sagen, ob wir endgültig damit rechnen können, dass unsere früheren Abreden in loyaler Weise eingehalten werden[33]". Unterzeichnet wurde nicht mehr von Josef Müller persönlich. Er war schwer erkrankt und starb am 30. Januar 1935 im Alter von 63 Jahren.

Der Fink Verlag feierte im Weihnachtsgeschäft 1934 mit seinem „Hummel-Buch" einen sensationellen Erfolg! Es enthielt eine bunte Mischung aus Kinderbildern und religiösen Motiven, begleitet von Dialekt-Gedichten der Wiener Volksschriftstellerin Margarete Seemann. Bodenständig und mit jungem Charme. „Eine Fünfundzwanzigjährige schickt dieses Buch in die Welt."[34] Unschuldig und heiter. „Das ist die hellherzige Künstlerin Sr. M. Innocentia (…). Die Sonne gehört als ein wesentliches zu ihr (…) Wie Musik und Licht ist alles, was sie schafft. Es ist kein Zug in ihren Bildern, der irgendeinem weh tun könnte."[35] In der Tat hatte diese heile Welt in jenen wenig fröhlichen Zeiten genau den populären Geschmack getroffen. Die erste Auflage, erschienen am 4. November 1934, war beinahe sofort vergriffen. Bis 1935 erschienen 20.000 Exemplare.[36]

Traueranzeige Josef Müller,
Verleger der Ars sacra
Obituary notice for Josef Müller,
publisher of the Ars Sacra Press

Stuttgart's projected *Hummel-Buch* remained a bone of contention. The convent had promised the Fink Press the rights to further pictures. Though the agreement had so far been only an oral one, Siessen insisted on their liberty to assign copyrights. The disappointment in Munich was great, and resulted in yet another enumeration of the expenditures from which others would now profit. "Last week, for example, we sent out 60,000 sample Hummel postcards to dealers, at the moment we are sending 70,000 cards of the enclosed little chimney sweep to private customers, along with 70,000 colored pictures, and next week we will send another 60,000 cards to dealers. That is altogether 190,000 free cards and 70,000 free pictures just between last week and next week."[32] The letter closed with the urgent request "to take a stance and tell us whether we can finally count on our past agreements being loyally adhered to."[33] The letter was no longer signed by Josef Müller in person. He was seriously ill and died on January 30, 1935, at the age of 63.

The sales success of the Fink Press's Hummel Book during the 1934 Christmas season was sensational. The book contained a colorful mixture of children's pictures and religious motifs, complemented by poems by the Viennese popular author Margarete Seemann. It was down to earth and filled with youthful charm – "A twenty-five-year-old sends this book into the world"[34] – innocent and cheerful – "This is the bright-hearted artist Sr. M. Innocentia (...). The sun is an essential part of her (...). Everything she creates is like light and music. There is not a single line in her pictures that could give pain to anyone."[35] The book's wholesome, intact world perfectly matched the popular taste at that less than cheerful time. The first edition, published on November 4, 1934, sold out almost instantly. By 1935, 20,000 copies had appeared.[36]

Arrest, 1933/1934
Captive, 1933/1934

Der Held, 1934
Retreat to Safety, 1934

Franz Goebel mit den Modelleuren Arthur Möller und Reinhold Unger im „Café am Dom" in München. Im Dezember 1934 schlägt damit die Geburtsstunde der M.I.Hummel-Figuren.
Franz Goebel with sculptors Arthur Möller and Reinhold Unger at the "Café am Dom" in Munich. This December 1934 event is the birth of M.I.Hummel Figurines.

Figuren-Unterseite mit Stempel
Goebel stamp on underside of figurine

Porzellan-Modelleur Arthur Möller (1886 – 1972)
Porcelain modeler Arthur Möller (1886 – 1972)

Anfang Dezember 1934 hielt ein aufmerksamer Vertreter einer fränkischen Porzellanmanufaktur ein solches „Hummel-Buch" in den Händen. Er war auf Durchreise in München und hatte – so sagt es die Legende – das Büchlein in einem Schaufenster entdeckt. In seiner Firma in Oeslau[37] bei Coburg, nahe der thüringischen Grenze, war man stets auf der Suche nach geeigneten Motiven, um sie in die Dreidimensionalität umzusetzen. Höchst angetan setzte er den Inhaber, Franz Goebel, von den einprägsamen Kinderbildern in Kenntnis. Seit 1929, dem Schwarzen Freitag an der New Yorker Börse und der folgenden Weltwirtschaftskrise, war die Situation der angesehenen Manufaktur schwierig geblieben. Mehr denn je hing das Überleben des Betriebs von neuen Ideen ab. Franz Goebel erkannte das unglaubliche Potenzial, das in den herzigen Hummel-Zeichnungen steckte, sofort. Kurz entschlossen fuhr er mit seinen beiden Modelleuren Arthur Möller und Reinhold Unger nach München, um dort mehr über die Künstlerin zu erfahren. Schließlich setzte man sich im gediegenen „Café am Dom" zusammen, um hier – so geht die Legende weiter – endgültig den Entschluss zu fassen, es mit einer Kinderfigurenserie zu versuchen.

Zurück in Oeslau machte sich ein Modelleur[38] sofort daran, einige der Hummel-Zeichnungen umzusetzen. Mitte Dezember 1934 stellte sich ein Herr[39] von der Firma W. Goebel in Sießen vor und wünschte Schwester Maria Innocentia zu sprechen. Einer ihrer Mitschwestern erzählte sie am selben Abend von dieser Unterredung: „… sie habe heute einen Besuch sehr schlecht behandelt. (…) Der sei mit einer Kiste voll Figürchen angekommen, die er ohne ihr Wissen ihrem Hummelbuch entnommen habe. Sie sei sehr aufgebracht gewesen und habe gesagt, sie werde nie ihre Erlaubnis geben, diese Figuren anzufertigen und in den Handel zu bringen (…). Nach langen Kämpfen sagte der Herr, von ihrem Jawort hinge es ab, ob er seine Fabrik schliessen und seine Angestellten arbeitslos entlassen müsse, bot dann an, einen Künstler anzustellen, der genau nach ihren Originalen arbeite, und keine Figur komme in den Handel, ehe sie nicht von Sr. M. Innocentia korrigiert wurde. Darauf ging die Künstlerin ein."[40]

Early in December of 1934, an alert salesman of a Franconian porcelain manufacturer got hold of the Hummel Book. While passing through Munich – or so the legend has it – he had discovered the booklet in a store window. His firm in Oeslau,[37] near Coburg, close to the Thuringian border, was always on the lookout for suitable motifs that could be rendered in three-dimensional

Entstehen einer „Mutterform"
The making of a "matrix mold"

Glasieren per Tauchbad im „Bottich"
Glazing by dipping in the "tub"

form. Strongly impressed, the salesman told the firm's owner, Franz Goebel, about these touching childhood images. The financial situation of the respected manufacturer had been critical ever since 1929's Black Friday at the New York stock exchange and the ensuing Depression. More than ever the survival of the firm depended on coming up with new ideas. Franz Goebel instantly recognized the enormous potential of these cute Hummel drawings. Without hesitating a moment, he traveled to Munich, together with his two modelers, Arthur Möller and Reinhold Unger, to learn more about the artist. Eventually they sat down at the popular "Café am Dom" ("Cathedral Café") – so the legend continues – to make their decision to try a series of children's figurines.

Returned to Oeslau, one of the modelers[38] instantly went to work converting a few of the Hummel drawings. In mid-December, 1934, a gentleman[39] of the firm W. Goebel presented himself at Siessen wishing to speak to Sr. Maria Innocentia. Late that day the latter told one of her fellow sisters about her conversation: "… that she had treated a visitor very badly today. (…) He had come with a box full of figurines, which he had taken from her Hummel book without her knowledge. She had been very upset and told the gentleman she would never permit these figures to be manufactured and sold (…). After lengthy arguments, the gentleman told her it would be up to her whether or not he had to close his factory and send his co-workers into unemployment. He then offered to hire an artist who would work exactly after her models and vowed that not one figure would come onto the market without having undergone correction by Sr. Maria Innocentia. Thereupon the artist gave her consent."[40]

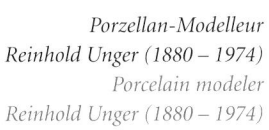

Porzellan-Modelleur
Reinhold Unger (1880 – 1974)
Porcelain modeler
Reinhold Unger (1880 – 1974)

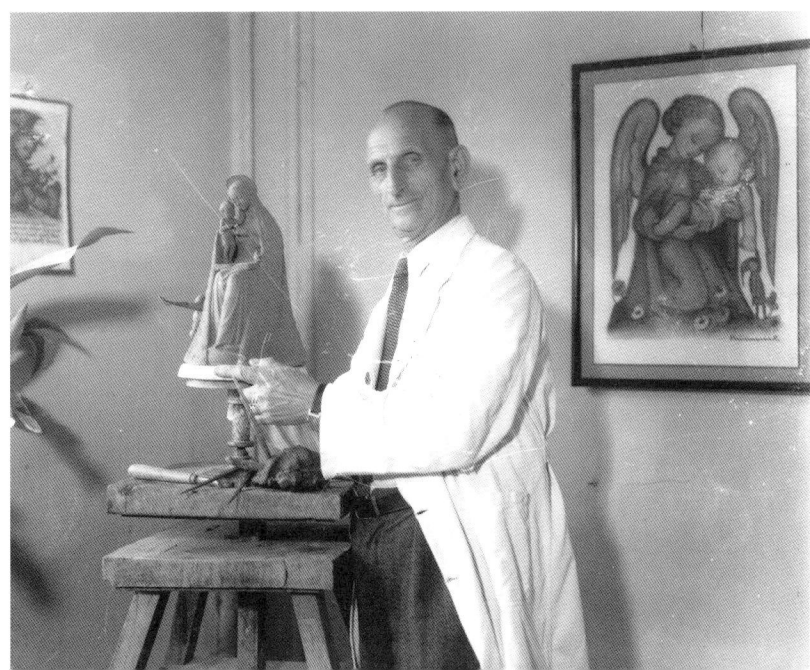

Besuch in Sießen: Franz Goebel (1904 – 1969) mit seiner erfolgreichsten Künstlerin (rechts)
Visit to Siessen: Franz Goebel (1904 – 1969) with his most renowned artist (right)

„Viel Freude in tausende von Menschenherzen hineinzutragen":
Weihnachtsbrief an die Familie, 1934
"To bring joy to the hearts of thousands":
Christmas letter to the family, 1934

Interessant an dem Bericht der Mitschwester ist auch ein kurzes Gespräch über finanzielle Dinge. Der Herr von der Firma Goebel habe mit ihr auch das Finanzielle besprechen wollen, aber sie habe ihn glatt abgewiesen mit den Worten: „Ich habe nichts mit Geld zu tun. Ich bin eine arme Franziskanerin und habe das Armutsgelübde abgelegt. Ich male. Alles andere geht die Vorgesetzten an."[41]

Wieder ist bald Weihnachten. Ein paar Tage der Stille. Es war viel dieses Jahr. Der Körper lässt es sie fühlen. Aber Schwester Laura sorgt sich doch allzu sehr über ihr blasses Aussehen! Maria Innocentia lächelt und beugt sich über den angefangenen Brief nach Hause. Diesmal hat sie ein wunderbares Geschenk! Sie wird schreiben, wie schön es ist, so vielen Leuten eine Freude gemacht zu haben. Von den unendlich vielen Briefen, die sie bekommen hat. Dass ihr tief empfundener Dank an die Eltern in über 15.000 Büchern Einzug in die Herzen der Menschen gehalten hat. Und sie wird schreiben von ihrer eigenen Kindheit und wie schön und warm Weihnachten war im Hummel-Haus.

Niemand konnte das vorhersehen. Im März 1935 präsentierte die Firma W. Goebel auf der Leipziger Frühjahrsmesse ihre ersten Hummel-Figuren. Franz Goebel berichtete hocherfreut von den „zahlreichen Orders"[42], die verbucht werden konnten. Er ahnt noch nichts von der Lawine, die er losgetreten hat. Noch weiß er nicht, dass in den nächsten Jahren ein deutlicher Aufschwung kommen wird. Dass man ihm gleich nach dem Krieg die Firma einrennen wird wegen seiner Hummel-Figuren. Dass die kleinen Figuren die Welt umrunden werden und ihre neue Heimat finden werden im Land der unbegrenzten Möglichkeiten. Dass es Streit geben wird um Millionengewinne. Dass auf sieben Jahrzehnte hin der Name Goebel untrennbar verbunden sein wird mit dem Signet „M.I. Hummel".

An interesting sidelight in this report by the fellow sister is a brief exchange about financial matters. The gentleman from the Goebel Company had wished to discuss the financial aspect with the artist, but she had brusquely cut him off with the words: "I have nothing to do with money. I am a poor Franciscan, who has made a vow of poverty. I merely paint. Everything else is the concern of my superiors."[41]

Soon it would be Christmas again, a time of quiet. Much has happened this year. She can feel the physical strain of it all. But Sister Laura is far too worried about her pallor! Maria Innocentia smiles and bends over the letter to her parents she has started. She has a wonderful present for them this time! She will write how lovely it is to have brought joy to so many people and about the innumerable letters she has received. That through the 15,000 copies of her book her deeply felt gratitude to her parents has entered into the hearts of countless people. And she will write about her own childhood, and how lovely and warm Christmas always had been at the Hummel home.

„Das kleine Geigerlein", 1935 modelliert von Arthur Möller, eine der ersten Figuren auf dem Markt
"The Little Fiddler," 1935 modelled by Arthur Möller, one of the very first figures on the market

No one could have foreseen it. In March of 1935 the firm of W. Goebel presented the first Hummel figurines at the Leipzig Spring Fair. Franz Goebel was overjoyed to report about the "numerous orders,"[42] he had been able to book. As yet he could not guess what an avalanche he was setting off. He did not yet know that already the next few years would bring a marked upswing. That right after the war people would besiege his firm about Hummel figurines. That the little figurines would travel around the world and find a new home in the land of unlimited opportunity. That there would be litigations concerning profits amounting to millions. That for seven decades to come the name Goebel would be inseparable from the signature "M.I. Hummel."

Geigenengel, 1934
Celestial Musician, 1934

Der Weihnachtsengel, 1934
Bearing Christmas gifts, 1934

M.I.Hummel®

Sammlerleidenschaft

Es geht die Geschichte, dass die Firma Goebel bei der Aufteilung der Besatzungszonen nicht zufällig auf amerikanischer Seite landete. Ausgerechnet bei Oeslau, heute Rödental, weist die Grenzlinie eine kleine Muldung in Richtung des ehemaligen DDR-Gebiets auf. Firmeninhaber Franz Goebel konnte sich nicht retten vor den GIs, die ihm jede noch so kleine Figur förmlich aus den Händen rissen.

Auch in Deutschland war die Begeisterung groß. Und nicht nur bei den Sammlern selbst, denn nach dem Krieg waren die begehrten Figuren ein lukratives Tauschobjekt, besser als bare Währung in einer Zeit, wo Lebensmittel und andere Naturalien kaum zu bekommen waren.

Seit jenen Zeiten ist die Anzahl der Liebhaber auf der ganzen Welt um ein Vielfaches gestiegen. 1977 wurde der „Goebel Collector's Club" gegründet – seit 1989 „M.I. Hummel Club" –, und bis ins neue Millenium hinein teilten über 200.000 Mitglieder weltweit ihre Begeisterung in großen Zusammenkünften, die abwechselnd in den USA und Europa stattfanden: in Look-Alike-Wettbewerben, wo Kinder wie Hummel-Figuren gekleidet werden, Informations- und Austauschmöglichkeiten in der clubeigenen Zeitschrift „Insights", Tauschbörsen und sozialen Engagements.

Und es gibt von der Mokkatasse bis zur Spieluhr ein reiches Angebot an Hummel-Artikeln, die jedes Liebhaberherz höher schlagen lassen.

Doch wo es um wertvolles Gut und bares Geld geht, wird auch kopiert und getäuscht. Fälschungen gab es von Anfang an, die erste soll bereits aus dem Jahr 1937 stammen. Noch Maria Innocentia selbst schrieb dankbar an Vater und Bruder, wie sehr sie deren unermüdlichen Einsatz gegen die unerlaubten Abbilder zu schätzen wusste. Manche Verwirrung entstand in den Kriegsjahren, wo in ungeklärter Rechtslage in Amerika nach den Ars-sacra-Vorlagen Figuren produziert wurden. So bietet bezeichnenderweise Filmheld Joseph Cotten seiner Partnerin Jennifer Jones in dem Film „Since you went away" von 1944 ausgerechnet eine dieser Fälschungen zum Geschenk an.

Apropos Kino: Der nostalgische Kontrast zum realen Leben, den die so berühmten Kinderfiguren verkörpern, ist bis heute gleichnishaftes Filmthema. Von der „Simpsons"-Folge bis zum Thriller haben sie ihren Auftritt. Unvergessen grandios in „About Schmidt" mit Jack Nicholson von 2002, stehen sie für eine illusorisch heile Welt, liebenswerte kleine Inseln einer sehnsuchtsvoll verlorenen Kindheit, Nestwärme und Heimat.

Collectors' Passion

The story goes that when Germany was divided into zones of occupation after the war, the Goebel Company did not wind up in the American Zone by accident. Exactly at Oeslau, now Rödental, the border forms a distinct little bulge into the territory of the former Russian Zone and later German Democratic Republic. Company owner Franz Goebel was positively swamped by GI's, who all but tore even the smallest figurine from his hands.

In Germany, too, the enthusiasm was tremendous. And not just among the collectors themselves; for after the war the beloved figurines were a lucrative object of barter, better than cash, at a time when groceries and produce were hard to come by.

Since then the number of Hummel fanciers has steadily grown world-wide. In 1977 the "Goebel Collector's Club" was founded – renamed the „M.I. Hummel Club" in 1989 – and up to the present century more than 200,000 members the world over shared their enthusiasm at gatherings that took place alternately in the U.S.A and in Europe; in look-alike contests, in which children are dressed as Hummel figures; in sources of information and opportunities for barter like the club journal *Insights*; in bartering marts and social engagements.

And the Hummel offering includes a rich variety of articles ranging from mocha cups to music boxes to captivate any fan's heart.

Naturally wherever there are valuables or cash, there will also be copying and counterfeiting. Forgeries existed from the beginning – the earliest are said to date from the year 1937. Maria Innocentia herself gratefully wrote to her father and brother, how much she appreciated their tireless struggle against the illicit copying. Confusion reigned especially during the war years, when, with the legal status being in limbo, figures were widely produced from Ars Sacra models in America. In the 1944 movie, "Since you went away," hero Joseph Cotten tellingly presents the heroine Jennifer Jones with one of these forgeries! Speaking of movies: to this day, the nostalgic contrast to real life, which the famous children's figurines suggest, is an emblematic motif in films ranging from the series "The Simpsons" to the occasional thriller. In "About Schmidt" with Jack Nicholson (2002), they stand in unforgettably grand manner for an illusory intact world, as lovable islets of a lost and longed-for childhood of security and home.

Die dunkle Zeit

Der Weg nach innen

The Dark Time – The Inward Path

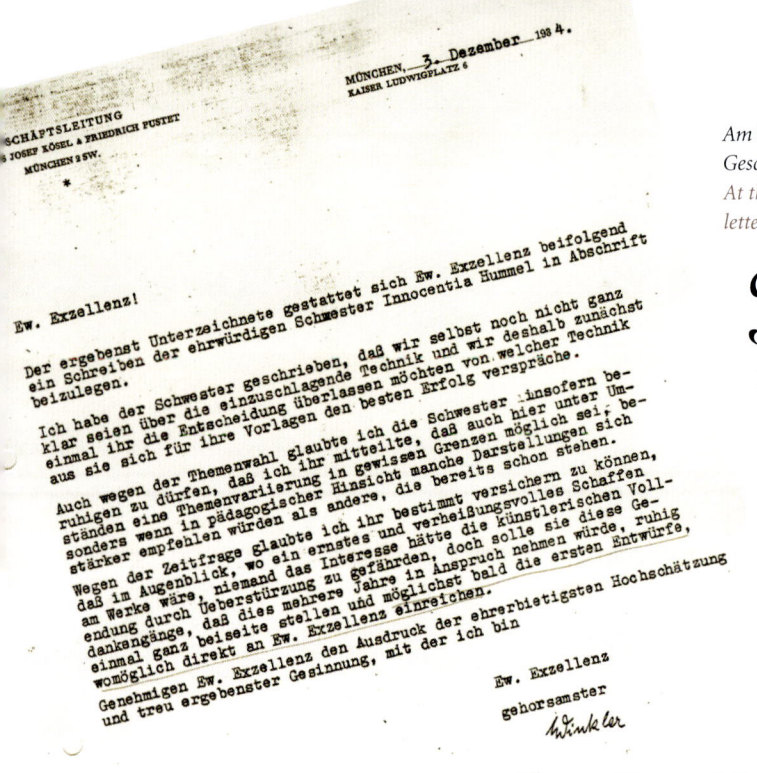

Am Beginn einer schwierigen Korrespondenz und eines künstlerischen Konflikts: Geschäftsbrief des Schulbibel-Verlegers Dr. Winkler an Bischof Michael Buchberger
At the start of a difficult correspondence and an artistic conflict: business letter from the publisher, Dr. Winkler, to Bishop Michael Buchberger

Anhänger mit Madonna von Maria Innocentias Rosenkranz
Pendant with Madonna from Maria Innocentia's rosary

„Tränen waren mein Brot bei Tag und bei Nacht; denn man sagt zu mir den ganzen Tag: ‚Wo ist nun dein Gott?‘ Das Herz geht mir über, wenn ich daran denke: wie ich zum Haus Gottes zog in festlicher Schar, mit Jubel und Dank in feiernder Menge. Meine Seele, warum bist du betrübt und bist so unruhig in mir? Harre auf Gott, denn ich werde ihm noch danken, meinem Gott und Retter, auf den ich schaue." (Psalm 42, 4-6)

Der Erfolg des „Hummel-Buchs" hatte nicht nur die Aufmerksamkeit kommerzieller Verwerter auf den Plan gerufen. Am 24. November 1934 war ein Schreiben seiner Exzellenz Dr. Michael Buchberger, des Hochwürdigsten Bischofs von Regensburg, an den Münchner Verlag Kösel & Pustet gegangen. Thema war die geplante Neuauflage der katholischen Schulbibel[1] für den süddeutschen Raum. Der Bischof drängte auf zeitgemäße Illustrationen und eine möglichst rasche Veröffentlichung, denn er fürchtete einerseits die zunehmend schwierige Lage für kirchenorientierte Verlage und andererseits, dass seinem Projekt eine gesamtdeutsche Einheitsschulbibel zuvorkommen könnte.[2] Eine Bestückung mit Hummel-Bildern würde eine weite Verbreitung des Werkes garantieren, denn „Schw. Hummel bzw. ihr Verlag hat auf Weihnachten einen ungeheuren Erfolg mit ihren Bildern gehabt – ein Beweis dafür, dass sie die Volksseele getroffen hat."[3]

Allerdings – und das kann nicht hoch genug eingeschätzt werden – war er einer der wenigen, der hinter der neuen Popularität die fähige Künstlerin sah und Maria Innocentia als solche verpflichten und fördern wollte: „Freilich bleibt zu beachten, daß es sich für unsere Zwecke um eine ernste und größere Aufgabe und Auffassung handelt als beispielsweise in dem Hummel-Buch."[4] Maria Innocentia reagierte erwartungsgemäß mit der „grössten Freude". Doch gleichzeitig zweifelte sie sehr, „dieser großen Arbeit schon gewachsen" zu sein. In aller

Bescheidenheit antwortete sie: „Ich will es einmal versuchen und mein ganzes Können daran setzen, die erwünschten Probebilder zu fertigen."⁵

Was für ein ehrgeiziger Auftrag für die 25-jährige Künstlerin! Etwa 20 Bilder aus dem Alten und 40 aus dem Neuen Testament sollten es sein.

Dr. Michael Buchberger, Bischof von Regensburg (1874 – 1961)
Dr. Michael Buchberger, Bishop of Regensburg (1874 – 1961)

My tears have been my meat day and night, while they continually say unto me, Where is thy God? When I remember these things, I pour out my soul in me; for I had gone with the multitude, I went with them to the house of God, with the voice of joy and praise, with a multitude that kept holiday. Why art thou cast down, O my soul? And why art thou disquieted in me? Hope thou in God, for I shall yet praise him for the help of his countenance." (Psalm 42:3-5)

The success of the *Hummel-Buch* had brought not only commercial interests into play. On November 24, 1934, a letter by his Excellency, Dr. Michael Buchberger, the Most Reverend bishop of Regensburg, had been sent to the Munich publishing house of Kösel & Pustet. The subject was the planned republication of the Catholic school bible[1] for the region of southern Germany. The bishop was anxious for it to have modern illustrations, as well as an early publication date, being concerned about both the increasingly precarious situation of church-oriented presses and the chance of his project being preempted by a uniform all-German bible.[2]

Illustrating the volume with Hummel pictures would guarantee a wide distribution, as "Sr. Hummel, or more precisely her publisher, had an immense success at Christmas with her pictures – proof that she has touched the soul of the nation."[3]

One should add that, greatly to his credit, the bishop was one of the few who could see the capable artist behind the popular novelty and wanted to engage and support Maria Innocentia as such: "It should be noted, to be sure, that ours is a greater and far more serious project and concept than found, for example, in the Hummel book."[4] As might be expected, Maria Innocentia responded with the "greatest delight." At the same time, however, she worried whether she was "as yet equal to so great a work." With due modesty, she replied: "I will make the attempt and apply all my ability to produce the desired trial pictures."[5]

Maria mit den sieben Schwertern, 1935/1936
Mother of Sorrows, 1935/1936

Frei in der Motivwahl und frei in der Ausführung, ein pädagogisches Werk, das maßgeblich sein konnte für ein paar Jahrzehnte. Der Regensburger Bischof hatte Maria Innocentia damit großes Vertrauen geschenkt. Gegen Ende ihrer Studienzeit in München war schon einmal ein Wettbewerb für dieses Projekt ausgeschrieben gewesen, an dem sie eigentlich hatte teilnehmen wollen. Doch dann hatte sie sich entschlossen, nach Sießen zu gehen. Der Wettbewerb scheiterte, denn kein einziger Entwurf der gut 20 Illustratoren hatte Gnade vor Bischof Buchbergers Augen gefunden.

Nun, zur Zeit dieses erneuten Angebots, stand Maria Innocentia unter massivem Druck. Sie war am Anfang ihres Ordenslebens. Nach ihrer Profess im Sommer 1934 hatte sie die künstlerische Leitung der Paramentenwerkstatt übertragen bekommen. Die Popularität ihrer Bilder bedeutete für die junge Schwester immer mehr Arbeit. Von München aus drängte Ars sacra mit Anregungen für neue Motive. Die Erstellung des Hummel-Buchs hatte enormen Einsatz von Maria Innocentia gefordert. Jedes Blatt, das im Probedruck von den Verlagen kam, musste beurteilt und gegebenenfalls korrigiert werden. Ebenfalls viel Zeit und Mühe würde die Bearbeitung der Figuren von der Firma Goebel in Anspruch nehmen. Maria Innocentia wusste um die Gefahr, die eine Festlegung auf die populären Motive in künstlerischer Hinsicht bedeutete. Bei der letztjährigen Tagung in Beuron war sie immer wieder darauf hingewiesen worden.

Nicht zu vergessen die Verantwortung, die auf Maria Innocentias Schultern spürbar wurde. Die wachsende Popularität der Hummel-Bilder bedeutete immer mehr finanzielle Rückenstärkung für die Klostergemeinschaft, besonders in diesen schwierigen Zeiten, als allen kirchlichen Orden, ganz besonders den Schulorden, ein eisiger Wind entgegenblies.[6] Es würde eine Entscheidung geben müssen.

Anfang April 1935 sandte Schwester Eligia Bischof Buchberger eine Absage. Die Künstlerin fühle sich der Sache nicht gewachsen. Man wolle sie stattdessen ab Mai für vier Aufbausemester nach München schicken, „von verschiedener Seite" nämlich „wurde dringend geraten, die Schwester weitere Studien machen zu lassen, denn trotz aller Begabung sei es notwendig, wieder etwas zu hören und zu sehen. So haben denn ihre Obern die Bestimmung getroffen, die Schwester Anfang Mai wieder nach München zu geben."[7]

Guter Hirte, 1933/1934
The Good Shepherd
(The Lord is My Shepherd), 1933/1934

Es ist vollbracht!, 1935/1936
It Is Finished!, 1935/1936

What an ambitious undertaking for a 25-year-old artist! She was to furnish 20 pictures from the Old and 40 from the New Testament, with freedom of choice regarding both motif and execution – a pedagogical work that would be authoritative for several decades to come. The bishop of Regensburg had thus put great confidence in Maria Innocentia. A competition for this project had, incidentally, been announced once before toward the end of her study period in Munich, and Berta had intended at the time to enter the contest. But then she had decided to go to Siessen. The competition had come to naught, as not a single submission from the more than 20 illustrators had found favor in Bishop Buchberger's eyes.

Now, at the time of the renewed offer, Maria Innocentia was under great pressure. She was standing at the beginning of her conventual life. After her First Profession in the summer of 1934, she had been assigned the artistic direction of the paraments workshop. Besides, the popularity of her pictures meant ever increasing work for the young sister. From Munich, Ars Sacra plied her with suggestions for new motifs. The production of the Hummel-Buch had demanded an enormous effort from Maria Innocentia. Every single sheet of page-proof that came from the presses had to be judged and, if need be, corrected. Checking the figurines for the Goebel Company would likewise require much time and energy. Maria Innocentia knew of the artistic risk that being pinned down to the popular motifs entailed: the congress at Beuron of the previous year had drawn attention to it again and again.

There was also the feeling of responsibility that was beginning to weigh on Maria Innocentia's shoulders. The growing popularity of the Hummel pictures signified increased financial support for the convent community, especially in these difficult times, when an icy wind had begun to blow against all ecclesiastical orders, especially the teaching orders.[6] A decision would have to be made.

Early in April of 1935, Sister Eligia sent Bishop Buchberger a cancellation notice. The artist, she wrote, did not feel up to it. She would instead be sent to Munich for four semesters of continued training. "Various sides" had "urgently advised to let the sister pursue additional studies, since regardless of talent it was imperative for her to hear and see something new again. Her superiors had therefore come to the decision to send the sister back to Munich by the beginning of May."[7]

Der abgewiesene Bischof war zutiefst gekränkt. Er wandte sich im Rückschreiben direkt an die Oberin des Klosters: „Ich kann Schwester Innocentia aus ihrem Versprechen nicht entbinden. (...) Die Künstler und die Lehrer der Kunst, die heute wirklich etwas geben können für eine echt kirchliche Kunst, sind sehr rar."[8] Trotz aller Versuche musste Bischof Buchberger schließlich doch auf die Hummel-Bibel verzichten. Noch im Juli 1935 hatte sich der Verlagslektor, Dr. Winkler von Kösel & Pustet, mit Maria Innocentia in München getroffen. „Nicht wenig überraschten die Äußerungen der Künstlerin, daß sie auf Zuraten Vieler sich für unfähig erklärte, den ihr gewordenen Auftrag durchzuführen und daß ihre Obern in dieser Richtung mitdirigierten."[9] Maria Innocentia hatte sogar einige Skizzen mitgebracht, die die begeisterte Zustimmung des Lektors fanden. Sie versprach, während ihres Münchner Studienaufenthalts daran weiterzuarbeiten, „zunächst als ganz privaten Versuch, weil sie sich eben als Ordensangehörige nicht ganz frei fühlt und anscheinend ihre Obern die Sache (...) ganz ad acta gelegt haben."[10]

Warum Maria Innocentia so offensichtlich davon abgehalten wurde, dieses Projekt zu übernehmen, bleibt ungeklärt. Sie hatte ihr persönliches Streben dem Gehorsam gegen die klösterliche Gemeinschaft untergeordnet. War es eine Entscheidung zugunsten der Auftragsarbeiten im bekannten Stil, deren Produktion einzuschränken man sich in diesen Zeiten auf lange Sicht kaum leisten konnte? Ob die Vorgesetzten befürchteten, die sensible junge Künstlerin würde niemals beides bewältigen können? Tatsache bleibt, dass hier entscheidende Weichen gestellt wurden.

Bibelszenen aus dem „Hummel-Buch":
Biblical scenes from the Hummel-Buch*:*

Gegrüßet seist Du, Maria!, 1934
Hail Mary, full of grace (Hail, O Favored One), 1934

Christi Geburt, 1934
The Birth of Christ, 1934

Vorsichtige Hinwendung zur Abstraktion; Bleistift- und Farbskizze zum gleichen biblischen Thema:
Linke Seite: Die Hochzeit zu Kana, 1935
Rechte Seite: Christus bei der Hochzeit zu Kana, 1935/1936
Tentative turn to abstraction; pencil and color sketches on the same biblical subject:
Left side: The Wedding at Cana, 1935
Right side: Christ at the Wedding at Cana, 1935/1936

The bishop, thus turned down, was deeply hurt. He sent his reply directly to the convent's Mother Superior: "I cannot release Sr. Innocentia from her promise. (...) The artists and teachers of art who today can really do something for a genuine ecclesiastical art are very few."[8] But despite all of his endeavors, Bishop Buchberger had to forgo the Hummel Bible at last. As late as July of 1935, Dr. Winkler, the chief lector of Kösel & Pustet, had met with Maria Innocentia in Munich. "It was not a little surprising to hear the artist state that, upon the advice of many, she declared herself unable to carry out the task offered to her and that her superiors were steering her in this direction."[9] Maria Innocentia had even brought some sketches along, which met with enthusiastic approval from the lector. She promised to continue working on these during her educational stay in Munich, "for the nonce as a purely private essay, since as a member of a religious order she does, of course, not feel completely free and her superiors have apparently put the matter (...) altogether to rest."[10]

It remains open to question why Maria Innocentia was so obviously kept from taking on this project. She had evidently subordinated her artistic aspirations to her obedience to the monastic community. Was it a decision in favor of the ongoing commissioned work in the recognized style, whose production one could not afford to curtail at this point? Did the superiors fear the delicate young artist would never be able to manage both tasks? In any case, a crucial change of course was being enacted here.

Die Flucht nach Ägypten, 1934
The Flight into Egypt, 1934

In Nazareth, 1934
In Nazareth, 1934

153

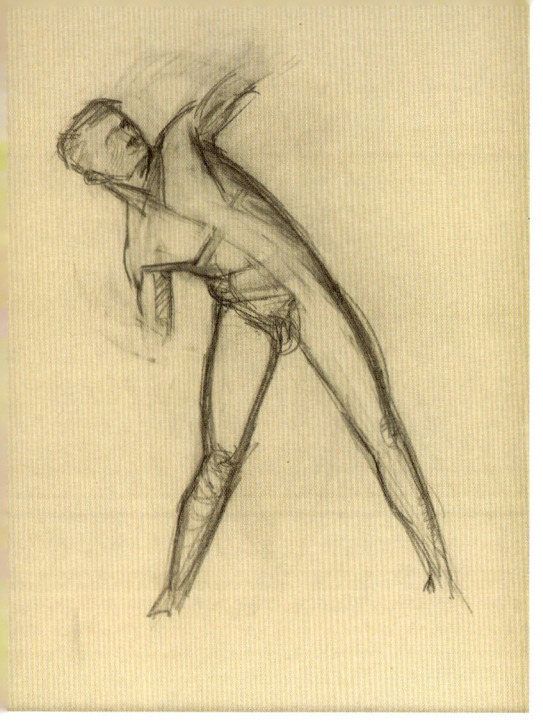

Vielleicht Maria Innocentias persönlichstes Werk: der Kreuzweg
Männlicher Akt, Bewegungsstudie, 1935/1936
Kreuzwegskizze, Jesus nimmt das Kreuz an, 1936
Jesus wird verurteilt, 1936

The Way of the Cross, perhaps Maria Innocentia's most personal work
Male nude: motion study, 1935/1936
Way of the Cross sketch: Jesus takes up the cross, 1936
Jesus is condemned, 1936

Und Maria Innocentias eigene Unsicherheit über ihre künstlerische Ausrichtung war derzeit groß genug. Die selbstbewusste Verve der früheren Studientage war einer verhaltenen Ernsthaftigkeit gewichen, das Bewusstsein um die Anforderungen gewachsen. Ob die Meisterin der naturnahen Darstellung fürchtete, sich allein auf unbekanntes Terrain zu begeben und an der Umsetzung idealer Werte zu scheitern? An den Ansprüchen des kunstsinnigen Bischofs, der etwas Bahnbrechendes von ihr erwartete?

Fortan wird sie sich gerade in ihrer religiösen Bildumsetzung immer wieder dem Vorwurf des „Kitschs" stellen müssen. Letzten Endes wird es zur Tragik der hochbegabten Künstlerin gehören, dass es ihr nicht gelingen wird, die beiden großen Sehnsüchte ihres Lebens – nach Gott und nach künstlerischer Freiheit – in wegweisender Qualität in Einklang zu bringen.

Das Kreuz tragen. Das Leben annehmen, wie es gegeben ist. In der Nachfolge Christi, Jahr um Jahr, Tag um Tag, Stunde um Stunde. Das Herz übervoll, möchte sie etwas Innigstes erarbeiten, ihrem Schmerz, ihrer Freude an ihrem Herrn und Gott Ausdruck verleihen. Er hat ihr die künstlerische Gabe geschenkt und die Leidenschaft dafür. Sie will einen Kreuzweg schaffen. 14 Stationen auf dem Weg nach Golgotha. Ein Kreuzweg ist Lebensarbeit. Sie wird ihn gehen und sie wird ihn malen, trotz allem. Ein gelebtes Gebet in diesen beiden Jahren ihrer Studienzeit. Im Zentrum der Bilder: das Kreuz. Schroff die dunklen Holzbalken. Massive gerade und bewegliche gebogene Linien überlagern sich. Meist sind es nicht mehr als zwei Akteure, um nicht abzulenken. Kühne, schnelle Striche formen die Körper. Sie nutzt die neuen Körperideale. Keine hungrigen Gestalten wie noch vor ein paar Jahren. Die Schergen strotzen vor Kraft, es sind die Siegerposen von den Modellen der Staatsschule, ein Speerwerfer als Henkersknecht, in wenigen Strichen, heftig, schwungvoll, fast grob auf das Papier gebannt.

Aus einem Skizzenheft, 1935/1936
From a sketchpad, 1935/1936

Besides, Maria Innocentia's own insecurity regarding her artistic direction was considerable at the time. The self-assured verve of her student days had yielded to a guarded earnestness, a growing awareness of the demands involved. Was she, so skilled in the rendering of images close to nature, afraid to venture unaided into unknown territory and perhaps to fail when it came to representing an ideal reality – and thereby to disappoint the art-loving bishop, who expected something innovative from her?

Particularly in her religious images she would hereafter time and again have to confront the charge of "kitsch." It will, in the end, be part of this highly gifted artist's tragedy that she will not succeed in reconciling her two profoundest longings – for God and for artistic freedom – with each other in a truly path-breaking degree.

To bear the cross, to accept life as it is given, in the Imitation of Christ, year after year, day by day, hour after hour. With a heart full to bursting, she longs to achieve something inmost that would express her sorrow, her joy in her Lord and God. He has given her the artistic talent. And the passion for it. She wants to create a Way of the Cross: fourteen stations on the way to Golgotha. A Way of the Cross is a life's work. She will walk it, and she will paint it, in spite of everything – as a lived prayer in these two years of study. At the center of the pictures will be the cross, its dark beams harsh, massive straight lines overlapped by mobile curved ones. For the most part no more than two actors, so as not to distract from the center. Bold, quick strokes compose the bodies, making use of the new physical ideal. No famished types, as still a few years ago: the executioners burst with strength, their victor's poses are those of the new models at the State School. One of the henchmen is a spear-thrower, dashed onto the paper with few, vehement strokes, spiritedly, almost crudely.

Aus der Fotovorlage komponiert:
Winterlicher Bergweg, 1935
Wintry mountain path
with photographic model, 1935

Ski Heil!, 1935
Good Skiing!, 1935

Etwa 50 Skizzen werden in diesen aufreibenden nächsten Jahren entstehen. Der Kreuzweg wird ihr vielleicht persönlichstes Werk werden, einzigartig und voll herber Abstraktion, aber nie vollendet.[11]

Wer in Sießen ahnte, wie sehr der Aufenthalt in München an Maria Innocentias Kräften zehren würde? Die Welt draußen hatte sich verändert. Von Anfang an, seit der Gründung der NSDAP, war klar gewesen, dass sich katholische Glaubenslehre und Nationalsozialismus nicht vertrugen. Deutschlands Katholiken, etwa ein Drittel der Bevölkerung, besaßen eigene Gesellschaftsstrukturen, unterhielten Vereine und Verbände, Gewerkschaften, Schulen, Krankenhäuser, Zeitschriften und Verlage. Um nicht an Einfluss zu verlieren, war Papst Pius XI. – trotz seiner grundsätzlichen Verurteilung des „Rassegedankens" – bereit, den Nationalsozialisten Zugeständnisse zu machen. Das Reichskonkordat 1933 sollte die wechselseitigen Rechte und Pflichten im Reichsgebiet besiegeln, und entgegen der vormals strikt anti-nationalsozialistischen Haltung ging nun aus Rom die Direktive an die deutschen Bischöfe, Treue gegen die „gottgesetzte Obrigkeit"[12] zu wahren. Der größere Teil der Kirchenoberen versuchte sich nun auf leisen diplomatischen Wegen[13] und Hitler hatte zunächst sein Ziel erreicht. Gleichzeitig aber war er entschlossen, die lästige Einflussnahme der Kirchen systematisch und rigoros zurückzudrängen und durch eigene Heilsverheißungen zu ersetzen. Gerade die Klöster waren ihm ein Dorn im Auge, galten sie doch als „Keimzellen" des Glaubens.[14] Wo es nur ging, begannen Schikanen in Form von Verwaltungshürden, Steuererhebungen, Diskriminierungen. Übergriffe auf Geistliche häuften sich.[15]

Maria Innocentias Mutter, Viktoria Hummel, berichtet, ihre Tochter habe trotz aller Freude an der Kunst und der Weiterbildung in ihrem zweiten Studium schwer an dem Druck des Hitlerregimes gelitten.[16]

Some fifty sketches will come into being during these exhausting two years. The Way of the Cross will turn out to be her perhaps most personal work, unique in its austere abstraction, but never completed.[11]

Who in Siessen had any inkling how much the stay in Munich would sap Maria Innocentia's energies? The world outside had changed. Ever since the founding of the NSDAP, it had been plain that the Catholic faith and the National Socialist ideology would not be compatible. Germany's Catholics, about one third of the total population, had their own separate social structures: they maintained clubs and associations, trade unions, schools, hospitals, journals and publishing houses. In spite of his principal condemnation of the "race concept," Pope Pius XI had been willing to make concessions to the Nazis, so as not to lose influence. The Reich Concordat of 1933 was to seal the mutual rights and obligations within the German Reich, and in lieu of Rome's previous, strictly anti-Nazi position, the new directive to the German bishops was to maintain loyalty to "divinely ordained authority."[12] The majority of the church princes were thereupon content with mild diplomatic gestures,[13] and Hitler had attained his immediate goal. At the same time, however, he was resolved to repress the irksome influences of the churches systematically and rigorously and to replace them with salvational promises of his own. Especially the monasteries, regarded as "germ cells" of the faith,[14] were a thorn in his side. Harassments cropped up wherever possible: administrative hurdles, special taxes, discriminations. Attacks on the clergy multiplied.[15]

Viktoria Hummel, Maria Innocentia's mother, recalled that despite her delight in art and in her continued education during her second course of studies, her daughter had suffered greatly under the pressures of the Hitler regime.[16]

Häschen mit Blumenkorb, 1937/1938
Little Rabbit with Flowers, 1937/1938

Plakatentwurf für das Künstlerbedarfsgeschäft Adrian Brugger, 1936
Poster sketch for the Adrian Brugger art supply store, 1936

München war 1933 zur „Hauptstadt der Deutschen Kunst" ernannt worden. Hier gedachte der ehemals erfolglose Postkartenmaler Hitler die Leitlinien für eine neue Ästhetik auszugeben. Noch im Jahr der Machtergreifung war mit pompösen Feierlichkeiten der Grundstein für das „Haus der Deutschen Kunst" gelegt worden. Funktional sollte das Gebäude den 1931 abgebrannten Glaspalast ersetzen, doch dieser erste Monumentalbau des jungen Regimes lag dem Führer besonders am Herzen. In seiner Lieblingsstadt sollte ein grandioser „Tempel deutscher Kunst" im klassizistischen Stil entstehen.[17] Hitler hatte bei jener Grundsteinlegung angekündigt, der NS-Staat werde zukünftig alle künstlerischen Belange dirigieren.

Der Treue des Staatsschul-Leiters für angewandte Kunst konnte er sich sicher sein. Die steile Karriere des Professors Richard Klein war untrennbar mit dem Aufstieg der Nationalsozialisten verbunden. Klein diente dem Regime als eine Art Chefdesigner für NS-Embleme. Kaum eine Großveranstaltung, wo er nicht zur Propagandaausstattung beitrug. Sein außerordentlich geschätztes Talent: einschlägige Symbole einprägsam in Szene zu setzen, vom Werbeplakat bis zur Ehrenmedaille. 1935 wurde Klein neben seiner Position als Direktor der Staatsschule zum „Reichskultursenator" ernannt und 1936 zum „Präsidialrat der Reichskammer der bildenden Künste".[18]

Kunst ausüben und verkaufen durfte nur, wer in der Bürokratie der Nationalsozialisten erfasst und für kompatibel befunden wurde. Ars sacra musste im Mai 1935 die Klosterverwaltung um den Nachweis ersuchen, dass Maria Innocentia bei der Reichskammer der bildenden Künste (RBK) gemeldet sei. „Jeder Künstler muss sich nämlich hier zwangsweise anmelden."[19] Eine fehlende Mitgliedsbescheinigung war faktisch mit einem Berufsverbot gleichzusetzen, da das Veräußern eines Werkes damit strafbar wurde. Dies war eine effektive Methode, künstlerisches Wirken im Sinne des Regimes zu steuern. Der Aufnahme in die RBK für Maria Innocentia wurde stattgegeben.

Wappen der „Hauptstadt der Bewegung" München, Entwurf von Richard Klein
Coat of arms of Munich as the "capital of the movement," design by Richard Klein

Munich had been named the "capital of German art" in 1933. Here the one-time hapless postcard painter Hitler planned to promulgate the guidelines of a new aesthetic. In the very year of his coming to power, the cornerstone for the "House of German Art" had been laid in a pompous ceremony. In practical terms the building was meant to replace the Glass Palace that had burned down in 1931; but as the first of the young regime's monumental structures, it was especially close to the "Führer's" heart. A grandiose classicistic "temple of German art" was to arise in his favorite city.[17] During the cornerstone ritual, Hitler had proclaimed that in future the NS state would direct all artistic concerns.

Lieber Besuch aus Massing: Maria Innocentia und ihre Eltern, August 1937
Cherished visitors from Massing: Maria Innocentia with her parents, August 1937

He could be assured of the loyalty of the head of the State School for Applied Art. The steep career of Professor Richard Klein was closely linked to the rise of the National Socialists. Klein served the regime as a kind of designer-in-chief of Nazi emblems. Nary a big party event where he did not contribute to the propaganda get-up. His special, much appreciated skill: staging appropriate symbols in an impressive manner, whether in the form of campaign posters or that of honor medals. In 1935, Klein was appointed "Reich Senator for Culture" alongside his post as director of the State School and, in 1936, "Presiding Councilor" of the "Reich Chamber of Pictorial Arts."[18]

Only artists who were registered in the Nazi bureaucracy and found to be compatible were allowed to practice and sell art. In May of 1935, Ars Sacra had to request proof from the convent administration that Maria Innocentia was on file with the Reich Chamber of Pictorial Arts (RBK), inasmuch as "every artist is forced to register."[19] Lack of a membership certificate was tantamount to a professional ban, as the sale of any work became a punishable offense. It was an effective way of keeping artistic production under the thumb of the regime. Maria Innocentia's admission to the RBK was approved.

Ex Libris A. Hummel, 1935/1939
Ex Libris A. Hummel, 1935/1939

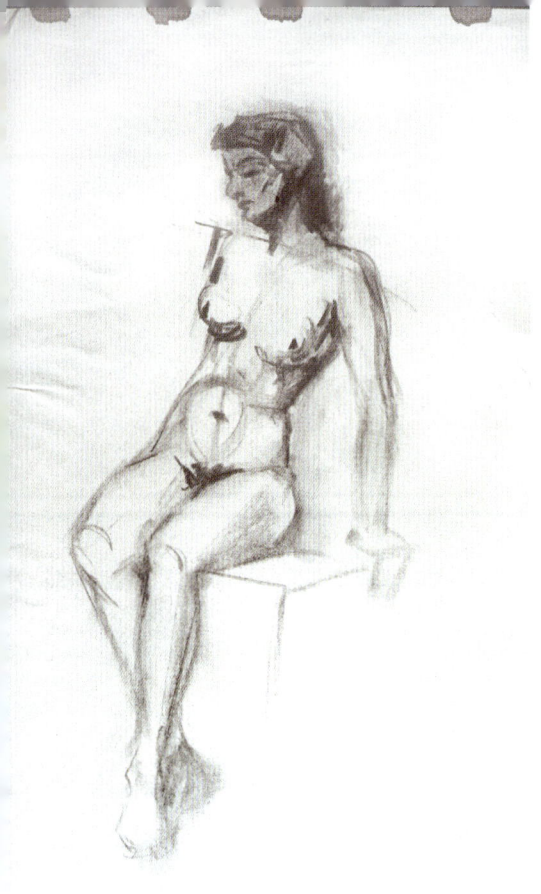

Weiblicher Akt, 1927/1936
Female nude, 1927/1936

Gloxinien im Topf, 1935/1936
Gloxinia pot, 1935/1936

Über Maria Innocentias zweite Studienzeit in „der Hauptstadt der Bewegung" ist wenig bekannt. Ihre Briefe nach Massing, die sie nun wieder häufiger schickte, geben nicht viel Aufschluss. Sie musste damit rechnen, dass Postsachen in fremde Hände gelangen könnten. Man kann vermuten, wie schwierig die Situation für sie damals war. Sie war auf sich gestellt. Sie konnte sich niemandem anvertrauen, außer vielleicht einigen Mitschwestern im Heim der Familienschwestern in der Blumenstraße, wo sie wieder wohnte, oder jemandem, der aus der Familie zu Besuch kam.

Der Blick muss sich nach innen wenden. Es ist nicht mehr das schnelle Erfassen, was Maria Innocentia interessiert. Nicht mehr das Spiel der Farben im flirrenden Licht. Der helle Untergrund des Papiers für die lichten Stellen. Der flüchtige Augenblick. Die kokette Pose des Modells. Nicht mehr der sorglose Pinselstrich, nicht mehr Leichtigkeit und Transparenz. Stattdessen vorsichtig ausloten, Tiefen ergründen. Bis dahin, wo lichtschluckende Stille ist. Arrangierte Blumen in Töpfen und Vasen: Die Farben sind gedämpft, gesättigt. Es bleibt wenig freie Fläche, die Gegenstände bekommen eine erdenschwere Dichte. Kopfstudien von alten Menschen, jungen Frauen, Männern mit Bart: Mit Bleistift oder Kohle die Physiognomie der Gesichter blockhaft erfasst, derselbe Kopf von oben, von unten, von den Seiten. Studieren, wie sich die Linien verkürzen, wie sich die Schädelknochen abzeichnen. Männliche Akte in kraftvollen Posen, wie es dem Geschmack der Zeit entspricht.

„Ich sage zu Gott, meinem Fels: ‚Warum hast du mich vergessen? Warum muss ich trauernd umhergehen, von meinem Feind bedrängt?' Wie ein Stechen in meinen Gliedern ist für mich der Hohn der Bedränger; denn sie rufen mir ständig zu: ‚Wo ist nun dein Gott?'" (Psalm 42, 10-11)

Not much is known about her second course of studies in the "capital of the movement." Her letters to Massing, which she now wrote again more frequently, reveal little, as she had to reckon with her mail getting into the wrong hands. One can guess how difficult things must have been for her. She was on her own. She could confide in no one, except perhaps a few fellow sisters at the Sisters of the Holy Family on Blumenstrasse, where she lodged again, or someone from the family coming to visit her.

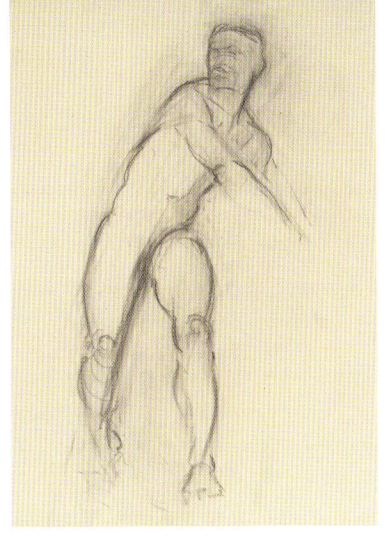

*Männlicher Akt,
Bewegungsstudie, 1935/1936*
Male nude, motion study, 1935/1936

*Kopfstudie eines Mannes und
Porträt eines Greises, 1935/1936*
Head sketch of a man and
Portrait of an old man, 1935/1936

Her gaze would turn inward. Maria Innocentia is no longer interested in the quick registering of things, the play of colors in a flickering light, the use of white space for the bright spots, the fleeting moment, the coquettish pose of the model. No longer for her the carefree brush stroke, the lightness and transparency. Instead, a careful plumbing, a probing of depths, all the way down to where silence engulfs all light. Flowers arranged in pots and vases, the colors muted, sated. There are few open spaces: objects acquire an earthen density. Head studies of old people, young women, bearded men: the physiognomy of the faces done block-like with pencil or charcoal, the same head from above, below, the sides. She studies how the lines foreshorten, how the skull bones appear in outline. Male nudes also in powerful athletic poses, as the taste of the time dictates.

"I will say unto God my rock, 'Why hast thou forgotten me? Why go I mourning because of the oppression of the enemy?' As with a sword in my bones, mine enemies reproach me; while they say daily unto me, Where is thy God?"
(Psalm 42:9-10)

Kopfstudien einer alten Frau und Porträt eines Mannes, auf die Hand gestützt, 1935/1936
Head sketch of an old woman and Portrait of a man leaning on his arm, 1935/1936

Hirsch an der Quelle, 1935/1936
Stag at a spring, 1935/1936

Tiere auf der Weide, 1935/1936
Animals in the pasture, 1935/1936

Liegende Katze, 1935/1936
Stretched-out cat, 1935/1936

Es weht ein anderer Wind als früher. Heroisches und Monumentales hat Konjunktur. Maria Innocentia probt den Rückzug. Arbeitet viel. Unverfängliches. Bukolische Szenen und musizierende Gruppen in antiken Gewändern. Religiöse Kunst ist nicht gern gesehen. Wenn, dann Themen aus dem Neuen Testament. Den Kreuzweg. Einmal malt sie einen Hirsch. Einfach einen trinkenden Hirsch an der Quelle. Wer weiß hier schon, dass es im „jüdischen" Alten Testament heißt: „Wie der Hirsch lechzt nach frischem Wasser, so lechzt meine Seele, Gott, nach dir. Meine Seele dürstet nach Gott, nach dem lebendigen Gott. Wann darf ich kommen und Gottes Antlitz schauen?" (Psalm 42, 2-3)

Ein ehemaliger Kommilitone beschreibt Maria Innocentia als „sehr zurückgezogen, introvertiert, immer gütig und freundlich".[20] Man habe sie gerngehabt. Sie sei fleißig und sehr begabt gewesen. Eine andere Studienkollegin erzählt, sie habe sich gewundert, dass Maria Innocentia „diese Kinderbilder" zeichnete, von einer Ordensschwester habe sie sich vielmehr religiöse Motive erwartet.

An der Staatsschule ist sie eine der Ältesten. „Die Hummel"! Jeder weiß, wer sie ist und dass sie schon so erfolgreich ist mit ihrer „Volkskunst". Sie fällt auf mit der Schwesterntracht. Sie spürt freundliche Neugier einerseits und Misstrauen andererseits. Sie hat wenig Kontakt zu den Mitstudenten. Auf Klassenfotos ist sie nicht zu sehen. Am Sonntag geht sie mit einer Kandidatin zur Messe in Sankt Michael, um Pater Rupert Mayer predigen zu hören. Dort wird jeder beobachtet, denn die Gestapo hat sich in der übervollen Kirche positioniert. Aber die Nazis haben es trotz seiner aufrührerischen Reden bisher noch nicht gewagt, den populären Pater verhaften zu lassen.

A different wind is blowing than before: what sells is the heroic and monumental. Maria Innocentia retrenches. She works a lot, does harmless things: bucolic scenes and musical groups in antique dress. Religious art is not welcome; if at all, then scenes from the New Testament. The Way of the Cross. One time she paints a stag, simply a stag drinking at a spring. Who, after all, would know here what the "Jewish" Old Testament says: "As the hart panteth after the water brooks, so panteth my soul after thee, O God. My soul thirsteth for God, for the living God: when shall I come and appear before God?" (Psalm 42:1-2)

Christkind mit Ochs und Esel, 1935/1936
(nachträglich mit „BH" signiert)
Infant Christ with ox and ass, 1935/1936
(signature "BH" added later)

A former fellow student describes Maria Innocentia as "quite withdrawn, introverted, always kind and friendly."[20] She was well liked. Hard-working and very gifted. Another colleague told how she was surprised that Maria Innocentia drew "these children's pictures": she would have expected a lot more religious motifs from a convent sister.

She is one of the oldest at the State School. "The Hummel!" Every one knows who she is and that she is already so successful with her "folk art." She stands out because of her habit. She senses friendly curiosity on the one hand and mistrust on the other. She has little contact with the other students. She does not appear on class photos. On Sundays she attends mass at St. Michael's, together with a candidate, to hear Father Rupert Mayer preach. Every one there is being observed: the Gestapo has stationed itself in the overcrowded church. But despite his seditious speeches, the Nazis have as yet not dared to arrest the popular priest.

Segelboote am Ufer, 1935
Seelandschaft, 1935
Sailboats on the Shore, 1935
Lakeside, 1935

Vom 18. bis 20. August 1936, in ihren Semesterferien, besuchte Maria Innocentia zusammen mit Schwester Laura die Porzellanfabrik Goebel in Oeslau. „Frohe Tage der Fa. Goebel in Oeslau" jubelte die örtliche Zeitung. „Anfang voriger Woche weilte (...) Schwester Innocentia aus Kloster Sießen für kurze Zeit in der Porzellanfabrik, um hier den Werdegang der nach ihren Zeichnungen geschaffenen wundervollen ‚Hummelfiguren' aus eigener Anschauung kennenzulernen. (...) Außer der Bewunderung für ihr großes künstlerisches Können ist es vor allem das Gefühl der Dankbarkeit, welches die in der Porzellanfabrik tätigen Männer und Frauen ihr entgegenbringen. Weiß doch jedermann im Betrieb, daß der seit wenigen Jahren eintretende, sich immer mehr geltend machende gewaltige Aufschwung im Beschäftigungsgrade der Firma neben der erhöhten Kaufkraft der Bevölkerung zu einem Großteil dem unermüdlichen schöpferischen Wirken der jungen Künstlerin aus dem Schwabenland zu verdanken ist."[21] Maria Innocentia äußerte sich nach ihrer Rückkehr nach Sießen sehr berührt von der Begeisterung der Arbeiter, die ihr zur Begrüßung und zum Abschied stehenden Beifall bekundet hatten.

Das vierte Semester in München geht seinen Gang. „Ich bin wieder so ziemlich im Geschirr", schreibt Maria Innocentia. „Male und pinsle halt drauflos, damit ich ‚der Welt' Besseres vorbringen kann. Ich hoffe, dass dieses Semester mein letztes hier ist."[22] Eines Tages hallen scharfe Schritte in den Gängen der Staatsschule wider. Alles ist in Hektik. Der Führer sei da! Er habe sich von Professor Klein porträtieren lassen und wolle nun die Klassenräume besichtigen! Die Studenten werden ihm der Reihe nach vorgestellt. Von einem aufgeregten Mädchen mit blonden Locken lässt er sich einige Arbeiten zeigen. Er treibt Konversation, lobt hier, kritisiert dort. Als er vor Maria Innocentia steht, wird sie ihm von Klein als „die berühmte Hummel" vorgestellt. Ohne ein Wort dreht er ihr den Rücken zu und verlässt mit seinem Tross den Raum. Später wird Maria Innocentia im Schwesternheim ganz verstört von seinen Augen berichten, einen Moment lang habe er ihr ins Gesicht geschaut.[23]

On August 20-22, 1936, during her summer vacation, Maria Innocentia, accompanied by Sister Laura, visited the porcelain factory Goebel in Oeslau. "Happy days for the Goebel Co. in Oeslau," the local paper rejoiced. "Early last week, Sister Innocentia of Convent Siessen (...) paid a brief visit to the porcelain factory in order to get to know the process of recreating the wonderful 'Hummel figures' from her drawings by direct observation. (...) Besides their admiration for her great artistic skill, it is above all feelings of gratitude that the men and women working at the factory have for her. For everyone in the firm knows that, apart from the populace's increased purchasing power, the tremendous employment growth evident in the company for the past few years is due in large measure to the tireless creative labors of the young artist from Swabia."[21] After her return to Siessen, Maria Innocentia expressed herself as greatly touched by the enthusiasm of the workers, who had both welcomed and bidden her farewell with standing ovations.

Porzellanmaler beim Dekorieren einer Hummel-Figur
Porcelain painter decorating a Hummel figurine

Figuren bei der Einfahrt in die Zugschmelze
Figurines entering the melting kiln

Die Figuren werden in Brennkapseln eingesetzt.
Figurines are put into saggars.

The fourth semester in Munich got underway. "I am pretty much back in harness," Maria Innocentia wrote, "painting and daubing away so that I can bring forth better things for 'the world.' I hope that this semester will be my last."[22] One day clanging steps echo through the hallways of the State School. Everybody is in an uproar: the "Führer" has come! He had himself portrayed by Professor Klein and now wants to inspect the classrooms! The students are presented to him one after the other. A flustered girl with blonde curls is allowed to show him some of her work. He makes conversation, praises here, criticizes there. When he comes before Maria Innocentia, she is introduced to him by Klein as "the famous Hummel." Without a word Hitler turns his back on her and leaves the room with his entourage. Later on Maria Innocentia would speak full of consternation about his eyes, how for one moment he had looked into her face.[23]

Garnierer bei der Arbeit
Assembling a figurine

Staatsschule für angewandte Kunst München

Das Jahr 1936 ist ein Jahr der Kriegserprobung. Das deutsche Expeditionskorps „Legion Condor" verwüstet aufseiten des aufständischen „Generalissimus" Francisco Franco die baskische Kleinstadt Guernica. Es ist das Jahr, in dem der Vertrag mit Mussolini die „Achse Berlin-Rom" begründet und Japan für den möglichen Kriegsfall als Bündnispartner des Deutschen Reichs gewonnen wird. Es ist andererseits das Jahr der demonstrativen Zurschaustellung einer sportlich-sauberen Nazi-Politik, da die Welt auf die Olympischen Spiele im herausgeputzten Berlin blickt.

Mitte November des Jahres erkrankte Maria Innocentia schwer an einer schlimmen Bauchgrippe mit „bedrohlicher, sehr schwerer Darmblutung".[24] Sobald sie wieder transportfähig war, wurde sie mit dem Auto nach Sießen geholt. Weihnachten musste sie auf der Krankenstation verbringen. „Ich sehe mein Leben als ein Neugeschenktes an", schrieb sie nach Massing. Es gehe „aufwärts", „doch für meine Verhältnisse (als Renngaul) viel zu langsam."[25] Dennoch beendete sie ihr Studium im April 1937 wieder mit Höchstnote: „Schwester Maria Innocentia ist ein sehr sensibler künstlerischer Mensch und hat sich durch großen Fleiß ein schönes Können angeeignet. Für das angestrebte Lehrziel, die Ausbildung in Malen, Zeichnen und Bildkomposition wird die Gesamtnote I erteilt."[26]

*Zeugnis mit „Gesamtnote 1"
und dem Stempel der nationalsozialistischen Bürokratie
Diploma with "overall grade of 1 [A]"
and rubber stamp of the Nazi bureaucracy*

The year 1936 is a year of testing for war. The German expeditionary corps "Legion Condor" devastates the small Basque town of Guernica in support of the insurgent "generalissimo" Francisco Franco. It is the year in which the treaty with Mussolini establishes the "axis Berlin-Rome" and Japan is won as a potential war ally of the German Reich. Alternatively it is the year of the ostentatious display of athletically "clean" Nazi politics, as the world watches the Olympic Games in a tricked-out Berlin.

In mid-November of that year Maria Innocentia succumbed to a severe intestinal flu with "ominous, very heavy intestinal bleeding."[24] As soon as she was capable of being transported, she was taken by car back to Siessen, where she once again spent Christmas in sickbay. "I regard my life as newly given to me," she wrote to Massing. Things were "coming along," "but for me (being a racehorse) much too slowly."[25] Nevertheless she finished her studies in April of 1937, once again with highest marks. "Sister Maria Innocentia is a very sensitive artistic person and by great industry has acquired a fine skill. For attaining her educational objective, i.e., training in painting, drawing and pictorial composition, she is assigned the overall grade of 1 [A]."[26]

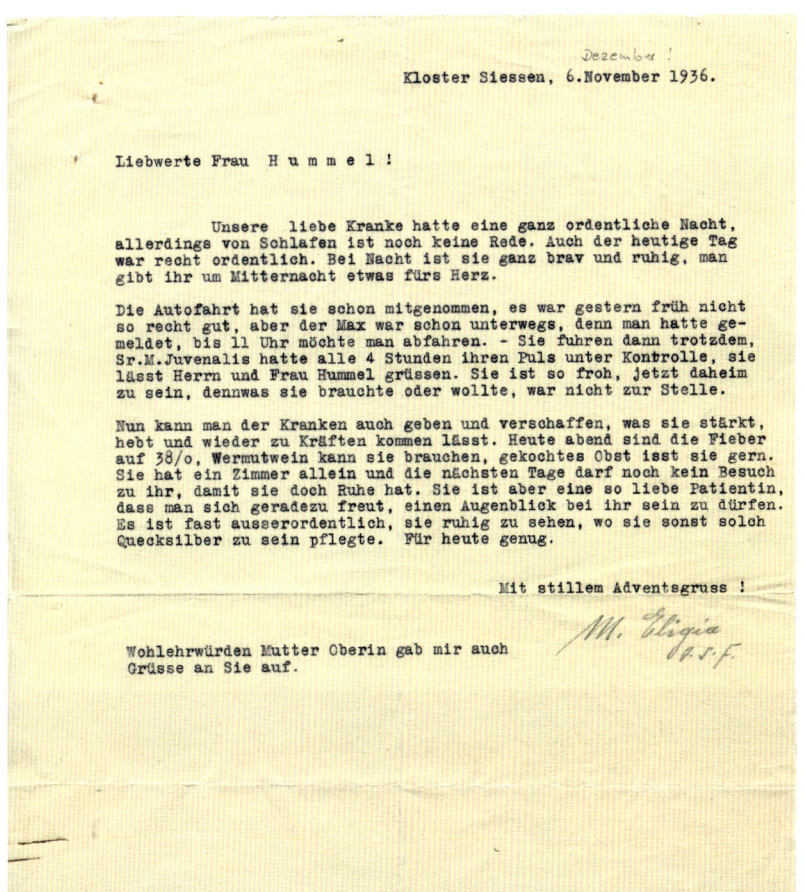

Besorgte Informationen an die Eltern über den Zustand der Kranken

Anxious reports to the parents about Maria Innocentia's illness

Nationalsozialistische Hetze: Zeitungsartikel aus dem nationalsozialistischen Blatt „Der SA-Mann", März 1937
Nazi smear campaign: article from the Nazi journal Der SA-Mann, *March 1937*

Zeitungen aus dem nationalsozialistischen Verlag Fritz Eher Nachf.
Newspapers from the Nazi press, Successors of Fritz Eher

Ein paar Wochen zuvor hatte ihretwegen im Sprechzimmer von Professor Klein eine sonderbare Konferenz stattgefunden. Grund hierfür war ein Artikel im „Kampfblatt der Obersten SA-Führung der NSDAP", dem „SA-Mann", gewesen. Das Blatt hatte am 20. März 1937 zu einem folgenschweren Schlag gegen Maria Innocentia und ihre „Kinderszenen" ausgeholt: „unzählige Abwandlungen desselben Typs wasserköpfiger und klumpfüßiger Wesen, denen zwecks innigen Humors stets der Rockaufhänger und die Stiefelstrippe der zerrissenen Schuhe ‚raushängt. (…) Nein, das ‚lieb' Vaterland' mag nicht ruhig sein, wenn man Dreckspatzen als Staatsjugend darstellt und an Dinge rührt, die ihm heilig sind. (…) In den Reihen deutscher Künstler ist für solche kein Platz, die zur Ausübung ihrer verantwortungsvollen Tätigkeit die erforderliche Zuverlässigkeit und Eignung nicht besitzen."

Lieb Jesulein, magst ruhig sein

Dr. Herbert Dubler, der Schwiegersohn des verstorbenen Josef Müller und neuer Verlagsleiter von Ars sacra, war entschlossen zu retten, was zu retten war: „Es gibt gar viele Fälle, wo die klösterliche Künstlerin sich nicht verteidigen kann – darf; nun ist doch der Verleger dazu da, für seine Produktion einzutreten. Wenn ich etwas herausgebe, so halte ich meine Haut dafür hin, wenn es sein muss."[27] Noch am Erscheinungstag des Artikels suchte er den viel beschäftigten Direktor der Staatsschule auf, von dessen Einfluss er sich viel versprach. Klein konstatierte über seine klösterliche Studentin: „Ja, die ist hundertprozentig begabt, aber was die da für einen Dreck zusammengemalt hat, ist entsetzlich." Er empfahl Dubler, lieber Zeichnungen einer Schülerin zu drucken, die offenbar in sehr persönlichem Kontakt zu ihrem Professor stand und der Unterhaltung beiwohnte. Dennoch entwickelte sich das Gespräch in launigem Ton. Klein sprach manches über „Saupfaffen" und „Geschäftskatholizismus" und dann versöhnlich darüber, dass auch von Parteiseite die meiste Kunst als „Kitsch" zu bewerten sei. Die Schriftleiter des SA-Mannes kenne er alle, er werde sehen, ob er ein Wörtchen an geeigneter Stelle einlegen könne.[28]

Lieb' Vaterland, magst ruhig sein!, 1934. Der Titel bezieht sich auf den Refrain des Kriegsliedes „Die Wacht am Rhein", das im wilhelminischen Kaiserreich den Status einer inoffiziellen Nationalhymne erreichte. Zum Vergleich (rechts): Ein Motiv der Müllerschen Verlagsanstalten aus dem Ersten Weltkrieg
"*Dear Fatherland, may'st be at ease*" *(Volunteers), 1934. The title alludes to the song "The Watch on the Rhine," a semi-official national anthem in the Wilhelminian age. For comparison (right): "Dear Fatherland, may'st be at ease": A World War I motif from the Müller Publishing Firm*

Dr. Herbert Dubler (1895 – 1970), Schwiegersohn von Maximiliane Müller und Verlagsleiter der Ars sacra
Dr. Herbert Dubler (1895 – 1970), son-in-law of Maximiliane Müller and director of Ars Sacra

A few weeks earlier, an odd conference had taken place about her in the office of Professor Klein. The reason for it was an article that had appeared in the *SA-Mann*, the "polemical journal of the supreme SA command of the NSDAP." On March 20, 1937, the paper had struck a momentous blow against Maria Innocentia and her "children's scenes": "endless variations of the same type of hydrocephalic and club-footed creatures, with the tab always sticking out of their coats and their laces hanging from torn shoes for cute humor. (...) No, the 'dear Fatherland' cannot be 'at ease' when mudlarks are presented as the national youth and things are touched on that are sacred to it. (...) There is no room in the ranks of German artists for such as lack the necessary dependability and aptitude for carrying out their high responsibility."

Dr. Herbert Dubler, the son-in-law of the deceased Josef Müller and current director of Ars Sacra, was resolved to save what could be saved: "There are many situations when the cloistral artist cannot, may not defend herself. Here it is the publisher's role to stand up for his products. If I publish something, I stake my life on it if necessary."[27] On the very day the article appeared, he called on the busy director of the State School, of whose influence he had great hopes. Klein observed about his monastic student: "Yes, she is a hundred percent gifted, but the rubbish she has painted up is really dreadful." He advised Dubler to print instead drawings of a student who evidently had close personal contact with her professor and was in fact present at the discussion. The exchange nevertheless developed in a genial manner. Klein made some remarks about "damned priests" and "commercial Catholicism" and then more conciliatorily about the fact that from the point of view of the Party, too, most art could be dismissed as "kitsch." He knew all the editors of the *SA-Mann*: he would try to put in a good word in the right place.[28]

Der Wanderbub, 1934
The Merry Wanderer, 1934

Wanderbub, 1935 modelliert von Arthur Möller. Ein Erfolgsmotiv, keine Figur wurde in so vielen verschiedenen Größen hergestellt.
The Merry Wanderer, 1935 modeled by master sculptor Arthur Moeller. A top hit: no other figurine was produced in so many different sizes.

Maria Innocentias Atelier, 1937
Maria Innocentia's studio, 1937

Doch die Würfel waren gefallen. Der Artikel war Auslöser für einen heftigen offiziellen „Anti-Hummel-Wind", der Maria Innocentia trotz ungebrochener Popularität von nun an in Deutschland entgegenpfiff. Mit Geschäften ins Ausland, vor allem in die USA, konnten sich allerdings die Nationalsozialisten sehr wohl anfreunden, denn „Hummel" brachte jede Menge Devisen! Von 1936 – 1939 führte Ars sacra über eine Million Reichsmark ab, davon allein im Jahr 1938 die stattliche Summe von 290.000 Reichsmark. Auch die Porzellanfirma Goebel dürfte üppig in die reichsdeutsche Staatskasse eingezahlt haben. Die Hummelkinder hatten nämlich in den wenigen Jahren die Herzen der Amerikaner im Sturm erobert.

Am Palmsonntag 1937 wurde in beinahe allen der 11.500 katholischen Pfarreien des Reichs die päpstliche Enzyklika „Mit brennender Sorge" verlesen. Endlich hatten sich die reichsdeutschen Bischöfe durchgerungen, die Zustände nicht länger zu tolerieren und öffentlich gegen den Nationalsozialismus Stellung zu beziehen. Hitler war außer sich vor Wut, als im Laufe jenes vorösterlichen Sonntags die Ungeheuerlichkeit bekannt wurde, dass das vom Papst persönlich unterzeichnete Schreiben in vielen Tausend Exemplaren heimlich gedruckt und unter die Leute verteilt worden war. Die Lage verschärfte sich.

„Flut ruft der Flut zu beim Tosen deiner Wasser, all deine Wellen und Wogen gehen über mich hin." (Psalm 42, 8)

Am 30. August 1937 legte Maria Innocentia die Ewige Profess ab, die endgültigen Gelübde für ihr ganzes Leben bis über den Tod hinaus.

Maria Innocentia ist erschöpft. Zu hoch waren die Anforderungen der letzten Monate. „Mit den Kindersachen will es nun gar nicht mehr gehen. Ich weiß nicht, was daran Schuld ist. Dagegen machen mir große Arbeiten ernsteren Charakters mehr Freude"[29], schreibt sie an ihren Vater.

Die martialische Bildsprache der Zeit hinterlässt ihre Spuren: Der Schutzengel, 1937
Influence from the period's martial iconography: The Guardian Angel, 1937

Ein dicker Gruß, 1937
Ein lieber Gruß, 1937
Easy Letters, 1937
Hard Letters, 1937

But the die was cast. The article unleashed a vehement official "Anti-Hummel wind" that henceforward blew against Maria Innocentia in Germany, despite her unbroken popularity. For trading abroad, on the other hand, especially to the United States, the Nazis could acquire a taste easily enough, for "Hummel" brought in any amount of foreign exchange. Between 1936 and 1939, Ars Sacra paid more than a million reichsmarks in taxes – in 1938 alone the stately sum of 290,000 marks. The porcelain company Goebel, too, must have paid plenty into the state coffers. For within just a few years, the "Hummel children" had taken the hearts of Americans by storm.

On Palm Sunday of 1937, the papal encyclica *Mit brennender Sorge* ("With burning care") was read in nearly every one of the 11500 Catholic parishes of the Reich. After a long struggle, the German bishops had at last decided not to tolerate the situation any longer and to publicly take a position against National Socialism. Hitler was beside himself with rage when in the course of the pre-Easter Sunday the enormity got about that the document, composed in a single night and signed by the Pope in person, had been secretly printed in many thousands of copies and distributed to the people. The situation was becoming increasingly tense.

"Deep calleth unto deep at the noise of thy waterspouts: all thy waves and thy billows are gone over me." (Psalm 42:7).

On August 30, 1937, Maria Innocentia made her Perpetual Profession, her final vows for life and beyond death.

She was exhausted. The demands of the last months had been too heavy for her. "The children's things aren't going at all any more now," she wrote to her father, "I don't know what is to blame for that. Instead, I take more pleasure in large works of a more serious nature."[29]

Der Wanderbub (mit Hund), 1935
modelliert von Arthur Möller
Strolling Along, 1935
modeled by Arthur Moeller

Buchdeckel: „Hui, die Hummel", 1939
Book cover Hui, die Hummel, *1939*

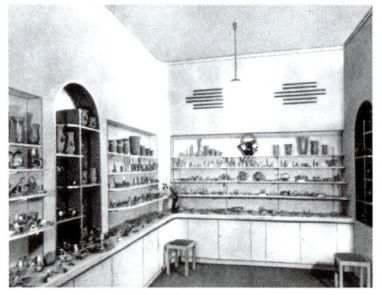

Messe-Stand der W. Goebel Porzellanfabrik in Leipzig
The booth of W. Goebel Porzellanfabrik at Leipzig Fair

Blick in eine Garnier-Stube der 30er-Jahre
A look into an assembling room in the early 30's

Doch es musste weitergehen. Nach ihrem Zusammenbruch in München lieferte sie bis in das Jahr 1939 etwa 80 weitere Motive an Ars sacra, die meisten davon Kinderbilder. Die umtriebige Maximiliane Müller sah ein, dass die Ressourcen ihrer populärsten Künstlerin nicht unendlich waren. Im Sommer 1938 fuhr ein Wagen der Ars sacra die überarbeitete Schwester in einen mehrwöchigen Erholungsaufenthalt nach Fribourg in der Schweiz. „Zeichenblock und Farben ruhen noch sanft im Koffer", berichtete Maria Innocentia den besorgten Eltern, „hab auch noch garnicht im Sinn, sie dort zu stören." Sie genoss die müßigen Spaziergänge in dem malerischen Städtchen und in der bergigen Gegend außen herum. Dann brach doch das alte Malertemperament durch und es juckte sie in den Fingern: „Manchmal packt mich schon die Lust, wie ehedem in Gäßchen und Winkeln zu malen, was als Schwester nicht gut geht."[30]

Zwischen Ars sacra und der Firma Goebel entbrannte ein Konkurrenzkampf, und Maximiliane Müller bat eindringlich, die Motive zuerst an sie zu schicken: „Es scheint mir wichtig für Ihren künstlerischen Ruf, dass das Publikum das betreffende neue Bild zuerst in der besseren Wiedergabe kennen lernt. (...) Die Bildausgaben haben für Kunstverständige Ihren Ruf begründet und erhalten ihn, nicht die Figürchen."[31] Der Verlag aktualisierte seinen Vertrag mit dem Kloster um zusätzliche Exklusivrechte. Unter anderem wurden „die Reproduktionsrechte der Hummeloriginale für (...) bebilderte Hummelbücher" zugesichert.[32] Denn im Herbstprogramm 1939 sollte unter dem Titel „Hui, die Hummel" ein zweites Hummel-Buch erscheinen. An die 70 neue Kindermotive.[33] Ein „lustiges Buch" in jenen dunklen Zeiten, als das deutsche Volk wie gelähmt auf die ersten Kriegsschauplätze blickte.

Es waren die letzten Wochen vor der Katastrophe. Am 16. August 1939 hatte sich ein großer Gratulantenkreis in Hitlers Sommerresidenz auf dem Obersalzberg eingefunden. Es war des Führers 25. „Militärjubiläum", seit er von München aus als Freiwilliger in den Ersten Weltkrieg gezogen war. Während der angehende Kriegsherr gegenüber den Botschaftern aus England und Frankreich jede militärische Absicht leugnete, stand die Wehrmacht bereit, sich in Richtung Osten in Bewegung zu setzen. Die Zivilbevölkerung erhielt noch Bezugsscheine für Lebensmittel und Kohle, vier Tage bevor am frühen Morgen des ersten September deutsche Soldaten die polnische Grenze überschritten. Der Zweite Weltkrieg hatte begonnen.

Maria Innocentia, 1939

But she had to keep going. Between her collapse in Munich and the year 1939, she delivered 80 new motifs to Ars Sacra, most of them children's pictures. The bustling Maximiliane Müller realized that the resources of her most popular artist were not limitless. In the summer of 1938, a car from Ars Sacra drove the overworked sister to Fribourg in Switzerland for several weeks of rest-cure. "Drawing block and paints are still resting peacefully in my suitcase," Maria Innocentia reported to her worried parents; "have as yet no intention of disturbing them there." She relished the leisurely walks through the picturesque town and the mountainous region around it. But then the old painter's temperament came through again, and her fingers began to itch: "Sometimes I do have a great mind to paint in alleys and corners, though as a sister I cannot well do that."[30]

A fierce competition erupted between Ars Sacra and the Goebel Company, and Maximiliane Müller asked emphatically that new motifs be sent to her first: "It seems to me crucial for your artistic reputation that the public gets to know a given new picture in the superior reproduction first. (…) It is the picture books that have established your reputation among the cognoscenti, and maintain it, not the figurines."[31] The press expanded its contract with the convent by additional exclusive rights. Among other things, it secured "the reproduction rights of the Hummel originals for (…) illustrated Hummel books."[32] For a second Hummel book was to appear in its fall program of 1939 under the title *Hui, die Hummel* ("Whoosh, the Hummel [Bumblebee]"), with 70 new children's motifs.[33] A "merry book" at that dark time, when the people of Germany were staring petrified at the first war fronts.

These were the final weeks before the catastrophe. On August 16, 1939, a large circle of congratulants had assembled at Hitler's summer residence on the Obersalzberg. It was the "Führer's" 25th "army anniversary" since the day he had marched from Munich into World War One as a volunteer. While the budding warlord was denying any and all military intentions vis-à-vis the English and French ambassadors, the *wehrmacht* stood poised to move eastward. Rationing cards for food and coal were issued to the civilian population already four days before, in the early morning hours of September 1, German soldiers crossed the border into Poland. World War Two had begun.

Maria Innocentia Berta Hummel

Lebensdaten

21. Mai 1909 Berta Hummel wird im niederbayerischen Massing geboren.

1. Mai 1915 Einschulung an der Massinger Volksschule

3. Mai 1921 Übertritt in die Höhere Mädchenschule, das Institut „Marienhöhe" der Englischen Fräulein

25. März 1926 Abschlusszeugnis Institut „Marienhöhe"

April 1927 – März 1931 Studium an der Staatsschule für angewandte Kunst, u. a. bei den Professoren Maximilian Dasio und Else Brauneis. Freundschaft mit zwei Franziskanerinnen aus dem württembergischen Kloster Sießen

18. März 1931 Abschlusszeugnis der Staatsschule mit Gesamtnote „Eins"

22. April 1931 Eintritt in das Franziskanerinnenkloster Sießen als Kandidatin. Tätigkeit in der dortigen Paramentenwerkstatt und als Zeichenlehrerin in der Mädchenschule in Saulgau; Auftragsarbeiten

Ab 1931 jährliche Ausstellung bei der Professfeier in Sießen, Teilnahme an den Künstlertagungen der Benediktinerabtei Beuron

Dezember 1932 / Januar 1933 Druck der ersten Fleißbildchen und Postkarten im Verlag für Christliche Kunst, München, und im Verlag Ver Sacrum, Rottenburg. Letzterer ließ Texte zu den Bildchen bald auch ins Französische, Englische und Spanische übersetzen.

März 1933 Beginn der Zusammenarbeit mit dem Münchner Verlag Ars sacra

30. Mai – 8. Juni 1933 Letzter Besuch im Elternhaus vor der Einkleidung

22. August 1933 Einkeidung, Annahme des Namens Maria Innocentia

Ab 1933 Dauerausstellung im „Hummelsaal" des Klosters

30. August 1934 Erst-Profess, Ablegung der zeitlichen Gelübde

4. November 1934 Erscheinen des „Hummel-Buchs" im Stuttgarter Fink Verlag. Bis Ende des Jahres werden 15.000 Bücher verkauft.

Dezember 1934 Beginn der Zusammenarbeit mit der Porzellanfabrik Goebel in Oeslau bei Coburg

1935 Erstausstellung der Hummel-Figuren bei der Leipziger Frühjahrs-Messe

5. Mai 1935 Beginn eines Aufbaustudiums an der Staatsschule für angewandte Kunst in München

23. März 1937 Angriff der Nationalsozialisten auf die Kinderbilder in der Zeitung „Der SA-Mann"

24. April 1937 Abschluss des Aufbaustudiums, abermals mit der Gesamtnote „Eins"

30. August 1937 Ewige Profess, Ablegung der Gelübde auf Lebenszeit

Oktober 1939 Erscheinen des zweiten Hummel-Buchs „Hui, die Hummel" im Verlag Ars sacra, München

4. November 1940 Räumung des Klosters Sießen durch die Nationalsozialisten

November 1940 und Oktober 1942 Aufenthalte bei der Familie in Massing

Juli 1944 Erkrankung an schwerer Bronchitis mit Rippenfellentzündung

November 1944 Überweisung an die Lungenheilstätte Wilhelmstift Isny im Allgäu

April 1945 Rückkehr nach Sießen

20. September 1945 Einlieferung in die Lungenfachklinik und Kinderheilstätte Wangen im Allgäu

9. September 1946 Rückkehr ins Kloster Sießen

6. November 1946 Tod von Maria Innocentia Berta Hummel in Sießen

9. November 1946 Beerdigung auf dem Klosterfriedhof in Sießen

Maria Innocentia Berta Hummel

Biographical Data

May 21, 1909 Berta Hummel is born in Massing in Lower Bavaria.

May 1, 1915 Enters elementary school

May 3, 1921 Enters "St. Mary's Heights," the girls' high school of the English Conventuals

March 25, 1926 Graduates from "St. Mary's Heights"

April 1927 – March 1931 Begins study at the State School of Applied Art, with Professors Maximilian Dasio and Else Brauneis, among others. Friendship with two Franciscan nuns from the Convent Siessen in Württemberg

March 18, 1931 Graduates from the State School with the overall grade of 1 [A]

April 22, 1931 Enters the Franciscan convent of Siessen as a candidate. Works in the paraments workshop of the convent and as an art teacher in the convent's girls' school. Does commissioned work.

From 1931 Annual exhibition at the Profession ceremonies in Siessen. Takes part in the artists' congresses at the Benedictine abbey of Beuron.

December 1932 / January 1933 The first "diligence pictures" and postcards are printed at the Christian Art Press, Munich, and at the Ver Sacrum Press, Rottenburg. Texts accompanying the pictures published by the latter press are soon also translated into French, English and Spanish.

March 1933 Beginning of the collaboration with the Ars Sacra Press, Munich

May 30 – June 8, 1933 Last visit at home prior to the Assumption of the Habit

August 22, 1933 Assumption of the Habit. Adopts the name Maria Innocentia

From 1933 Permanent exhibition in the "Hummel Hall" at the convent

August 30, 1934 First Profession, taking of temporal vows

November 4, 1934 Publication of the *Hummel-Buch* at the Fink Press, Stuttgart. By the end of the year, 15,000 copies have been sold.

December 1934 Beginning of the collaboration with the porcelain manufacturing company Goebel in Oeslau near Coburg

1935 First exhibition of Hummel figurines at the Leipzig Spring Fair

May 5, 1935 Start of the further studies at the State School of Applied Art in Munich

March 23, 1937 Attack on the children's pictures by the Nazi newspaper *Der SA-Mann*

April 24, 1937 Completion of the further studies, again with overall grade of 1 [A]

August 30, 1937 Perpetual Profession, taking of life-long vows

October 1939 Publication of the second Hummel Book, *Hui, die Hummel*, by the Ars Sacra Press, Munich

November 4, 1940 Eviction from the convent by the National Socialists

November 1940 and October 1942 Stays with the family in Massing

July 1944 Succumbs to severe bronchitis and pleurisy

November 1944 Tansfer to sanatorium Wilhelmstift Isny in the Allgäu

April 1945 Return to Siessen

September 20, 1945 Hospitalized at the pulmonary clinic and children's sanatorium Wangen in the Allgäu

September 9, 1946 Return to convent Siessen

November 6, 1946 Death of Maria Innocentia Berta Hummel in Siessen

November 9, 1946 Burial in the convent cemetery in Siessen

Das „Pinsele" geht heim

Letztes Schenken

The "Paintbrush" is laid aside – Last Gifts

Maria Innocentia, 1939

„Meine lieben Eltern und Geschwister! Heute komme ich mit einer traurigen Nachricht – wir sind obdachlos geworden –, unser Kloster muß bis Donnerstag ganz und gar geräumt sein – wissen noch nicht wohin – u. was werden wird."[1] Es ist der 1. November 1940. Am Tag zuvor hatten sich der Einsatzführer Drautz aus Heilbronn und Kreisleiter Siller aus Saulgau von der Generaloberin M. Augustina Steinhauser die Klosteranlage zeigen lassen.

Drautz durchmisst mit hallendem Stiefelschritt die Klosterkapelle. Unwirsch klopft er mit dem Fingerknöchel auf eine der Kirchenbänke. Die müssen raus! Wir brauchen Platz hier! Dann lässt er die religiösen Zeichen entfernen, unter anderem zwei große Seitenaltarbilder der Schwester Maria Innocentia. Die Kapelle soll zunächst als Lagerraum für Holzwolle und Säcke herhalten.

Bis zum 15. Dezember 1940 sollten 1300 Auslandsdeutsche aus der Südbukowina im Kloster Sießen eintreffen. Nachdem die mit Holzwolle gestopften Säcke auf Feldbetten in den Räumen verteilt waren, würde der Lagerkommandant in der Kapelle das Kino für die Insassen einrichten.

Innerhalb von acht Tagen hatten die Franziskanerinnen beinahe die gesamten Klostergebäude vollständig zu räumen. Nur ein kleiner, durch eine Bretterwand abgeteilter Teil im Südflügel mit Pfarreck sollte den Schwestern bleiben. Der ganze Rest war durch die Volksdeutsche Mittelstelle[2], die dem SS-Führer Heinrich Himmler unterstellt war, kurzerhand beschlagnahmt und als Auffanglager den Umsiedlern aus Osteuropa und dem Elsass zugewiesen worden.

Die Klosterleitung erhob Protest an die Präsidialkanzlei in Berlin. Sie sah sich nicht in der Lage, in so kurzer Zeit an die 280 Schwestern und Kandidatinnen auswärts unterzubringen, vor allem die älteren und kranken Ordensfrauen. Doch jeder Einspruch wurde abgeschmettert. Im Gegenteil: Zur Strafe plante die Gauleitung zusätzlich die Beschlagnahmung der gesamten Landwirtschaft, die den Klosterfrauen ihren Lebensunterhalt sicherte. „Bei uns ist nichts unmöglich! Schicken Sie die Schwestern heim! Ihr Jesus soll für sie sorgen!"[3], tönte Drautz. Die Franziskanerinnen mussten sich fügen. Etwa 50 Ordensfrauen wurden ausgewählt, um vorerst den Klosterbetrieb in den verbliebenen Räumlichkeiten aufrechtzuerhalten. Einige waren von der Lagerleitung zwangsverpflichtet worden für die Lagerküche und die Wäscherei.

Klosteranlage Sießen, 1963
Convent Siessen, 1963

My dear parents and siblings! Today I have sad news for you – we have become homeless – our convent has to be completely vacated by Thursday – as yet no idea whereto – and what will happen."[1] It is the first of November, 1940. The day before, the *Einsatzführer* (task force leaders), district leader Drautz of Heilbronn and district leader Siller of Saulgau, had the Mother Superior M. Augustina Steinhauser show them the buildings of the convent.

Drautz' echoing boot steps traverse the convent chapel. Testily he raps his knuckles on the old church pews. These will have to go! We need the room here! He orders all religious tokens to be removed, including two large side altar pieces by Sister Maria Innocentia.

For the moment, the chapel was to be used as storage space for sacks and wood-shavings for paillasses. By December 15, 1300 ethnic Germans from the southern Bukovina were to arrive at the Siessen convent. Once the paillasses had been distributed to camp beds in the various rooms, the camp commandant would convert the chapel into a film theater for the inmates.

Within one week the Franciscans were to clear out almost the entire convent building. Only one small area in the south wing, sectioned off by a wooden partition, was to remain for use by the sisters. All the rest had been confiscated without further ado by the Volksdeutsche Mittelstelle (Transit Agency for Ethnic Germans)[2] under SS-Führer Heinrich Himmler and assigned as a reception camp for the groups being resettled from Eastern Europe and the Alsace.

The convent administration lodged a protest with the presidential office in Berlin, saying they were simply unable to relocate some 280 sisters and candidates, especially elderly and ailing convent women, in so short a time span. But every one of their objections was simply thrown back at them. To punish them, the Gau (province) administration, in fact, made plans for the additional confiscation of the convent's farmland, from which the sisters derived their livelihood. "Nothing is impossible with us! Send the sisters home! Let their Jesus take care of them!"[3] Drautz vociferated. The Franciscans had to submit. Some fifty members of the order were selected to keep the convent running, for the time being, on the remaining premises. Some had been conscripted by the camp administration for the camp kitchen and the laundry.

Maria Innocentias Rosenkranz
Maria Innocentia's rosary

Am 5. November wurde in der beschlagnahmten Kapelle zum letzten Mal eine gemeinsame Messe gefeiert, bevor ein Großteil der Schwestern das Kloster in eine ungewisse Zukunft verlassen musste. Es war ungewöhnlich ruhig an diesem Tag. In den Tagen und Nächten zuvor hatte fieberhaftes Treiben geherrscht. Durch die Klostereinfahrt waren unablässig Möbelwagen, Bulldogs, Autos und Pferdefuhrwerke ein- und ausgefahren, alles, was nur irgendwie in der Lage war, eine Transportmöglichkeit zu bieten. Die Nachricht von der Räumung des Klosters hatte sich unter den Bauern der Gegend wie ein Lauffeuer verbreitet, und viele waren gekommen, um das klösterliche Eigentum wegschaffen zu helfen, damit es nicht in die falschen Hände gelangte.

Eine beauftragte Schwester ging auf den Nachbarhof, um die Bauern um einen Gefallen zu bitten: ob sie das große romanische Kreuz bei sich auf dem Hof in Obhut nehmen würden? Die Nazis hatten regelmäßige Kontrollen angekündigt, bei denen sie jeden Winkel der Klosteranlage durchsuchen würden. Jenes Kreuz vorantragend, waren einst 1722 die Dominikanerinnen in den barock erstrahlten Gebäudekomplex umgezogen. Es war das wertvollste Erbe des Klosterbesitzes.

Du kommst doch wieder, Schwester Innocentia, gelt? Das Mädchen Resele drückt sich verschreckt hinter dem Rock ihrer Mutter herum. Maria Innocentia spürt plötzlich die Anstrengung der vergangenen Woche wie Blei in allen Gliedern. Sie weiß keine Antwort.

Sie hatte nach Massing geschrieben, ob ihre Familie ihr Obdach gewähren könnte. Zunächst für 14 Tage. „Wir schaffen Tag u. Nacht u. müssen gewärtig sein, dass man uns noch alles beschlagnahmt."[4] Auch alle ihre Bilder bat sie nach Massing bringen zu dürfen.

Die alte Heimat Massing:
Hummel-Sommerhaus, 1927
The old home Massing:
Summer house of the Hummels, 1927

Massing vom Kirchberg aus, 1928/1929
Massing viewed from the Kirchberg, 1928/1929

On November 5, mass was celebrated for the last time by all in the confiscated chapel, before a majority of the sisters had to leave their convent for an uncertain future. The quiet on that day was unusual. During the days and nights before, a feverish commotion had reigned. Trucks, tractors, cars, and horse-drawn vehicles, everything that could provide any transportation, had rolled ceaselessly in and out of the convent drive-way. Word of the evacuation had spread like wildfire among the region's farmers, and many had come to help move the convent's property, so it would not fall into the wrong hands.

Alte Häuser, 1929/1930
Old houses, 1929/1930

A sister was dispatched to the neighboring farm to ask the owners for a favor. Would they take the great Romanesque cross into their keeping on the farm? The Nazis had announced regular controls, during which they would search every nook and cranny of the convent complex. Back in 1722, the Dominicans had moved into the building complex, newly renovated in sumptuous Baroque form, bearing that Romanesque cross in front of them. It was the most precious heirloom in the possession of the convent.

You'll come back again, Sister Innocentia, won't you? Fearfully, the little girl Resele clings to her mother's skirt. Maria Innocentia suddenly feels the strain of the past week like lead in every limb. She has no answer.

She had written to Massing to ask if her family could put her up temporarily, for two weeks perhaps. "We labor day and night, yet must be prepared to see everything get confiscated anyway."[4] She also asked to be able to bring all of her pictures.

Lichtblick in harter Zeit: Maria Innocentia mit ihrer kleinen Nichte Traudl und im Kreise ihrer Familie (rechts), 1940
A ray of light in a dark time: Maria Innocentia with her little niece Traudl and her family (right), 1940

So fuhr sie noch einmal über die Rottaler Hügel in die Heimat ihrer Kindheit. Die Eltern nahmen großen Anteil an dem Schicksal der Sießener Schwestern und taten alles, um ihrer Tochter die Situation zu erleichtern. Der Vater Adolf Hummel hatte selbst Schwierigkeiten mit der nationalsozialistischen Ortsführung. Man hatte ihm gedroht, ihn trotz seines Alters an die Front zu schicken, wenn er sich nicht besser einordne. Maria Innocentias Bruder Ady und seine Frau Wally wohnten ebenfalls im Elternhaus, sie hatten eine kleine Tochter von etwa fünf Monaten. Wie schön hätte ein Wiedersehen unter anderen Umständen sein können!

Doch alles ist rastlose Unruhe. Jeden Morgen, wenn Maria Innocentia ihr Ordensgewand anlegt, tut sie es in bewusster Erinnerung. „Der Herr bekleide dich mit dem neuen Menschen, der nach Gott geschaffen ist in Gerechtigkeit und wahrer Heiligkeit", hört sie die Worte ihrer Einkleidung, als wäre es gestern gewesen. Jetzt sind sie zum Aufruf geworden: „Legt die Rüstung Gottes an …!" (Eph, 6, 11) Den Gürtel für Reinheit, den Mantel für Demut. „Alles für Sießen u. seine Sendung!", ruft sie in die Ungewissheit hinein gen ihre Wahlheimat.⁵ So oft sie kann, schreibt sie an die Mutter Oberin. Das Rad ist nicht zurückzudrehen. Bei ihrer Einkleidung hatte sie an Neuanfang gedacht und nicht an Abschied. Doch so sehr es schmerzt, sie scheint nicht mehr zu der Welt zu gehören, die sie als junges Lausmädel verlassen hat.

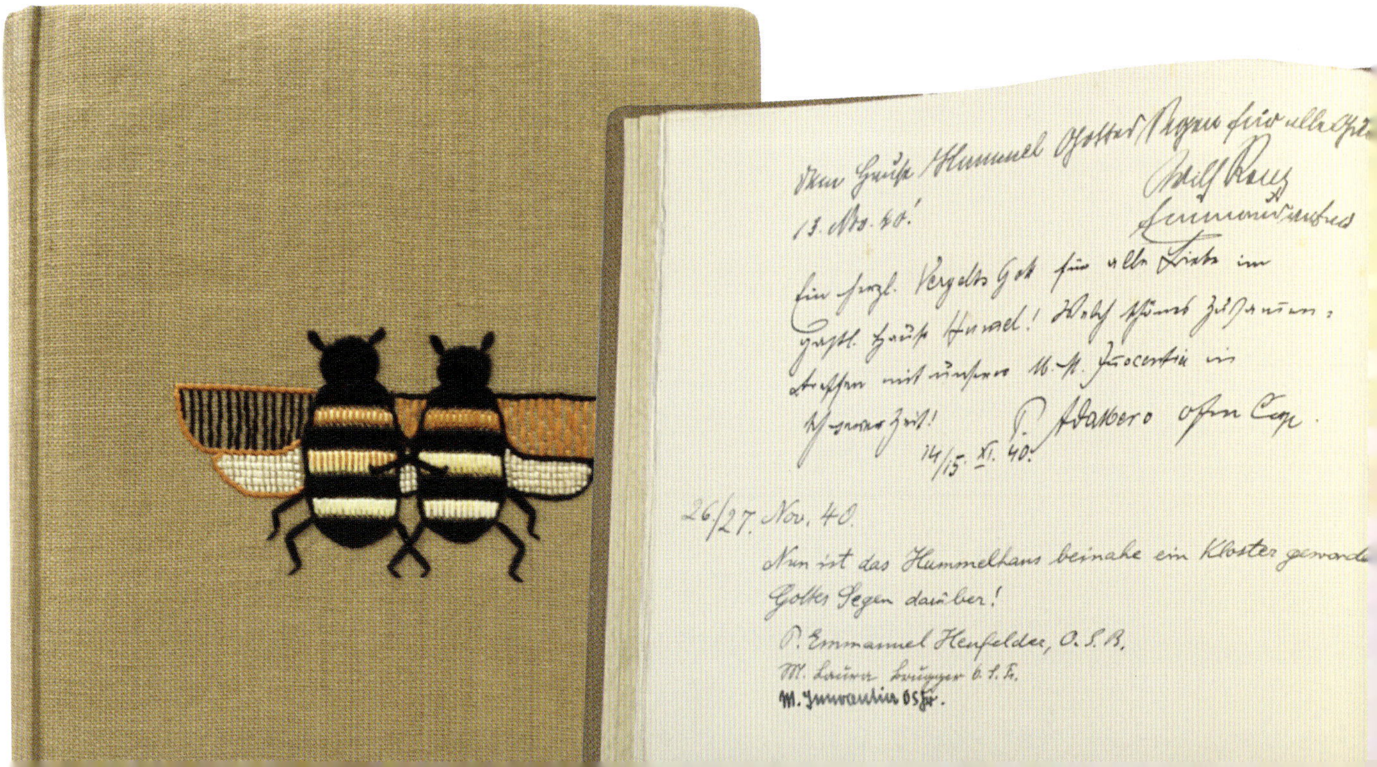

„Nun ist das Hummelhaus beinahe ein Kloster geworden." Gästebuch mit Unterschriften von Pater Emmanuel Heufelder, Maria Innocentia und M. Laura Brugger, die sie in Massing abholte. „Von der lieben Klosterheimat vertrieben hat Gott mich zu meinen Lieben geführt u. ich durfte das Glück u. die Wärme meines Elternhauses in so reichem Maße genießen, daß ich in inniger Dankbarkeit nur das Eine sagen möchte: Gott lohne Euch alles 1000-fach!" "The Hummel House is almost a convent now." Visitors' book with signatures by Father Emmanuel Heufelder, Maria Innocentia and M. Laura Brugger, who accompanied her from Massing. "Expelled from my beloved convent home, God has led me to my dear ones, and I could savor the happiness and warmth of my parental home in such a rich measure that in inmost gratitude I want to say only one thing: May God reward you for everything a thousand-fold."

Thus she got to travel once more over the hills of the Rott Valley into the village of her childhood. Her parents greatly sympathized with the fate of the Siessen sisters and did everything to relieve their daughter's situation. The father, Adolf Hummel, was in trouble with the local Nazi authorities himself: threats had been voiced to send him to the front in spite of his age, unless he fell in line with the reigning order. Maria Innocentia's brother Ady and his wife Wally, who had a five-months-old baby daughter, were also living with the parents. How lovely this reunion could have been under different circumstances!

But everything is in constant turmoil. Every morning, when Maria Innocentia puts on her habit, she does so as a conscious act of memory. "The Lord clothe you with the New Man, who is created in the image of God in righteousness and true holiness," she hears the words of her Assumption of the Habit rite as if it had been yesterday. Now they have become a call to arms: "Put on the whole armor of God!" (Eph. 6:11) The cincture for purity, the cloak for humility. "All for Siessen! And its mission!" she calls out in her uncertainty in the direction of her adopted home.[5] As often as possible she writes to Siessen. The wheel cannot be turned back. At her Assumption of the Habit she had thought about a new beginning, not about parting. But as much as it hurts, she no longer seems to belong to the world she had left as a young hoyden.

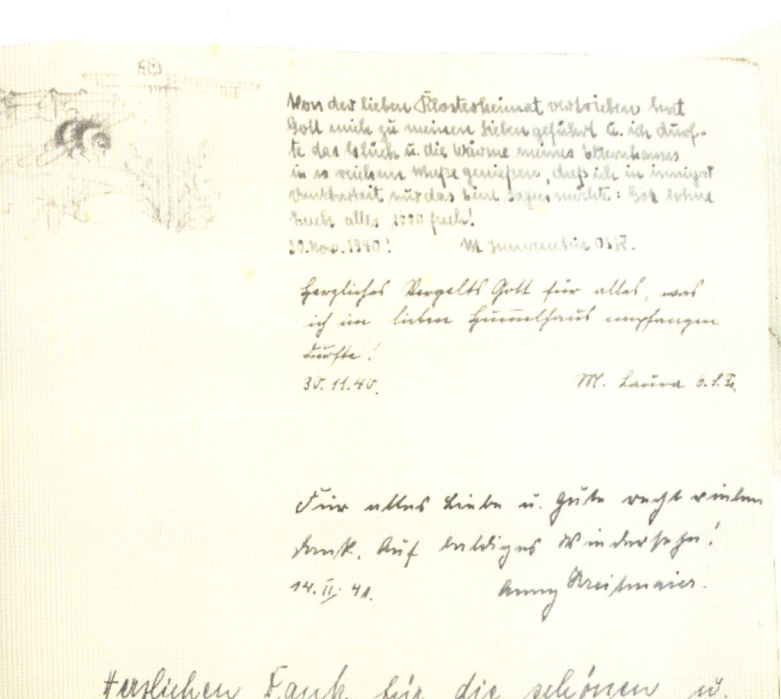

183

Mit ihren Zeichnungen gelang es Maria Innocentia, die Mitschwestern in den harten Zeiten aufzuheitern. Für das weinende Mädchen bat sie eine von ihnen, Modell zu stehen, und brachte alle durch das realistische Porträt zum Lachen. „Die große Neuigkeit" war eines Tages die erleichternde Zusicherung, dass der verbliebene Teil des Klosters zunächst nicht beschlagnahmt werden würde.

In a hard time, Maria Innocentia managed to cheer up her fellow sisters with her drawings. She asked one of them to sit for the picture of the weeping girl and made everyone laugh by the extreme realism of the portrait. The "great news" was the comforting assurance that for the present the remaining part of the convent would not be confiscated.

Die große Neuigkeit, 1941
Telling Her Secret, 1941

Warum so traurig?, 1941/1944
Why So Sad?, 1941/1944

Maria Innocentia mit ihrer Werkstattleiterin M. Eligia Stadler OSF, 1940
Maria Innocentia with the head of the atelier M. Eligia Stadler OSF, 1940

Nach etwa fünf Wochen kehrte Maria Innocentia in ihr Kloster zurück. „Fragt mich nicht über die ersten Eindrücke", schrieb sie entsetzt der Familie. „Aber es ist doch noch ein Stück Klosterheimat u. ich freue mich, daß ich zu denen gehören darf, die in Siessen sein dürfen. Mutter Oberin gab mir ein schönes Zimmer als Atelier, das ich mit Schwester Laura bewohnen darf."[6] Bedenkt man, welch engen Raum die ungefähr 50 Schwestern sich in dem abgetrennten Gebäudetrakt teilen mussten, kann man an der Einrichtung eines Ateliers für die Künstlerin den Wert einschätzen, den sie und ihre Arbeit nach wie vor für das Kloster hatten. Andererseits aber auch die Bedingungen, unter denen ein kreatives Schaffen stattfinden sollte. In diesem Winter würde sie nochmals ihren Arbeitsraum wechseln müssen. In keinem ihrer Briefe nach Massing fehlt der Wunsch, dass der Krieg endlich vorübergehen möge.

Erstaunlich sind die übereinstimmenden Berichte der noch lebenden Mitschwestern über die Art und Weise, wie Maria Innocentia ihre Rolle in der Gemeinschaft aufnahm. Die alte Fröhlichkeit und Schlagfertigkeit scheint in all den Unbilden wieder sehr präsent. Doch der Krieg forderte seine Opfer. Kaum eine Schwester, die nicht irgendeinen männlichen Verwandten an der Front wusste, kaum eine, die nicht von den sich häufenden Todesnachrichten betroffen war. Maria Innocentia blieb trotz ihrer immer kränklicheren Konstitution als starke und humorvolle Persönlichkeit in Erinnerung, die den anderen oft Mut zusprechen konnte und stets ein aufmunterndes Wort oder einen Scherz auf den Lippen hatte.

Zwei Engel auf einer Wolke, 1940/1942
Two angels on a cloud, 1940/1942

Glücksbringer: Fliegenpilz, Glücksklee und Hummel, 1939/1942
Good luck charms: toadstools, four-leaf-clover and bumblebee, 1939/1942

After some five weeks, Maria Innocentia returned to her convent. "Don't ask me about my first impressions," she wrote aghast to her family. "And yet it is a little piece of my cloistral home, and I am glad that I may be among those who are allowed to stay in Siessen. Mother Superior has given me a nice room for a studio, in which I can lodge together with Sister Laura."[6] If one considers the narrow space the more than 50 sisters had to share in the partitioned-off building tract, one can judge from the assignment of a studio for the artist how valuable her work continued to be for the convent – as well as the cramped conditions under which creative work would have to be carried on. She would have to shift her work area once more this winter. In each and every of her letters to Massing she includes the fervent wish that the war would finally come to an end.

One marvels at the unanimous accounts of still living fellow sisters about the manner in which Maria Innocentia resumed her role in the community. Despite all the tribulations, her old mirth and quick wit seem to have been fully present again. Yet the war exacted its sacrifices. There was hardly a single sister who did not have some male relative at the front, hardly one who was not affected by the growing number of casualty reports. Despite her progressively sickly constitution, Maria Innocentia is remembered by all as a strong and humorous personality, who was often able to lift the spirits of the others and who always had an encouraging word or a jest on her lips.

Offenbar hatte sich trotz der widrigen Umstände eine Art Arbeitsalltag eingestellt. Die Verlage und die Firma Goebel waren benachrichtigt über die schwierigen Verhältnisse. Größer denn je war die Nachfrage nach „lustigen Sachen". Die Anpassung an die jeweiligen Bedürfnisse im In- und Ausland nahm zuweilen skurrile Züge an, und so schrieb Maximiliane Müller: „Für Amerika brauchen Sie gar nicht anders zu arbeiten als für Deutschland, man könnte höchstens jetzt sagen, dass statt der Engerl mit Flügeln Kinder am Platze sind, aber keine Negerkinder wegen der ‚Rassenschande' und wegen der Franzosen, welche schwarze Soldaten gegen uns in Bereitschaft haben. Diese Auswechslung der Engel in Kinder (...) ist auch für Amerika gut."[7] Maximiliane Müller und Herbert Dubler hatten in Lugano in der Schweiz eine Dependance von Ars sacra gegründet, um das Überleben des Verlags zu sichern. Im Kriegsdeutschland gab es für die „Hummel"-Produkte keine Papierzuteilung mehr.[8] Dieses faktische Druckverbot hatte einen wachsenden Schwarzmarkthandel zur Folge. Andererseits blühte bereits das Geschäft mit Fälschungen, gegen die Verlag und Porzellanfirma entschieden vorzugehen versuchten.

Maria Innocentia führte ihre Korrespondenz mit den Geschäftspartnern nun meist selbst, pragmatisch und direkt. Sie war nicht immer einverstanden mit der profitablen Vermarktung ihres Namens. Franz Goebel musste sich mit Kritik auseinandersetzen: „Vor allem vermisse ich die Berücksichtigung der mir eigenartigen Abtönung der Farben, wie ich es seiner Zeit in Oeslau eingehendst gezeigt habe. Ich weiss, daß das mehr Arbeit gibt – aber lieber weniger und gut, als viel und schlecht."[9] Auch gegen Maximiliane Müller konnte sie gelegentlich ihren Unmut kaum verhehlen. Denn die drängte in der schwierigen Lage des Verlags weiterhin auf immer neue Motive. Viel Rücksicht auf die gegenwärtige Situation der Künstlerin leistete sie sich dabei nicht: „Ich will mich bessern, soviel es mir möglich ist, aber zuviel kann ich leider nicht versprechen, denn auch ich werde getrieben – von der Not, die unerbittlich ist. Mehr brauche ich wohl nicht zu sagen."[10]

„Außerdem weiß ich nicht, in welcher Art ich für Amerika arbeiten soll." Brief an die Verlegerin Maximiliane Müller (1876 – 1963)
"Besides, I have no idea in what manner to work for Americans." Letter to the publisher, Maximiliane Müller (1876 – 1963)

Erlaubnis zur Weiterführung des Verlags Ars sacra unter der Bedingung, ausschließlich für den Export zu arbeiten
Permit to keep the Ars Sacra Press going on condition that it would publish exclusively for export

Evidently something of a regular work schedule established itself despite the adverse circumstances. The publishers and the Goebel Company had been informed of the difficult situation. The demand for "jolly things" was bigger than ever. Adapting to the various requirements within the country and abroad at times took on bizarre forms. Thus Maximiliane Müller wrote: "You don't have to work differently for America than for Germany; at most one could say that children are now in order instead of little angels with wings; just no Negro children because of the 'Rassenschande' (racial disgrace) and because of the French, who have black soldiers in readiness against us. Replacing angels with children (…) is also good for America."[7] Maximiliane Müller and Herbert Dubler had opened a branch of Ars Sacra in Lugano in Switzerland to insure the survival of the firm. In war-time Germany no paper was allotted any longer for "Hummel" products,[8] which amounted to a ban on printing. The result was a growing black market trade. At the same time, traffic in counterfeits already flourished, though both the press and the porcelain company tried to take steps against it.

Foto und Zeichnung:
Ein schwerer Geschenkkorb, 1944
Photograph and drawing:
Spring Basket, 1944

Entwürfe für Amerika:
Jesus in Krippe mit Engel, 1940
Mädchen schüttelt Baum, 1940
Sketches for export to the United States
Jesus in the Manger with Angel, 1940
Shaking the tree, 1940

Maria Innocentia now conducted the correspondence with her business partners mostly herself, pragmatically and directly. She was not always in agreement with the marketing of her name for profit. Franz Goebel had to confront her criticism: "Above all I miss the shading of colors unique to me, which I thoroughly demonstrated in Oeslau at the time. I know that that makes more work – but better less and good than more and bad."[9] Toward Maximiliane Müller, too, she sometimes could hardly conceal her displeasure, as the latter tried to offset the precarious state of the publishing house by continuing to press for ever new motifs, without much regard for the situation of the artist: "I will do better as best I can, but unfortunately I cannot promise much, as I am driven as well – by necessity, which is inexorable. I trust I do not need to say more."[10]

Hummel auf Blütenzweig, Dezember 1941
Bumblebee on a flowering branch, December 1941

Während der harten Kriegszeit wurde jeder Schwester ein fünftägiger Heimatbesuch gestattet. Im Oktober 1942 machte sich Maria Innocentia zu einem Urlaub nach Massing auf.

Elfeinhalb Jahre ist es her, dass Maria Innocentia ihre alte Heimat, ihr Elternhaus und den Weg einer freien Künstlerin verlassen hat. Auf jenem Wandbehang, ihrer Abschlussarbeit an der Staatsschule, hatte sie damals die Straße ihres Lebens vorgezeichnet. Zur Kirche hinauf würde sie gehen, wo ein ins Gebet versunkener Franziskanermönch zu sehen ist. Hinter der Kirche geht es auf die Sonne zu, das Licht Gottes, am Wegesrand das Lamm, Sinnbild der Unschuld und des Opfers. Es sollte diesmal ein letztes Wiedersehen mit Massing sein, dem „Hummel-Nest" ihrer Kindheit.[11]

Die Verhältnisse im Sießener Lager wurden unterdessen immer unerträglicher. Alles war hoffnungslos überfüllt, zu Spitzenzeiten stieg die Bewohnerzahl auf über 2000 Personen an. Die Räumlichkeiten und sanitären Anlagen waren für höchstens 500 Personen ausgelegt. Die Insassen klagten über starken Wanzenbefall und die Schikanen der Lagerleitung. „Heim ins Reich", hatte es für die deutschstämmigen Slowenen und Bessarabier, Russen und Elsässer geheißen. Die örtliche Hitlerjugend war damit betraut, sich um die Umsiedlerkinder zu kümmern. Sie lehrte sie stramme deutsche Lieder, in deren Takt sie hinter ihren Betreuern zum Arbeitseinsatz auf den Feldern marschierten. Schwimmen brachten sie ihnen bei, indem sie die Kleineren nackt in den nahe gelegenen See warfen. Im Sommer staute sich die Luft zum Ersticken und im Winter starben die Kinder an Lungenentzündung und Tuberkulose. Pannen bei den zugewiesenen Aufgaben wurden hart bestraft. Eines Tages erhängte sich ein 17-jähriger Slowene, weil er den technischen Anforderungen der komplizierten Heizanlage nicht gewachsen war und dafür nicht weiter die Verantwortung tragen wollte.

During the hard war years, every sister was allowed a five-day home visit. In October of 1942, Maria Innocentia set out for a vacation in Massing.

It had been eleven and a half years since she left both her native village, her parental home and her initial career choice as a freelance artist. On the wall-

Das „Hummel-Nest", 1942. „Das waren schöne Tage daheim! Herzliche Vergelt's Gott für alle Liebe u. Güte." Zeichnung in das Gästebuch der Eltern zur Geburt des Neffen Alfred
The "Hummel Nest," 1942. "Lovely days being at home! God reward you for all your love and kindness." Drawing in the parents' visitors' book on the occasion of the birth of nephew Alfred

Wandbehang Massing, 1931
Wall-hanging: Massing, 1931

hanging that had been her final project at the State School, she had mapped out her new road. Up to the church she would travel, where a Franciscan monk can be seen absorbed in prayer. Behind the church, the traveler would head toward the sun, the light of God, past the lamb by the wayside, the emblem of innocence and sacrifice. It would be her last return to Massing, the "Hummel nest" of her childhood.[11]

Meanwhile the conditions in the Siessen camp grew increasingly intolerable. The camp was hopelessly overcrowded. At peak times the number of inhabitants rose to above 2000 – the rooms and sanitary installations had been designed for no more than 500. The inmates complained about an infestation of bedbugs and chicaneries from the camp command. "Home into the Reich" had been the motto for the Slovenes, Bessarabians, Russians, and Alsatians of German extraction. The local Hitler Youth was charged with looking after the children of the resettlers. They taught them snappy German songs, to whose beat the children then marched behind their caretakers to work in the fields. And they taught the little ones to swim by throwing them naked into the nearby lake. In summer the air was stiflingly stagnant, in winter the children died of pneumonia and consumption. Any slip-up in assigned work was punished severely. One day a young 17-year-old Slovene hanged himself because he was not equal to the demands of the complicated heating system and no longer wanted to bear the responsibility for it.

Porträt Viktoria Hummel, April 1929
Portrait of Viktoria Hummel, April 1929

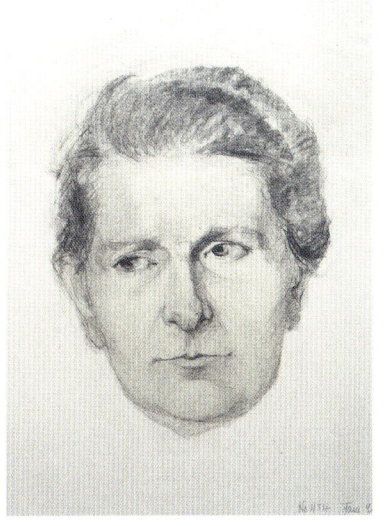

Porträt Adolf Hummel, März 1929
Portrait of Adolf Hummel, March 1929

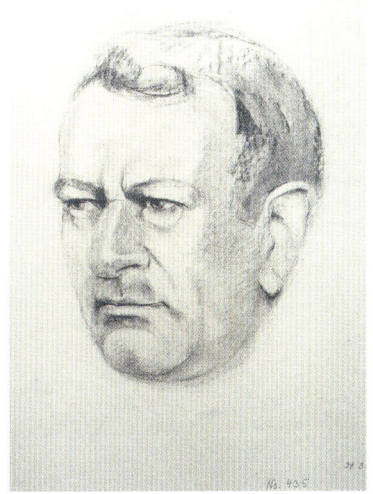

Messlatte für den Nachwuchs des Hummel-Hauses (Entwurf), 1941
Measuring tape for a new generation of little Hummels (sketch), 1941

Kopf hoch und schlucken, 1941/1944
Hold your Head High
and Swallow Hard, 1941/1944

Den Klosterfrauen war der Kontakt zu den Lagerbewohnern untersagt, beide Seiten hatten im Falle einer Missachtung drakonische Strafen zu befürchten. Doch das Elend hinter der Bretterwand war zu groß. Die Schwestern brachten heimlich Lebensmittel und Kleidung für die Kinder. Gauleiter Drautz suchte mit allen Mitteln Vorwände, um sich der restlichen Franziskanerinnen zu entledigen. Die Ökonomin des Klosters wurde wegen angeblicher Veruntreuung von Lebensmitteln verhaftet. Kaum ein Monat ohne Kontrollgänge der Gestapo durch den verbliebenen Teil des Klosters. Kein Tag ohne die Angst im Nacken, dass nun doch alles aufgegeben werden müsse.

Wieder einmal sind Stiefelschritte der Gestapo auf den Gängen zu hören. Harsche Stimmen fordern immer dieselben Formulare und die Herausgabe von angeblich versteckten Gütern. Da befestigt Maria Innocentia die Zeichnung einer kleinen gelben Ente an der Tür des Refektoriums, dort wo alle sie sehen können. Das Tierchen hält den Schnabel nach oben und darunter steht: „Kopf hoch und schlucken!" Keine von den Schwestern verliert ein Wort darüber. Aber wenn es in den nächsten Tagen arg wird, zwinkern sie sich heimlich zu, recken den Kopf ein wenig und ahmen die Schluckbewegung der kleinen Ente nach.[12]

Ab Mitte 1944 stieg die Anzahl der Todesfälle aufgrund epidemischer Krankheiten im Lager erheblich an. Aus Südfrankreich waren Anhänger des Deutschland-Kooperateurs Philippe Pétain[13] dazugestoßen. Schlecht ernährt kamen die erschöpften Familien nach den Strapazen einer einmonatigen Transport-Odyssee in Sießen an. Besonders hart traf es die Kinder. Mindestens einmal in der Woche wurde ein kleiner Holzsarg aus dem Lager getragen.

The convent women were prohibited from all contact with the camp inmates, on pain of draconic penalties imposed on both parties. But the misery behind the wood partition was too extreme: the sisters smuggled in food and clothing for the children. Gauleiter [governor] Drautz searched for any available pretexts to get rid of the remaining Franciscans. The convent economist was arrested for supposedly misappropriating provisions. Hardly a month went by without the Gestapo making control rounds through the remaining section of the convent, no day without besetting fears that now everything would have to be given up after all.

Skizze eines liegenden Soldaten, 1942
Sketch of a lying soldier, 1942

Maria Innocentias Bruder Ady, der in München stationiert war, hatte einen ungewöhnlichen Auftrag für seine Schwester an Land gezogen: Trauerkarten für gefallene christliche Soldaten der Wehrmacht.
Maria Innocentia's brother Ady, who was stationed in Munich, obtained an unusual commission for his sister: obituary cards for fallen Christian wehrmacht soldiers.

Soldaten-Andenken, 1942
Praying soldier, 1942

Once again Gestapo boots can be heard in the corridors. Harsh voices keep demanding the same questionnaires and the surrender of supposedly hidden goods. On this afternoon, Sister Maria Innocentia pins a drawing of a little yellow duck to the door of the refectory, where all can see it. The little animal is holding up its beak, and below it are the words "Heads high and swallow hard!" Not one of the sisters says a word about it. But whenever things get really bad the next several days, they secretly wink at each other, raise their heads a little, and mimic the swallowing motion of the little duck.[12]

By mid-1944, the number of deaths due to epidemic diseases rose drastically in the camp. From southern France, adherents of the collaborator Philippe Pétain[13] had been added. Families arrived in Siessen malnourished and exhausted from the hardships of a month-long transport Odyssey. The children were especially hard-hit. Nearly every week a small wooden coffin was borne away for burial.

Im Atelier: die letzte Aufnahme von Maria Innocentia, 1944 entstanden bei einem Besuch ihres Bruders Franz
In her studio: the last photograph of Maria Innocentia, taken by her brother Franz in 1944

In der Julihitze 1944 erkrankte Maria Innocentia an einer Bronchitis mit Rippenfellentzündung. Fünf Wochen war sie kaum ansprechbar, bis der Arzt endlich eine Besserung ihres Zustandes konstatierte. Zur Sicherheit sollte sie zur Röntgenaufnahme ins örtliche Krankenhaus überwiesen werden. „Das Schlimme ist eben, daß um die Lunge zu fürchten ist. Ich hoffe aber nicht"[14], schrieb sie nach Massing.

Ein Röntgenbild von Mitte Oktober zeigte außer der Rippenfellentzündung am linken Lungenflügel noch eine beschattete Stelle. „3 Monate liegen". lautete darauf die Anweisung der Spezialistin, eine große Enttäuschung für Maria Innocentia, die auf baldige Besserung gehofft hatte. Dennoch durfte sie ihre besorgte Familie nach der Diagnose beruhigen: „Ich kann wieder ganz gesund werden, muß nur jetzt das ‚Opfer des Liegens' bringen."[15] Viktoria Hummel hatte stärkendes Malzbier geschickt, „ich hab Vertrauen dazu, schon deßhalb, weil es von ‚daheim' ist u. Mama alles darauf hält. Man kann ja sonst so wenig tun."[16] Hundefett, Lebertran und ein warmes Leibchen mit Katzenfell sollen das Übrige zur Heilung beitragen. Maria Innocentia war in ihrem Atelier untergebracht, unter Tags stets bei offenem Fenster nach Süden. Frischluft sei gut für die Lunge, hatte man im Saulgauer Krankenhaus geraten.

Kalanchoe am Fenster, 1943/1944
Kalanchoe at the window, 1943/1944

Villa Vogelfrei „geschlossen" und Skizze, 1944/1945
Villa Vogelfrei (Outlaw) "closed" and Sketch, 1944/1945

Kloster Sießen, Klosterkirche
Convent Siessen, convent church

During the July heat of 1944 Maria Innocentia came down with bronchitis and pleurisy. For five weeks she was nearly unresponsive, until the physician called in from Saulgau could finally diagnose an improvement in her condition. To make sure, she was to be referred to the local hospital for an X-ray test. "The bad news is that one might have to fear for the lung; but I hope not,"[14] she wrote to Massing.

An X-ray taken in mid-October showed, besides the pleurisy, a shadow on the left lung. Thereupon the woman pulmonologist ordered "three months of bed rest," a major disappointment for Maria Innocentia, who had hoped for a quick recovery. Even so she was able to reassure the worried family after the diagnosis: "I can get completely well again, just have to make the 'sacrifice of lying down.'"[15] Viktoria Hummel had sent malt beer to strengthen her: "I have great confidence in it, if only because it is from 'home' and Mama sets such store by it. There is so little else to be done anyway."[16] Dog's fat, cod-liver oil, a warm bodice made of cat's fur were to speed the healing further. Maria Innocentia had been put up in her studio, always with the southern window open during the day. Fresh air would be good for the lungs, the Saulgau hospital had advised.

Aschenbrödel, 1944
Cinderella, 1944

Maria Innocentias Taschenuhr wurde später in Massing aufbewahrt, mit der Aufschrift: „Uhr von Inno Bertl".
Maria Innocentia's pocket watch, preserved in Massing, with the inscription "Inno Bertl's watch."

Maria Innocentias Zustand blieb bedenklich instabil. Anfang November empfahl die Ärztin eine Luftveränderung und überwies sie in das Wilhelmstift Isny im Allgäu, eine Fachklinik für Lungenkrankheiten. Maria Innocentia musste dort einer ernüchternden Diagnose ins Auge blicken. „Leider ist der Lungenbefund nicht so harmlos, wie man ihn mir in Saulgau vorgestellt hat", schrieb sie deprimiert nach Massing, und eine neue, gequälte Unruhe ist ihrem atemlosen Schreibstil anzumerken. „So muß ich aber glauben, daß ich ‚krank' bin – obwohl es mir gar nicht so ist. O liebste Eltern, das waren jetzt schwere Tage – schon das Fortgehen von Siessen – die Angst – das Fremde – u. so vieles – vieles –. Das Eine dürft Ihr schon hoffen, daß ich noch heilbar bin – aber natürlich mit viel Geduld." Dringend äußerte sie am Ende des Briefes noch eine bemerkenswerte Bitte, die sie in vielen ihrer folgenden Briefe wiederholen würde: „Wenn Ihr mir schreibt – bitte nie meinen Namen, für keinen Fall ‚Hummel' am äußeren Couvert. In der Heilstätte wissen es nur die Schwestern, daß ich hier bin, nicht aber die Patienten – Mutter Oberin wünscht, daß es nicht bekannt wird. Es wäre mir auch sehr lieb, wenn Ihr darüber nicht mit den Leuten reden würdet, wenigstens nicht über die Art der Erkrankung – gelt – bitte."[17]

Die Tage und Wochen gingen dahin. Die Stimmung wechselte. Maria Innocentia war auf eigenen Wunsch mit einer Sießener Mitschwester in ein Zimmer gelegt worden, die sich wegen ihrer Lungenkrankheit ebenfalls in Isny aufhielt. An guten Tagen siegte die Zuversicht. Dann schrieb sie in aufmunterndem Elan nach Sießen, man möge sich nicht zu viel um sie sorgen: „Im Übrigen ist bei uns der Frohsinn zu Haus und alle, die kommen, sollen davon zu kosten bekommen. Wie oft fahren wir im Geiste nach Sießen – natürlich mit dem ersten Zug (…). O Sießen, mein Sießen!"[18]

Die düsteren Gedanken kommen von selbst. Maria Innocentia muss an ihre Geschwister und an ihre Kindheit denken. An das „Eckerlsitzen", wenn sie etwas angestellt hatten. „Das Winkelstehen steht manchen Schwestern so gut an", hatte vor nicht allzu langer Zeit der Vikar der Klinik gesagt. Sie schreibt der Mutter Oberin nach Sießen: „Ich hoffe, daß ich mich ‚im Eckerl' auch gut ausnehme u. der liebe Gott jeden Tag zufriedener sein wird mit seinem borstigen Pinsel, den er in die Ecke geworfen hat. Ob er ihn wohl noch einmal gebrauchen wird? Bisweilen benützt man solch abgenützte Pinsel zu allerhand Dreckarbeiten."[19]

Ansichtskarte des Sanatoriums Wilhelmstift in Isny und Postkarte an die Familie in Massing
Picture postcard of the sanatorium Wilhelmstift in Isny and postcard to the family in Massing

*Skizze „Grüß Gott, tritt ein", 1940er
Druckstock für Holzschnitt
Massinger Haus, 1928*
Sketch: "Hello, come in," 1940's
Printing block for woodcut of
a Massing house, 1928

Über den Dächern, 1928/1930
High above the roofs, 1928/1930

Maria Innocentia's state of health remained gravely unstable. Early in November the woman doctor recommended a change of air and referred her to the Wilhelmstift at Isny in the Allgäu, a clinic specializing in lung diseases. There Maria Innocentia had to face a sobering diagnosis. "The condition of the lung is unfortunately not as harmless as presented to me in Saulgau," she wrote downcast to Massing, and a new, tormented unrest is noticeable in her breathless style. "So now I must think that I am really 'ill' – although I don't feel as if I am. O dearest parents, these have been hard days – just the departure from Siessen – the anxiety – the strange surroundings – and so much else – so much –. One thing you can surely hope, that I am still curable – but of course only with lots of patience." Interestingly, she concludes with an urgent request, one she would reiterate in many of her subsequent letters: "If you write to me – please never include my name, on no account 'Hummel' on the envelope. At the sanatorium only the nurses know that I am here, but not the patients – Mother Superior does not wish that it become public. I would also greatly prefer if you did not talk to people about it, at least not about the nature of the disease – all right? – please?"[17]

Days and weeks passed with changing outlooks. By her own wish, Maria Innocentia had been assigned a room together with a fellow sister from Siessen, who had likewise been referred to Isny for a pulmonary illness. On good days confidence prevailed, and she would write to those in Siessen with reassuring élan that they should not worry about her too much: "Overall, cheerfulness dwells with us, and all who come here shall get a taste of it. How often do we travel back to Siessen in spirit – on the earliest train, of course (…). O Siessen, my Siessen!"[18]

The black thoughts come by themselves. Maria Innocentia has to think of her siblings and her childhood, for example of the "corner sitting," after they had been up to some mischief. "Standing in the corner really becomes many a sister," the vicar at the clinic had said not long ago. Now Maria Innocentia writes to the Mother Superior in Siessen: "I hope that in the 'corner' I'll cut a good figure, too, and that the good Lord will be satisfied every day with his bristly paintbrush, which he has cast into the corner. Will he use it once more? Sometimes one employs such worn-out brushes for all kinds of dirty work."[19]

Das zerstörte Verlagsgebäude der Ars sacra nach einer Bombennacht vom 9. auf den 10. März 1943
The bombed press building of Ars Sacra after an air raid on the night of March 9-10, 1943

Zum 31. Dezember kündigte Maria Innocentia vorläufig ihren Vertrag mit Ars sacra. Eine Last weniger. „Doch glaube ich, daß Sie mein Handeln im Hinblick auf die Zeitlage und meinen gegenwärtigen Gesundheitszustand sicher verstehen werden."[20]

Anfang Februar 1945 kam die erste Entwarnung. Die Tomografie der Lunge fiel derart gut aus, dass der Chefarzt von einem „reinsten Wunder" sprach. „Jetzt glaube ich, daß mich der lb. Gott noch einmal gesund haben will u. dankbar nehme [ich] das geschenkte Leben aus seiner Hand an. Ich fühle oft schon richtig Schwung – ein Zeichen, daß ich gesunde"[21], jubelte Maria Innocentia nach Massing. Die Entlassung erfolgte „auf eigenen Wunsch", „gebessert", aber „arbeitsunfähig". Maria Innocentia hatte unbedingt darauf gedrängt, nach Sießen gebracht zu werden. Von Osten rückten die amerikanischen, von Westen die französischen Soldaten vor und die Lage für einen Krankentransport würde immer unberechenbarer werden.

Eine Sießener Mitschwester hatte bei ihrer Entlassung fassungslos ausgerufen: „Du gehst nach Sießen, wo sie nichts zu essen haben und du hier so gut versorgt wirst?" Diese Nachricht nahm Maria Innocentia derart mit, dass sie vor der Heimfahrt eine Herzspritze benötigte.

Gott um Demut bitten ist ihr leises Gebet. „Nun das will ich lernen, ‚das Pinsele' sein, ob im Kasten liegend, wartend auf die Hand des Meisters, ob schon benützt u. dann weggelegt, damit es gereinigt werde von allem Schmutz, ob in der Hand des Meisters, daß er es führe und damit Freude schaffe oder aber – ausgebraucht – gerade recht zum Wegwerfen."[22]

Am 23. April 1945, gerade acht Tage, nachdem Maria Innocentia in ihr Kloster zurückgekehrt war, rollten die französischen Panzer in Sießen ein. Einsatzführer und Lagerleiter wurden verhaftet und von bewaffneten Soldaten nach Saulgau abgeführt. Unter dem Hakenkreuz über dem Haupteingang kam das jahrelang verhüllte Christusbild des Klosters wieder zum Vorschein. Am 30. April, an demselben Tag, an dem im fernen Berlin Adolf Hitler und seine frisch angetraute Eva in ihrem unterirdischen Führerbunker Selbstmord begingen, bekamen die Ordensfrauen von den französischen Alliierten ihre Eigentumsrechte bestätigt. Das „tausendjährige" Dritte Reich und der Zweite Weltkrieg hatten ein Ende.

As of December 31, Maria Innocentia canceled her contract with Ars Sacra for the time being. One burden less. "But I think that you will surely understand my action in view of the current situation and the present state of my health."[20]

Early in February of 1945, a first "all-clear" was sounded. The tomography of the lung was so positive that the head physician spoke of a "sheer miracle." "Now I do think that the good Lord wants me to be well once more, and I thankfully accept the newly given life from his hand. I already feel downright vigorous – a sign, that I am recovering,"[21] Maria Innocentia exulted in a letter to Massing. Her discharge took place "at her own wish" and with the remark "improved" but "unfit for work." She had insisted on being taken back to Siessen. From the east, American troops were advancing, French forces from the west, and the road situation for a sick transport was becoming increasingly unpredictable.

Maria Innocentias Atelier, 1946
Maria Innocentia's studio, 1946

At her release, a fellow sister from Siessen had exclaimed in total perplexity: "You are going to Siessen, though you are so well taken care of here, while in Siessen they have nothing to eat?" This bit of news took such a toll of Maria Innocentia that she had to be given a cardiac injection before the trip.

Pleading with God for humility is her silent prayer. "I want to learn now just to be 'the little paintbrush,' whether lying in the box, waiting for the hand of the master, or already used and put aside to be cleaned of all dirt, whether in the hand of the master for him to wield and create pleasure, or else – used up – just good enough to be thrown away."[22]

On April 23, 1945, just eight days after Maria Innocentia had returned to her convent, French tanks rolled into Siessen. The *Einsatzführer* and the camp commandant were arrested and taken to Saulgau by an armed guard. The crucifix over the main entrance, hidden for years under a swastika, came into view again. On April 30, the day on which in far-away Berlin Adolf Hitler and his newly wed Eva took poison in their underground "Führer" bunker, the sisters were restored their property rights by the French allied forces. The "thousand-year" Reich and the Second World War had come to an end.

Verschiedene Gutachten der Tuberkulose-Fürsorge des Staatlichen Gesundheitsamts Saulgau
Medical certificates of the tuberculosis service of the State Public Health Office in Saulgau

Dennoch blieben die Verhältnisse chaotisch. Die französische Verwaltung war überfordert mit all den Menschen, die sich im hoffnungslos überfüllten Lager aufhielten. Es würde noch fünf lange Monate dauern, bis auch die letzten 1200 Insassen am 30. Oktober das Lager räumen konnten. Die französischen Pétain-Sympathisanten, die seit Kriegsende in gelähmter Angst vor der Rache ihrer Landsleute verharrten, erwartete ein grausames Schicksal. Eine Augenzeugin aus dem Kloster berichtet, dass eines Mittags schwarze Lastwagen mit französischer Kennung einfuhren, um die internierten Pétain-Anhänger abzuholen. Die Männer von ihnen seien vermutlich alle erschossen worden.

Bis zum Sommer ging es trotz allem stetig aufwärts mit Maria Innocentias Gesundheit. Sie nahm wieder zu und wurde kräftiger.[23] Bis am 19. Juli 1945 ein Bluterbrechen einen neuerlichen Krankheitsschub auslöste.

Seit beinahe zwei Monaten hatte die Familie in Massing nichts mehr von Maria Innocentia gehört. Am frühen Abend des 16. September fuhr eine einsame Fahrradfahrerin die Birkenallee nach Sießen hinauf. Als sie im Klosterhof von ihrem klapprigen Gefährt sprang, kam ihr eine der Schwestern aus der Pforte entgegengelaufen. „Centa Hummel! Sie schickt der Himmel!" Niederbayern oblag amerikanischer Besatzung, und es war in jenen unmittelbaren Nachkriegsmonaten keine Seltenheit, dass alle Verbindungen zwischen den verschiedenen Zonen gekappt waren. Eines Tages hatte Centa die Ungewissheit nicht mehr ausgehalten und war mit einem alten Fahrrad, das noch nicht einmal Bremsen hatte, nach Westen aufgebrochen. Die Fahrt war mehr als abenteuerlich gewesen, denn ohne Passierschein gab es zwischen den Zonen keine Einreiseerlaubnis, und die Franzosen galten nicht als zimperlich, was die Behandlung der ehemaligen Kriegsgegner anbelangte. Centa hatte über 700 Kilometer zurückgelegt, also mehr als die doppelte Strecke als gewöhnlich, um den patrouillierenden Soldateneinheiten zu entgehen.

Even so conditions remained chaotic. The French military administration was overtaxed by the masses of people in the hopelessly overcrowded camp. It would be five more months before, on October 30, the last 1200

Die Aufteilung Deutschlands in vier Besatzungszonen: amerikanische, britische, französische und russische Zone, um 1945
The division of Germany into four occupied zones: American, British, French and Russian, about 1945

Skizzenblatt mit Mariendarstellungen und Skizzenblatt mit Tieren, 1946
Sketch sheet with Madonnas and Sketch sheet with animals, 1946

inmates were able to leave the camp. The Pétain French, who ever since the end of the war had been paralyzed with fear of revenge from their countrymen, met with a grim fate. According to an eyewitness account from the convent, black trucks with French license plates drove up one day to pick up the interned Pétain adherents. The men among them, the report says, were presumably all shot.

Nonetheless Maria Innocentia's health kept improving steadily into the summer. She regained weight and kept getting stronger.[23] Until on July 19, 1945, a vomiting of blood signaled a new phase of illness.

For nearly two months the family in Massing had not heard anything from Maria Innocentia. In the early evening of September 16, a solitary bicyclist came riding up the birch alley to Siessen. As she jumped off her rickety bike in the convent yard, a sister came running towards her from the convent gate. "Centa Hummel! Heaven has sent you!" Lower Bavaria was in the American occupation zone, and it was not infrequent in those immediate months after the war for all communication between the different zones to be disrupted. One day Centa had been able to bear the uncertainty no longer and had started out west on an ancient bicycle that did not even have any brakes. The trip had been more than adventurous, for one could not cross from one zone into another without a permit, and the French were not known to treat their former enemies with kid gloves. Centa had traveled for some 440 miles, more than twice the normal distance, to evade the military border patrols.

Kinderheilstätte Wangen im Allgäu

„Besuch und ärztliche Untersuchung der Schwester": Passierschein in die französische Zone nach Wangen für Dr. Franz Hummel
"Visit and medical examination of the sister": Franz Hummel's pass for Wangen in the French Zone

Maria Innocentia liegt in dem kleinen Raum, der ihr letztes Atelier war. Sie sieht wieder stark ausgezehrt aus und die Augen sind glasig vom Fieber. „Die lassen mich hier einfach liegen!", begehrt sie plötzlich ein einziges Mal auf. Centa, die am Bett sitzt, bricht es das Herz.

Auf Centas Betreiben wurde die Kranke zum Arzt nach Saulgau gebracht. „Wegen Erkrankung an Lungentuberkulose mit Lungenblutung dringend sofort zur Spezialbehandlung und Heilstättenkur in die Heilstätte nach Wangen"[24], lautete die Empfehlung.

Die Vorgesetzten hatten lange gezögert, Maria Innocentia in Behandlung zu geben – zu lange? Ob man der Kranken die Reise in eine Fachklinik nicht zumuten wollte? Das Alleinsein in fremder Umgebung? Ob religiöse Schicksalsergebenheit einen festen Entschluss hemmte? Hätte ein rechtzeitig klares Wort der Mutter Oberin vielleicht bessere Heilungschancen bedeutet?

Am 20. September wurde Maria Innocentia in Begleitung zweier Schwestern in die überfüllte Lungenheilstätte oberhalb des malerischen Städtchens Wangen im Allgäu eingeliefert. Centa war solange bei ihr geblieben und fuhr dann mit ihrem Fahrrad dem Krankenauto nach, um sicherzugehen, dass ihre Schwester gut untergebracht war. Der Chefarzt Prof. Dr. Heinrich Brügger kümmerte sich persönlich um die prominente Patientin. Die Tuberkulose hatte sich auch auf den zweiten Lungenflügel ausgebreitet: „Bei der Aufnahme am 20. September 1945 bestand ein ausgesprochen doppelseitiger Befund. Ich halte die Prognose nicht für günstig. (...) Irgendwelche operativen Maßnahmen kommen bei Sr. Innocentia nicht in Frage, da es sich um einen doppelseitigen Befund handelt, der progredient ist und die Patientin nicht über besonders gute Abwehr verfügt."[25]

linke Seite:
Ernste Beratung unter Kollegen: Schreiben des Direktors der Klinik Professor Brügger an Maria Innocentias Bruder „Dr. med. Franz Hummel" und Ansichtskarte der Kinderheilstätte Wangen. In dem vor allem auf Kinder spezialisierten Lungenkrankenhaus arbeiteten auch Franziskanerinnen aus dem Kloster Sießen in der Krankenpflege.
left side:
Consultation among colleagues: letter from the clinic director, Professor Brügger, to Maria Innocentia's brother "Dr. Franz Hummel, M.D." and Picture postcard of the sanatorium, Wangen. The pulmonary clinic, which was mainly for children, included several Franciscan nuns from Convent Siessen on its nursing staff.

Maria Innocentia was lying in the small room that was her last studio. She once again looked gaunt, and her eyes were glassy from the fever. "They just let me lie here!" she protested for once. Centa's heart broke as she sat by the side of the bed.

At her insistence, the patient was taken to the physician in Saulgau. His recommendation: "Due to acute pulmonary tuberculosis with bleeding from the lungs, to be referred at once for specialized treatment to the sanatorium in Wangen."[24]

The superiors had hesitated for a long time to send Maria Innocentia to medical care – too long? Did they not want to impose a long journey to a specialized clinic upon the sick woman? Or being alone in strange surroundings? Did religious resignation to fate hamper a firm decision? Might a timely, resolute word from the Mother Superior have meant a greater chance of recovery?

On September 20, Maria Innocentia, accompanied by two sisters, was admitted to the overcrowded tuberculosis sanatorium above the picturesque town of Wangen in the Allgäu. Centa, who had remained with her, followed the ambulance on her bicycle to make sure that her sister would be properly accommodated. The head physician, Prof. Dr. Heinrich Brügger, took on the prominent patient in person. The consumption had spread to the second lung. "At her admission on Sepember 20, 1945, double-sided tuberculosis was plainly diagnosed. The prognosis is not favorable in my judgment. Operative procedures are out of the question, as Sr. Innocentia's (…) condition is progressive and the patient does not have a particularly strong immune system."[25]

An „Meine Lieben" nach Massing: Seit Monaten benutzte Maria Innocentia zum Schreiben ihrer Briefe nur noch Bleistift.
To "My dear ones" in Massing: for months now, Maria Innocentia had been using nothing but pencil for her letters.

Porträt Franz Hummel, 1930
Portrait of Franz Hummel, 1930

Noch einmal Kinderbilder:
„Einige nette kleine Sachen", 1946
Zur eiligen Gratulation
Der richtige Osterhase
Once more children's pictures:
"A few nice little things," 1946
Quick Congratulation
The Real Easter Bunny

Sowohl Maria Innocentias Bruder Franz Hummel, der Chefarzt im niederbayerischen Arnstorf geworden war, als auch Maximiliane Müller und Herbert Dubler in der Schweiz hatten sich schon seit einiger Zeit um Sanatoriumsplätze für die schwer kranke Künstlerin bemüht. Franz hatte einen amerikanischen Major getroffen, der ein großer Hummel-Verehrer war und sein Militärflugzeug schicken wollte, um Maria Innocentia abzuholen. Man wartete auf die Zustimmung der Klosterleitung.

Drei Monate nach Maria Innocentias Einweisung nach Wangen lautete der Bericht von Chefarzt Dr. Brügger: „Schwester Innocentia geht es zur Zeit leidlich. Die Temperaturen sind ruhig geworden. An und für sich würde ich einen Aufenthalt in der Schweiz sehr befürworten, nur weiß ich nicht recht, ob der Zeitpunkt nicht etwas verfrüht ist. Ich befürchte, daß der Gesundheitszustand von Schwester Innocentia durch die gewiß nicht leichte Reise geschädigt werden kann und daß erneut Temperaturen auftreten. Das wäre in dem jetzigen Zustande sehr bedauerlich. Wenn die Angehörigen oder Sie sich sehr viel versprechen von dem Aufenthalt in der Schweiz, so müßte man sie vielleicht doch hinschicken. Ich selbst bin aber zurückhaltend damit. Schwester Innocentia selbst möchte jetzt auch nicht fort. Wir werden weiterhin alles tun für sie, was möglich ist."[26] Maria Innocentia selbst verhielt sich passiv: „Ich überlasse es ganz den Vorgesetzten", schrieb sie nach Massing.[27]

Stunde um Stunde sickert die Zeit in die lähmende Stille hinein. „Für mich heißt es jetzt nur immer: warten, warten – warten – zum Leben oder zum Tod."[28] Zu Centa, die zu Besuch gekommen ist, sagt sie: „Weißt du, ich glaube, ich bin das Kriegsopfer der Familie." Opfer an der Brüder statt, die unversehrt aus dem Krieg zurückgekommen sind.

Zu der Tuberkulose kam der Befund einer neuen Herzschwäche. Maria Innocentia sehnte sich in ihr geliebtes Kloster zurück. An besseren Tagen kam der alte Schalk durch: „Wenn von Sießen ein Auto kommt, wird man mich fast beaufsichten müssen, daß ich mich nicht in einen Apfelsack schmuggle und so mit nach Sießen fahre. – Aber was wäre das dort für eine Enttäuschung, wenn statt der Äpfel ‚die Hummel' herausrollen würde."[29] An anderen, fiebrigen und schwachen Tagen bat sie immer wieder: „Aber nicht wahr, liebe Mutter Oberin, wenn mir nicht mehr zu helfen ist u. das Krankenhaus hergerichtet ist, dann, dann darf ich doch heim – o bitte, bitte."[30]

For some time both Maria Innocentia's brother, Franz Hummel, who had become head physician in Arnstorf in Lower Bavaria, and Maximiliane Müller and Herbert Dubler in Switzerland, had endeavored to find a first-rate sanatorium for the desperately ill artist. Franz had met an American major, who was a great Hummel fan and offered to send his military plane to fetch Maria Innocentia. What was still needed was the consent of the convent administration.

Three months after Maria Innocentia's admission to Wangen, head physician Dr. Brügger wrote in his summary report: "Sister Innocentia is doing passably at the moment. Her temperatures have stabilized. In general I would highly recommend a stay in Switzerland, except that I am not sure if at the moment it is not too soon for that. I fear that Sr. Innocentia's condition might be adversely affected by the demands of the journey and that her temperature could go up again, which would be very regrettable given her present state. If the family or she herself expect a great deal from a stay in Switzerland, one should perhaps send her there. I myself have some reservations, however. Sister Innocentia also does not want to leave now. We shall continue to do everything possible for her."[26] Maria Inocentia herself remained passive: "I leave it altogether to my superiors,"[27] she wrote to Massing.

*Muttergottes, 1946,
untertitelt von Viktoria Hummel
mit „Bertas letztes Bild"*
*"Berta's last picture":
Mother of God, 1946,
with subtitle by Viktoria Hummel*

Hour by hour time elapses into petrifying silence. "For me, there is now only waiting, waiting, - always waiting – for life, or for death."[28] Centa, who has come to visit, she tells: "You know, I think I am our family's war sacrifice." Sacrifice as substitute for the brothers, who have returned from the war unharmed.

Added to the consumption was the diagnosis of a weak heart. Maria Innocentia yearned to be back in her beloved convent. On better days, the old roguish spirit came to the fore again: "If a car should come from Siessen, I would have to be watched, lest I smuggle myself into an apple sack and travel to Siessen that way. – But what a disappointment it would be if, instead of apples, 'the Hummel' were to come tumbling out."[29] On other days of fever and weakness, she would beg again and again: "But dear Mother Superior, when I am past all help and the clinic is fixed up, then I may come home, yes? Oh, please, please!"[30]

Muttergottes-Ikone aus Maria Innocentias Krankenzimmer
Mother-of-God icon from Maria Innocentia's sick-room

Beinahe ein Jahr verbrachte Maria Innocentia in der Lungenheilstätte Wangen. Sie bekam ein Einzelzimmer, wo sie die häufigen Besuche ihrer Familie empfangen und sogar ein wenig zeichnen konnte. „Einige nette kleine Sachen"[31], ganz zart und fein, als wolle sie zum Abschied noch einmal mit leiser Wehmut über die Seiten ihres Skizzenblocks streichen. Die Farben so duftig und hell wie schon lange nicht mehr.[32] Ihre Briefe nach Massing unterzeichnete sie jetzt mit „Eure Inno".

Am 9. September 1946 wurde Maria Innocentia mit dem Auto von der Generaloberin von Wangen abgeholt und nach Sießen gebracht. Das geschwächte Herz hatte eine weitere Behandlung unmöglich gemacht.

Vom Krankenzimmer schreibt sie ein letztes Mal in die alte Heimat an die Eltern. „Sehr freue ich mich auf Euer Kommen. Ich würde vorschlagen bald, weil es sonst kalt wird u. Ihr bei mir frieren müßtet."[33]

Es war ein unwirtlicher Herbst 1946. Die Blätter an den Bäumen verfärbten sich früh. Die Tage waren dunkel. Am 11. Oktober bat Maria Innocentia um die Sterbesakramente. Im Beisein ihrer Mutter erwartete sie von nun an, „mit brennender Lampe dem Herrn entgegenzugehen"[34]

Letzte Post an die Eltern: „Sehr freue ich mich auf Euer Kommen. (...) Auf Wiedersehen!"
Last letter to the parents: "I am so looking forward to your coming. (...) Good-bye till then!"

For almost a year Maria Innocentia stayed at the Wangen sanatorium. She was given a single room, where she could receive her family and even do some drawing. "A few nice little things,"[31] very soft and delicate, as if she wanted to caress the pages of her sketchbook one last time in a wistful farewell. Colors as light and gossamery as they had not been for a long time.[32] Her letters to Massing she now regularly signed with "Your Inno."

On September 9, 1946, Maria Innocentia was picked up by car by the Mother Superior and brought back to Siessen. Her weakened heart had rendered further treatment impossible.

From her sick-room at the convent, she wrote one last time to her parents at her old home, asking them to come to Siessen. "I would suggest soon, because then it will get cold and you would freeze here."[33]

The autumn of 1946 was not a genial one. The leaves on the trees turned early, the days were gloomy. On October 11, Maria Innocentia asked for the last rites. In the presence of her mother she expected from now on "to walk toward the Lord with my lamp burning."[34]

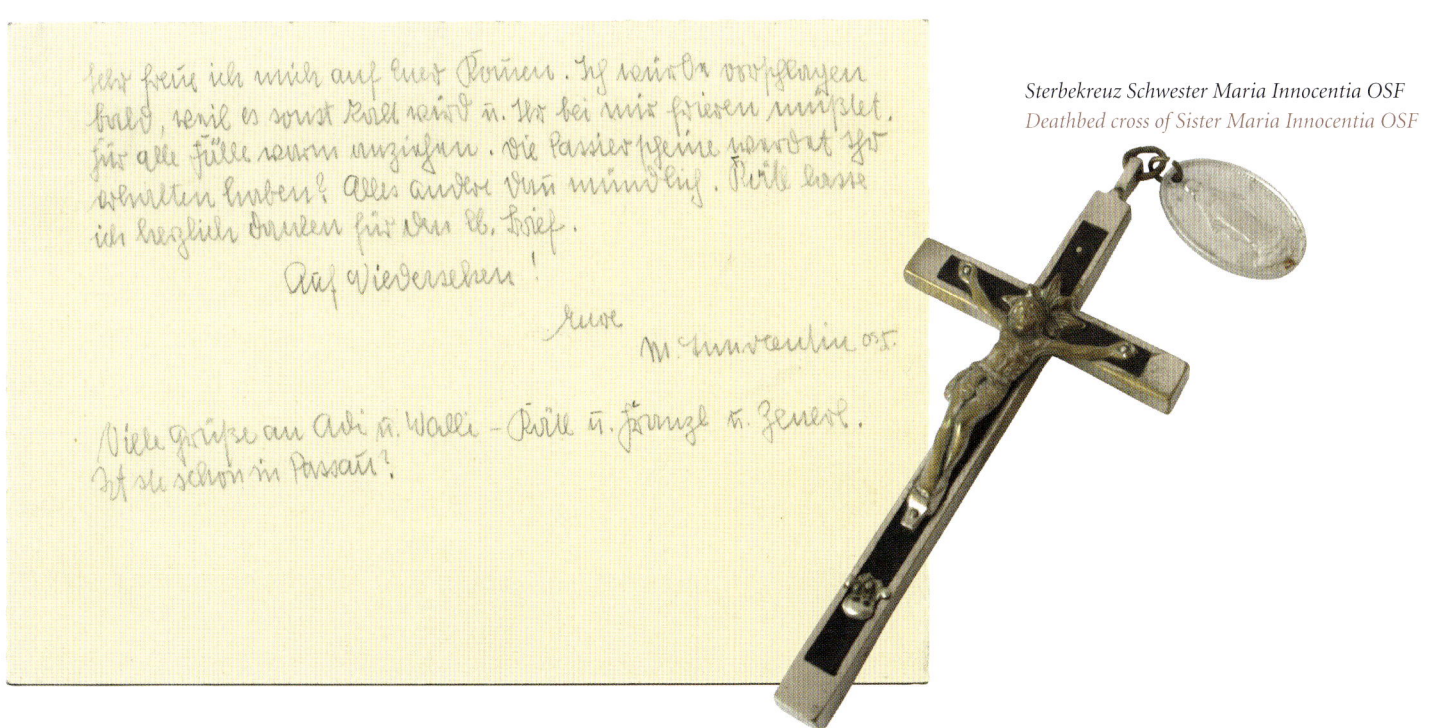

Sterbekreuz Schwester Maria Innocentia OSF
Deathbed cross of Sister Maria Innocentia OSF

Am Morgen des 6. November empfing sie noch einmal – ein letztes Mal – die heilige Kommunion. Den ganzen Vormittag beteten die Mitschwestern am Krankenbett. Kurz vor zwölf Uhr öffnete die Sterbende noch einmal ihre Augen, mit einem Blick wie aus der Ferne nahm sie noch einmal Abschied von ihrer Mutter, die an ihrem Bett saß. Als mittags die Angelusglocke zu läuten begann, starb Maria Innocentia, in der einen Hand die Sterbekerze, in der anderen Rosenkranz und Sterbekreuz.[35]

Es schneit. Maria Innocentia hatte sich so sehr Schnee gewünscht für ihre Beerdigung. In großen Flocken schneit es auf den Weg zum Klosterfriedhof. Es ist still, trotz der vielen Menschen, die gekommen sind. Die Farben des Herbstes verschwinden. In kürzester Zeit ist alles weiß.[36]

„In stiller Trauer":
Totenbrief der Mutter
"In quiet mourning":
Requiem letter of the mother

Massing den 12. Nov. 1946

Meine Lieben!

Nachdem die Teilnahme und die Nachfrage so groß ist möchte ich einen kurzen Bericht über das Ableben unserer Jnnocentia geben.
Am Allerheiligentag bei Tisch, kam ein telefonischer Anruf von Sießen. Die Verständigung war nur durch Vermittlung möglich. Die Schwester habe Herzschwäche, es solle jemand kommen. Nachdem schon Briefe von Herzschwächen kamen, waren wir schon auf das Schlimmste gefaßt. Mit bangen Herzen fuhren Papa und ich am Allerseelentag, Samstag, früh hier weg. Unterwegs konnten wir telefonieren und erfuhren daß sich Jnno. wieder besser fühle. Gott sei Dank sie lebt! Am Sonntag früh trafen wir sie besser als wir hofften. Am Montag früh und vormittag war Jnno so frisch da ß sich Papa entschloß nachmittags heimzufahren. Beim Abschied waren beide recht tapfer, so schwer es war. Papa war ihr doch so viel, er verstand sie, besonders in der Kunst, am besten. Ich begleitete ihn zur Bahn, wie oft gingen seine Blicke nach dem schönen Kloster, mit der bangen Frage, werde ich Dich wohl wiedersehen? Joh ging erst um 5 Uhr zu Jnno. Ich traf sie recht müde und verändert. Die frischen, klaren, großen und strahlenden Augen, die sie noch vormittags hatte, steckten viel tiefer. Die blauen Ringe um die Augen fielen mir besonders auf. Die kommende Nacht brachte Herzbeschwerden, der Dinstagnachmittag brachte wieder eine große Herzschwäche, ebenso die Nacht war schlimm. Am Mittwoch den 6. um 9Uhr holte man Mutter Oberin und mich. Auch H.H. Superior kam, er betete die Sterbegebete. Sie wurde bewußtlos und kamm wieder zu sich. Noch ein langer Blick zu ihrer lieben geistigen Mutter, ein langer Blick zu mir „zu a-ll den lieben Mitschwestern die um ihr Bett standen,-unterm Angelus läuten gab unser liebes gutes Kind den Geist auf. Mutter Oberin sagte: O, seliges Sterben, unter dem Geläute aller Glocken ging sie in den Himmel! Wie wird ihr die lb. Mutter Gottes

die sie so sehr verehrte, entgegengekommen sein! Die Trauer und der Schmerz um Jnno. ist in Sießen groß, zumal sie bis zur letzten Stunde auf ein Wunder hofften. Mutter Oberin sagte, bei Tisch waren alle Schwestern aufs tiefste ergriffen, es wurde kein Wort gesprochen. Jnno. war ja so beliebt, aber der lb. Gott hatte sie noch lieber.
Meine Lieben, es war für mich bestimmt schwer, a-ber ich weiß nichtwie mir war, ich ha-tte trotz allem einen Trost in mir, und mußte Gott danken, da-ß ich so ein Kind haben durfte. Wa-s ich diese schweren Tage erlebte möchte ich nicht missen. Daß ich bei Jnno in den letzten Stunden beistehen durfte ist mir ein großer Trost . Für Papa wäre das zu schwer gewesen, er ha-t sie noch so gesehen, wie ers ertragen konnte.
Am Freitag kamen nach 9stündiger Autofahrt Papa mit Kinder.
In der Kapelle im Klosterhof war Jnno aufgebahrt. Sie lag so schön und voll da , sie lächelte, ma-n hätte sie immer ansehen können.
Am Samstag um 8Uhr war die Beerdigung. Es war eine selten schöne ergreifende Feier. Nach der Aussegnung von der Kapelle wurde die Bahre von 8 Schwestern im Leichenzug unter dem Gesang Miserere, von den Schwestern gesungen, in die Kirche getragen, mit Kränzen und Blumen geschmückt. Das ist in Sießen Brauch (daß) die Tote darf zum Letztenmal bei der Gemeinschaft sein. Nach dem Requiem, das ein Hofrat aus Wien spielte, wurde eine geordnete Prozeßion a-ufgestellt von kl. Kinder , über 100Zöglinge, Adspirantine Apostolantinen, Verwandte, Bahre, Geistlichkeit, Besuche, MutterOberin mit Convent, und Weltleute. Die Schwestern sangen da-s Requiem und am Grabe wunderbar. Was uns sehr lieb war, es wurde nichts gesprochen. Es waren viele hohe Persöhnlichkeiten da, man sah die Männer in Tränen aufgelöst, noch beim kontolieren. Blumen und Kranzspende war groß und schön. Der Abschied vom Gra-be war schwer. Was das heißtwenn Elterndem zweiten erwachsenen Kinde in's Grab schauen muß, da-s weiß nur der, der das gleiche Loos teilt. Solche gibt es heute viele. Der lb. Gott verlangt scheint von jedem ein Kriegsopfer und so wollen wir uns mit den millionen trösten. Jnno sagte öfters:o, last mich heimgehn, ich ka-nn Euch doch vom Himmel mehr helfen. Und so wollen wir weiter beten, zu ihr, sie möge uns als

On the morning of November 6, she again – and for the last time – received Holy Communion. All morning her fellow sisters prayed at her bedside. Shortly before noon the dying artist once more opened her eyes. With a look as if from far away, she took a last leave of her mother, who was sitting by her bed. As the Angelus bells began to chime at noon, Maria Innocentia died, death candle in one hand, cross and rosary in the other.[35]

It is snowing. Maria Innocentia had wished so much for snow at her funeral. It is snowing in large flakes on the way to the convent cemetery. And it is very still, despite the many people who have come. The autumn colors vanish. In a short time everything is a pure white.[36]

```
                    2.Blatt

erste Hilfe ,unsern braven Schwiegersohn von der Gefang-
schaft heimbitten. Bitte unterstützt uns im Gebete.
Meine Lieben!
Wir ha-ben am Dinstag hier in Massing den Trauergottes-
dinst für die Pfarrei. So unendlich leid es uns tut
Können wir mit dem besten Willem unsere lieben Verwand-
ten nicht bitten,den wir haben keine Übernachtungs-
möglichkeit. Alle Häuser sind hier überbelegt. Wir
haben 5 Erwachsene Eva-kuirte im Haus, im ga nzen sind
uns 22 Personen.Die lieben Verwandten werden das einsehen
Wir bitten auch unsere Verwandten hier in Massing und
Umgebung nicht,außer Geschwister. Unser Verwandtkreis
ist ja so groß,wie soll man jetzt so viel Menschen versor
gen.
Verzeiht meine Fehler, ich schreibe so selten,und bin
mit Maschinenschreiben nicht recht bewandert, und
das viele schreiben rüttelt immer wieder a-ll das
Schwere auf.

             Jn stiller Trauer
```

Viktoria Hummel am Grab ihrer Tochter, 1963
Viktoria Hummel, at the grave of her daughter, 1963

Epilog

„Leg dich einmal ins Gras, nimm ein kleines Blümchen, einen Grashalm, sieh sie Dir genau an, vergleiche, wie verschieden u. mannigfaltig ihre Gestaltung ist, dann gehe heim u. zeichne, was Du beobachtet u. gesehen hast, Du wirst sehen, wie notwendig es ist, erst richtig ‚schauen' zu lernen, dann aber wie wichtig es ist, das Wesen zu erfassen. Nehme an, das hilflose, schwankende des Grashalms, das stärrige u. stachelige des Gestrüpps, das ‚Stillblühen' des Veilchens", schrieb Maria Innocentia einst an ihren Bruder Franz.

Was für ein wunderbar zartes und leises Vermächtnis!

Die Eltern in Massing, die Mitschwestern in Sießen, die Geschwister Centa, Ady, Franz und Kätl, Maximiliane Müller, die Professoren Brauneis und Dasio und Resele, das Mädchen mit den dunklen Locken, haben es miterlebt, wie nach dem Krieg im Sturm der Begeisterung eine beispiellose Erfolgsgeschichte die Welt umrundete. Wie Franz Goebel seiner Manufaktur den Durchbruch verschaffte. Wie seine gewinnbringenden Porzellanfigürchen der Marke „M.I. Hummel" die Wohnzimmervitrinen bevölkerten. Wie der berühmte Name zum Inbegriff des naiv-nostalgischen Miniaturidylls avancierte. Es entstand ein Millionengeschäft, hinter dem die Schöpferin selbst still zurücktrat.

Seit einigen Jahren beginnt die Öffentlichkeit, sich mit dem „anderen", reichen und vielfältigen Werk der Künstlerin auseinanderzusetzen. Im Kloster Sießen und im eigens eingerichteten Museum der Familie Hummel in Massing wird dieses Erbe sorgfältig bewahrt.

Was außerdem noch bleibt, ist die einzigartige Geschichte der Bertl, Berta, Maria Innocentia Hummel.

Epilogue

"Lie down in the grass some time," Maria Innocentia once wrote to her brother Franz, "take a little flower or a blade of grass, look at them closely and compare how different and manifold their shapes are. Then go home and draw what you have seen and observed. You will realize, first, how necessary it is to learn to really 'look,' and then, how important it is to grasp the essence – say, the helpless, swaying character of the grass blade, the stiff and prickly one of the shrubbery, the 'still blooming' of the violet."

What a wonderfully tender, soft-spoken legacy!

The parents in Massing, the fellow sisters in Siessen, the siblings Centa, Ady, Franz und Kätl, Maximiliane Müller, the professors Brauneis and Dasio, and Resele, the little girl with the dark curls – they all witnessed how after World War II an unparalleled success story went around the world in a frenzy of enthusiasm. How Franz Goebel achieved a breakthrough for his manufacture. How his lucrative porcelain figurines with the "M.I. Hummel" trademark populated the glass cabinets in people's living rooms. How the famous name became the epitome of the naive-nostalgic miniature idyll. The result was a multi-million business, behind which the creator herself quietly retreated.

For some years, however, the public has also begun to acquaint itself with the artist's rich and multifarious "other" work – a heritage carefully preserved at the Siessen convent and at the museum organized for the purpose by the Hummel family in Massing.

What remains besides is the singular story of Bertl, Berta, Maria Innocentia Hummel.

Fußnoten

Hummel Bertl – zeichne mich!

1. In Eningen bei Reutlingen, dessen Bürgern wohlgemerkt seit jeher nachgesagt wird, sie seien die „geborenen Krämer". Vgl. Franz J. Tschudy, Leben und Werk der Schwester Maria Innocentia Hummel, in: 50 Jahre „M.I. Hummel"-Figuren 1935 – 1985, Museum der Deutschen Porzellanindustrie Hohenberg, 6. Juli – 13. Oktober 1985.
2. Jakob Hummel war hiermit in die Zunft der Kaufleute aufgenommen.
3. Ein siebtes Kind, der Nachzügler Josef, geboren am 2. März 1920, starb kurz nach der Geburt.
4. Möglich war dies nicht zuletzt durch die Unterstützung der elterlichen Bäckerei, die die Familie mit den Grundnahrungsmitteln versorgen konnte.
5. Berta wurde am Freitag nach Christi Himmelfahrt geboren, der nach Bauernregel wegen der hohen Regenwahrscheinlichkeit „Schauerfreitag" genannt wird. Der seltsame Spitzname ist in der Familiengeschichte immer wieder belegt.
6. Dieser Orden wurde im 19. Jahrhundert von Karolina Gerhardinger in Neunburg vorm Wald gegründet und hatte sich die schulische Erziehung von Mädchen auf der ganzen Welt zur Aufgabe gemacht.
7. Archiv Kloster Sießen, „Bericht über Frl. Berta Hummel, nun M. Innocentia O.S.Fr." vom 19. Juli 1934
8. Eigentlich Congregatio Jesu, 1609 von der Engländerin Mary Ward zur Bildung von Mädchen gegründeter Orden nach den Ordensregeln der Jesuiten
9. Alte Bezeichnung für Heimweh
10. Archiv Hummel Massing, aus einem Bericht der Mutter von 1947
11. Ebd., Brief an die Eltern vom 13. Dezember 1925
12. Das Fach „Zeichnen" wurde natürlich mit „hervorragend" bewertet, ebenso wie Religionslehre, Geschichte, Erdkunde, Handarbeiten und Turnen. In allen anderen Fächern erhielt sie mit „lobenswert" eine Zwei.

Ein außergewöhnliches Talent

1. Mit diesen Worten beginnt Thomas Manns „Gladius Dei" (1902), ein heiterironisches Zeitporträt, nicht zuletzt über das selbstgerechte „Fachurteil" so manches saturierten Münchner Kunsthändlers.
2. Heute noch legen z. B. die Villen von Wilhelm von Kaulbach (1805 – 1874), Franz von Lenbach (1836 – 1904), Adolf von Hildebrand (1847 – 1921) und Franz von Stuck (1863 – 1928) prächtiges Zeugnis davon ab. Das Lenbachhaus und die Stuckvilla werden als viel besuchte Museen genutzt.
3. Pablo Picasso, 1898. Zitiert nach: Christoph Stölzl, Unordnung und gedämpftes Leuchten. In: Die Zwanziger Jahre in München, München 1979, S. XXI.
4. Die „Jugend – Münchner illustrierte Wochenschrift für Kunst und Leben", 1896 gegründet, hatte dem Jugendstil seinen Namen gegeben. Daran lässt sich gut ablesen, wie einflussreich die Zeitschrift um die Jahrhundertwende – und bis zum Ersten Weltkrieg – in der Tat war.
5. Eine der wichtigsten deutschen Kunst- und Literaturzeitschriften, 1899 gegründet und u. a. von Otto Julius Bierbaum herausgegeben. Zu den Autoren gehörten neben vielen anderen Hugo von Hofmannsthal, Rainer Maria Rilke und Robert Walser.
6. So u. a. Hermann Hesse, Thomas Mann, Ludwig Thoma, Frank Wedekind, Karl Arnold, George Grosz, Olaf Gulbransson, Alfred Kubin, Heinrich Zille, Hugo von Hofmannsthal, Erich Kästner und Heinrich Mann
7. Der andere war der Zeichner und Schriftsteller Thomas Theodor Heine.
8. Joachim Ringelnatz, München, in: Die Weltbühne 17, Nr. 21, 1921. Zitiert aus: Das Gesamtwerk in sieben Bänden, Bd. 5, Zürich 1994, S. 237
9. „Zehn Jahre Kunstpest, Eine kunstmedizinische Betrachtung", anlässlich der Ausstellung „10 Jahre neue Kunst in München" in der Galerie Hans Goltz. In: Völkischer Beobachter vom 29. März 1923
10. Der Kunstkritiker, Kulturhistoriker und Diplomat Wilhelm Hausenstein setzte sich auch vor 1933 gegen den Nationalsozialismus und Antisemitismus ein. Nach der Machtergreifung Hitlers wurde er fristlos aus seiner Redak-

Footnotes

Hummel Bertl – will you draw me?

1. In Eningen, near Reutlingen, whose inhabitants have always been said to be "born merchants." Cf. Franz J. Tschudy, "Leben und Werk der Schwester Maria Innocentia Hummel," in: *50 Jahre "M.I. Hummel"-Figuren 1935 – 1985* (Hohenberg: Museum of the German Porcelain Industry, July 6 – October 13, 1985).
2. This certified Jakob Hummel's admission to the merchants' guild.
3. A seventh child, Josef, a late-comer, born March 2, 1920, died shortly after birth.
4. Owing in no small measure to the support from the parental bakery, which supplied the family with staple foods.
5. Berta was born on the Friday after Ascension Day, known among peasants as "Shower Friday" because of the likelihood of its being a rainy day. The odd nickname is repeatedly documented in the family history.
6. This order was founded in the 19th century in Neunburg vorm Wald by Karolina Gerhardinger for the specific purpose of providing schooling for girls world-wide.
7. Archive Convent Siessen, "Bericht über Frl. Berta Hummel, nun M. Innocentia O.S.Fr.," July 19, 1934.
8. Actually Congregatio Jesu, an order founded in 1609 and based on the rules of the Jesuits by the Englishwoman Mary Ward for the education of girls.
9. Archive Hummel Massing, from an account by the mother of 1947.
10. Ibid., letter to the parents of December 13, 1925.
11. She naturally received a grade of "Outstanding" [A] in Art, but the same also in Religion, History, Geography, Needlework, and Gymnastics. In all her other subjects she received a "Laudable" or 2 [B].

An Exceptional Talent

1. As the opening sentence of Thomas Mann's "Gladius Dei" (1902) has it, a humorously ironic period portrait, satirizing, among other things, the self-satisfied "professional judgment" of many a well-heeled Munich art dealer.
2. Even today the villas of Wilhelm von Kaulbach (1805 – 1874), Franz von Lenbach (1836 – 1904), Adolf von Hildebrand (1847 – 1921), and Franz von Stuck (1863 – 1928) are sumptuous testimony of this. The Lenbach House and the Stuck Villa serve as much-visited museums.
3. Pablo Picasso, 1898. Quoted from: Christoph Stölzl, "Unordnung und gedämpftes Leuchten," in: *Die Zwanziger Jahre in München* (Munich, 1979), p. xxi.
4. The journal *Jugend – Münchner illustrierte Wochenschrift für Kunst und Leben*, founded in 1896, is the source of the name "Jugendstil" (Art Nouveau) – an indication how influential the journal was around the turn of the century and up to WWI.
5. One of the most important German art and literature journals, founded in 1899 and edited by Otto Julius Bierbaum among others. Its authors included Hugo von Hofmannsthal, Rainer Maria Rilke, Robert Walser and others.
6. Hermann Hesse, Thomas Mann, Ludwig Thoma, Frank Wedekind, Karl Arnold, George Grosz, Olaf Gulbransson, Alfred Kubin, Heinrich Zille, Hugo von Hofmannsthal, Erich Kästner, and Heinrich Mann, among others.
7. The other was the draftsman and writer Thomas Theodor Heine.
8. Joachim Ringelnatz, "Munich," in: *Die Weltbühne*, 17, No. 21, 1921. Quoted from: *Das Gesamtwerk in sieben Bänden*, vol. 5 (Zurich, 1994), p. 237.
9. "Zehn Jahre Kunstpest, Eine kunstmedizinische Betrachtung", about the exhibition "10 Jahre neue Kunst in München" in the Gallery Hans Goltz. In: *Völkischer Beobachter*, March 29, 1923.
10. The art critic, cultural historian, and diplomat Wilhelm Hausenstein polemicized against National Socialism and anti-Semitism already before 1933. After Hitler's coming to power he was summarily dismissed from his post as editor of the *Münchner Neueste Nachrichten*, and ejected from the Reich Chamber for Literature, for refusing to remove the names of Jewish artists from his art-historical work.

teurstätigkeit bei den Münchner Neuesten Nachrichten entlassen und 1936 aus der Reichsschrifttumskammer ausgeschlossen, weil er sich geweigert hatte, aus seinem kunsthistorischen Werk die Namen jüdischer Künstler zu entfernen. Berta besaß in späteren Jahren eine Fra-Angelico-Monografie von Wilhelm Hausenstein, die sie sehr schätzte.

11 Wilhelm Hausenstein, München. Sinn und Verhängnis einer Stadt. In: Die Welt um München, München 1929, S. 70
12 Diesen „Ehrentitel" an die bayerische Landeshauptstadt verlieh Hitler offiziell 1935, in Erinnerung an die Anfänge der NSDAP in München.
13 In der Luisenstraße 37, ein Gebäude, das ein paar Jahre später dem Krieg zum Opfer fiel. Zu Bertas Studienzeiten wurde die Schule zweimal umbenannt, ab 1928 hieß sie anlässlich ihres 60-jährigen Bestehens offiziell „Staatsschule für angewandte Kunst", ab 1937 „Akademie für angewandte Kunst".
14 Dies war keineswegs überall in Deutschland so. Bemühungen, die Kunstausbildungen gleichberechtigt zusammenzulegen, hatte es 1919 schon einmal gegeben, als der damalige Direktor der Kunstgewerbeschule, Richard Riemerschmid, eine „Einheitskunstschule" nach dem Vorbild des Weimarer Bauhaus anstrebte. Erst 1946 wird der Lehramtszweig endgültig an die Akademie verlegt, die sich nun in dieser Vereinigung „Hochschule der bildenden Künste" nennen darf, dann seit 1953 bis heute als „Akademie der bildenden Künste" ihren vorerst letzten Namen trägt.
15 Zur Geschichte der Kunstgewerbeschule siehe Wolfgang Kehr, Kunsterzieher an der Akademie. In: Thomas Zacharias (Hrsg.), Tradition und Widerspruch – 175 Jahre Kunstakademie München, München 1985, S. 287 ff.
16 Franz von Stuck war Professor an der Akademie von 1895 bis 1928. Interessanterweise hatte er wiederum vor seinem eigenen Akademiestudium als junger Mann ein handwerkliches Studium an der (damals noch Königlichen) Kunstgewerbeschule studiert.
17 Olaf Gulbransson zeichnete u. a. für den „Simplicissimus" und trat 1929 die Nachfolge auf dem Lehrstuhl Franz von Stucks an der Akademie an. Für kurze Zeit hatte er Mitte der 20er-Jahre auch an der Staatlichen Kunstgewerbeschule unterrichtet.
18 Zur Geschichte der Kunstgewerbeschule siehe Wolfgang Kehr, Kunsterzieher an der Akademie. In: Thomas Zacharias (Hrsg.), Tradition und Widerspruch – 175 Jahre Kunstakademie München, München 1985, S. 292
19 Archiv Hummel Massing, Brief an den Vater vom 15. Juni 1927
20 Ebd., Brief an die Freundin „Zenzerl" vom 12. Juni 1927
21 Ebd., Brief an die Eltern vom 7. Oktober 1928
22 Ebd., Brief an die Eltern vom 12. März 1929
23 Vgl.: Gisela Kleine, Gabriele Münter und Wassily Kandinsky, Frankfurt 1998, S. 91
24 Grund hierfür scheinen Auseinandersetzungen mit dem neuen Konkurrenten Professor Richard Klein gewesen zu sein, der ebenfalls Zeichnen unterrichtete. Glücklicherweise war er künstlerisch nicht von seinem Lehrberuf abhängig, sondern besaß auch darüber hinaus einen Ruf als Maler, Grafiker und Medailleur.
25 Archiv Kloster Sießen, nach einem Bericht von M. Laura Brugger
26 Archiv Hummel Massing, Postkarte an ihre Schwester Viktoria Hummel vom 22. Juni 1928
27 Vgl.: Christoph Stölzl, Unordnung und gedämpftes Leuchten. In: Die Zwanziger Jahre in München, München 1979, S. XXI.
28 Bayerische Staatszeitung, 7./8. Juni 1931
29 Archiv Hummel Massing, Holzschnitt-Postkarte an den Bruder Adolf Hummel vom 18. Dezember 1927
30 Ebd., Brief an die Eltern vom 10. Februar 1928
31 Archiv Kloster Sießen, Prüfungszeugnis der Staatsschule für angewandte Kunst, unterzeichnet am 18. März 1931: „Der Ministerialkommissär M. Dasio" und „Der Direktor Carl Sattler"

Der andere Weg

1 P. Hilarin Felder, Die Ideale des hl. Franziskus von Assisi, Paderborn, 1924, S. 167. Dieses Buch war seinerzeit eine gängige Ausgabe, die auch Berta

11 Wilhelm Hausenstein, "München. Sinn und Verhängnis einer Stadt," in: *Die Welt um München* (Munich, 1929), p. 70.
12 This "honorary title" Hitler formally bestowed upon Munich is 1935, in commemoration of the rise of the Nazi Party there.
13 The school was located at No. 37 Luisenstrasse, a building that was destroyed during the war some years later. During Berta's years, the school was renamed twice: to "State School of Applied Arts" in 1928, on the occasion of its sixtieth anniversary, and then, in 1937, to "Academy of Applied Arts."
14 This was not uniformly the case throughout Germany. Efforts to combine the various training programs in the arts into one with equal rights had been initiated once before in 1919, when the then director of the Arts and Crafts School, Richard Riemerschmid, aimed at a unified arts school on the model of the Weimar Bauhaus; but these were thwarted by the backwardness of his colleagues. Not until 1946 was the teacher training branch finally transferred to the Academy, thereafter called College of the Fine Arts and then, after 1953, Academy of Fine Arts, its current name.
15 On the history of the School of Arts and Crafts, see Wolfgang Kehr, "Kunsterzieher an der Akademie," in: Thomas Zacharias, ed., *Tradition und Widerspruch – 175 Jahre Kunstakademie München* (Munich, 1985), pp. 287 ff.
16 Franz von Stuck was professor at the Academy from 1895 until 1928. As a young man, he himself had undergone vocational training as a craftsman at the (then still Royal) School of Arts and Crafts, prior to his academic studies.
17 Olaf Gulbransson worked as a caricaturist for the *Simplicissimus*, among other things; in 1929 he became the successor of Franz von Stuck at the Academy. During the twenties, he had also briefly taught at the State School of Arts and Crafts.
18 On the history of the School of Arts and Crafts, see Wolfgang Kehr, "Kunsterzieher an der Akademie," in: Thomas Zacharias, ed., *Tradition und Widerspruch – 175 Jahre Kunstakademie München* (Munich, 1985), p. 292.
19 Archive Hummel Massing, letter to the father of June 15, 1927.
20 Ibid., letter to her girlfriend "Zenzerl" of June 12, 1927.
21 Archive Hummel Massing, letter to parents of October 7, 1928.
22 Ibid., letter to the parents of March 12, 1929.
23 Cf. Gisela Kleine, *Gabriele Münter und Wassily Kandinsky* (Frankfurt, 1998), p. 91.
24 The reason seems to have been conflicts with the new competitor, Professor Richard Klein, who likewise taught drawing. Fortunately, Dasio was not dependent on his teaching profession as an artist but enjoyed an independent reputation as a painter, graphic artist, and medal maker.
25 Archive Convent Siessen, according to an account by M. Laura Brugger.
26 Archive Hummel Massing, postcard to her sister Viktoria Hummel, June 22, 1928.
27 Cf. Christoph Stölzl, "Unordnung und gedämpftes Leuchten," in: *Die Zwanziger Jahre in München* (Munich, 1979), p. xxi.
28 *Bayerische Staatszeitung*, June 7/8, 1931.
29 Archive Hummel Massing, woodcut postcard to the brother Adolf Hummel of December 18, 1927.
30 Ibid., letter to the parents of February 10, 1928.
31 Examination report of the State School of Applied Arts, dated March 18, 1931, signed "The Ministerial Commissioner, M. Dasio" and "The Director, Carl Sattler."

The Other Way

1 P. Hilarin Felder, *Die Ideale des hl. Franziskus von Assisi* (Paderborn, 1924), p. 167. The book was a widely known edition at the time, and one that Berta may well have read. A few years later she portrayed the author.
2 Liturgical vestments, covers for chalice, altar, and lectern, wall-hangings, and banners for church interiors. To this day paraments are often designed and executed with extraordinary artistic display.
3 Archive Convent Siessen, from the "Prospekt für die Kandidatinnen" from before 1932. It was this prospectus that Berta must have studied before she applied to the convent.

gelesen haben dürfte. Berta porträtierte den Verfasser ein paar Jahre später sogar einmal.
2 Liturgische Gewänder, Gedecke für Kelch, Altar und Lesepult, Behänge und Fahnen für den Kirchenraum. Auch heute noch werden Paramente oft mit großem künstlerischem Aufwand entworfen und angefertigt.
3 Archiv Kloster Sießen, aus dem „Prospekt für die Kandidatinnen" vor 1932. Diesen muss auch Berta studiert haben, bevor sie sich im Kloster bewarb.
4 Bis heute ist in katholischen Haushalten (v. a. im süddeutschen Raum) ein Stubenwinkel dem mit Blumen, Ähren o. Ä. aus der Kräuterweihe geschmückten Kreuz Christi vorbehalten. Im Hummel-Haus war der „Herrgottswinkel" in der Essecke, sodass man den Erlöser jeden Tag beim Tischgebet vor Augen hatte.
5 Archiv Kloster Sießen, nach einem mündlichen Bericht von M. Kostka Hartmann 1994
6 Archiv Hummel Massing, Postkarte an die Eltern vom 13. Juni 1929
7 Vielleicht kam die Verehrung für den später durch sein mutiges Engagement gegen die Nazis berühmt gewordenen Seelsorger auch durch dessen Verbindung mit der Schwesternschaft der Heiligen Familie zustande, die er 1914 mitbegründet hatte. Es war die Schwesternschaft, die auch Bertas Wohnheim führte. Pater Rupert Mayer wurde 1987 durch Papst Johannes Paul II. seliggesprochen.
8 Zitiert nach: Schwestern von der Heiligen Familie (Hg.), „Schwestern von der Heiligen Familie – 75 Jahre im Dienst für die Familie", München, 1998, S. 22
9 Archiv Kloster Sießen, aus einem Bericht von M. Kostka Hartmann 1972
10 Ebd.
11 Vgl. Archiv Hummel Massing, Brief an die Eltern vom 3. Mai 1930
12 Ebd., Brief an die Eltern vom 20. März 1931
13 Ebd.
14 Ebd.
15 Ebd.
16 Die Veranstaltungen fanden im bekannten Britsch-Institut statt. Die Schulkinder sollten in dieser Lehrmethode dazu angehalten werden, frei nach ihren eigenen Vorstellungen zu malen und nicht nach Vorgaben, wie es damals üblich war. Vgl. Egon Kornmann, Wege zum Bildverständnis, erschienen 1933 im Verlag Bruckmann, München
17 Archiv Hummel Massing, Brief an die Eltern vom 15. Januar 1930
18 Ebd., Brief an die Mutter vom 14. Mai 1931
19 Alter Ausdruck für wallfahren
20 Archiv Kloster Sießen, aus dem „Prospekt für die Kandidatinnen" vor 1932

Klosterkind und Künstlerin
1 Archiv Hummel Massing, Brief an die Eltern vom 25. April 1931. Laut Personalblatt des Klosters war Bertas Eintrittstag der 22. April.
2 Ebd., Brief an die Eltern vom 4. Mai 1931. Es war Berta aufgrund des klösterlichen Zeitplans also nie möglich, länger als zwei Stunden an einer Sache zu arbeiten.
3 Ebd.
4 Ebd., Brief an den Vater vom 14. Juni 1931. Mit „Krägelchen" ist eine kurze Pelerine gemeint. Das der Kandidatinnen war noch kurz, später im Postulat würde es um einige Zentimeter „gewachsen" sein.
5 Ebd., Brief an die Eltern vom 29. Juni 1931
6 Ihren ersten Auftrag hatte sie aus Massing mitgebracht, eine Prozessionsfahne mit Bruder-Konrad-Motiv. Konrad von Parzham (1818 – 1894) war Laienbruder aus dem Kapuzinerorden und wurde 1934 heiliggesprochen. „Bruder Konrad" stammte wie Berta aus dem Rottal und war in dieser Gegend natürlich besonders populär.
7 Die lückenlose Dokumentation im Kloster wurde von Schwester Laura erstellt. Da im Krieg einiges verloren ging, konnte man später aus beiden Sammlungen gegenseitig ergänzen.
8 Archiv Hummel Massing, Brief an die Eltern vom 29. Juni 1931
9 Ebd., Brief an die Eltern vom 19. Oktober 1931
10 Ebd., Brief an die Eltern vom 14. November 1931

4 To this day in Catholic households, especially in southern Germany, a corner of the room is reserved for a crucifix decorated with flowers, grain stalks, etc., from the consecration of the herbs. At the Hummel home, the "Herrgottswinkel" was in the dining area, so that one would have the Redeemer daily before one's eyes during grace.
5 Archive Convent Siessen, from an oral account of M. Kostka Hartmann, 1994.
6 Archive Hummel Massing, postcard to the parents of June 13, 1929.
7 Perhaps the veneration for this pastor, who later became famous for his courageous opposition to the Nazis, was due in part also to his connection with the Sisterhood of the Holy Family, which he had helped to found in 1914. It was this sisterhood that ran Berta's boarding-house. In 1987, Father Rupert Mayer was beatified by Pope John Paul II.
8 Quoted from: Sisters of the Holy Family, eds., *Schwestern von der Heiligen Familie – 75 Jahre im Dienst für die Familie* (Munich, 1998), p. 22.
9 Archive Convent Siessen, from an account by M. Kostka Hartmann, 1972.
10 Ibid.
11 Archive Hummel Massing, letter to the parents of May 3, 1930.
12 Ibid., letter to the parents of March 20, 1931.
13 Ibid.
14 Ibid.
15 Ibid.
16 The seminars were held at the noted Britsch Institute. School children were to be encouraged by this teaching method to paint freely according to their own imaginations rather than from models, as was the standard method then. Cf. Egon Kornmann, *Wege zum Bildverständnis* (Munich: Bruckmann, 1933).
17 Archive Hummel Massing, letter to the parents of January 15, 1930.
18 Ibid., letter to the mother of May 14, 1931.
19 Archive Convent Siessen, from the "Prospekt für die Kandidatinnen," from before 1932.

Convent Child and Craftswoman
1 Archive Hummel Massing, letter to the parents of April 25, 1931. According to the convent's personnel records, the day of Berta's arrival was April 22.
2 Ibid., letter to the parents of May 4, 1931. The convent schedule thus never allowed more than two hours of uninterrupted work on a given project.
3 Ibid.
4 Ibid., letter to the parents of June 14, 1931. By "little collar" is meant a short tippet or cape. The one for the candidates was still quite short; the postulants' cape will have "grown" by an inch or so.
5 Ibid., letter to the parents of June 29, 1931.
6 Her first commission Berta had brought with her from Massing, a procession banner with a Brother Konrad motif. Konrad of Parzham (1818 – 1894) was a lay brother of the Capuchin order, who was canonized in 1934. "Brother Konrad" was from the Rott Valley like Berta and thus, of course, particularly popular in the region.
7 The complete documentation in the convent was compiled by Sr. Laura. Though some things were lost during the War, the two collections could be made to complement and complete each other again later.
8 Archive Hummel Massing, letter to the parents of June 29, 1931.
9 Ibid., letter to the parents of October 19, 1931.
10 Ibid., letter to the parents of November 14, 1931.
11 Ibid., letter from Else Brauneis, "My dear little Bertl," of October 26, 1931.
12 Ibid., letter to the parents of March 11, 1932.
13 Ibid., letter to the parents of May 5, 1932.
14 Ibid., letter to the parents of July 20, 1932.
15 Ibid., letter from M. Laura Brugger to Adolf Hummel, October 21, 1932.
16 Soon the series was printed not only with a German text but also in French, English, and Spanish translation. A separate edition was issued for Switzerland with Roman letters instead of the German Sütterlin script.
17 Archive Hummel Massing, letter to the parents of December 16, 1932.

11 Ebd., Brief von Else Brauneis an „Meine liebe kleine Bertl" vom 26. Oktober 1931
12 Ebd., Brief an die Eltern vom 11. März 1932
13 Ebd., Brief an die Eltern vom 5. Mai 1932
14 Ebd., Brief an die Eltern vom 20. Juli 1932
15 Ebd., Brief von M. Laura Brugger an Adolf Hummel vom 21. Oktober 1932
16 Schon bald wurde diese Serie nicht nur mit deutschem Text gedruckt, sondern auch ins Französische, Englische und Spanische übersetzt. Für die Schweiz wurde eine gesonderte Ausgabe in Druckbuchstaben statt der deutschen Sütterlin-Schrift gefertigt.
17 Archiv Hummel Massing, Brief an die Eltern vom 16. Dezember 1932
18 Ebd., Brief an die Eltern vom 18. Januar 1933
19 Das letzte halbe Jahr vor der Einkleidung wurde Postulat genannt, dann folgte ein einjähriges Noviziat, das mit der Einkleidungsfeier begann. Nach diesem Jahr als Novizin kommt die Erst-Profess. Das Ablegen von zunächst zeitlichen Gelübden vor der endgültig „Ewigen Profess" ist eine kirchenrechtliche Vorschrift, um doch noch die Möglichkeit zum Rücktritt zu gewähren.
20 Archiv Hummel Massing, Brief an die Eltern vom 18. Januar 1933
21 Ebd.
22 Spottgedicht von Karl Kinndt, in: „Simplicissimus" 37, Jg. Nr. 41, S. 482
23 Archiv Hummel Massing, Brief an den Vater vom 14. Juni 1931
24 Ebd., Brief an die Eltern vom 22. Mai 1933
25 Ebd., Brief an den Vater vom 15. Juni 1933
26 Ebd.
27 Ebd., Brief an die Eltern vom 18. Juli 1933
28 Ebd., „Einkleidung unseres lieben Kindes Berta Hummel am 22. August 1933 – Kloster Sießen bei Saulgau", Bericht des Vaters Adolf Hummel
29 Ebd., Bericht des Vaters Adolf Hummel, Abschrift der Festpredigt mit dem Thema: „Der Meister ist da und ruft dich" (Johannesevangelium, 11. Kap.). Festprediger war ein Vetter der Hummels, zu dem auch Berta Briefkontakt hatte, Pater Guardian Adalbero Hugo OFMCap. von dem „Käppele" in Würzburg.
30 Die „Bräutchen" waren mit Blumenkindern bei einer Hochzeit vergleichbar. Bertas „Bräutchen" war Maria Hugo, eine kleine Kusine aus Wolfratshausen bei München.
31 Archiv Hummel Massing, aus dem Bericht des Vaters Adolf Hummel
32 Ebd.

Hummel um die Welt

1 Archiv Irmin Nauer-Dubler, Schreiben an Josef Müller vom 9. März 1933
2 Birgit Franz und Constanze Lindner Haigis, 100 Jahre Ideen, München und Zug, 1996, S. 55
3 Gemeint sind nach heutiger Auffassung die zweidimensionalen Reproduktionsrechte.
4 Archiv Irmin Nauer-Dubler, Brief an Sr. Eligia Stadler vom 11. März 1933
5 S. Fußnote 3
6 Es handelte sich hierbei um die Motive: „Herz Jesu", Osterkarte „Alleluja", Osterkarte „Fröhliche Ostern", Erstkommunionbild „Mädchen", Erstkommunionbild „Knabe" und „Jesulein, ich hab dich so lieb".
7 Archiv Irmin Nauer-Dubler, Brief an Sr. Eligia Stadler vom 17. März 1933
8 Beide schufen Kinderbuchklassiker, die bis heute ihren Reiz nicht verloren haben.
9 Eine Hummel'sche Version von „Max und Moritz" hing lange Zeit im klösterlichen Atelier.
10 Zum Thema Kinderbilder und Vorbilder vgl. Ulrich Gertz, Einige Anmerkungen zu den „Hummel"-Figuren, in: 50 Jahre „M.I. Hummel-Figuren 1935 – 1985, Museum der Deutschen Porzellanindustrie Hohenberg, 1985, S. 20 ff., und Dieter Struss, M.-I.-Hummel-Figuren, Augsburg, 1993, S. 36 ff.
11 Archiv Irmin Nauer-Dubler, Zusammenfassung des Besuches im Kloster an Sr. Eligia Stadler vom 7. April 1933
12 Ebd., Brief an Josef Müller vom 10. April 1933
13 Ebd., Brief an Josef Müller vom 14. Juni 1933

18 Ibid., letter to the parents of January 18, 1933.
19 The final six-month period of the candidacy is called postulancy, which is followed by a one-year novitiate beginning with the Assumption of the Habit ceremony. The novitiate is followed by the First or Simple Profession: the making of a provisional temporal vow, prior to the "Perpetual Profession," is prescribed by canon law so as to leave open the possibility of a last-minute withdrawal.
20 Archive Hummel Massing, letter to the parents of January 18, 1933.
21 Ibid.
22 Lampoon by Karl Kinndt, in *Simplicissimus* 37, vol. 41, p. 482.
23 Archive Hummel Massing, letter to the father of June 14, 1931.
24 Ibid., letter to the parents of May 22, 1933.
25 Ibid., letter to the father of June 15, 1933.
26 Ibid.
27 Ibid., letter to the parents of July 18, 1933.
28 Ibid., "Assumption of the habit of our dear child Berta Hummel on August 22, 1933 – Convent Siessen near Saulgau," account of the father, Adolf Hummel.
29 Ibid., account of the father, Adolf Hummel, copy of the ceremonial sermon on the theme: "The master is here and calls you" (Gospel of John, Ch. 11.). The preacher was a cousin of the Hummels, Father Guardian Adalbero Hugo OFMCap. from the "Käppele" in Würzburg, with whom Berta was also in correspondence.
30 Die "bridelets" were comparable to the flower girls at a wedding. Berta's "bridelet" was Maria Hugo, a young cousin from Wolfratshausen near Munich.
31 Archive Hummel Massing, from the account of the father, Adolf Hummel.
32 Ibid.

Hummel World-Wide

1 Archive Irmin Nauer-Dubler, letter to Josef Müller of March 9, 1933.
2 Birgit Franz and Constanze Lindner Haigis, *100 Jahre Ideen* (Munich and Zug, 1996), p. 55.
3 I.e., the reproduction rights.
4 Archive Irmin Nauer-Dubler, letter to Sr. Eligia Stadler of March 11, 1933.
5 See footnote 3.
6 These included the motifs "Sacred Heart," Easter card "Alleluja," Easter card "Happy Easter," First Communion picture "Girl," First Communion picture "Boy" and "Little Jesus, I love you so."
7 Archive Irmin Nauer-Dubler, letter to Sr. Eligia Stadler of March 17, 1933.
8 Both wrote classic children's books that retain their appeal even today.
9 A Hummel version of "Max and Moritz" hung in the convent studio for a long time.
10 On the subject of children's pictures and models, see Ulrich Gertz, "Einige Anmerkungen zu den 'Hummel'-Figuren," in: *50 Jahre M.I. Hummel-Figuren 1935-1985* (Museum der Deutschen Porzellanindustrie Hohenberg, 1985), pp. 20 ff., and Dieter Struss, *M.-I.-Hummel Figuren* (Augsburg, 1993), pp. 36 ff.
11 Archive Irmin Nauer-Dubler, summary of the visit to the convent sent to Sr. Eligia Stadler, April 7, 1933.
12 Ibid., letter to Josef Müller of April 10, 1933.
13 Ibid., letter to Josef Müller of June 14, 1933.
14 Prior to assuming the habit, Berta had signed her works B.H., B. Hummel, Berta Hummel, Bertl Hummel, Berta, and Bertl.
15 Maximiliane Müller adds: "If the custom to 'shoot in' the New Year is insufficiently known elsewhere, it would have to be left off. In Bavaria, the New Year is greeted with mortar salutes."
16 Archive Irmin Nauer-Dubler, letter to Sr. Eligia Stadler of July 19, 1933.
17 Ibid., letter to Maximiliane Müller of July 20, 1933.
18 From an anecdote by M. Laura Brugger.
19 Archive Irmin Nauer-Dubler, letter to Sr. Eligia Stadler of November 25, 1933.

14 Bis zu ihrer Einkleidung signierte Berta mit B.H., B. Hummel, Berta Hummel, Bertl Hummel, Berta und Bertl.
15 Hierzu ergänzt Maximiliane Müller: „Wenn die Sitte, das neue Jahr ‚anzu schiessen', auswärtig zu wenig bekannt ist, müsste es wegbleiben. In Bayern wird sie doch jedes neue Jahr mit Böllerschüssen begrüßt."
16 Archiv Irmin Nauer-Dubler, Brief an Sr. Eligia Stadler vom 19. Juli 1933
17 Ebd., Brief an Maximiliane Müller vom 20. Juli 1933
18 Nach einer Anekdote von M. Laura Brugger
19 Archiv Irmin Nauer-Dubler, Brief an Sr. Eligia Stadler vom 25. November 1933
20 Ebd., Brief an Josef Müller vom 15. Februar 1934
21 Ebd., Brief an Josef Müller vom 12. März 1934
22 Bisher wurden einfarbige Bilder in Kupfertiefdruck und farbige im Buchdruck-Verfahren hergestellt.
23 Archiv Irmin Nauer-Dubler, Brief an Josef Müller vom 15. Februar 1934
24 Ebd., Brief an Josef Müller vom 13. Juni 1934
25 Ebd., Brief an Eligia Stadler vom 21. Juni 1934
26 Ebd.
27 Ebd., Brief an Josef Müller vom 13. Juni 1934
28 Ebd., Zusammenfassung des Besuches im Kloster an Sr. Eligia Stadler vom 24. Juli 1934
29 Ebd., Der Verlag kämpfte mit allen nur möglichen Argumenten um seine erfolgversprechendste Künstlerin: „Wenn die Bilder von Schwester Innocentia im Verlaufe der nächsten Jahre überall bekannt und eingeführt sind, so werden Sie doch recht viele Anfragen bekommen von den verschiedensten und grossenteils auch unzuverlässigen Verlagen sowie von Zeitschriften und Kalendern um Überlassung von Abdruckrechten, sei es für Gotteslohn oder gegen geringe Vergütung. Wie nützlich ist es da für Sie, wenn Sie sich dabei auf den starken Standpunkt stellen können, dass Sie dem ‚Ars sacra' Verlag generell Ihre Reproduktionsrechte übertragen haben, man möge sich an diesen wenden, viel unproduktive Arbeit und auch Enttäuschungen werden Ihnen so erspart bleiben."
30 Archiv Kloster Sießen, nach dem damaligen Ritus
31 Zitiert nach Birgit Franz und Constanze Lindner Haigis, 100 Jahre Ideen, München und Zug, 1996, S. 66
32 Archiv Irmin Nauer-Dubler, Brief an Sr. Eligia Stadler vom 7. November 1934
33 Ebd.
34 Beginn der Einführung in „Das Hummel-Buch", Stuttgart 1934
35 Ebd., S. 15
36 Bis heute wird das Buch im Fink Verlag aufgelegt. Leider wurde in den 50er-Jahren der teils im Dialekt geschriebene Text durch eine hochdeutsche Variante ersetzt; dies zeigte sich zwar im deutschsprachigen Raum als massenkompatibler, die Gedichte verloren jedoch erheblich an ihrem volkskünstlerischen Charme. Deshalb ist die aktuelle Ausgabe auch wieder in leichter Mundart erhältlich.
37 Heute Rödental
38 Vermutlich Arthur Möller, er fertigte auch die erste offizielle Hummel-Figur: „Geigerlein mit Hund" (Hum 1).
39 Es ist nicht geklärt, ob es sich bei dem Besuch um Franz Goebel persönlich handelt oder ob er seinen Vertreter Steiner schickte, der auch später immer wieder in Sießen war. Aus einem Brief vom 19. Dezember 1934 aus dem Goebel-Archiv geht hervor, dass Herr Steiner im Dezember 1934 im Kloster vorsprach. Die Mitschwester M. Innocentias spricht in ihrem Bericht von 1971 allerdings vom „Eigentümer der Firma Göbel".
40 Archiv Kloster Sießen, aus einem Bericht von M. Rosa Staehle, 1971
41 Ebd.
42 Archiv der Goebel Porzellanmanufaktur GmbH, Schreiben an „Sr. M. Innocentia Hummel" vom 8. März 1935

Die dunkle Zeit
1 Die „Schulbibel" war eine Auswahlbibel für den Unterricht. Die Texte aus

20 Ibid., letter to Josef Müller of February 15, 1934. "Deutscher Gruß" (German salute) meant "Heil Hitler."
21 Ibid., letter to Josef Müller of March 12, 1934.
22 Until then monochrome pictures were printed in copper gravure, colored ones in letter press.
23 Archive Irmin Nauer-Dubler, letter to Josef Müller of February 15, 1934.
24 Ibid., letter to Josef Müller of June 13, 1934.
25 Ibid., letter to Eligia Stadler of June 21, 1934.
26 Ibid.
27 Ibid., letter to Josef Müller of June 13, 1934.
28 Ibid., summary of the visit to the convent, sent to Sr. Eligia Stadler, July 24, 1934.
29 Ibid. The press fought with every possible argument for its most promising artist: "If Sister Innocentia's pictures come to be known and introduced everywhere in the next few years, you will surely receive many requests, from the most diverse and often also unreliable publishers as well as from journals and calendar makers, for reproduction rights for love or a pittance. How useful will it be for you, therefore, to have the powerful standpoint that you have generally ceded all reproduction rights to the 'Ars Sacra' Press, so that people should direct their inquiries there. You will be spared much unproductive labor and many disappointments."
30 Archive Convent Siessen, the ritual as it was observed at the time.
31 Quoted from Birgit Franz and Constanze Lindner Haigis, *100 Jahre Ideen* (Munich and Zug, 1996), p. 66.
32 Archive Irmin Nauer-Dubler, letter to Sr. Eligia Stadler of November 7, 1934.
33 Ibid
34 Opening of the introduction to: *Das Hummel-Buch* (Stuttgart, 1934).
35 Ibid., p. 15.
36 The book is still available from the Fink Press. Unfortunately, the original text, written partly in dialect, was replaced by a High German variant. Though this proved more compatible with a mass readership nationwide, the poems lost much of their folk art charm.
37 Now Rödental.
38 Probably Arthur Möller, who also created the first official Hummel figure, "Little Fiddler with Dog" (Hum 1).
39 It is not clear whether the visitor was Franz Goebel himself or his representative Steiner, who regularly visited Siessen in later years. A letter in the Goebel archive dated December 19, 1934, would indicate that it was Steiner who visited the convent in December of 1934. M. Innocentia's fellow sister, however, refers to the "owner of the Göbel firm" in her record of 1971.
40 Archive Convent Siessen, from a report by M. Rosa Staehle, 1971.
41 Ibid.
42 Archive of the Goebel Porcelain Manufacturing Co., Ltd., letter to Sr. Maria Innocentia Hummel of March 8, 1935.

The Dark Time
1 The "School Bible" was a bible anthology for the classroom. The stories of the Old and New Testaments were told in a simplified style suitable for children.
2 Hitler had even advocated a "purged" Scripture, in which Old Testament revelation would be altogether excluded, in line with the Nazis' anti-Jewish propaganda.
3 Central Episcopal Archive of Regensburg, letter to Dr. Winkler, Kösel and Pustet, Publishers, of December 29, 1934.
4 Ibid., November 24, 1934. The *Hummel-Buch* had even included six Bible illustrations. But the bishop clearly had expectations that went beyond that in terms of further artistic development.
5 Ibid. Letter to Michael Buchberger of December 20, 1934.
6 In 1934, the school of St. Anna in Bad Saulgau, where Maria Innocentia had also taught, was closed by the Nazis, as were the Private Seminar for Home Economics Teachers and, in 1935, the Private Teacher Seminar in Siessen; by 1937 almost all the Catholic schools had been closed. Meanwhile, the

dem Alten und Neuen Testament waren für Kinder in vereinfachtem Stil erzählt.
2 Hitler hatte sich sogar für eine „Reinigung" der Heiligen Schrift ausgesprochen, in der die Offenbarung des Alten Testaments innerhalb der nationalsozialistisch-judenfeindlichen Propaganda strikt abgelehnt wurde.
3 Bischöfliches Zentralarchiv Regensburg, Brief an Dr. Winkler, Verlag Kösel & Pustet, vom 29. Dezember 1934
4 Ebd., vom 24. November 1934. Im „Hummel-Buch" waren sogar sechs Bibel-Illustrationen enthalten. Der Bischof hatte jedoch im Sinne einer künstlerischen Weiterentwicklung ganz offensichtlich Ansprüche, die darüber hinausgingen.
5 Ebd., Brief an Michael Buchberger vom 20. Dezember 1934
6 1934 wurde die Schule St. Anna in Bad Saulgau, wo auch Maria Innocentia unterrichtet hatte, von den Nationalsozialisten geschlossen, ebenso 1934 das Priv. Hauswirtschaftslehrerinnen-Seminar und 1935 das Priv. Lehrerinnen-Seminar in Sießen; bis 1937 fast sämtliche Ordensschulen. Das Kloster gründete 1932 in Südafrika und 1936 in Brasilien Missionsstationen. Für diese neue Aufgabe meldeten sich begeistert viele junge, frei gewordene Lehrerinnen.
7 Ebd., Schreiben an Michael Buchberger vom 8. April 1935
8 Bischöfliches Zentralarchiv Regensburg, Brief an die Generaloberin M. Gertrudis Bosch vom 12. April 1935
9 Bischöfliches Zentralarchiv Regensburg, Brief Dr. Winkler an Michael Buchberger vom 11. Juli 1935
10 Ebd.
11 Um die 50 Kreuzwegskizzen entstanden in den Jahren 1935 – 1936. Bei einigen ist die Parallelität zu Bewegungsstudien aus Maria Innocentias zweiter Münchner Studienzeit deutlich zu erkennen. Obwohl die Bestandsaufnahme von ca. 30 Kreuzwegskizzen im Hummel Archiv in Massing schon in den 1960er Jahren bekannt war, wurde eine weitere Fassung aller 14 Stationen im Kloster Sießen erst 1978 von M. Witgard Erler wiederentdeckt, weil niemand sie nach dem Tod von M. Laura Brugger dem Hummel-Werk zugeordnet hatte. Als Franziskanerin war ihr der Gedanke, in Jesu Nachfolge seinen Leidensweg zu gehen, sehr präsent. „Ich habe es wohl vor, einmal einen Kreuzweg zu machen, aber so was ist Lebensarbeit." Vgl. Archiv Hummel Massing, Brief Maria Innocentia an die Eltern vom 3. Januar 1934 und zur Thematik Genoveva Nitz, „Der Kreuzweg", in: Die andere Berta Hummel, Unbekannte Werke einer bekannten Künstlerin, Regensburg, 1986, S. 94 ff.
12 Formulierung des Münchner Kardinals Michael Faulhaber, der sich vor Hitlers „Machtergreifung" sehr kritisch gegen die Nationalsozialisten verhalten hatte
13 Doch nicht alle Bischöfe ließen sich einschüchtern. Zu nennen sind hier etwa Konrad von Preysing, Bischof von Eichstätt und später von Berlin, und Clemens August Graf von Galen, Bischof von Münster, die aktiv Widerstand leisteten und die Bevölkerung dazu aufriefen. Hitler wagte aufgrund ihrer Popularität nicht, sie mit Restriktionen zu belegen. Auch Johann Baptist Sproll, dessen Diözese Rottenburg (Stuttgart) das Kloster Sießen zugeordnet war, war ein erklärter Nazi-Gegner. Maria Innocentia kannte den Bischof persönlich und hatte ihm sogar eine Kinderzeichnung gewidmet.
14 Auch Bischof Buchberger hatte in seinem Brief an die Oberin von Sießen erwähnt, er habe kein Verständnis für die Zurückweisung der Hummel-Illustrationen: „angesichts der vielen Mühen und Opfer, die wir Bischöfe jetzt für Weiterbestand und Weiterwirken der Klöster bringen müssen, glaube ich, daß man eine schon gegebene Zusage einem Bischof gegenüber nicht einfach zurücknehmen darf."
15 In Rom erzürnte sich der Papst, er habe nicht mit den Nationalsozialisten „verhandelt", damit jetzt seine Priester „misshandelt" würden.
16 Archiv Hummel Massing, aus einem Bericht von Viktoria Hummel, 1947
17 „Tempel" ist hier übrigens durchaus wörtlich zu nehmen. Die NS-Propagandasprache bediente sich bekanntlich gerne religiöser Terminologie. So war z. B. die „Kunstpolitische Kampfschrift zur Gesundung deutscher Kunst im Geiste nordischer Art" (1937) des Malers und Schriftstellers Wolfgang

Siessen convent had been establishing missionary stations in South Africa, in 1932, and Brazil, in 1936, and many young teachers who had lost their positions enthusiastically applied for these new opportunities.
7 Ibid. Letter to Michael Buchberger of April 8, 1935.
8 Central Episcopal Archive, Regensburg, letter to the Mother Superior, M. Gertrudis Bosch, of April 12, 1935.
9 Central Episcopal Archive, Regensburg, letter from Dr. Winkler to Michael Buchberger of July 11, 1935.
10 Ibid.
11 Some 50 Way of the Cross sketches were made in the years 1935 – 1936. Some of them clearly show parallels to motion studies done during Maria Innocentia's second study period in Munich. Although nearly thirty sketches to the Way of the Cross had been registered in the Hummel Archive in Massing in the 1960s, further version with all 14 stations in Kloster Siessen was rediscovered only in 1978 by M. Witgard Erler, because after the death of Sr. Laura Brugger, no one had identified them as part of the Hummel corpus. As a Franciscan, the thought of walking Jesus' road of thorns in an Imitatio Christi was very present to her. "I do want to do a Way of the Cross someday, but something like that is life's work." Cf. Archive Hummel Massing, letter from Maria Innocentia to her parents of January 3, 1934. On the subject generally, see Genoveva Nitz, "Der Kreuzweg", in: *Die andere Berta Hummel, Unbekannte Werke einer bekannten Künstlerin* (Regensburg, 1986) pp. 94 ff.
12 The formulation is that of the Munich cardinal Michael Faulhaber, who prior to Hitler's assumption of power had been highly critical of the National Socialists.
13 Not every bishop could be intimidated, however. One should mention here Konrad von Preysing, bishop of Eichstätt and later of Berlin, and Clemens August Count von Galen, bishop of Münster, who put up resistance and called upon the populace to resist. Because of their popularity, Hitler did not dare to impose restrictions on them. Johann Baptist Sproll, to whose dioces of Stuttgart-Rottenburg the convent Siessen belonged, was like wise a declared opponent of the Nazis. Maria Innocentia knew the bishop personally and had even dedicated one of her children's drawings to him.
14 In his letter to the Mother Superior of Siessen, Bishop Buchberger had similarly said about his inability to understand the rejection of the Hummel illustrations project: "in view of the many efforts and sacrifices we bishops now have to make for the sake of the continued existence and work of the monasteries, I do not think one may simply retract an assent already given to a bishop."
15 In Rome, the Pope was incensed, saying he did not "treat" with the Nazis so they could now "mistreat" his priests.
16 Archive Hummel Massing, from an account of Viktoria Hummel, 1947.
17 "Temple" is to be taken quite literally. The Nazis, as is well known, liked to use religious terminology in their propaganda. Thus, e.g., the "Art-political polemic for the recovery of German art in the Nordic spirit" by the painter and writer Wolfgang Willrich (1937), was entitled "The Cleansing of the Temple of Art" in allusion to Jesus' Cleansing of the Temple in Jerusalem. Willrich was one of the organizers of the exhibition "Entartete Kunst" ("Degenerate Art"), which opened its gates in July of 1937 in Munich, shortly after Maria Innocentia had finished her second course of studies.
18 Richard Klein (1890 – 1967), a native of Munich, was a trained sculptor and had also studied at the Academy under Franz von Stuck. "A very important artist" even the student Berta had reverentially called him four years earlier in a letter to her parents. Incidentally, Professor Klein had fully appreciated her talent, saying there was only one student in his class of 1931 with whom he could "do anything" while otherwise handing out low grades by the dozen (cf. Archive Hummel Massing, letter to the parents of March 14, 1931). By 1944 he was one of the privileged "artists in the war effort" who were exempted from military service and work in the arms industry. On the subject, see Munich Municipal Museum, ed., *München – "Hauptstadt der Bewegung"* (Munich, 1993), pp. 36f., and Thomas Zacharias, *(Art) reine Kunst, Die Münchner Akademie um 1937*, p. 10.

Willrich überschrieben: „Die Säuberung des Kunsttempels", in Anlehnung an die Tempelreinigung Jesu in Jerusalem. Willrich gehörte zu den Organisatoren der Ausstellung „Entartete Kunst", die, kurz nachdem Maria Innocentia ihr zweites Studium beendet hatte, im Juli 1937 in München ihre Pforten öffnete.

18 Richard Klein (1890 – 1967) stammte aus München, war gelernter Bildhauer und hatte später an der Akademie u. a. bei Franz von Stuck studiert. „Ein sehr bedeutender Künstler", hatte sogar die Studentin Berta noch vor vier Jahren voller Ehrfurcht an ihre Eltern geschrieben. Professor Klein hatte ihre Begabung übrigens sehr zu schätzen gewusst, es gäbe eine Einzige, mit der er in seiner Klasse 1931 „was anfangen" könne, hatte er konstatiert und ansonsten reihenweise schlechte Noten verteilt (vgl. Archiv Hummel Massing, Brief Berta an die Eltern vom 14. März 1931). 1944 gehörte er zu den privilegierten „Künstlern im Kriegseinsatz", die von Wehrdienst und Arbeit in der Rüstungsindustrie freigestellt wurden. Zum Thema siehe Hrsg. Münchner Stadtmuseum, München – ‚Hauptstadt der Bewegung', München 1993, S. 365 f., und Thomas Zacharias, (Art) reine Kunst, Die Münchner Akademie um 1937, S. 10.
19 Archiv Irmin Nauer-Dubler, Brief an Sr. Eligia Stadler vom 4. Mai 1935. Die dem Propagandaministerium zugehörige RBK war 1933 gegründet worden, und die Mitgliedschaft war verpflichtend für alle deutschen Künstler. Jüdische Künstler und Künstler der Avantgarde waren ausgeschlossen.
20 Ebd., mündlicher Bericht des Kommilitonen Blasius Spreng
21 Aus der Coburger Nationalzeitung vom 22. August 1936, immerhin der „Amtlichen Tageszeitung der Nationalsozialistischen Deutschen Arbeiterpartei des Bezirks Coburg"
22 Archiv Hummel Massing, Brief Maria Innocentia an ihre Schwester Katharina vom 6. November 1936
23 Archiv Kloster Sießen, nach einem mündlichen Bericht von M. Cäcilia Denkinger 1985 und 1994
24 Ebd., Ärztliches Attest vom 4. Dezember 1936
25 Archiv Hummel Massing, Brief Maria Innocentia an die Mutter vom 19. Dezember 1936
26 Archiv Kloster Sießen, Abgangszeugnis vom 24. April 1937
27 Ebd., Brief an Eligia Stadler vom 15. März 1938
28 Archiv Irmin Nauer-Dubler, aus dem Protokoll der Besprechung Dubler-Klein
29 Archiv Hummel Massing, Brief Maria Innocentia an den Vater vom 12. Juni 1938
30 Ebd., Brief Maria Innocentia an die Eltern vom 15. Juli 1938
31 Archiv Irmin Nauer-Dubler, Brief an Maria Innocentia vom 8. März 1937
32 Ebd., vom 6. Juli 1939
33 Die Verse stammten diesmal von dem berühmten Theologen Dr. Joseph Bernhart, „in Rücksicht auf seine wissenschaftlichen Arbeiten allerdings nur unter Pseudonym und unter Diskretion." (Ebd., vom 25. Mai 1939)

Das „Pinsele" geht heim
1 Archiv Hummel Massing, Brief Maria Innocentias an die Familie Hummel vom 1. November 1940
2 Die sogenannte „VoMi", unterstellt dem Stellvertreter Hitlers, Rudolf Hess, und der Waffen-SS unter Heinrich Himmler, koordinierte alle Aktionen, die deutsche Volksgruppen im Ausland betrafen. Als „Volksdeutsche" wurden etwa zehn Millionen Menschen bezeichnet, die zwar nach Sprache und Kultur deutscher Abstammung waren, die jedoch keine deutsche Reichsbürgerschaft besaßen. Zur Thematik vgl. Melanie Schmitt, Das Umsiedlungslager der volksdeutschen Mittelstelle im Kloster Sießen 1940 – 1945, Bad Saulgau, 2003
3 Zitiert nach August Hagen, Kloster Sießen, Stuttgart, 1960, S. 81
4 Archiv Hummel Massing, Brief an die Familie vom 2.[?] November 1940
5 Archiv Kloster Sießen, Brief an die Generaloberin M. Augustina Steinhauser vom 7. November 1940
6 Archiv Hummel Massing, Brief an die Familie vom 16. Dezember 1940

19 Archive Irmin Nauer-Dubler, Estate of Ars Sacra, letter to Sr. Eligia Stadler of May 4, 1935. The RBK, which was part of the Ministry for Propaganda, had been established in 1933. Membership in it was obligatory for all German artists. Jewish artists and artists of the avant-garde were excluded.
20 Ibid., oral account by the fellow student Blasius Spreng.
21 From the Coburger Nationalzeitung of August 22, 1936, the "official daily of the National Socialist German Workers Party of the district of Coburg."
22 Archive Hummel Massing, letter from Maria Innocentia to her sister Katharina, November 6, 1936.
23 Archive Convent Siessen, according to an oral account by M. Cäcilia Denkinger, 1985 and 1994.
24 Ibid., medical certificate of December 4, 1936.
25 Archive Hummel Massing, letter from Maria Innocentia to her mother, December 19, 1936.
26 Archive Convent Siessen, diploma of April 24, 1937.
27 Ibid., letter to Eligia Stadler of March 15, 1938.
28 Archive Irmin Nauer-Dubler, from the minutes of the Dubler-Klein conference.
29 Archive Hummel Massing, letter from Maria Innoentia to her father, June 12, 1938.
30 Archive Hummel Massing, letter from Maria Innocentia to her parents, July 15, 1938.
31 Archive Irmin Nauer-Dubler, letter to Maria Innocentia of March 8, 1937.
32 Ibid., letter of July 6, 1939.
33 This time the accompanying verses were by the famous theologian Dr. Joseph Bernhart, "under pseudonym and discretion in consideration of his work as a scholar" (ibid., May 25, 1939). The book's title plays on the name "Hummel" meaning "bumblebee" in German.

The "Paintbrush" is laid aside
1 Archive Hummel Massing, letter from Maria Innocentia to the Hummel family, November 1, 1940.
2 The so-called "VoMi," under Hitler's deputy Rudolf Hess and Heinrich Himmler's Waffen SS, coordinated all actions concerning groups of ethnic Germans abroad. As Volksdeutsche the Nazis classified some 10 million people who by language and culture were of German stock but did not hold citizenship in the Reich. On this subject, cf. Melanie Schmitt, Das Umsiedlungslager der volksdeutschen Mittelstelle im Kloster Siessen 1940-1945 (Bad Saulgau, 2003).
3 Quoted from August Hagen, Kloster Siessen (Stuttgart, 1960), p. 81.
4 Archive Hummel Massing, letter to the family of November 2 [?], 1940.
5 Archive Convent Siessen, letter to Mother Superior M. Augustina Steinhauser of November 7, 1940.
6 Archive Hummel Massing, letter to the family of December 16, 1940.
7 Archive Irmin Nauer-Dubler, letter from Maximiliane Müller to Maria Innocentia, August 25, 1939.
8 Because of this, Maria Innocentia requested permission in 1942 to print a few motifs at the smaller press Mandt in Stuttgart, which evidently was not affected by the paper rationing. "I don't think it will damage you in any way if at least a few Hummel cards can still be found in Germany." Ars Sacra gave the green light, and thus a few prints could still appear in Germany during those years. Cf. Maria Innocentia's letter to Maximiliane Müller of September 3, 1942, Archive Irmin Nauer-Dubler.
9 Archive of the Goebel Porcelain Manufacturing Co., Ltd, letter to Franz Goebel of August 13, 1941.
10 Archive Irmin Nauer-Dubler, letter from Maximiliane Müller to Maria Innocentia, October 21, 1942.
11 Maria Innocentia used the phrase "Hummel nest" (with pun on "Hummel" = bumblebee) frequently in her letters hereafter, and always a little wistfully.
12 After an anecdote by M. Laura Brugger.
13 Philippe Pétain was the head of the right-wing conservative Vichy regime,

7 Archiv Irmin Nauer-Dubler, Brief Maximiliane Müller an Maria Innocentia vom 25. August 1939
8 1942 bat Maria Innocentia aus diesem Grund, ein paar Motive bei der kleineren Verlagsanstalt Mandt in Stuttgart drucken zu dürfen, die von der Papierzuteilung offensichtlich nicht betroffen war. „Ich glaube nicht, daß es ihnen schaden wird, wenn wenigstens ein paar Hummelkarten in Deutschland noch zu finden sind." Ars sacra gab grünes Licht, und so konnten in jenen Jahren doch noch einige Druckerzeugnisse erscheinen. Vgl. Brief von Maria Innocentia an Maximiliane Müller vom 3. September 1942, Archiv Irmin Nauer-Dubler
9 Archiv der Goebel Porzellanmanufaktur GmbH, Schreiben an Franz Goebel vom 13. August 1941
10 Archiv Irmin Nauer-Dubler, Brief Maximiliane Müller an Maria Innocentia vom 21. Oktober 1942
11 Den Ausdruck „Hummel-Nest" verwendete Maria Innocentia fortan in ihren Briefen häufig und immer ein wenig wehmütig.
12 Nach einer Anekdote von M. Laura Brugger
13 Philippe Pétain leitete das rechts-konservative Vichy-Regime, der Regierung des südlichen Teils Frankreichs, der nach der Kriegsniederlage am 22. Juni 1940 nicht von Deutschland besetzt war. Pétain geriet im eigenen Land wegen seiner Kooperation mit Hitler zunehmend in die Kritik, wurde 1944 nach Landung der Alliierten in der Normandie interniert und schließlich in Sigmaringen untergebracht, unweit vom Kloster Sießen.
14 Archiv Hummel Massing, Brief an die Familie vom 4. September 1944
15 Ebd., Brief an die Eltern vom 22. Oktober 1944
16 Ebd., Brief an die Familie vom 1. November 1944
17 Ebd., Brief an die Eltern vom 15. November 1944. Dennoch schrieb sie einen Monat später sehr berührt von der Reaktion der Menschen: „Bei den Patienten bin ich noch unbekannt – aber es fängt schon an ‚zu mungeln'. Es gibt begeisterte Hummelverehrer unter den Soldaten (ist auch ein Lazarett hier). Einer machte Scherenschnitte nach meinen Karten. Kürzlich wurde ein braves Mädchen hoffnungslos entlassen. In ihrem großen Leid vertraute sie der Krankenschwester an – einen Trost habe sie immer noch, wenn sie ganz traurig sei u. verzagen möchte, dann hole sie ‚ihren Schatz' hervor (…). ‚Dieser Schatz' war eine Schachtel, die mit ‚Hummelkarten' gefüllt war." (Brief an die Familie vom 13. Dezember 1944)
18 Archiv Kloster Sießen, Brief an Generaloberin M. Augustina Steinhauser vom 7. Januar 1945
19 Ebd., vom 15. Januar 1945
20 Archiv Irmin Nauer-Dubler, Schreiben „An den Verlag Josef Müller" vom 20. Dezember 1944
21 Archiv Hummel Massing, Brief an die Familie vom 3. Februar 1945
22 Ebd.
23 Sie kam bei einer Größe von 163 cm immerhin von unter 50 kg wieder auf 56 kg Gewicht.
24 Archiv Kloster Sießen, Amtsärztliches Zeugnis vom 17. September 1945
25 Archiv Kloster Sießen, Arztbericht Dr. Brügger vom 26. Oktober 1945
26 Ebd. vom 13. November 1945
27 Vgl. Brief an die Familie vom 10. November 1945, Archiv Hummel Massing
28 Archiv Hummel Massing, Brief an Centa Hummel vom 28. September 1945
29 Archiv Kloster Sießen, Brief an Generaloberin M. Augustina Steinhauser vom 8. Oktober 1945
30 Ebd., vom 8. Januar 1946
31 Ebd., Brief an Ady Hummel vom 28. Februar 1946
32 Diese letzten Zeichnungen wurden bereits 1947 im Fink-Verlag unter dem Titel „Letztes Schenken" veröffentlicht.
33 Archiv Hummel Massing, Brief an die Eltern vom 17. September 1946
34 Archiv Kloster Sießen, „Totenbrief für Schwester Maria Innocentia Hummel", November 1946
35 Ebd.
36 Ebd., M. Radegundis Wespel, Grußwort bei der Eröffnung des Berta-Hummel-Museums in Massing 1994

the government of the southern part of France, which had not been occupied by Germany after the defeat of June 22, 1940. Pétain came increasingly under attack in his own country because of his cooperation with Hitler. After the landing of the Allies in Normandy in 1944, he was interned and at length brought to Sigmaringen, not far from Siessen.
14 Archive Hummel Massing, letter to the family of September 4, 1944.
15 Ibid., letter to the parents of October 22, 1944.
16 Ibid., letter to the family of November 1, 1944.
17 Ibid., letter to the parents of November 15, 1944. Nevertheless she wrote a month later about being greatly touched by the reactions of the people. "I am still unknown among the patients – but there are already 'rumors.' There are great Hummel fans among the soldiers (this is also a military hospital). One soldier is making silhouettes after my cards. Recently a brave girl was discharged as incurable. In her great sorrow she confided to the nurse that she always had one consolation left: whenever she gets very sad and wants to despair, she takes out 'her treasure' (…). This 'treasure' was a box filled with 'Hummel cards'" (letter to the family of December 13, 1944)
18 Archive Convent Siessen, letter to the Mother Superior M. Augustina Steinhauser of January 7, 1945.
19 Ibid., January 15, 1945.
20 Archive Irmin Nauer-Dubler, letter "To the Publishing House Josef Müller" of December 20, 1944.
21 Archive Hummel Massing, letter to the family of February 3, 1945.
22 Ibid.
23 With a height of 5'4", her weight rose from 110 back to 124 lbs.
24 Archive Convent Siessen, official medical certificate of September 17, 1945.
25 Archive Convent Siessen, medical report by Dr. Brügger of October 26, 1945.
26 Ibid., November 13, 1945.
27 Cf. letter to the family of November 10, 1945, Archive Hummel Massing.
28 Archive Hummel Massing, letter to Centa Hummel of September 28, 1945.
29 Archive Convent Siessen, letter to Mother Superior M. Augustina Steinhauser of October 8, 1945.
30 Ibid., January 8, 1946.
31 Ibid., letter to Ady Hummel of February 28, 1946.
32 These last drawings were published already in 1947 by the Fink Press under the title *Letztes Schenken* ("Last Gifts").
33 Archive Hummel Massing, letter to the parents of September 17, 1946.
34 Archive Convent Siessen, requiem letter for Maria Innocentia, November 1946.
35 Ibid.
36 Ibid., M. Radegundis Wespel, greeting at the opening of the Berta Hummel Museum in Massing, 1994.

Bildnachweis

Soweit nicht anders bezeichnet, stammen alle künstlerischen Abbildungen aus dem Werk der Berta Maria Innocentia Hummel

Abkürzungen:
ARS AG: ARS AG, Baar, Schweiz
HM: aus dem Archiv Hummel Massing
KS: aus dem Archiv des Klosters Sießen
ND: aus dem Archiv Irmin Nauer-Dubler

Fotos aus dem Stadtmuseum München sind dem Katalog: München – Hauptstadt der Bewegung, München 1993 entnommen.
Abbildungen aus dem Simplicissimus stammen aus dem Katalog: Simplicissimus, München 1977

Schuber und Buchcover:
Hui, die Hummel!, ARS AG; Schönwetter, ARS AG; alle anderen s.u.
Inhaltsverzeichnis und Kapitelseiten:
S.u.
Hummel Bertl – zeichne mich!
10/11 Wappen, 1942, Wasserfarbe und Blattgold, 228 x 159 mm, KS; Hummel-Haus, 1913; Berta mit Matrosenkragen, 1919; Massing, Marktplatz 1928/1929; Marktplatz im Winter, 1928, Bleistift, 235 x 320 mm; alle übrigen HM
12/13 Zeichnung Adolf Hummel; Großeltern, 1928, Rötel, 270 x 433 mm, mit fotografischer Vorlage; Taufschleife; Abschrift Eheurkunde; Berta, 1910/1911; Stammbaum; alle HM
14/15 Adolf Hummel in Uniform; Viktoria Hummel, 1913; Großmutter, 1910; Viktoria Hummel, 1916/1917; Porträt Großmutter, 1927, Pittkreide, 350 x 300 mm; Porträt Viktoria Hummel, 1927, Bleistift, 235 x 153 mm; alle HM
16/17 Kätl, Viki und Berta im Winterdirndl, 1915; Essecke der Familie Hummel; Hummelkinder Berta, Viki, Franzl und Kätl, 1923/1925, Tinte und Wasserfarbe, 66 x 50, 65 x 45, 68 x 53 und 65 x 45 mm; alle HM
18/19 Buben, 1929/1930, Bleistift, 70 x 100 mm; Hummelkind Ady, 1923/1925, Tinte und Wasserfarbe, 64 x 45 mm; „Feldpost“; alle HM
20/21 „Bericht über Frl. Berta Hummel“, 1934, KS; Klassenfoto 1919; Volksschulhaus Massing, 1928/1929; Kätl und Viki am Klavier, 1920; Erstkommunion, 1918; Strafarbeit, 1921; alle übrigen HM
22/23 Urkunde des bayerischen Königs an Adolf Hummel; Aufgang zur Volksschule Massing, 1928, Aquarell, 333 x 240 mm; Sommerhaus, 1922; Fahrpreisermäßigung Simbach-Massing; Institut „Marienhöhe“ in Simbach, Postkarte; „Gewürzkasten“, 1921; „Spulen und Model“, 1923; alle HM
24/25 „Marienhöhe“, 1927/1928, Lithografie, 251 x 171 mm, HM; Berta und Centa, HM; Zwergerl auf dem Reck, 1934, Bleistift, 90 x 75 mm, KS; Ehrenurkunde, 1923, HM; Briefe an die Eltern, 13.06.1921 und 26.03.1922, HM; Bewertungsblatt, HM; Hummelkind Centa, 1923/1425, Tinte und Wasserfarbe, 66 x 45 mm, HM
26/27 Personalausweis; Berta mit Kätzchen, 1925; Elmar, Kopfstudie, 1925/26, Tusche, 195 x 135 mm; Jahreszeugnis 1925; Schulausflug, 1925; Hausordnung „Marienhöhe“; alle HM
28/29 Berta im Harlekinkostüm, 1925, HM; Bertas erster Ölmalkasten, KS; Brief 13.12.1925, HM; Maria im Walde, 1926/1927, Wasserfarbe, 320 x 460 mm, HM; Berta vor Ölbild, 1926/1927, HM; Segelschiff, 1926/1927, Öl auf Leinwand, 660 x 875 mm, HM
30/31 Palette, Pinsel und Ölfarbe aus dem Ölmalkasten (auch auf folgenden Seiten), KS; Einladung Schlussfeier; Absolvia, 1926; Berta, 1926/1927; Familie Hummel, 1926; Berta mit „Lord“, 1926/1927; Kätl und Viki am Klavier, 1926, Bleistift, 145 x 165 mm; Dirigent im Frack, 1926, Bleistift, 238 x 321 mm; alle übrigen HM
Centa Hummel
32/33 Bilder: Centa mit Absolvia-Mütze, 1928, Farbstift, 300 x 278 mm; Centa, März 1931, Öl, 319 x 241 mm; Centa, 1927/1928, Grafit, 240 x 183 mm; alle HM
Ein außergewöhnliches Talent
36/37 Selbstporträt, 1928, Bleistift, 320 x 220 mm; Münchner Dächer, 1928/1930, Aquarell, 235 x 400 mm; Im Stadtteil Au, 1929, Aquarell, 405 x 275 mm; alle HM
38/39 München, Viktualienmarkt, 1929/1930, Aquarell, 251 x 348 mm, HM; Bulldogge Simplizissimus; Mobilmachung, 2. August 1914, Stadtmuseum München; Gautag München-Oberbayern der NSDAP am 3. Juli 1932, Stadtarchiv München
40/41 Passbild, 1928, HM; Bestimmungen der Staatlichen Kunstgewerbeschule, KS; Kindertapete, 1927, Bleistift, 93 x 94 mm, HM; Kindertapete, 1927, Bleistift und Wasserfarbe, 61 x 95 mm, HM; Brief 27.04.1927, HM
42/43 Zeitungsartikel Umbenennung, 1928; Kunstgewerbeschule in der Luisenstraße, Postkarte; Fahrpreisermäßigung; Porträt eines alten Mannes, 1930, Kohle, 250 x 176 mm; Porträt Margret, 1930, Kohle, 305 x 194 mm; Margret, sitzend, 1930, Kohle, 280 x 175 mm; alle HM
44/45 Betrunkenen-Perspektive, 1929, Bleistift, 99 x 54 mm; Neujahrsmusikanten, 1929, Bleistift, 100 x 55 mm; Skizzenblatt mit Karikaturen, 1931, Bleistift, 195 x 175 mm; Viehmarkt Massing, 1931, Farbstift und Bleistift, 210 x 285 mm; Fronleichnamsprozession in Massing, 1931, Farbstift und Bleistift, 210 x 270 mm; alle HM
46/47 Chinoiserie, 1927, Farbstift, 143 x 202 mm; Brandgasse Massing, 1928, Holzschnitt, 96 x 79 mm; Pfau, 1927, Wasserfarbe, 107 x 108 mm; Visitenkarte; Verschiedene Kopfskizzen, 1928, Bleistift, 109 x 150 mm; alle HM
48/49 Malausflug mit Professor Dasio 1927/1928; Professor Friedrich Wirnhier, Porträtfoto; Professor Maximilian Dasio, Porträtfoto; Bauer mit Hut, 1930, Aquarell, 164 x 147 mm; alle HM
50/51 Maria Graser, 1928, Rötel, 290 x 245 mm; Bäuerin, 1927/1928, Kohle, Original beschnitten; Bäuerin, 1929/1930, Kohle, 260 x 188 mm; Johann Huber, 1928, Rötel, 310 x 220 mm; Kleinkinderstudien, 1928, Rötel, 190 x 140 mm; alle HM
52/53 Berta mit Malklasse, 1927; Dasio, 1930, Grafit, 260 x 180 mm; Dasio, 1930, Holzschnitt, 105 x 70 mm; Dasio mit Zeitung, 1930, Aquarell, 268 x 188 mm; Johann Huber, 1929, Aquarell, 353 x 250 mm; Porträt Mann mit Hut, 1929/1930, Pastell, 335 x 265 mm; alle HM
54/55 Dame in Rot, 1930, Aquarell und Bleistift, 500 x 280 mm; Salzburg, Blick auf den Dom, 1929/1930, Aquarell, 410 x 291 mm; Studienausflug 1927/1928; alle HM
56/57 Porträt einer jungen Frau mit Kopftuch, 1929/1930, Aquarell, 490 x 270 mm; Biedermeier-Zimmer, 1929/1930, Aquarell, 463 x 361 mm; Signaturen (auch auf den übrigen Seiten); Studienausweis, 1927; alle HM
58/59 Akt, 1927/1930, Rötel, 464 x 200 mm; Akt, 1927/1930, Holzschnitt, 174 x 105 mm; Akt, 1927/1930, Kohle, 196 x 386 mm; Engel mit Blumen, 1931, Bleistift, 50 x 30 mm; Schaufensterdekoration, 1928; alle HM
60/61 Berta 1930/1931, HM; Porträt einer Frau, 1929/1930, Kohle und Pittkreide, 270 x 195 mm, HM; Porträt einer jungen Frau, 1929/1930, Kohle, 290 x 235 mm, HM; Dame in Blau, 1929/1930, Aquarell und Bleistift, 500 x 300 mm, HM; Auseinandersetzung, 1930, Stadtarchiv München; Die Münchner Ludwigstraße zum Siegestor, 1929, Aquarell, 463 x 605 mm, HM
62/63 Prüfungszeugnis, Abschrift, 1931; Telegramm 15. 3. 1931; Silberhochzeit, 1931; Gabentisch mit Wandbehang; Selbstporträt, 1929, Rötel, 252 x 187 mm; alle HM
Der andere Weg
68/69 Vogelpredigt des hl. Franziskus, 1935, Kohle, 720 x 360 mm, KS; „Das kleine Geheimnis“, HM; Kruzifix mit Kerze und Büchern, 1929/1930, Aquarell, 525 x 353 mm, HM
70/71 Gebirgslandschaft mit Wald, 1929/1930, Aquarell, 555 x 405 mm, HM; Porträt Jakob Huber, 1929, Aquarell, 352 x 244 mm, HM; Der rote Fäustling, 1927, Farbstift, 200 x 125 mm, HM; Knieende Madonna, 1931, Farbstift, 90 x 35 mm, KS; Herrgottswinkel im Hummel-Haus, HM; Stube mit Herrgottswinkel, 1929/1930, Aquarell, 352 x 457 mm, HM
72/73 Einsiedler, 1927, Tusche, 220 x 319 mm; Romanischer Kreuzgang, 1929/1930, Aquarell, 271 x 398 mm; Malausflug an den Chiemsee; Dampfer auf dem Chiemsee, 1929/1930, Aquarell, 347 x 465 mm; alle HM
74/75 St. Annaplatz und Kirche, Postkarte, HM; Maria-Theresien-Wohnheim in der Blumenstraße, KS; Passbild Berta Hummel, HM; M. Kostka Hartmann OSF, KS; Schmerzensmutter, 1935, Kohle und Pastell, 890 x 485 mm, KS
76/77 Rosen, 1927/1928, Bleistift, 210 x 162 mm, HM; Pater Rupert Mayer, Archiv des Erzbistums München; Stillleben mit Obst und Blumenstock, 1928/1930, Aquarell, 557 x 417 mm, HM
78/79 Familienausflug, 1928; Hummel-Schwestern, 1928; Chrysantheme, 1929/1930, Aquarell, 510 x 345 mm; Rote Primeln, 1929/1930, Aquarell, 520 x 380 mm; alle HM
80/81 Porträt Brauneis, 1930, Aquarell und Bleistift, 270 x 187 mm, HM; Porträt Dasio, 1930, Aquarell und Beistift, 270 x 208 mm, HM; Münchner Hauptbahnhof, Postkarte, HM; Klassenfoto, KS
82/83 Altes Massinger Haus, 1929/1930, Aquarell, 285 x 220 mm; Massinger Häuser, 1929/1930, Aquarell, 440 x 330 mm; Berta mit „Lord“, 1930; Der Hund „Lord“, 1929/1930, Aquarell und Bleistift, 340 x 340 mm; alle HM
Tagesordnung
84/85 12 Kalenderblätter, 1935, Kohle und Pastell, alle ca. 340 x 660 mm, ARS AG
Klosterkind und Künstlerin
88/89 Brief 25.04.1931, HM; Fußweg durch die Birkenallee nach Sießen, Aufnahme Metz Tübingen, 1949, KS; Franziskanerinnenkloster Sießen, Luftaufnahme Aero-Ex. München, 1962, KS
90/91 Bruder Konrad Fahne, 1931, Applikation, Gold- und Seidenstickerei, KS; Kasel-Entwurf, 1931/1933, Farbstift und Bronzegold, 200 x 145 mm, KS; M. Laura Brugger, KS; Entwurf Messgewand, 1930/1931, Wasserfarbe und Bronzegold, 222 x 155 mm, HM
92/93 Kloster Sießen, 1954, KS; Postkarte mit Unterschriften, HM; Berta und Centa, 1931, HM
94/95 J. Hummel Firmenzeichen, 1929, Wasserfarbe, 170 x 207 mm, HM; Porträt Adolf Hummel, 1931, Bleistift, 320 x 232 mm, HM; Entwurf für die Fahne der Anzenberg-Kongregation: Maria mit Kind, Engel und Anzenbergkirche, 1931, Kohle und Pastell, 890 x 525 mm, KS; Bruder-Konrad-Fahne, 1931, HM
96/97 Madonna im Rundbogen, 1931/1933, Bleistift, 70 x 55 mm, KS; Muttergottesfahne, 1931, Maße unbekannt, KS
98/99 Kloster Sießen, Aufnahme Junkers Luftbild Leipzig, 1931, KS; Unterschrift Else Brauneis, HM; Berta 1932, HM; Porträt der Professorin Else Brauneis, 1930, Grafit, 350 x 275 mm, HM
100/101 Christkind mit König (und Detail Stern), 1931, Bleistift, 60 x 70 mm, KS; Christkind mit Hirt, 1931, Bleistift, 60 x 70 mm, KS; Christkind, Engel mit Kerze, 1931, Öl auf Pappe, 350 x 420 mm, KS; Lesendes Kind, 1928, Wasserfarbe, 130 x 165 mm, HM
102/103 Kreuzgarten, 1934; Kinderstudien, 1932/1933, Kohle, 540 x 370 mm; Schreibendes Mädchen, 1932/1933, Kohle, 540 x 370 mm; Lesendes Mädchen, 1932/1933, Kohle, 410 x 260 mm; alle KS
104/105 Hochzeit Kätl, 1932, HM; Berta und Centa, HM; Tierliebe, 1932, Kohle und Pastell, ca. 450 x 300 mm, ARS AG; Missionsmadonna, 1932/33, Kohle und Pastell, 765 x 1240 mm, ARS AG; Mitgliedsurkunde Deutsche Gesellschaft für Christliche Kunst, HM
106/107 Marktplatz in Massing um 1930, HM; Berta-Hummel-Straße, 1929, Aquarell, 310 x 230 mm, HM; Zeitungsrezension Beuroner Tagung, 1932, HM; Auf dem Schulweg, Beim Beten, Beim Spielen, Kohle und Pastell, 450-460 x 310 mm, ARS AG
108/109 Blätter aus dem Simplicissimus; Hitler und Hindenburg, 21. März 1933, Stadtmuseum München
110/111 Stempelentwürfe Sießen, 1931/1933, Grafit, 270 x 194 mm, KS
112/113 Marktszene mit Druckstock, 1928, Holzschnitt, 66 x 80 mm; Postulantin Berta, Juni 1933; Familie Hummel, 1933; Berta und Familie, 1933; alle HM
114/115 Straßenkarte; Speisekarte; Bericht Adolf Hummel zur Einkleidung seiner Tochter, 22. August 1933; alle HM
116/117 Prozession der eingekleideten Novizinnen, 1959, KS; Einzug der Postulantinnen in die Klosterkapelle, 1959, KS; Porträt Adalbero Hugo, 1930, Grafit, 350 x 237 mm, HM
118/119 Gruß Maria Hugo; Porträt Maria Hugo, 1928, Rötel, 192 x 190 mm; Erinnerungsbildchen; Abschiedsfoto; alle HM
70 Jahre Handarbeit
120/121 alle Fotos Romy Gallina, ARS AG
Hummel um die Welt
124/125 Fotokarte Resele mit Ball, KS; Maria Innocentia mit Kind, KS; Verlagshaus Ars sacra, ND; Brief Ars sacra 14.3.1933, ND
126/127 Liebreich Holdseligste, 1933, Kohle und Pastell; St. Franziskus, 1933, Kohle und Pastell, 870 x 685 mm; Alleluja-Engel 1931/1933, Kohle und Pastell, 345 x 400 mm; alle ARS AG
128/129 Frohe Ostern, 1932/1933, Tinte, 80 x 57 mm, KS; Ehepaar Müller, ND; Englein mit Christkind im Wägelchen, 1929/1932, Tusche, 48 x 108 mm, KS; Alleluja-Engel, 1932/1933, Tinte, 82 x 60 mm, KS
130/131 Briefkopf, ND; Porträt Josef Müller, ND; Rezension, 1933, HM (mit Abbildung: Hansel merk dir das, ARS AG); Grabkreuz-Entwürfe, 1933/1934, Grafit, 100 x 293 mm, KS
132/133 Im Kreuzgarten: Maria Innocentia mit Kind, 1934, KS; Anneliese, 1933/1934, Kohle und Pastell, ARS AG; Glück zum Neuen Jahr!, 1932/1933, Kohle und Pastell, 340 x 525 mm, ARS AG; Gebet vor der Schlacht, 1933, Kohle und Pastell, ca. 550 x 360 mm, ARS AG; Ich bring dir Glück, 1933, Kohle und Pastell, 335 x 550 mm, ARS AG
134/135 Schwester Maria Innocentia, 1934; Maria Innocentia mit Kindern, 1934; alle KS
136/137 Bericht von Adolf Hummel zur Profess, HM; Klosterkapelle, 1954, KS; Erinnerungen für das Familienalbum, HM; Maria Innocentia im Kreis ihrer Lieben, 1934, KS
138/139 Titelblatt (Entwurf), Farbstift, 233 x 162 mm, KS; Zum 50sten, 1934, Wasserfarbe, Tusche und Farbstift, 123 x 170 mm, KS; Traueranzeige Josef Müller, Verleger der Ars sacra, ND; Arrest, 1933/1934, Kohle und Pastell, 370 x 510 mm, ARS AG; Der Held, 1934, Kohle und Pastell, 830 x 580 mm, ARS AG
140/141 alle Fotos: Archiv der Goebel Porzellanmanufaktur
142/143 Franz Goebel, HM; Brief an die Familie (21.12.1934), HM; „Das kleine Geigerlein“, ARS AG; Geigenengel, 1934, Kohle und Pastell, 430 x 630 mm, ARS AG; Der Weihnachtsengel, 1934, Kohle und Pastell, 410 x 650 mm, ARS AG
Sammlerleidenschaft
144/145 Lizenzprodukte und Figurenabbildungen (weiße und farbige „Gänseliesl“, 1936; „Hui, die Hummel“, Mädchen und Junge, 1936; Alter Mann mit Zeitung, 1948, unveröffentlicht): ARS AG; Clubzeitschrift „Insights“ und Logo: Archiv der Goebel Porzellanmanufaktur; Hummel-Sammlungen, HM, mit Dank an Ruth und Robert L. Miller und David May; Fälschungen, HM
Die dunkle Zeit
148/149 Brief an Bischof Buchberger (3.12.1934), Bischöfliches Zentralarchiv Regensburg; Medaille, HM; Dr. Michael Buchberger, Archiv des Erzbistums München
150/151 Maria mit sieben Schwertern, 1935/1936, Wasserfarbe und Bronzegold, 145 x 240 mm, ARS AG; Guter Hirte, 1933/1934, Kohle und Pastell, 510 x 650 mm, ARS AG; Es ist vollbracht!, 1935/1936, Kohle und Pastell, 540 x 660 mm, ARS AG
152/153 Hochzeit zu Kana, 1935, Bleistift und Farbstift, 215 x 152 mm, KS; Christus bei der Hochzeit zu Kana, 1935/1936, Tempera, 220 x 200 mm, KS; Gegrüßet seist Du, Maria!, 1934, Farbstift, 430 x 465 mm, ARS AG; Christi Geburt, 1934, Farbstift, 440 x 500 mm, ARS AG; Die Flucht nach Ägypten, 1934, Farbstift, 410 x 490 mm, ARS AG; In Nazareth, 1934, Farbstift, 430 x 490 mm, ARS AG
154/155 Männlicher Akt, Bewegungsstudie, 1935/1936, Grafit, 450 x 330 mm; Kreuzwegskizze, Jesus nimmt das Kreuz an, 1936, Wasserfarbe, 108 x 103 mm; Kreuzwegskizze, Jesus wird verurteilt, 1936, Wasserfarbe, 124 x 129 mm; Aus einem Skizzenheft, 1935/1936, Bleistift, 278 x 200 mm; alle KS
156/157 Winterlicher Bergweg mit Fotovorlage, 1935, Kohle und Pastell, 660 x 460 mm, KS; Ski Heil!, 1935, Kohle und Pastell, 630 x 458 mm, KS; Häschen mit Blumenkorb, 1937/1938, Kohle und Pastell, 440 x 500 mm, ARS AG, KS
158/159 Plakatentwurf, 1936, Tempera, 340 x 245 mm, KS; Wappen Richard Klein, Stadtarchiv München; Maria Innocentia und Eltern, 1937/1939, KS; Ex libris A. Hummel, 1935/1939, Stempelfarbe, 53 x 32 mm, KS
160/161 Weiblicher Akt, 1927/1936, Kohle, 430 x 290 mm, HM; Gloxinien im Topf, 1935/1936, Aquarell, 495 x 445 mm; Männlicher Akt, 1935/1936, Grafit, 450 x 330 mm; Porträt eines Greises, 1935/1936, Grafit, 295 x 190 mm; Kopfstudien einer alten Frau, 1935/1936, Grafit, 390 x 330 mm; Porträt eines Mannes, auf die Hand gestützt, 1935/1936, Grafit, 370 x 295 mm; Kopfstudie eines Mannes, 1935/1936, Bleistift, 350 x 300 mm; alle übrigen KS
162/163 Hirsch an der Quelle, 1935/1936, Tempera, 226 x 212 mm, KS; Tiere auf der Weide, 1935/1936, Tempera, 180 x 185 mm, KS; Liegendes Katzentier, 1935/1936, Kohle, 290 x 360 mm, KS; Christkind mit Ochs und Esel, 1935/1936, Wasserfarbe und Farbstift, 120 x 100 mm, ARS AG
164/165 Segelboote am Ufer, 1935, Kohle und Pastell, 337 x 665 mm, ARS AG; Seelandschaft, 1935, Kohle und Pastell, 337 x 664 mm, ARS AG; alle Fotos: Archiv der Goebel Porzellanmanufaktur
166/167 Zeugnis, KS; Informationen an die Eltern, HM
168/169 Zeitungsartikel „SA-Mann“, 1937, HM (mit Abbildungen Lieb' Vaterland magst ruhig sein und Kannst dich verlassen, ARS AG); Zeitungen Fritz Eher, Stadtmuseum München; Lieb Vaterland, magst ruhig sein!, 1934, Kohle und Pastell, 420 x 595 mm, ARS AG; Lieb' Vaterland magst ruhig sein, ND; Dr. Herbert Dubler, ND
170/171 Wanderbub, 1934, Farbstift, ca. 150 x 105 mm, ARS AG; Wanderbub, 1935, ARS AG; Maria Innocentias Atelier, 1937, KS; Der Schutzengel, 1937, Kohle und Pastell, 498 x 896 mm, ARS AG; Ein dicker Gruß, 1937, Kohle und Pastell, 590 x 470 mm, ARS AG; Ein lieber Gruß, 1937, Kohle und Pastell, 605 x 480 mm, ARS AG; Wanderbub, 1935, ARS AG
172/173 Buchdeckel: „Hui, die Hummel“, 1939, ARS AG; Fotos S. 172, Archiv der Goebel Porzellanmanufaktur; Fotos Maria Innocentia, 1939, HM
Das „Pinsele“ geht heim
178/179 Maria Innocentia, 1939, HM; Kloster Sießen, 1962, KS
180/181 Rosenkranz; Hummel-Sommerhaus, 1927, Bleistift und Wasserfarbe, 220 x 253 mm; Massing vom Kirchberg aus, 1928/1929, Aquarell, 264 x 494 mm; Alte Häuser, 1929/1930, Bleistift, 180 x 140 mm, 192 x 136 mm und 275 x 180 mm; alle HM
182/183 Maria Innocentia mit Nichte Traudl und mit Familie, 1940, HM; Gästebucheinträge, Schrift HM, Zeichnung KS
184/185 Warum so traurig?, 1941/1944, Kohle und Pastell, 540 x 390 mm, ARS AG; Die große Neuigkeit, 1941, Kohle und Pastell, 540 x 440 mm, ARS AG; Maria Innocentia mit M. Eligia Stadler OSF, 1940, HM; Zwei Engel auf einer Wolke, 1940/1942, Collage, 215 x 270 mm, KS; Fliegenpilz, Glücksklee und Hummel, 1939/1942, Kohle und Pastell, 363 x 363 mm, 365 x 367 mm und 365 x 365 mm, KS
186/187 Brief an Maximiliane Müller, 1939, ND; M. Müller, ND; Erlaubnis zur Weiterführung des Verlages Ars sacra, ND; Ein schwerer Geschenkkorb, 1944, Kohle und Pastell, ca. 450 x 350 mm, Bild ARS AG, Foto HM; Jesus in Krippe mit Engel, 1940, Tinte, 106 x 103 mm, ARS AG; Mädchen schüttelt Baum, Tinte, 97 x 126 mm, ARS AG
188/189 Hummel auf Blütenzweige, Dezember 1941, Farbstift, 148 x 104 mm, KS; Das Hummel-Nest, 1942, KS; Wandbehang Massing, 1931, Applikation, 835 x 1290 mm, HM; Porträt Viktoria Hummel, April 1929, Kohle, 280 x 260 mm, HM; Porträt Adolf Hummel, März 1929, Kohle, 280 x 260 mm, HM; Entwurf Messlatte, 1941, Kohle und Pastell, 1600 x 100 mm, KS
190/191 Kopf hoch und schlucken, 1941/1944, Kohle und Pastell, 325 x 425 mm, ARS AG; Skizze liegender Soldat, 1942, Bleistift, 85 x 155 mm, KS; Soldaten-Andenken, 1942, Bleistift und Farbstift, 165 x 196 mm, KS; Maria Innocentia, 1944, HM
192/193 Kalanchoe am Fenster, 1943/1944, Kohle mit Pastell, 600 x 440 mm, ARS AG, KS; Villa Vogelfrei „geschlossen“, 1944/45, Farbstift, 105 x 82 mm, KS; Skizze, 1944/45, Bleistift, 149 x 114 mm, KS; Kloster Sießen, Klosterkirche, HM; Aschenbrödel, 1944, Kohle und Pastell, 400 x 420 mm, ARS AG
194/195 Taschenuhr, HM; Sanatorium Wilhelmstift in Isny, Postkarte, HM; Postkarte an die Familie (22.11.1944), HM; Skizze: „Grüß Gott, tritt ein“, 1940er, Bleistift, 220 x 170 mm, KS; Druckstock, 1928, HM; Über den Dächern, 1928/1930, Aquarell, 235 x 400 mm, HM
196/197 Verlagsgebäude Ars sacra, ND; Maria Innocentias Atelier, 1946, KS
198/199 Gutachten, HM; Besatzungszonen, Stadtmuseum München; Skizzenblatt Mariendarstellungen, 1946, Bleistift, 230 x 190 mm; Skizzenblatt mit Tieren, 1946, Bleistift, 240 x 210 mm; alle übrigen KS
200/201 Schreiben Dr. Brügger an Franz Hummel (17.10.1945); Ansichtskarte Wangen; Passierschein; Brief (18.09.1945); alle HM
202/203 Porträt Franz Hummel, 1930, Aquarell, 287 x 226 mm, HM; Zur eiligen Gratulation, 1946, Farbstift und Bleistift, 86 x 78 mm, ARS AG; Der richtige Osterhase, 1946, Farbstift und Bleistift, 148 x 133 mm, ARS AG; Muttergottes, 1946, Bleistift und Farbstift, 121 x 87 mm, KS
204/205 Muttergottes-Ikone; Postkarten an die Eltern (17.09.1946); Sterbekreuz; alle HM
206/207 Totenbrief der Mutter, HM; Viktoria Hummel am Grab ihrer Tochter, 1963, KS

Picture Credits

Where not otherwise stipulated, all art reproductions are taken from the œuvre of Berta Maria Innocentia Hummel.

Abbreviations:

ARS AG: ARS AG, Baar - Switzerland
HM: Archive Hummel, Massing
CS: Archive Convent Sießen
ND: Archive Irmin Nauer-Dubler

Photograps from the Municipal Museum, Munich, are taken from the catalogue: *München – Hauptstadt der Bewegung* (Munich, 1993).
Illustrations from the *Simplicissimus* are taken from the catalogue: *Simplicissimus* (Munich, 1977).

Slipcase and book cover:

Baby and the Bee, ARS AG; Sunny Weather, ARS AG; all others q.v. below

Contents:

Q.v. below

Hummel Bertl – will you draw me?

10/11 The Hummel family coat of arms, 1942, water color and gold leaf, 9 x 6 ¼ in., CS; The Hummel House, 1913; Berta in a sailor shirt,1919; Market square, Massing, 1928/1929; Market square in winter, December 1928, pencil, 9 ¼ x 12 ½ in.; all others HM

12/13 Drawing by the father, Adolf Hummel; Grandparents Anglsperger, reading, 1928, red chalk, 10 ¾ x 17 in. and photographic model; Berta's christening bow; Marriage license; Berta, 1910/1911; Family tree; all HM

14/15 Adolf Hummel in his World War I uniform; Viktoria Hummel, 1913; Grandmother, 1910; Viktoria Hummel, 1916/1917; Portrait Creszentia Anglsperger, 1927, pittchalk, 13 ¾ x 11 ¾ in.; Portrait of Viktoria Hummel, 1927, pencil, 9 ¼ x 6 in.; all HM

16/17 Kätl, Viki and Berta in winter dirndls, 1915; The Hummel dining area; Hummelchildren Berta, Viki, Franzl und Kätl, 1923/1925, ink and watercolor, all ca. 2 ½ x 2 in.; all HM

18/19 Two boys quarreling, 1929/1930, pencil, 2 ¾ x 4 in.; Hummel child Ady, 1923/1925, ink and watercolor, 2 ½ x 1 ¾ in.; "field-post;" all HM

20/21 "Report on Miss Berta Hummel," 1934, CS; Class photo, 1919; Berta's elementary school, photograph of 1928/1929; Berta's sisters Kätl and Viki at the piano, 1920; Berta at her first communion, 1918; Penalty assignment, 1921; all others HM

22/23 Certificate from the king of Bavaria; Elementary school, Massing, August 1928, watercolor, 13 x 9 ½ in.; Summer house, 1922; application for reduced train fare, Simbach-Massing; The Institute "Marienhöhe" ("St. Mary's Heights"), picture postcard; Drawing class works, 1921 and 1923; all HM

24/25 "St. Mary's Heights," Simbach, 1927/1928, lithograph, 10 x 6 ¾ in., HM; Berta and Centa, HM; Little gnome on the horizontal bar, 1934, pencil, 3 ½ x 3 in., CS; Certificate, 1923, HM; Letters to the parents in Massing, HM; School report card, HM; Hummel child Centa, 1923/1925, ink and watercolor, 2 ½ x 1 ¾ in., HM

26/27 Berta's identity card; Berta with kitten, 1925; Elmar, head sketch, 1925/26, India ink, 7 ½ x 5 ¼ in.; year-end report card, 1925; Class excursion, 1925; House rules and daily schedule at "St. Mary's Heights;" all HM

28/29 Berta in a harlequin costume, 1925, HM; Berta's first oil paint box, CS; Letter, 1925, HM; The Virgin in the Woods, 1926/1927, water color, 12 ½ x 18 in., HM; Berta working on her first large-format oil painting, 1926/1927, HM; Sailing ship, oil on canvas, 26 x 34 ½ in., HM

30/31 Palette, paintbrush und colors from the oil paint box (also on following pages), CS; Invitation to the musical graduation ceremony; Graduation, 1926; Berta, 1926/1927; The Hummel family,1926; Berta with "Lord," 1926/1927; Kätl and Viki at the piano, 1926, pencil, 5 ¾ x 6 ½ in.; The Conductor, July 1926, pencil, 9 ¼ x 12 ¾ in.; all others HM

Centa Hummel

32/33 Paintings and drawings: Centa, 1928, color pencil, 11 ¾ x 11 in.; Centa, 1931, oil, 12 ½ x 9 ½ in.; Centa, 1927/1928, graphit, 9 ½ x 7 ¼ in.; all HM

An Exceptional Talent

36/37 Self-portrait, 1928, pencil, 12 ½ x 8 ¾ in.; Munich, bird's-eye view, 1928/1930, watercolor, 9 ½ x 15 ¾; Munich, city district Au, 1929, watercolor, 16 x 10 ¾ in.; all HM

38/39 Market in Munich, 1929/1030, watercolor, 10 x 13 ¼ in., HM; Bulldog cover Simplizissimus; Mobilization, 1914, Municipal Museum, Munich; NSDAP gau celebration, 1932, City Archive Munich

40/41 Berta's passport picture, 1928, HM; From the Rules of the State School of Arts and Crafts, Munich, CS; Wallpaper for children, 1927, pencil, 3 ¾ x 3 ¾ in., HM; Wallpaper for children, 1927, pencil, 2 ½ x 3 ¾, HM; Letter, 1927, HM

42/43 Newspaper article, 1928; State School on Luisenstrasse, postcard; Application for reduced train fare Munich – Massing; Portrait of an old man, 1930, charcoal, 9 ¾ x 7 in.; Portrait Margret, 1930, charcoal, 12 x 7 ¾ in.; Margret, seated, 1930, charcoal, 11 x 7 in.; all HM

44/45 Topsy-turvy, 1929, pencil, 4 x 2 ¼ in.; New Year's music, 1929, pencil, 4 x 2 ¼ in.; Caricature sketches, 1931, pencil, 7 ¾ x 5 ¾ in.; Cattle market, 1931, colored pencil and pencil, 8 ¼ x 11 ¼ in.; Corpus Christi Procession, 1931, crayon and pencil, 8 ¼ x 10 ¾ in.; all HM

46/47 Chinoiserie, 1927, crayon, 9 ¼ x 6 in.; Massing, Brandgasse, 1928, woodcut, 3 ¾ x 3 in.; Peacock, 1927, watercolor, 4 ¼ x 4 ¼ in.; Berta's calling card; Head Studies, 1928, pencil, 4 ¼ x 6 in.; all HM

48/49 Painting excursion with Professor Dasio, 1927/1928; Professor Friedrich Wirnhier; Professor Maximilian Dasio; Peasant with hat, 1930, watercolor, 19 ¾ x 11 in.; all HM

50/51 Portrait of Maria Graser, 1928, red chalk, 11 ½ x 9 ¾ in.; Peasant woman, 1927/1928, charcoal, cropped; Peasant woman1929/1930, charcoal, 10 ¼ x 7 ½ in.; Johann Huber, night watchman, 1928, red chalk, 12 ¼ x 8 ¾ in.; Young children (study), 1928, red chalk, 7 ½ x 5 ½ in.; all HM

52/53 Berta in her Painting class, 1927; Portrait of Professor Maximilian Dasio, 1930, graphite, 10 ¼ x 7 in.; Portrait of Professor Maximilian Dasio, March 1930, woodcut, 4 ¼ x 2 ¾ in.; Portrait of Professor Maximilian Dasio reading his newspaper, 1930, watercolor, 10 ¼ x 7 in.; Johann Huber, 1929, watercolor, 14 x 9 ¾ in.; Potrait of a man with hat, 1929/1930, pastel chalk, 6 ½ x 5 ¾ in.; all HM

54/55 Lady in red, 1930, watercolor and pencil, 19 ¾ x 11 in.; Salzburg, view of the cathedral, 1929/1930, watercolor, 16 ¼ x 11 ½ in.; Study excursion 1927/1928; all HM

56/57 Portrait of a young woman with head-scarf, 1929/1930, watercolor, 9 ¾ x 6 ½ in.; Biedermeier interior, 1929/1930, watercolor, 18 ¼ x 14 ¼ in.; Signatures (also on following pages); Berta's student ID, 1927; all HM

58/59 Male nude, 1927/1930, red chalk, 18 ¼ x 7 ¾ in.; Male nude, 1927/1930, woodcut, 6 ¾ x 4 ¼ in.; Female nude, 1927/1930, charcoal, 7 ¾ x 15 ¼ in.; Angel with flowers, 1931, pencil, 2 x 1 ¼ in.; Window decoration, 1928; all HM

60/61 Berta 1930/1931, HM; Portrait of a woman, 1929/1930, charcoal and pittchalk, 10 ¾ x 7 ¾ in., HM; Portrait of a young woman, 1929/1930, charcoal, 11 ½ x 9 ¼ in., HM; Lady in blue, 1929/1930, watercolor and pencil, 19 ¾ x 11 ¾ in., HM; Altercation with Nazis, 1930, City Archive, Munich; Munich, Ludwigstrasse, view towards the Siegestor, 1929, watercolor, 18 ¼ x 23 ¾ in., HM

62/63 Final report, 1931; Telegram of March 15, 1931; Silver wedding, 1931; Table for presents, 1931; Self portrait, 1929, red chalk, 10 x 7 ¼ in.; all HM

The Other Way

68/69 St. Francis preaching to the birds, 1935, charcoal, 28 x 14 in., CS; "The Little Secret" by Cassian Carg, HM; Crucifix with candle and books, 1929/1930, watercolor, 20 ¾ x 14 in., HM

70/71 Alpine forest Wooded mountain landscape, 1929/1930, watercolor, 21 ¾ x 16 in., HM; Portrait of Jakob Huber, 1929, watercolor, 13 ¾ x 9 ½ in., HM; Red mitten, 1927, color pencil, 3 ½ x 4 ¼, HM; Kneeling Virgin with Child, 1931, crayon, 3 ½ x 1 ¼ in., CS; Herrgottswinkel ("Lord's corner") at the Hummel home, HM; Living room with crucifix, 1929/1930, watercolor, 13 ¾ x 18 in., HM

72/73 Hermitage with hermit, 1927, India ink, 8 ½ x 12 ½ in.; Romanesque cloister, watercolor, 10 ¾ x 15 ¾ in.; Painting excursion to the Chiemsee; Chiemsee steamer, 1929/1930, watercolor, 13 ¾ x 18 ¼ in.; all HM

74/75 St. Anna in Munich, postcard, HM; Boarding house Maria Theresia on Blumenstrasse, CS; Passport photograph of Berta Hummel, HM; M. Kostka Hartmann OSF, CS; Mater dolorosa, 1935, charcoal and crayon, 35 x 19 in., CS

76/77 Roses, 1927/1928, pencil, 8 ¼ x 6 ¼ in., HM; The Jesuit priest Rupert Mayer, Archepiscopal Archive, Munich; Still life with fruit and potted plant, 1928/1930, watercolor, 22 ¾ x 16 ½ in., HM

78/79 Family excursion, 1928; The four Hummel sisters, 1928; Chrysanthemum, 1929/1930, watercolor, 20 x 13 ½ in.; Red primula, 1929/1930, watercolor, 20 ½ x 15 in.; all HM

80/81 Portrait Brauneis, 1930, watercolor and pencil, 10 ¾ x 7 ¼ in., HM; Portrait of Professor Maximilian Dasio, 1930, watercolor and pencil, 10 ¾ x 8 ¼ in., HM; Munich central station, postcard, HM; Class picture, CS

82/83 Massing, old house in sunlight, 1929/1930, watercolor, 11 ¼ x 8 ¾ in.; Massing, old houses, 1929/1930, watercolor, 17 ¼ x 13 in.; Berta with her boxer "Lord," 1930; The dog "Lord," 1929/1930, watercolor and pencil, 13 ½ x 13 ½ in.; all HM

Daily Schedule

84/85 12 calendar sheets, 1935, charcoal and crayon, all ca. 13 ¼ x 26 in., ARS AG

Convent Child and Craftswoman

88/89 Letter, 1931, HM; Footpath to Siessen, CS; Franciscan convent of Siessen, postcard, 1962, CS

90/91 Brother Konrad Banner, 1931, appliqué and silk embroidery with gold thread, CS; Design for a chasuble, cross and IHS, 1931/1933, colored pencil and bronze gold, 8 x 5 ½ in., CS; M. Laura Brugger, CS; Design for a chasuble, 1931/1933, colored pencil and bronze gold, 8 x 5 ½ in., HM

92/93 Convent courtyard, Siessen, 1954, CS; postcard with signatures from "St. Mary's Heights," HM; Berta and Centa, 1931, HM

94/95 J. Hummel trademark, 1929, watercolor, 6 ½ x 8 in., HM; Portrait of Adolf Hummel, March 1931, pencil, 12 ½ x 9 ¼ in., HM; Design for Banner of the Congregation Anzenberg: Madonna and child, Angel and the Anzenberg Church, 1931, charcoal and crayon, 35 x 20 ½ in., CS; Brother Konrad banner, 1931, HM

96/97 Madonna under a round arch,1931/1933, pencil, 2 ¾ x 2 in., CS; Mother of God banner, 1931, CS

98/99 Convent Siessen from the air, 1931, CS; Signature Else Brauneis, HM; Berta 1932, HM; Portrait of Professor Else Brauneis,1930, graphite, 13 ¾ x 10 ¾ in., HM

100/101 Christ Child with King, 1931, pencil, 2 ¼ x 2 ¾ in., CS; Christ Child with Shepherd, 1931, pencil, 2 ¼ x 2 ¾ in., CS; Christ Child, angel with candle, 1931, oil on cardboard, 13 ¾ x 16 ½ in., CS; Child reading, 1928, watercolor, 5 ¼ x 6 ½ in., HM

102/103 In the cloister garden, 1934; Sketches of children, 1932/1933, charcoal, 21 ¼ x 14 ½ in.; Girl writing, 1932/1933, charcoal, 21 ¼ x 14 ½ in Girl reading, 1932/1933, charcoal, 16 x 10 ¼ in.; all CS

104/105 Wedding of Berta's sister Kätl, 1932, HM; Berta und Centa, HM; Pet-Loving, charcoal and crayon, ca. 17 ½ x 11 ½ in., ARS AG; Madonna of the Missions, 1932/33, charcoal and crayon, 30 x 48 ¾ in., ARS AG; Membership certificate Society for Christian Art, HM

106/107 Massing, Market Square, ca. 1930, HM; Berta-Hummel-Street, 1929, watercolor, 12 x 9 in., HM; Newspaper reviews of the congress in Beuron,1932, HM; On the Way to School, Child's Prayer, Making Repairs, charcoal and crayon, 17 ½ -18 x 12 in., ARS AG

108/109 Pages from the Simplicissimus; Hitler and Hindenburg, 1933, Municipal Museum, Munich

110/111 Rubber stamp designs for the Siessen convent, 1931/1933, graphite, 10 ½ x 7 ½ in., CS

112/113 Hummel house with market scene, 1928, woodcut, 2 ½ x 3 ¼ in.; Postulant Berta, June 1933; The family at the summer house, 1933; Family, 1933; all HM

114/115 Road map; Menu of the Hotel Kleber Post; Adolf Hummel on his daughter's Assumption of the Habit, August 22, 1933; all HM

116/117 Procession to the Assumption of the Habit ceremony, 1959, CS; Portrait of Father Adalbero Hugo, 1930, graphite, 13 ¾ x 9 ¼ in., HM; Festive entrance into the parish church, CS;

118/119 Greeting of Maria Hugo; Portrait of Maria Hugo, 1928, red chalk, 7 ½ x 7 ½ in.; Memento of a solemn day; Taking leave; all HM

70 Years of Handcraft

120/121 all photograps by Romy Gallina, ARS AG

Hummel World-Wide

124/125 Resele with ball, photo card, CS; Maria Innocentia with child, CS; Ars Sacra Press on Munich's Friedrichstrasse, ND; Letter Ars Sacra, 1933, ND

126/127 Virgin Mother, 1933, charcoal and crayon; St. Francis, 1933, charcoal and crayon, 34 x 26 ½ in.; Alleluja Angel, 1931/1933, charcoal and crayon, 13 ½ x 15 ½ in.; all ARS AG

128/129 Happy Easter, 1932/1933, ink, 3 x 2 in., CS; Josef and Maximiliane Müller, ND; Christ Child with angels in toy cart, 1929/1932, India ink, 3 x 2 ½ in., CS; Alleluja Angel, 1932/1933, ink, 3 x 2 ½ in., CS

130/131 Letterhead of the press's New York branch, ND; Portrait Josef Müller, artist unknown, ND; Newspaper, 1933, HM (Little Nurse, ARS AG); Sketches, 1933/1934, graphite, 4 x 11 ½ in., CS

132/133 In the cloister garden: Maria Innocentia with a child, 1934, CS; Anneliese (Heidi), 1933/1934, charcoal and crayon, ARS AG; Town Crier, 1931/1933, charcoal and crayon, 13 ¾ x 20 ½ in., ARS AG; Prayer before Battle, 1933, charcoal and crayon, ca. 21 ½ x 14 in., ARS AG; Good luck chimney sweep, 1933, charcoal and crayon, 13 x 14 in., ARS AG

134/135 Sister Maria Innocentia, 1934; Maria Innocentia with children, 1934; all CS

136/137 Adolf Hummel's account of the Profession ceremony, 1934, HM; Convent chapel, 1954, CS; Mementos for the family album, HM; Maria Innocentia surrounded by her loved ones, 1934, CS

138/139 Title page of the "Hummel-Buch" (sketch), 1934, colored pencil, 9 x 6 ½ in., CS; For the father's fiftieth birthday, 1934, watercolor, India ink and colored pencil, 5 x 6 ½ in., CS; Obituary notice for Josef Müller, ND; Captive, 1933/1934, charcoal and crayon, 14 ½ x 20 in., ARS AG; Retreat to Safety, 1934, charcoal and crayon, 32 ½ x 22 ¾ in., ARS AG

140/141 all photograps: Archive of the Goebel Porcelain Manufacturing Co., Ltd.

142/143 Franz Goebel, HM; Letter to the family, 1934, HM; "The little fiddler," 1935, ARS AG; Celestial Musician, 1934, charcoal and crayon, 17 x 24 ¾ in., ARS AG; Bearing Christmas gifts, 1934, charcoal and crayon, 16 x 25 ½ in., ARS AG

Collector's Passion

144/145 Licensed products and illustrations of the figurines (Goose Girl, white and colored, 1936; Hummel Rings, girl und boy,1935; Old Man Reading Newspaper, 1948, unpublished), ARS AG; "Insights" and logo, Archive of the Goebel Porcelain Manufacturing Co., Ltd.; Hummel-collections, HM, with thanks to Ruth and Robert L. Miller and David May; Fakes, HM

The Dark Time

148/149 Letter to Dr. Michael Buchberger, 1934, Central Episcopal Archive, Regensburg; Pendant, HM; Dr. Michael Buchberger, Archepiscopal Archive, Munich

150/151 Mother of Sorrows, 1935/1936, watercolor and bronze gold, 5 ¾ x 9 ½ in., ARS AG; The Good Shepherd, 1933/1934, charcoal and crayon, 20 x 25 ½ in., ARS AG; It Is Finished!, 1935/1936, charcoal and crayon, 21 ¼ x 26 in., ARS AG

152/153 The Wedding at Cana, 1935, pencil and color pencil, 8 ½ x 6 in., CS; Christ at the Wedding at Cana, 1935/1936, tempera, 8 ½ x 7 ¾ in., CS; Hail Mary, full of grace, 1934, color pencil, 17 x 18 ¼ in., ARS AG; The Birth of Christ, 1934, color pencil, 17 ¼ x 19 ½ in., ARS AG; The Flight to Egypt, 1934, color pencil, 16 x 19 ¼ in., ARS AG; In Nazareth, 1934, color pencil, 17 x 19 ¼ in., ARS AG

154/155 Male nude, 1935/1936, graphite, 17 ¾ x 13 in.; Way of the Cross sketch: Jesus takes up the cross, 1936, watercolor, 4 ¼ x 4 in.; Jesus is condemned, 1936, watercolor, 4 ¾ x 5 in.; From the sketchpad for the Way of the Cross, 1935/1936, pencil, 11 x 7 ¾ in.; all CS

156/157 Wintry mountain path with photographic model, 1935, charcoal and crayon, 26 x 18 in., CS; Good Skiing!, 1935, charcoal and crayon, 24 ¾ x 18 in., CS; Little Rabbit with Flowers,1937/1938, charcoal and crayon, 17 ¼ x 19 ½ in., ARS AG, CS

158/159 Poster sketch, 1936, tempera, 13 ¼ x 9 ½ in., CS; Coat of arms of Munich, design by Richard Klein, City Archive Munich; Maria Innocentia with her parents, 1937, CS; Ex Libris A. Hummel, 1935/1939, Stamp color, 2 x 1 ¼ in., CS

160/161 Female nude, 1927/1936, charcoal, 17 x 11 ¼ in., HM; Gloxinia pot, 1935/1936, watercolor, 19 ½ x 17 ½ in.; Male nude, motion study, 1935/1936, graphite, 16 x 8 ¼ in.; Portrait of an old man, 1935/1936, graphite, 11 ½ x 7 ½ in.; Head sketch of an old woman, 1935/1936, graphite, 15 ¼ x 13 in.; Portrait of a man leaning on his arm, 1935/1936, graphite, 14 ½ x 11 ½ in.; Head sketch of a man, 1935/1936, pencil, 13 ¾ x 11 ¾ in.; all others CS

162/163 Stag at a fountain, 1936/1936, tempera, 11 x 8 ½ in., CS; Animals on the pasture, 1935/1936, tempera, 6 ½ x 7 in., CS; Stretched-out cat, 1935/1936, charcoal, 11 ½ x 14 in., CS; Infant Christ with ox and ass,1935/1936, watercolor and color pencil, 4 ¾ x 4 in., ARS AG

164/165 Sailboats on the Shore,1935, charcoal and crayon, 13 ¼ x 26 in., ARS AG; Lakeside,1935, charcoal and crayon, 13 ¼ x 26 in., ARS AG; all photographs: Archive of the Goebel Porcelain Manufacturing Co., Ltd.

166/167 Diploma, CS; Report to the parents, HM

168/169 SA-Mann, 1937, HM (Volonteers and You Can Count on Me, ARS AG); Newspapers, Municipal Museum, Munich; "Dear Fatherland, may'st be at ease" (Volonteers), 1934, charcoal and crayon, 16 ½ x 23 ½ in., ARS AG; "Dear Fatherland, may'st be at ease," ND; Dr. Herbert Dubler, ND

170/171 The Merry Wanderer, color pencil, 17 x 19 ¼ in., ARS AG; The Merry Wanderer, 1935, ARS AG; Maria Innocentia's studio, 1937, CS; The Guardian Angel, 1937, charcoal and crayon, 19 ½ x 35 ¼ in., ARS AG; Easy Letters, 1937, charcoal and crayon, 23 ¼ x 18 ½ in., ARS AG; Hard Letters, 1937, charcoal and crayon, 23 ¾ x 18 ¾ in., ARS AG; Strolling Along, 1935, ARS AG

172/173 Book cover "Hui, die Hummel," 1939, ARS AG; Photographs p. 172, Archive of the Goebel Porcelain Manufacturing Co., Ltd.; Maria Innocentia, 1939, HM

The "Paintbrush" is laid aside

178/179 Maria Innocentia, 1939, HM; Convent Siessen, 1962, CS

180/181 Rosary; Summer house of the Hummels, 1927, pencil and watercolor, 8 ¾ x 10 in.; Massing viewed from the Kirchberg, 1928/1929, watercolor, 10 ½ x 19 ½ in.; Old houses, 1929/1930, pencil, 7 x 5 ½ in., 7 ½ x 5 ¼ in. and 10 ¾ x 7 in.; all HM

182/183 Maria Innocentia with her little niece Traudl and her family, 1940, HM; Visitors' book with signatures, HM and CS

184/185 Why so sad?, 1941/1944, charcoal and crayon, 21 ¼ x 15 ¼ in., ARS AG; Telling Her Secret, 1941, charcoal and crayon, 21 ¼ x 17 ¼ in., ARS AG; Maria Innocentia with M. Eligia Stadler OSF, 1940, HM; Two angels on a cloud, 1940/1942, Collage, 8 ½ x 10 ½ in., CS; Good luck charms, 1939/1942, charcoal and crayon, all ca. 14 ¼ x 14 ¼ in., CS

186/187 Letter to Maximiliane Müller, 1939, ND; Maximiliane Müller, ND; Permit to keep the Ars Sacra Press going, ND; Spring Basket, charcoal and crayon, ca. 17 ¾ x 13 ¾ in., drawing ARS AG, photograph HM; Jesus in the Manger with Angel, 1940, ink, 4 x 4 in., ARS AG; Shaking the tree, 1940, ink, 3 ¾ x 5 in., ARS AG

188/189 Bumblebee on a flowering branch, December 1941, color pencil, 5 ¾ x 4 in., CS; The "Hummel Nest," 1942, CS; Wall hanging: Massing, 1931, appliqué, 32 ¾ x 50 ¾ in., HM; Portrait of Viktoria Hummel, April 1929, charcoal, 11 x 10 ¼ in., HM; Portrait of Adolf Hummel, March 1929, charcoal, 11 x 10 ¼ in., HM; Measuring stick for a new generation of little Hummels (sketch), 1941, charcoal and crayon, 63 x 4 in., CS

190/191 Hold your Head High and Swallow Hard, 1941/1944, charcoal and crayon, 12 ¾ x 16 ¾ in., ARS AG; Sketch of a lying soldier, 1942, pencil and color pencil, 6 ½ x 7 ¾ in., CS; Memento of a soldier, 1942, pencil and color pencil, 6 ½ x 7 ¾ in., CS; Maria Innocentia, 1944, HM

192/193 Kalanchoe at the window, 1943/1944, charcoal with crayon, 23 ½ x 17 ¼ in., ARS AG, CS; Villa Vogelfrei "closed," 1944/45, color pencil, 4 x 3 ¼ in., CS; Sketch, 1944/45, pencil, 5 ¾ x 4 ½ in., CS; Convent Siessen, convent church, HM; Cinderella, 1944, charcoal and crayon, 15 ¾ x 16 ½ in., ARS AG

194/195 Maria Innocentia's pocket watch, HM; Picture postcard of Wilhelmstift in Isny, HM; Postcard to the family, 1944, HM; Sketch: "Hello, come in," 1940's, pencil, 8 ½ x 6 ½ in., CS; Printing block for woodcut of a Massing house, 1928, HM; High above the roofs?, 1928/1929, watercolor, 9 ½ x 15 ¾ in., HM

196/197 Ars Sacra Press, 1943, ND; Maria Innocentia's studio, 1946, CS

198/199 Medical opinions, HM; Occupied zones, Municipal Museum, Munich; Sketch sheet with Madonnas, 1946, pencil, 230 x 190 mm, 9 x 7 ½ in.; Sketch sheet with animals, 1946, pencil, 9 ½ x 8 ¼ in.; all others CS

200/201 Letter from Dr. Brügger, 1945; Picture postcard Wangen; Pass; Letter to the Family, 1945; all HM

202/203 Portrait of Franz Hummel, 1930, watercolor, 11 ¼ x 9 in., HM; Quick Congratulation, 1946, colored pencil and pencil, 3 ¼ x 3 in., ARS AG; The Real Easter Bunny, 1946, colored pencil and pencil, 5 ¾ x 5 ¼ in., ARS AG; Mother of God, 1946, pencil and color pencil, 4 ¾ x 3 ½ in., CS

204/205 Mother-of-God icon; Postcards to the parents, 1946; Deathbed cross; all HM

206/207 Death letter of the mother, HM; Viktoria Hummel, at the grave of her daughter, 1963, CS

Danksagung

Alfred Hummel für seine hilfsbereite Unterstützung bei allen Fragen und den stets offenen Zugang
zum Werk- und Dokumentenarchiv der Familie Hummel in Massing

Der Klostergemeinschaft Sießen für ihre Gastfreundschaft, vor allem Sr. Claudia Maria Mühlherr,
dem Hummel-Team und ganz besonders Sr. M. Witgard Erler, ohne deren unglaubliche
Sachkenntnis und Präzision diese Biografie nicht hätte geschrieben werden können

Centa Hummel für ihre Bereitschaft, ihre oft schmerzliche Erinnerung mit der Autorin zu teilen

Dr. Genoveva Nitz für ihre tags und nachts zur Verfügung stehende Kompetenz

Ulrike Hübner und Johannes Potzler für unermüdliche Lesebereitschaft

Prof. Dr. Ernest Bernhardt-Kabisch für die exzellente Übersetzung

Ute Freudenberger für ihr Vertrauen und alle tatkräftige und mentale Unterstützung

Dagmar Treuner und Herbert Hennig von der Goebel Porzellanmanufaktur GmbH

Renato Turri von der ARS AG

Marcel Nauer, ehemaliger Inhaber der arsEdition GmbH

Stefanie Hummel, Katharina Zellhuber und Dajana Fascicolo vom Berta Hummel Museum im Hummelhaus in Massing

und der Grafikerin dieses Buches, Romy Gallina, für die wunderbare kreative Zusammenarbeit

Acknowledgements

I am deeply grateful to the following individuals:

Alfred Hummel for his active support in all matters and ever ready access to the works and documents
in the archives of the Hummel family in Massing;

The convent community at Siessen for their hospitality, especially Sr. Claudia Maria Mühlherr,
the Hummel-Team, and above all Sr. Witgard Erler, without whose incredible knowledge and precision
this biography could not have been written;

Centa Hummel for her willingness to share memories, also of sad moments, with the author;

Dr. Genoveva Nitz for making her competence available day and night;

Ulrike Hübner and Johannes Potzler for tireless reading;

Prof. Dr. Ernest Bernhardt-Kabisch for the excellent translation;

Ute Freudenberger for her trust and her active support;

Dagmar Treuner and Herbert Hennig of the Goebel Porcelain Manufacturing Co., Ltd.;

Renato Turri of ARS Corporation;

Marcel Nauer, former owner of the arsEdition Co., Ltd.;

Stefanie Hummel, Katharina Zellhuber, and Diana Fascioli of the Berta Hummel Museum im Hummelhaus in Massing;

and Romy Gallina, the book's graphic artist, for her marvellous creative collaboration.

Adressen / Addresses

Das Berta Hummel Museum im Hummelhaus
Berta-Hummel-Straße 2
D-84323 Massing
info@hummelmuseum.de
www.hummelmuseum.de

Franziskanerinnen-Kloster Sießen
D-88343 Bad Saulgau
www.klostersiessen.de

Goebel Porzellanmanufaktur GmbH
Coburger Straße 7
D-96472 Rödental
goebel@goebel.de
www.goebel.de

M.I. Hummel Club Zentrale
Postfach 1147
D-96466 Rödental
mihummelclub@goebel.de
www.goebel.de

ARS AG Licensing & Merchandising
Blegistraße 3
CH-6340 Baar
info@arsag.de
www.arsag.ch

Verlag arsEdition GmbH
Friedrichstraße 9
80801 München
verlag@arsedition.de
www.arsedition.de

M.I.Hummel Originalbilder
jacques.nauer@gmx.ch

Schöne Geschenke für Hummelfreunde
Handsome Gifts for Hummel Fans

www.mi-hummel.de

ISBN 978-3-7607-2970-1

ISBN 978-3-7607-2971-8

ISBN 978-3-7607-2969-5

ISBN 978-3-7607-2968-8

Jeder Titel: 48 S. / € 6,95 (D)

Spiralaufsteller / 160 S.
€ 12,95 (D) / ISBN 978-3-7607-3253-4

Hummel-Magnete je € 2,50 (D)*

€ 12,95* (D) / ISBN 978-3-7607-2898-8

* unverbindliche Preisempfehlung

Limitierte Sammleredition
Limited Collectors Edition

Zum 100. Geburtstag präsentiert arsEdition eine exklusive Geschenk-kassette für Hummel-Liebhaber: die Biografie der weltberühmten Künstlerin in einer wertvoll ausgestatteten Schatulle mit acht hochwertigen Kunstdrucken. Ein Muss für den begeisterten Sammler in limitierter Auflage!

On the occasion of the Hummel centennial arsEdition presents a special gift box for Hummel lovers: a richly appointed casket containing the biography of the world-famous artist together with eight high-quality art prints of both familiar motifs and largely unknown ones from earlier creative phases. A must for the devoted collector, in a limited edition!

M.I. Hummel Jubiläums-Edition
Kassette mit 8 Kunstdrucken und Biografie / 32 x 39 cm
€ 98,00 (D) / ISBN 978-3-7607-3283-1

Die Autorin / The Author

Dido Nitz, 1970 in München geboren, studierte Germanistik, Anglistik, Kunstgeschichte und Buchwissenschaft und lernte Leben und Werk der Maria Innocentia Berta Hummel kennen, als sich die Aufarbeitung von deren künstlerischer Vielseitigkeit noch in den Kinderschuhen befand. Beim Aufbau eines Hummel-Museums in New Braunfels, Texas, war sie fasziniert von der Begeisterung, die das Phänomen „M.I. Hummel" bei den amerikanischen Mitarbeitern und den Besuchern aus aller Welt hervorrief.
Büchermachen ist ihr Beruf und Leidenschaft. Die Autorin lebt und arbeitet in ihrer Heimatstadt München.

Dido Nitz, born in Munich, Germany, in 1970, studied German and English Literature, Art History and Library Science. She encountered the life and works of Maria Innocentia Berta Hummel at a time when the critical appraisal of the latter's artistic versatility was still in its infancy. While participating in the establishment of a Hummel Museum in New Braunfels, Texas, she was fascinated by the enthusiasm the phenomenon "M.I. Hummel" elicited from the American colleagues and the visitors from all over the world.
Book production is her profession and her passion. Dido Nitz lives and works in her native city of Munich.

Impressum

In einigen Fällen war es nicht möglich, für den Abdruck der Bilddokumente die Rechteinhaber zu ermitteln. Honoraransprüche der Autoren, Verlage und ihrer Rechtsnachfolger bleiben gewahrt.

© 2009 arsEdition GmbH, München
Alle Rechte vorbehalten

Gesamtkonzeption und Text: Dido Nitz
Übersetzung : Ernest Bernhardt
Gestaltungskonzept und Layout: Romy Gallina

M.I. Hummel® wird verwendet unter
Lizenz von Goebel © Ars AG, Baar / Schweiz

ISBN 978-3-7607-2964-0
Printed by Tien Wah Press
www.arsedition.de

Imprint

For some illustrations it was not possible to identify the copyright holders for the purpose of obtaining permission to reprint. Honorarium claims by authors, publishers, or their assignees guaranteed.

© 2009, arsEdition Ltd., Munich
All rights reserved

Overall conception and text: Dido Nitz
Translation: Ernest Bernhardt
Design concept and layout: Romy Gallina

M.I. Hummel® is used under License from
Goebel © Ars AG, Baar / Switzerland

ISBN 978-3-7607-2964-0
Printed by Tien Wah Press
www.arsedition.de